DATE DUE

JACK AND JACKIE

Also by Christopher Andersen

*Young Kate: The Remarkable Hepburns
and the Shaping of an American Legend*

Citizen Jane

The Best of Everything (with John Marion)

The Serpent's Tooth

The Book of People

Father

Susan Hayward

The Name Game

JACK and JACKIE

Portrait of an American Marriage

Christopher Andersen

William Morrow and Company, Inc.
New York

B
05834 a
(1)

Grateful acknowledgement is made to the following for permission to use the
photographs in this book:

AP/Wide World Photos: 21, 22, 50

John F. Kennedy Library: 1, 7, 8, 9, 10, 13, 14, 15, 17, 18, 28, 29, 30, 31,
33, 34, 35, 36, 37, 38, 39, 40, 41, 42, 43, 44, 45, 46, 47, 49, 51, 52, 53

Movie Star News: 23, 24, 25, 26, 27

New Bedford Standard Times: 5, 48

Cecil Stoughton/John F. Kennedy Library: 32

UPI/Bettmann Archive: 2, 3, 4, 6, 11, 12, 16, 19, 20, 54, 55

Copyright © 1996 by Christopher P. Andersen

ISBN 0-688-14760-7

Printed in the United States of America

To Valerie, Kate, and Kelly

Preface

From the very beginning, theirs was destined to be one of the most celebrated unions of the twentieth century: he the handsome, charismatic young standard-bearer of one of America's most powerful families, she the darkly beautiful thoroughbred. By the time it ended with gunshots in Dallas, John Fitzgerald Kennedy and his wife, Jacqueline, were indisputably the First Couple of the World.

The way we would come to view them mirrored the disillusionment and growing cynicism of the age. By the 1980s, Camelot was dismantled brick by brick and the Kennedy myth irreparably shattered. Even those of us who vividly recall where we were and what we were doing the moment we heard the news of JFK's assassination have had our memories of the President and his First Lady virtually obliterated by the avalanche of scandalous revelations. Jack's womanizing ways became fodder for the tabloids, while his widow transmogrified into the larger-than-life Jacqueline Onassis, more a creature of legend than a flesh-and-blood woman, mother, wife.

Whatever powerful forces drew these two remarkable people together also propelled them to the summit of power and prestige. And these same forces enabled them to survive one soul-crushing personal crisis after another—until only one remained to bear the heaviest burden of all.

They were outlandishly rich, impossibly attractive, brilliant, elegant, youthful, *exciting*. Glamour and power and sex and money—not to mention the dreams and aspirations of a generation—were embodied in the forty-three-year-old President and his thirty-one-year-old wife. They seemed truly blessed by the gods, so it should have come as no surprise when their story took on the dimensions of a Greek tragedy.

Given all that Jack and Jackie Kennedy came to symbolize, the tangled nature of their relationship is worth exploring—now more than ever. For this, the saga of their time together remains one thing above all else: a great American love story.

Love *(luv) n.*   *1: intense affection and warm feeling for another   2: strong sexual desire for another person   3: a strong fondness or enthusiasm   4: a beloved person   5: a zero score in tennis.*

Emotionally, they were in many ways the two most isolated, most alone people I ever met. They both wanted desperately to connect, but hadn't the faintest idea how. That's what made their love story so achingly poignant. And it was, in every sense of the word, a love story.

JFK's close friend Chuck Spalding

We are like two icebergs—the public life above the water, the private life is submerged. It is a bond between us.

Jacqueline Kennedy

JACK AND JACKIE

He had a wedding to go to, but Jack was in agony, and the pain he endured was not merely physical. For years, he had suffered debilitating back spasms from a slipped disc—a chronic condition that battalions of Harvard-educated doctors seemed powerless to alleviate. Not that he had allowed this infirmity to get in the way of his socializing, or to curb even slightly his prodigious sexual appetites.

To be sure, the word *irresistible* applied to Black Jack Bouvier as it did to few other men. Jack was tall, tanned, rakishly handsome, the Ivy League–educated heir to a not-inconsequential fortune. He was charming and fun; men as well as women loved being in his company. He remained a bachelor until his mid-thirties, when he decided to finally take the plunge with a girl scarcely out of college.

Earlier this evening, he had performed admirably at the wedding rehearsal. The bride's face had lit up when she saw him. And tomorrow the crème de la crème of New York and Washington society would be in attendance at St. Mary's Church in Newport, Rhode Island, as Black Jack walked down the aisle with his strikingly beautiful daughter Jacqueline. Certainly no one was prouder of the bride. He had watched her blossom into an elegant, supremely self-assured, utterly enchanting young woman. But there were always nagging doubts at times like these, and Black Jack dealt with them—along with the recurring pain in his back—the best way he knew how: He sat in his suite at Newport's Viking Hotel and drank himself into a stupor.

A series of increasingly incoherent telephone calls to his sisters followed late that evening and into the early-morning hours. By ten o'clock the next morning, it had become painfully clear that Jack Bouvier would be in no condition to walk his adored Jacqueline down the aisle and give her away to the *other* handsome Jack in her life—a man who was to an uncanny degree her father's mirror image—John Fitzgerald Kennedy.

As the rest of the wedding party assembled at Hammersmith Farm, the Auchincloss family estate in Newport, the mother of the bride unleashed a blistering tirade against her ex-husband. She was accustomed to what she referred to as Black Jack's "wanton depravity." But to pass out drunk in his hotel room on his daughter's wedding day—that surpassed even the notorious Black Jack's capacity for wickedness. "I knew he would do this to us," Janet told her trembling daughter. "Why you wanted him here in the first place I will never know!"

To be sure, Jacqueline herself was crestfallen upon hearing news of her father's condition. He had seemed so pulled-together the night before at the rehearsal. Throughout their young lives, Jackie and her sister, Lee, had been used as unwilling pawns in their parents' marital wars. Brimming with social ambition and moral rectitude, their mother made certain during the time they were married that the girls did not miss a single detail of their father's reckless spending, his gambling and drinking, and most of all, his philandering. When Black Jack's fortunes on Wall Street began to falter, Janet and the girls moved into a massive thirteen-room Park Avenue apartment owned by Janet's banker father, James T. Lee. Grandfather Lee then joined in the chorus of rebukes.

Outnumbered and largely guilty of the accusations leveled against him, Black Jack did not fight back. When Janet did divorce him on grounds of adultery in 1940, Black Jack agreed to all his ex-wife's terms in the interest of harmony. His energies would better be expended lavishing gifts, praise, and affection on Jackie and Lee.

The effect of all this bickering was to cast Black Jack in the sympathetic role of hapless, unjustly maligned underdog—at least in the eyes of his young daughters. Where they harbored a wary respect for their iron-willed mother, it was their much-misunderstood father whom they adored. To Jackie in particular, Black Jack became the standard against which other men were measured. He was also her model for what to expect of men in general. Black Jack taught Jacqueline that men (the exciting ones, anyway) were congenitally prone to infidelity. That they meant no harm by it; this was simply one of the immutable laws of nature.

She also appreciated early on the necessity of "marrying well." When Janet became the third wife of monied, socially prominent Hugh D. Auchincloss, the balance of power shifted dramatically. While Black Jack's entire real estate holdings consisted of a four-room apartment at 125 East Seventy-fourth Street in Manhattan (by then the Bouvier family estate, Lasata, had been sold), the Auchinclosses divided their time between two lavish properties: Merrywood, a Georgian mansion set on forty-six rolling acres in Virginia's hunt country, and Hammersmith Farm, the twenty-eight-room shingled "cottage" with its sweeping views of Newport's glistening Narragansett Bay.

Black Jack had gamely continued to pay the girls' monthly allowances, as well as to foot the cost for their college tuitions, their horses, and even their charge accounts at Bloomingdales and Saks. But he was clearly no match for the enormously wealthy Auchincloss clan. Jackie and Lee owed the opulence of their surroundings to their stepfather, "Uncle Hughdie."

For her part, Janet had wasted no time trying to forge a bond between the hot-blooded Catholic Bouvier girls and their WASP stepfamily. In 1945, Janet gave birth to their half-sister, Janet, and two years later to a half-brother, Jamie. There were already several Auchincloss stepsiblings in place. Hugh Dudley III (called "Yusha" by his Russian mother), Nina (who also happened to be writer Gore Vidal's half-sister), and Thomas. Of these, Jackie was closest to Yusha, who was only two years her senior and, in his own words, "completely captivated" by her.

This latest shift in the balance of power was evident by the time Black Jack arrived in Virginia in April 1953 for Lee's marriage to Michael Canfield, Harvard-educated adopted son of the legendary publisher Cass Canfield. That time, the father of the bride had no difficulty giving his daughter away. But when he rode to Merrywood for the reception, he was so overcome by the grandeur of the place that he nearly broke down. Surely, there was no way for him to compete with this. Over the next few months, his resentment toward his ex-wife and the Auchinclosses continued to fester.

Defying Janet's orders barring him from Jackie's wedding, Black Jack was determined to make his daughter proud. He devoted July to perfecting his tan and toning his physique at East Hampton's Maidstone Club. He also began assembling his formal wardrobe—custom-made gray suede shoes (to be worn with carefully ironed silk socks), custom-tailored shirt, vest, cutaway, striped pants, mother-of-pearl studs and gold cuff links. And to set everything off, a family heirloom: Grandfather Bouvier's pearl stickpin.

Upon his arrival in Newport for what was being billed as the Wedding of the Year, Black Jack was treated like a visiting pasha. He was whisked by limousine from the train station to the Viking Hotel, where he was given one of the most desirable suites, the best table in the dining room, and round-the-clock room service.

So solicitous was the staff, in fact, that it was later suggested that Janet had concocted the whole debacle—that she had personally ordered the management of the Viking Hotel to ply Black Jack with liquor. She had even phoned old drinking buddies of her ex-husband and urged them to "show Jack a good time." Janet had also seen to it that Black Jack was excluded from all the prewedding dinners and cocktail parties—a crushing blow to Bouvier, who had expected to be invited to at least one event. As a result, he had little more to do than drink with his old pals or alone in his room—and gradually become obsessed with his role in the wedding ceremony itself.

Conspiracy theories notwithstanding, Black Jack's twin sisters, Michelle and Maude, dispatched their husbands—Harrington Putnam and John E. Davis, respectively—to try to sober him up. When the two men arrived, they found him sprawled across the bed in his underwear.

Janet declared that he would not be allowed inside St. Mary's. If he even tried, he would be physically barred at the door. But the Bouviers pleaded with Janet to give Black Jack another chance. They could clean him up in time for the ceremony, they insisted. Jackie told her mother to delay the proceedings long enough to let her father walk her down the aisle.

But the formidable Janet, who once pulled a knife on a maid for failing to fold the towels properly, would have none of it. Jacqueline's stepfather, Hughdie Auchincloss, was enlisted to fill in for Black Jack. By some bizarre coincidence, Janet had already arranged days in advance for Hughdie's formal wear—including tails—to be cleaned, pressed, and hanging in his closet.

All of this Sturm und Drang amounted to little more than a minor annoyance for the man who was really at the controls: Joseph P. Kennedy. Although he left such details as the color of the bridesmaids' gowns and what flowers would be used in the centerpieces to Janet Auchincloss, the father of the groom had orchestrated the all-important press coverage with the military precision of a seasoned battlefield commander.

"As in all things, Papa Joe was the ringmaster," said JFK intimate Chuck Spalding. "He treated the wedding like one of those big Hollywood productions he used to finance. He knew that this was the wedding of a future American president and that it would be written about in history books. This was Joe's grand scheme. He wasn't about to let a little thing like Black Jack's, shall we say, temporary incapacity, screw things up." When asked by a *New York Times* reporter to explain Jack Bouvier's absence from the proceedings at the church, it was Joe who delivered what was to become the party line: Jackie's father, he told the *Times,* had been stricken with the flu and was confined to his bed.

One Auchincloss who was in fact fond of Black Jack was Jackie's stepbrother Yusha. "He and I were friends. I spoke to him at the wedding rehearsal the night before and he seemed fine," Yusha recalled. Fellow usher Paul "Red" Fay, a war buddy of JFK, concurred. "Black Jack was in great shape at the rehearsal. That's why it was such a total shock when he didn't show up. Jackie was crushed."

While Janet reminded everyone that she had predicted this would happen, the Auchincloss step- and half-siblings felt nothing but sympathy for Jackie. "It was a very unfortunate circumstance," Yusha later observed with typical Auchincloss understatement. "I was very disappointed that Jackie's father couldn't give her away as she wanted. It was very upsetting to Jackie, and therefore very upsetting to me."

One who chose not to get involved at this juncture was the groom. While the rest of the wedding party was in a state of turmoil, Jack was being knocked into a rosebush during a last-minute game of touch football with his brothers and a couple of ushers. The scratches on his face, later clearly visible at the ceremony and during the reception afterward, would be retouched in the wedding photographs.

Jackie was enough of a trouper to go along with the plan to replace her father with her stepfather. She sobbed a little behind closed doors at Hammersmith Farm, but when she emerged she was radiant. "Aside from the usual confusion and excitement," said one of the bridesmaids, "you would never have guessed that anything was wrong. Jackie was absolutely beautiful, ethereal, the perfect storybook bride, and from the way she carried herself, it looked as if she didn't have a care in the world."

September 12, 1953, was a perfect day for a wedding. It was cloudless, crisp, and breezy enough to churn up whitecaps on Narragansett Bay. Rosecliff, Marble House, the Breakers, and Newport's other palatial summer "cottages" glistened like fairy tale castles in the morning sun.

Joe Kennedy, former Ambassador to the Court of St. James's and tycoon *extraordinaire*, scarcely noticed the weather as his limousine pulled up to St. Mary's. What truly excited him were the multitudes who clogged the downtown streets in hopes of catching a glimpse of the wedding party. He had pulled enough strings and called in enough IOUs to ensure the marriage of the young senator from Massachusetts, albeit a rising star in the Democratic Party firmament, got the kind of publicity previously accorded only movie stars and royalty. It was truly gratifying for Joe to see that money and influence still counted for something.

As was his custom, Joe virtually ignored his long-suffering wife, Rose. Teeth clenched in a fixed, for-the-cameras grin, he grasped her forearm roughly and steered her into the Gothic stone church without exchanging a word. Rose, accustomed to such unloving treatment, was content in the knowledge that her blue lace gown had cost her husband a then-staggering thousand dollars.

All three tribes that were being united by marriage—the staunchly Republican Bouviers, the equally Republican Auchinclosses, and the Kennedys—were each heavily represented. Although Janet had pleaded with Jack to limit the guest list to this discreet group (along with a smattering of Vanderbilts and Astors), Jack and Joe ignored her. Instead, they added to the guest list numerous senators, congressmen, assorted Boston political cronies, and Joe's business associates. By the time they were finished, at least seven hundred had been invited to the wedding, and an additional six hundred to the reception.

Joe had also brushed aside Janet's request that the ceremony not be "too Catholic." After all, the Auchinclosses were Protestant, and neither the Bouviers nor the Kennedys (with the glaring exception of Rose) were particularly devout. "If he could have," observed a family friend, "Joe would have gotten the Pope himself to perform the ceremony." He did the next best thing. Richard

Cardinal Cushing, Archbishop of Boston, was enlisted to conduct the Nuptial High Mass and bestow the Apostolic Blessing of Pope Pius XII on the newlyweds. Among those other esteemed clergymen who assisted the raspy-voiced Cushing were the Very Reverend John J. Cavanaugh, former president of Notre Dame, and the head of the Christophers movement, the Very Reverend James Kellor of New York. Tenor Luigi Vena was also imported from Boston, to sing "Ave Maria" and "Jesu, Amor Mi."

When Jackie arrived, the crowd of three thousand frenzied onlookers who had been straining at police barricades set up across the street suddenly surged forward and nearly crushed the startled bride. On the arm of the stalwart Hugh Auchincloss, Jackie blinked with wonder as she entered the church. The interior was awash in white chrysanthemums and pink gladioli, and light streaming through the stained-glass windows, in the words of one guest, "made you feel as if you were inside an Impressionist painting."

Jack stood waiting at the altar with brother Bobby, his best man. They looked, said Jackie's Bouvier cousin John Davis, "too tanned and too handsome to be believed." Jackie's sister, Lee, was the matron of honor, and Jackie's little half-siblings also had roles to play. Janet was flower girl and Jamie, clad in short black velvet trousers and a ruffled white silk shirt straight out of a portrait by Thomas Gainsborough, took his responsibilities as page seriously.

Lee and the eleven bridesmaids wore pale pink taffeta dresses with claret-colored satin sashes and bandeaux on their heads reminiscent of Mary, Queen of Scots. They walked slowly down the aisle ahead of the bride, and once Jackie was in full view an audible gasp went up from the crowd. She had decided to build her entire wedding outfit around the slightly yellowed rose-point lace veil she was borrowing from her grandmother. Instead of a white dress that would clash with the antique veil, she had chosen an ivory silk taffeta gown with an off-the-shoulder neckline and cap sleeves. All ruffles and flourishes, the dress, which took fifty yards of material to make, was tightly fitted at the waist and cascaded down in waves. The veil itself, shirred into a back-of-the-head cap festooned with tiny orange blossoms, trailed to the ground.

The dress, described by one fashion writer as "atrocious," was not Jackie's first choice. She had wanted something simple, elegant, and modern, but Jack had demanded that she wear something "more traditional." To save a few Auchincloss dollars, Janet had turned to Ann Lowe, an African-American dressmaker whose work appeared on some of society's grandest dames. Several times Jackie had secretly visited her Lexington Avenue workshop for fittings. Even after a flood destroyed Jackie's and all the bridesmaids' gowns five days before the wedding, Ann Lowe miraculously managed to come through on time—though in the process she actually lost money on the deal. At the wedding, Lowe was on hand to personally hold up the train so it would not get trampled. (Still, when later asked who made her bridal gown, Jackie never gave Ann Lowe credit by name. She only allowed that the dress had been made by a "colored woman dressmaker," and not a pricey couturier.)

During the ceremony, Jackie clutched a bouquet of pink and white orchids, stephanotis, and miniature gardenias. She also wore, unseen beneath a mountain of ivory silk taffeta, a blue garter for luck. There was only one tense moment, when Bobby searched frantically through his pockets for the ring before finally pulling it out with a look of triumph.

With all eyes on the bride and groom, no one had noticed usher Chuck Spalding slip into the church with a still-under-the-weather Black Jack. "Jack [Kennedy] had come over and said, 'Do me a favor, go get Black Jack and bring him to the church,' " Spalding recalled. "I got him into a pew, but it was one interesting maneuver. We had an arm around him, sort of holding him up. He'd had more alcohol that day than he needed, but he shook it off." (No one else remembered seeing Bouvier in the church that day, but Spalding insisted he was there for the final few moments of the ceremony.)

After Cardinal Cushing pronounced Jackie and Jack man and

wife, the guests began spilling out of the church and into the five hundred cars that would ferry them to the luncheon reception at Hammersmith Farm. As he waited on the church steps for his limousine, Joe could not have been more pleased. Those in attendance shared his enthusiasm. "The ceremony," *The New York Times* would proclaim in the next morning's edition, "far surpassed the Astor-French wedding of 1943." For the son of a Boston saloon-keeper, albeit a phenomenally wealthy one, beating the Astors on their home turf was nothing if not satisfying.

At Hammersmith Farm, several tents were set up on the West Lawn to accommodate the thirteen hundred guests, along with dozens of umbrella-topped tables that occasionally took off in the breeze. An army of servants in black uniforms scurried about the grounds, righting upended tables and balancing trays crowded with champagne glasses.

Next to the brick fireplace in the white-paneled living room, Jackie and Jack stood in the receiving line for nearly three hours. At times the line stretched out the door and several hundred feet down the manicured front lawn. Like any good Boston pol, the groom seized this opportunity to forge new alliances and cement old ones. "The senator made a huge fuss over each of our wives when they came to him in the reception line, introducing them to Jackie and telling her that without their husbands he would never have been elected," recalled JFK crony Kenneth P. O'Donnell. "From that day on, Kennedy could do no wrong in our wives' eyes—which of course was what he had in mind at the time."

Much to the relief of both Rose and Janet, one of those who chose not to crash the party was Joe's longtime mistress, the actress Gloria Swanson. This did not stop the senior Kennedy, often referred to as "the Ambassador," from pinching several young women in full view of Rose and his own children. Jackie observed Jack eyeing his father's antics with envy. "Don't," Jackie whispered into the groom's ear, "get any ideas."

Society bandleader Meyer Davis, who had also played at the ill-fated wedding of Jackie's parents, was imported to provide his patented brand of schmaltzy dance music. For the first dance, Jack had selected "I Married an Angel." Beneath the blue-and-white-striped canopy, Jack and Jackie danced for just a few bars before stepfather Hugh cut in.

At the head table, the newlyweds endured an off-key serenade from the boisterous Kennedy siblings and the customary round of toasts. It was then that Joe Kennedy cornered Florida's George Smathers, Jack's closest colleague in the Senate. "Now, you're going to have to speak for the groom," Joe told Smathers. "I want you to be funny. I want you to be clever. I want you to say everything that you can think of that's going to make Jack look good. I don't want the Bouviers to be outshining us." He was dead serious.

"Well, okay, Mr. Ambassador," Smathers replied nervously. "I wish somebody had told me this a little while ago. But anyway I'll do it the best I can." Smathers later recalled that he didn't think he was "very good, really. But I got a big hand," he added, "it went off fine."

Jackie, meanwhile, was showing off the diamond bracelet Jack had given her as a wedding present and her two-carat diamond-and-emerald engagement ring. The happy couple then cut the five-tier four-foot-high wedding cake—the gift of a Quincy, Massachusetts, baker.

Filling the upstairs rooms were hundreds of wedding gifts, not including the two truckloads that had yet to be uncrated. As they streamed through the rambling house and the Frederick Law Olmsted–designed gardens, guests buzzed about Black Jack's absence. It was not long before Joe Kennedy's official story—that Jackie's father had the flu—was contradicted by people who had seen him drinking heavily at his hotel the night before. Black Jack, who was also to have been in the receiving line at the reception, indeed was not among the celebrants. Still ashamed, he had slunk back to his hotel room and packed for the trip back to New York. He made the trip by ambulance.

With the party still in full swing, Jackie went to the top of the stairs and, with an "eeny, meeny, miny, mo," tossed her bouquet down to the squealing bridesmaids. She made sure that it would be caught by Nancy Tuckerman, the woman who in the end could justly claim to have been Jackie's closest and most trusted friend.

Jackie then scurried to her white-and-yellow bedroom to change. It was in this room, her haven since childhood, that she felt free enough to cry once again out of sight of her guests. "She was heartbroken," Yusha said. "She worshipped her father and she wanted him to be there. But she accepted it."

Moments later, Jackie emerged wearing a tailored gray Chanel suit and clutching a green velvet hat that her mother had given her. Jackie thought the hat was ugly and refused to put it on. A huge diamond pin, a gift from Joe Kennedy, sparkled on her lapel. Jackie rejoined her new husband on the second-floor landing, bussed each of her bridesmaids on the cheek, and cornered her stepfather to thank him for filling the void left by Black Jack. Jack Kennedy, meanwhile, had sought out the members of his Senate staff and asked them to take a few days off while he honeymooned. He suggested they spend a few days in Boston before heading back to Capitol Hill. "I don't want to think of you back here working," he told them, "while I'm having a good time."

They then left in a blizzard of rice and pink confetti, climbed into their waiting limousine, and headed for the local airport where a private plane was waiting to take them to New York. But they were scarcely out the driveway and onto Ocean Drive when they became stuck in a colossal traffic jam caused by several hundred out-of-town chauffeurs drunk on French champagne. Mindful that Black Jack had pursued millionairess Doris Duke while on his honeymoon with Janet, Jackie playfully needled Jack as she had throughout their courtship. "I'll bet you're already dreaming of your carefree old bachelor days," she purred. Jack merely smiled.

The newlyweds spent their first two nights as man and wife at the Waldorf-Astoria, then flew to Acapulco. Jackie had been to the Mexican resort years before with her mother, and ever since had fantasized about a pink villa that clung to the side of a cliff overlooking the Pacific. Jackie had mentioned the villa in passing, and Joe, who would do anything for his cherished daughter-in-law, sprang into action. The owner, it turned out, owed Joe Kennedy a few favors.

Jackie and her father-in-law had, in fact, forged a special bond of mutual respect and affection early on in her courtship with Jack. It had not been easy. The staunchly Republican Auchin-closses were, of course, opposed to virtually everything the Kennedys stood for politically. Just as firmly planted in the GOP camp despite his flamboyant ways, Black Jack detested Joe Kennedy for personal reasons. As head of the Securities and Exchange Commission in the 1930s, the senior Kennedy had cracked down on certain questionable Wall Street practices, hurting Bouvier's brokerage firm. Bouvier and others charged that it was only after Joe Kennedy had used these same loopholes to build one of America's greatest fortunes that he made them unavailable to his competition.

Over time, Jackie and the Ambassador warmed to each other more and more. She found him lovable, crusty, and wise. He delighted in her beauty, sophistication, and playful wit. They shared private jokes, and confidences. She knew that it was Joe who had urged his son to marry her, even if his motivation had as much to do with the need for a presidential aspirant to be married as it did any regard for her worth as a person. Ironically, next to Black Jack, she felt a deep, almost spiritual attachment to her new father-in-law.

Once they were ensconced in their Acapulco honeymoon retreat, Jackie sat down and wrote a warm note to Black Jack, forgiving him for not showing up to give the bride away. The note gave her father, holed up in his apartment since the wedding, enough courage to face the outside world again. "They had a deep love for one another," said Yusha Auchincloss, "and Jackie knew how much pain he had caused himself. She understood his weaknesses and was willing to overlook them."

Black Jack showed the letter to only one person, his Wall Street partner and confidant John Carrere. It read more like a letter between former lovers than one from daughter to father. "Jackie was always talking about her father, and it was pretty clear that they worshipped each other," George Smathers said. Indeed, Black Jack sometimes referred to Jacqueline as "all things holy." Jackie's devotion to her father was no less intense. "Marrying Jack Kennedy," Smathers said, "was as close as she was ever going to get to marrying Black Jack Bouvier."

———

There were all sorts of reserves in him.
There were a great many things nobody knew
about him, that he didn't share.

family friend Kay Halle

———

"If he was capable of loving any one woman, then that woman was Jackie," said former NBC newswoman Nancy Dickerson, who both dated Jack Kennedy and covered his political career. "But it couldn't have been easy for either one of them. All his life he was trained to view women as objects to be conquered, possessed. Jack really had no respect for women. You can hardly blame him. After all, Jack learned at the foot of the master."

Just as Black Jack Bouvier provided the model for what Jackie would come to regard as her ideal man, Joseph P. Kennedy set a rather twisted example for his own children. It is, in fact, difficult to imagine any father exerting a more profound and far-reaching control over the lives of his offspring than Joe Kennedy.

He was the son of Boston ward heeler P. J. Kennedy (his grandfather had fled the Irish potato famine in the 1840s), but Joe Kennedy knew precious little of poverty. P. J.'s saloon and various investments generated enough income for him to winter in Palm Beach, buy a seaside mansion staffed with servants, and hire a retired admiral to skipper his sixty-foot yacht. He could also afford to send Joe to the elite Boston Latin prep school and then to Harvard.

Still, from an early age P. J.'s freckle-faced, blue-eyed son was determined to make his own mark. At age twelve he took his first job delivering hats to the fashionable Protestant ladies on Beacon Hill—careful to identify himself only as "Joseph," never revealing his Irish surname. He peddled papers on the docks, sold candy aboard a boat that gave tours of Boston harbor, and was paid to light lamps and stoves for Orthodox Jews on the Sabbath.

At Harvard, Joe excelled at baseball and even managed to get into the WASP-dominated Hasty Pudding society. But he was a mediocre student; ironically, Joe Kennedy did so poorly in a banking and finance course that he had to drop it after a single semester. Nevertheless, one year after his graduation in 1912, Joe managed to take control of East Boston's Columbia Trust Company. At twenty-five, he was the youngest bank president in the country. He vowed to a local newspaper that he would become "a millionaire by the age of thirty-five."

By this time Joe—who had distinguished himself as an "unctuous, totally unabashed social climber," in the words of one Harvard classmate—was already hotly pursuing Rose Fitzgerald, eldest daughter of Boston's legendary Mayor John Francis ("Honey Fitz") Fitzgerald. The Mayor was best known for doling patronage jobs to his cronies, belting out "Sweet Adeline" at the slightest provocation, and carrying on a public affair with a cigarette girl named "Toodles" Ryan. But he had also hoped Rose would marry into a more socially prominent Catholic family, and toward that end sent her to the finest convent schools in Europe capped off by a year at New York's exclusive Sacred Heart Convent.

After she returned home to Boston, more than four hundred guests attended Rose's coming-out party, including a pair of congressmen and the Governor. And while Rose would never be fully accepted by the Protestant blue bloods who ran "proper" Boston society, "Fitzie" (as he was also called) was not eager to see her marry a lace-curtain Kennedy.

Over her father's protests, the usually obedient Rose fell hard for the dashing young bank president. In the summer of 1914, he gave her a two-carat diamond ring—Rose later recalled he never actually asked for her hand, but treated their marriage as if it were a fait accompli—and they were wed on October 7.

They moved into a modest house in the Boston suburb of

Brookline, and precisely nine months and two weeks after the wedding ceremony Rose gave birth to the first of their nine children, Joseph Patrick Kennedy, Jr. On May 29, 1917, John Fitzgerald arrived, followed in rapid succession by Rosemary in 1918, Kathleen in 1920, and Eunice in 1921. After a three-year hiatus, Patricia arrived in 1924, then Robert Francis the following year, Jean Ann in 1928, and, last, Edward Moore in 1932.

There were strains on the marriage even before Jack's arrival. While his peers volunteered for service in the Great War, Joe preferred to stay home and make money on the war effort—a glaringly unpatriotic stance that embarrassed not just the Kennedy clan but the Fitzgeralds as well.

Joe's reputation suffered another blow when, after being hired to run Bethlehem Steel's Fore River shipyard in Quincy, Massachusetts, he threatened to fire thousands of striking workers rather than honor a promised pay hike. Assistant Secretary of the Navy Franklin Roosevelt, seeing Fore River's production of warships as crucial to the war effort, weighed in on the side of the workers and settled the dispute. Joe, now viewed as a headstrong obstructionist incapable of managing a large work force, was given a stern dressing-down by his superiors and promptly demoted.

Rose could overlook these career setbacks. She found it more difficult to ignore Joe's philandering. Mrs. Kennedy was well aware that Joe's long nights at the office were really spent in the company of hatcheck girls and nightclub chorines. In January 1920, frustrated and humiliated by her husband's infidelities and his interminable absences, Rose left Joe Jr., Jack, and Rosemary in the care of two nannies and returned to the welcoming bosom of the Fitzgeralds. After a two-week separation, it was clear to the devoutly Catholic Rose that annulment or divorce was out of the question. She would have no choice but to return to her husband.

While she denied him sex for anything other than reproducing, Joe continued his various extracurricular pursuits. Both were suddenly united by crisis, however, when two-year-old Jack was unexpectedly stricken with scarlet fever. The boy was taken to Boston City Hospital, where on several occasions he came perilously close to dying. Shaken, Joe offered to give the church half his worldly goods if his son's life were spared. When Jack recovered, Joe parted with only $3,500—a far cry from the $1.5 million or so that he would have donated if he had honored his pledge.

No sooner had Jack returned to the family after a three-month stay at a sanatorium in Maine than the Kennedys moved into larger quarters on Brookline's Abbotsford Road. It was there that Rose plunged into the business of running her household with a frightening Prussian efficiency—this despite the fact she was so absentminded she had to pin little notes on her clothing to remind herself of the day's tasks.

Rose kept a three-by-five card file on each child, making note of immunizations, childhood diseases, gains in height and weight, shoe sizes, any medication that had been prescribed for the child, and so forth. The children lined up each morning for inspection, with Rose paying particular attention to any loose threads or dangling buttons. As for play, Rose used folding partitions to divide the wraparound porch at Abbotsford Road into separate pens so "they could be with each other and entertain one another for hours at a time, with a minimal risk that they would push one another down or stick one another with something sharp."

From his little open-air cell, Jack could watch the passing parade of humanity on the street. But neither he nor his siblings were allowed to interact with other children in the neighborhood for fear of catching some dread infectious disease—or, worse yet, having their minds polluted by outside influences.

"They did not speak to other parishioners at church, or socialize with the neighbors," recalled another Abbotsford Road resident. "If anybody tried to strike up a conversation with Rose, she literally walked right past them, smiling but not uttering a word. The Kennedy children didn't play with other children. Everybody thought they were terrible snobs. But it was a way for the parents to maintain complete control over their children's lives."

With each new addition to the family, Rose hired another nursemaid, issued a new set of instructions and became more emotionally withdrawn from her own brood. She would later claim she tried to be home by 5:30 each afternoon to help them with their homework, but in fact she spent most of her days outside the home shopping, socializing, praying, and, when Joe was on the road, taking long trips in the opposite direction.

Even when Rose was present for her children in body, she was absent in spirit. Obsessed with discipline and order, "Madame" (as she insisted on being addressed by the servants) seemed to relish doling out corporal punishment. "I saw it as a duty," she later explained, "never to be done in anger or a fit of irritability. I'd just tell them not to do something and spank them with the ruler if they did it. If a child is walking with me on the sidewalk and runs in front of an approaching car, I quickly paddle him then and there, and so he is not apt to run out again. If he goes near a stove which is hot, I hold his finger near the stove to show him he will be burned. Or if he takes my sharp scissors . . . I stick the point into his arm or finger to show the seriousness of such a point in his eye. If this reasoning does not avail, I used to have my ruler in my desk and would use it." When the ruler wasn't handy, she settled for a hairbrush or coat hanger.

Of paramount importance was punctuality. "We were," Eunice later said with pride, "computerized at an early age." Rose put a clock in each child's room so that they would have no excuse for being late. Dinner was served at a specific time, and a child who was even a few minutes late could expect a stiff dressing-down. The children—male and female—were required to stand whenever Rose entered the room and were forbidden to leave the dinner table until she made her exit.

Each week, the children were dressed up in their starch-collared Sunday best and, prayer books in hand, marched off to mass. When they returned, Rose quizzed them on the day's sermon. At dinner, Rose picked one of the children to say grace—

not just a rote prayer, but something that incorporated a thought for the day.

Proud of her own slim figure, Rose kept an eagle eye on the waistlines of her offspring. The girls were berated for gaining so much as a pound, while Jack was given extra helpings of dessert to beef up his scrawny physique. While the Kennedy women would spend a lifetime obsessed with their weight, the favorable treatment shown Jack at the dinner table led to competition between Joe Jr. and Jack for their mother's affection.

Determined that they be a match for any adversary on the playing field, Jack's mother hired a physical education teacher who had the children outside doing calisthenics at 7 A.M. All the children were also required to take swimming, tennis, sailing, and golf lessons. Even "fun" had a purpose. Rose supervised the parlor games that would become a staple of Kennedy family life, and drilled the children with math problems, brain teasers, and impromptu spelling bees.

Rose was a cold, unforgiving presence in the house on Abbotsford Road. Yet for all her domination of daily life, she kept her distance emotionally. When the family bought a summer house in Hyannis Port on Cape Cod, she went so far as to have her own cottage built on the beach, where she spent solitary hours in religious contemplation.

More so than his brother and sisters, the highly sensitive, sickly Jack craved his mother's affection and openly resented her for withholding it. When informed that Rose was departing on yet another two-week vacation with her sister, Jack confronted her. "Gee," he said, "*you're* a great mother to go away and leave your children all alone." Years later, Jack still simmered with anger over his mother's detached preoccupation with "managing" her children rather than loving them. "She was never there when we really needed her," he said. "My mother never really held me and hugged me. Never! Never!"

Nor, in fact, did Joe Sr. Beneath the boisterous, all-for-one façade, there was very little real intimacy expressed among the family members. As a result, Jack would have a lifelong aversion to touching and being touched in a nonsexual way. "He absolutely hated to be touched," Jack's friend George Smathers later recalled. "If you put your hand on his shoulder, he would literally pull away. He just wasn't brought up in a family where there was a lot of hugging and that sort of thing. It just made him terribly uncomfortable. It wasn't like he could help himself. Jackie eventually broke through that wall, but it took her a long, long time."

In Rose's defense, many mothers of her wealth and position—particularly those of Irish heritage bred in New England—seldom if ever indulged in excessive displays of affection, even toward their own children. Lest the child be spoiled, kisses and hugs were dispensed sparingly, if at all. (Years later, Kathleen "Kick" Kennedy confessed to her boyfriend at the time that "the thing about me you ought to know is that I'm like Jack, incapable of deep affection.")

Nevertheless, Jack never forgave his mother for her dogma-ridden, robotic approach toward child rearing. His unfulfilled need for some sign of maternal affection almost certainly launched him on a lifelong search for it in affairs with countless women. It also may have contributed to his later difficulty in connecting with women on anything but a physical level. "He never got over the way he was treated by Rose," said Chuck Spalding. "It had a profound effect on the way he related to women throughout his life. But I think Joe had an even greater impact on Jack."

The senior Kennedy spent even less time than Rose did with the children. Joe was not present for the birth of several of them, and traveled so extensively on business that an entire month passed before he set eyes on his daughter Patricia. And as the day-to-day supervisor and resident disciplinarian (Joe never had to spank the children), Rose could easily be cast as the villain. But, whereas Rose sought only to instruct, Joe lavished attention on the children: He asked questions about their activities and their schoolwork, and seemed genuinely interested in them as individuals.

Not that Joe came remotely close to indulging the children. Jack later remembered his father as being "stern," "brusque," and "rather curt" toward his offspring. He wanted them to excel, and to that end he embarked on a single-minded campaign not only to educate them, but to instill in them a fierce, win-at-any-cost sense of competition.

His two eldest were already locked in a battle for their parents' attention that often turned bloody. Early on Joe Jr., whose quick-tempered aggressiveness contrasted sharply with Jack's even-tempered disposition, asserted himself as a sort of substitute father figure in his parents' absence. This did not sit well with the second son. As a young senator, in fact, Jack would remember his martyred older brother as "a bully. I always had the problem of my older brother. Physically we used to have some fights which, of course, he always won. It was a problem in my youth."

Rose was well aware of the "problem," though she was seldom around to witness some of the more violent incidents. "During the earlier years of their boyhood," Rose said, "there were fights, few of which I saw but some of which I have been told were real battles. Joe Jr. was older, bigger, stronger. But Jack, frail though he was, could fight like fury when he wanted to." Still, their mother conceded, "Joe was so much stronger than Jack, and if there was any physical encounter, Joe really whacked him, considerably. So when they were young, everybody was trying to protect Jack, more or less, from Joe."

According to a family friend, Jack actually spent much of his childhood "trying to keep his brains from being bashed in" by his scrappy, mercurial older brother. In her memoirs, Rose recalled an incident—related to her by the staff—when Joe exploded in a rage over some imagined slight and tore after his skinny brother—"across the lawn, through the marsh, and down the beach. He then ran along the old breakwater." It took Eddie Moore, Joe's aide-de-camp and Ted Kennedy's namesake, to break up the fight. "It chilled me to think what could have happened if Eddie hadn't turned up at the right time," Rose conceded. No one turned up to save Jack when, at Joe's insistence, they raced their bikes around the block in opposite directions and crashed head-on, leaving Jack with a wound that required twenty-eight stitches.

On another occasion in the summer of 1929, their governess Gertrude Frazer witnessed a similar incident—again, out of Rose's sight. "We found the boys on the pier arguing," Frazer remembered. "Before long, fists were flying, and soon the older boy lost his balance and fell overboard. His brother jumped right in after him."

Joe Sr. was even more removed than Rose from such unseemly scenes of sibling rivalry, though he would have applauded their fighting spirit. Above all else, the senior Kennedy instilled in his progeny the drive to win—at Monopoly, Scrabble, checkers, cards, sailing, swimming, golf, tennis, football, virtually any competitive endeavor. "Touch football was not a matter of strategy with the Kennedy family," said Tom Bilodeau, a contemporary of Joe Jr. "It was a matter of blood and thunder. There was blocking and roughhousing, so when you got into one of their games you tried to get on the side that had the most weight or else you'd get killed. Whichever one Joe was on, Jack would always take the opposite team. They were in a constant state of competition."

Years later when all three were students at Harvard, Bilodeau recalled sailboat races at Hyannis Port. "When the wind was heavy," said Bilodeau, who then weighed nearly 215 pounds, "both Joe and Jack vied for my affection." At the start of one race, Bilodeau's bulk gave Jack an advantage over his brother. "But when we came down to the finish line the wind let up and we started slowing down. Jack turned to me and said, 'Over the side, boy.' So right out there in open water, I proceeded to just go over the side." Jack won the race.

At the core of this win-at-all-costs mentality was a burning desire to please the paterfamilias. By comparison, Rose's attention was a very poor consolation prize. Indeed, the sheer force of Joe's personality was so overwhelming that Rose seemed to wither in her husband's presence. He was, unmistakably, the boss. When the Old Man was around, they hung on his every word and competed for his approval; during the remaining 90 percent of the time when he was away on business, they were content to worship him from afar.

Joe inspired the same sort of awe on Wall Street. In 1924, he spearheaded efforts to fend off a hostile takeover of the Yellow Cab Company. With that one deal, he made good on his promise to become a millionaire at age thirty-five—several times over.

From that point on, Joe seized on any opportunity to turn a profit—the bigger the gamble the better. Nor did he let legalities get in the way. A master at stock manipulation, he conspired with other investors to artificially drive up stock prices, then dump them at a huge profit. Prohibition offered other, more blatantly illegal opportunities to make money. At the height of the no-holds-barred Roaring Twenties, Joe Kennedy financed bootleg whiskey and rum-running schemes that involved the likes of organized crime figures Frank Costello and Meyer Lansky.

Even if he had acquired his wealth by more "respectable" means, there was no way the barkeep's son would be admitted into polite society. Joe was blackballed from Boston's most exclusive clubs, and his wife, Rose, summarily excluded from every important function. "Such a lovely person," said one leader of Boston society who considered the Kennedys hopelessly nouveau riche, "but what a dreadful voice she has."

Furious at his own inability to crack Boston's rigid caste system and concerned that his daughters would not be invited to the proper debutante parties when they came of age, Joe packed up his family to a manor house in the well-heeled (and presumably more ethnically tolerant) Riverdale section of the Bronx. Later, they moved into a twenty-room Westchester mansion once owned by brewery magnate August Busch.

At this point, Joe was also determined that his children would never dirty their hands in the pursuit of money. In 1925 he set up a $1 million trust fund for each Kennedy child. By the time Jack was able to collect the first installment in 1938 at the age of twenty-one, his fund alone was worth an estimated $6 million. That figure doubled by the time he assumed the presidency.

Ensconced in a Manhattan office suite, Joe cast about for new industries in which to invest. He quickly zeroed in on a fledgling billion-dollar-a-year business that was being virtually ignored by New York's hidebound bankers. Although it ranked as the nation's sixth-largest industry, Hollywood relied on only a half-dozen banks for nearly all its financing. Most of this money went to only the biggest studios. The slack was taken up by loan sharks who charged usurious interest rates or, in some cases, helped themselves to a healthy slice of the gross.

Joe saw Hollywood as a potential gold mine, likening it to "another telephone industry." First he bought a chain of thirty small movie houses in northern New England, then sold them off to finance the purchase of a small studio called Film Booking Offices (FBO). Where other studios were turning out silent classics starring Charlie Chaplin and Lillian Gish, FBO carved out a niche with low-budget features starring the likes of football legend Red Grange and cowboy star Tom Mix.

Predictably, this was not enough for Joe. Intent on connecting with Hollywood's elite, he coaxed the Harvard Business School into conducting a seminar. Then he invited the giants of the medium, including Adolph Zukor, Harry Warner, Marcus Loew, and Cecil B. De Mille, to speak at the seminar. For Harvard's hidebound faculty members, it was a rare chance to rub elbows with filmland aristocracy; for the producers and directors, the invitation carried with it tremendous snob appeal. From that point on, Kennedy was welcomed into the bosom of the industry.

Joe boarded the fabled Twentieth Century Limited and moved to Hollywood, leaving Rose and the children behind. If she was hurt, Rose did not admit it. Neither did the children, who lived vicariously through their father's letters. On return trips, he came loaded down with presents: cowboy hats and chaps for the boys, Mary Pickford dolls for his daughters.

On the cusp of adolescence, Joe Jr. and Jack—themselves

viewed as "gods" by their younger sisters and their new brother Bobby—saw the Old Man as omnipotent. He would set the standard for them in all things, including sex.

Joe Sr.'s philandering took a glamorous turn on November 11, 1927, when he first met Gloria Swanson over lunch at Manhattan's Savoy Plaza Hotel. Having gone over budget producing her latest project, a film version of Somerset Maugham's steamy *Sadie Thompson*, the headstrong Swanson needed a healthy infusion of capital—and some sage financial advice. Ironically, Joe Kennedy had tried to scuttle *Sadie Thompson* by sending a protest telegram to the notoriously prudish film censor Will Hays. Over lunch Swanson reminded Kennedy of the telegram, but was clearly willing to overlook it in exchange for a loan.

For all his womanizing, Joe had never encountered anyone remotely as exciting as Swanson. Tinier even than five-foot three-inch Rose, with mesmerizing pale blue eyes and a seductive mouth, she had been divorced from Wallace Beery and was currently wed to the Marquis Henri de la Falaise. A French noblewoman by marriage, she could rightfully lay claim to a grander title. Swanson was the reigning queen of Hollywood, and arguably the most desirable woman in the world.

Kennedy flew into action, setting up an independent film company, Gloria Productions, to produce Swanson's first talkie. She was impressed by the brash, take-charge Irish American—and convinced he could make her one of the richest women in the country. "I felt fortunate to have him taking charge of my finances," she later said. "He was a Harvard graduate, he had shaken up Wall Street, and he wasn't a goddamned stuffed shirt like every other banker I'd ever met."

Joe shared her contempt for those stuffed shirts. "Take Boston," he told her. "The Cabots and the Lodges wouldn't be caught dead at pictures, or let their children go. And that's why their servants know more about what's going on than they do. The working class gets smarter every day, thanks to radio and pictures. It's the snooty Back Bay bankers who are missing the boat."

By this time, Joe had purchased an oceanfront villa in Palm Beach, Florida, and invited Swanson and her husband there. Kennedy arranged for one of his minions to take the hapless marquis fishing, and while Rose read in another room, he pounced on his glamorous houseguest.

"With one hand he held the back of my head, with the other he stroked my body and pulled at my kimono," Swanson remembered. "He insisted in a drawn-out moan, 'no longer, no longer. *Now.*' He was like a roped horse, rough, arduous, racing to be free. After a hasty climax he lay beside me, stroking my hair . . ." Within two months, Swanson later conceded, "Joseph Kennedy had taken over my entire life . . . I was literally owned by him. My whole life was in his hands."

During the next three years, they conducted their affair right under the nose of Joe's long-suffering wife. He paid the rent for Swanson's Rodeo Drive bungalow in Beverly Hills, invited her to Hyannis Port (where nine-year-old Kick watched with her friend while Swanson obligingly autographed the wall of the garage that doubled as a clubhouse wall), and even took her along with Rose on a tour of Europe. Rose dismissed the whole relationship as "a complicated business detail," and behaved as if she and her husband's mistress were the coziest of friends. Swanson could only marvel at Rose's imperturbability. "Was she a fool," asked Swanson, "or a saint? Or just a better actress than I was?"

The Kennedy-Swanson affair was, in fact, common knowledge on both coasts. What no one except the principals knew was that the devoutly Catholic Joe spent most of their affair trying to convince Swanson that she should have his child. To convince Gloria of his devotion to her, he pointed out that Rose had not gotten pregnant following Jean's birth in 1928—confirmation that he had remained true to Swanson. (The next and final Kennedy child, Teddy, did not arrive until 1932.)

For her part, Swanson, who had a child of her own, resisted Joe's attempts to impregnate her. "He was completely irrational on this topic," she said. "I have no idea why he wanted us to have a child, except for some need to fulfill his enormous ego. I wanted no part of it."

The impact of his father's very public affair with Swanson, occurring when Jack was between the highly impressionable ages of ten and fourteen, was clear and lasting. During one visit to Hyannis Port, Joe took Swanson out for a sail on the family yacht, the *Rose Elizabeth*. They were making love topside when Jack, who had stowed away below deck, suddenly popped up. Stunned and confused about what he had witnessed, Jack dove overboard and headed for shore. "But Joe wasn't upset," Swanson recalled. "He just laughed, then he fished Jack out of the water. I was embarrassed, of course, and Jack was shaking, almost crying. He didn't really understand what we had been doing or how to react. Joe thought the whole episode was hilarious."

It was not the only time Jack caught Swanson and his father together. During a later visit to the house in Westchester, Swanson was locked in a passionate embrace with Joe when she suddenly realized Jack was only a few feet away, staring at them. "I automatically pushed myself away from Joe and tried to recoup," she said. "But Joe pulled me back to him and kissed me again, this time much more forcefully. He was doing it for Jack's benefit! I was ashamed, but here was Joe putting on a show for his little boy. Teaching him a lesson, perhaps. This time Jack just stood there with no emotion registering on his face at all, then wandered off as if nothing unusual had happened."

Toward the end of their affair, Joe asked Swanson to introduce his two eldest boys to the world of sex. "By then I can't say I was very surprised at anything Mr. Kennedy had to tell me. But I often wondered how all this affected the children, especially Jack. And if in the White House he was doing the same thing to Jackie that his father did to Rose . . ."

Ultimately, it was Joe who dumped Swanson for another, younger actress—Nancy Carroll. But not before wrecking her film career and her marriage. The first film made under the Gloria Productions banner, *Queen Kelly*, was such an unqualified disaster that it left even the stalwart Joe shaken. In her memoirs, Swanson recalls Kennedy's reaction after first screening the film. "He slumped into a deep chair. He turned away from me, struggling to control himself. He held his head in his hands, and little high-pitched sounds escaped from his rigid body, like those of a wounded animal whimpering in a trap. He finally found his voice. It was quiet, controlled. 'I've never,' he said, 'had a failure in my life.' "

There were conquests too numerous to mention in the coming decades for both father and son, but Joe never allowed Jack to forget the Swanson affair. By way of reminding his son who was the true swordsman of the family, Joe often bragged to Jack *and* to Jackie about his fling with Swanson.

In fact, Joe had no qualms about flouting his marriage vows. While the Kennedy youngsters were growing up, he brought his paramours along on family outings, made passes at the school-mates of his teenage daughters and even his sons' dates.

Mary Pitcairn, a friend of the family who dated John Kennedy, remembered that the senior Kennedy had a habit of kissing all young female visitors good night. Once while visiting Jack's sister Eunice at Hyannis Port, Pitcairn was in her nightgown and ready for bed when Joe came in, grabbed her and kissed her on the mouth—in full view of his daughter. Pitcairn felt sorry for Eunice, but instead of being upset she acted "as if this was standard pro-cedure. I think all this bothered Jack. He was a sensitive man and I think it confused him. What kind of object is a woman? To be treated as his father treated them? And his father's behavior was blatant. There was always a young, blond beautiful secretary around."

"He was completely amoral," admitted Joe's close friend, the noted journalist Arthur Krock. "I think only a Roman Catholic could possibly describe how you could be amoral and still religious. That is, how you can carry an insurance policy with the deity and at the same time do all those other things. Yes, he was amoral. Sure he was ... It never bothered me at all because Rose acted as if they [the other women] didn't exist and that was her business, not mine."

Rose had responded by splurging on clothes and jewelry. Realizing she was a "nobody" compared to the electrifying Miss Swanson, Joe's loyal spouse decided "I could make the most of what I had by keeping my figure trim, my complexion good, my grooming perfect, and by always wearing clothes that were interesting and becoming."

That left Rose little time to spend with Jack, who was attended to by a procession of nurses and governesses. Following his near-fatal bout with scarlet fever, the frail Jack had suffered whooping cough, measles, chicken pox, German measles, bronchitis, ear infections, anemia, and tonsillitis, among other things. Confined to bed much of the time, he became a voracious reader, devouring the works of Sir Walter Scott, Kipling, and Robert Louis Stevenson. Jack was also, in stark contrast to his older brother, rather a slob; he slouched around the house with his shirttail hanging out and seemed to make it a point never to be on time for anything.

After a somewhat disappointing final year at Riverdale Country Day School, Jack was shipped off to boarding school just as his brother had been. Joe wanted his eldest son enrolled at the Choate School in Wallingford, Connecticut, so that he could move easily among the WASP blue bloods who still sat at the top of America's social heap.

But Rose had an entirely different agenda. With Joe away on business she seized the opportunity to send Jack to Canterbury, a Catholic boarding school perched high on a hill overlooking another pristine Connecticut town, New Milford.

Jack arrived at Canterbury in September 1930. He was thirteen. Homesickness soon began to take its toll. His grades began to slip, as did his weight. His vision became blurry, and he got his first pair of reading glasses. And after a series of fainting spells, Jack collapsed with severe abdominal pains. He was rushed to nearby Danbury Hospital, where an emergency appendectomy was performed. Jack did not bounce back from the routine surgery as quickly as most patients and was sent home to recuperate.

The following year, Jack transferred to Choate, where his health continued to slide. He spent weeks at a time in the infirmary, suffering from coughing jags, dizzy spells, and a strange swelling in the neck that was later diagnosed as the mumps. By and large, however, the battery of physicians who saw him during his prep school years were unable to diagnose what was at the root of what Jack himself called his "wasting disease."

Without exception, anyone who ever knew Jack Kennedy will agree on one thing: that however much pain or discomfort he was in, he *never* complained. When he was not in the Choate infirmary, he made efforts to join in with other students on the football field or in the swimming pool. He set himself apart from his husky, athletic brother by becoming the class clown, the wisecrack artist whose good-natured irreverence made him one of the best-liked boys at school—this despite the fact that his protruding Kennedy teeth (later corrected by Rose's on-call orthodontist) and gaunt visage earned him the unfortunate nickname "Rat Face."

Still, he made few real friends. One major exception was Kirk LeMoyne "Lem" Billings, who was almost certainly the closest and most loyal friend JFK would ever have. Jack was a sophomore and Lem a junior when they both went out for the Choate yearbook, *The Brief,* in 1933. Billings, whose ancestors had come over on the *Mayflower,* had one important thing in common with Jack: He, too, had been all but eclipsed by an overachieving older brother.

Not long after his father died, Billings was invited to spend Christmas with the Kennedys at Hyannis Port. The following February, Jack was back in the infirmary at Choate, once again with symptoms—stomach pains, hives, weight loss, fever—that baffled the doctors. At one point, the diagnosis was leukemia, and the student body was sent to chapel to pray for their classmate's recovery. After a month, the hives disappeared, Jack recovered his appetite, and the doctors were once again left scratching their heads.

During the summer of 1934, Billings was visiting Hyannis Port when Jack was rushed to the Mayo Clinic with unremitting abdominal pain. While his friend soaked up the sun back on Cape Cod, Jack was in Minnesota being flushed out with enemas. By way of irony, Billings, who at six foot two and 175 pounds was the picture of robust health, accidentally scalded himself in one of the showers at the Kennedy compound and had to be hospitalized for three weeks. Jack could not muster much in the way of compassion for his injured pal. "Tough about your burns," he wrote, "but to get back to a much more interesting subject . . . my bowels have utterly ceased to be of service and so the only way that I am able to unload is for someone to blow me out from the top down or from the bottom up."

At only seventeen, Jack was already capable of writing letters so bawdy they might have been written by a sailor twice his age. In graphic detail, he described how "the doctor first stuck his finger up my ass. I just blushed because you know how it is. He wiggled it suggestively and I rolled 'em in the aisles by saying, 'You have good motion!' I was certainly feeling great as I know you would having a lot of strangers looking up my asshole . . . My poor bedraggled rectum is looking at me very reproachfully these days."

Predictably, a teenager surrounded by buxom blond nurses could scarcely get his mind off sex. Complaining about the state of his "implement" (or, occasionally, his "vital organ"), Jack wrote Billings that he worried his "vitality" was being "sapped" by as many as six enemas a day. "My penis," he lamented, "looks as if it had been run through a wringer."

Jack's flamboyant use of profanity might have been expected of a seventeen-year-old, particularly one raised by such an oppressively prudish mother. But the tone of Jack's letters reveals far more about the relationship between Jack and the young man who became his roommate at Choate.

Even the salutation "Dear Crap!!" makes it clear that Jack felt comfortable tweaking his friend with the filthiest language he could conjure up ("You dirty-minded shit." "You slimy fuck." "Have you got laid yet? You bitch!"). At the same time, he opened up to Billings in a way he could to no one else. Jack's brashness and bravado scarcely concealed an almost tender affection for his tagalong pal.

The unlikely pair shared a passion for gossip, a cutting sense of humor, and a deep-seated need to thumb their noses at authority (as leading members of the troublemaking Muckers Club, they came perilously close to being expelled). But there was never any doubt that Jack was the star and Lem merely a supporting player—even when they jointly signed a letter asking to be admitted into the French Foreign Legion. Jack jokingly referred to the comparatively impoverished Billings, who attended Choate on a scholarship, as "our poor relation." In keeping with a lifelong penchant for bestowing nicknames on practically everyone, Jack also variously referred to his friend as "LaMoan" and "Pneumoan" and "Delemma" and "Lemmer."

Billings was more than willing to serve as jester at the Kennedy Court—a part he played until Jack's death, and beyond. Continuing on the Kennedy family payroll, Billings grew particularly close to Robert Kennedy and his children. His role in the Kennedy saga ended only with his mysterious death, possibly as the result of a drug overdose, in 1981. "I'm sure," Eunice Kennedy Shriver eulogized at Billings's funeral, "he's already organizing everything in heaven so that it will be completely ready for us—with . . . everything ready for a big, big party." She went on to say that "Jack's best friend was Lem and he would want me to remind everyone of that today. I am sure the Good Lord knows that heaven is Jesus and Lem and Jack and Bobby loving one another."

Lem Billings's contribution to the rise of JFK cannot be overestimated, for Lem was the first person apart from his younger siblings who openly worshipped Jack. He was content to bask in

Kennedy's reflected glory, and proved his unshakable loyalty repeatedly over the years. An unrepentant speed demon always in danger of losing his license, Jack would order Billings to switch places with him in the driver's seat whenever they heard the wail of a police siren. Billings willingly complied, taking the rap for his friend on several occasions.

Equally profound was Billings's impact on Jack's sexual sense of self. So close were the two preppies that on a visit to New York Jack decided he and Lem Billings should lose their virginity together. They donned formal attire, took a cab to a house of ill repute in Harlem and paid three dollars for a white prostitute. Billings waited in the hall while Jack went ahead, but when it was finally his turn he balked. After Jack harangued him for half an hour, Billings finally relented and went into the bedroom with the girl.

Later that night, they knocked on the door of the Manhattan apartment owned by fellow Choate classmate Rip Horton. Jack and Lem were, Horton recalled, "in a total panic. They were frightened to death they'd get VD." So frightened that they went straight to Lenox Hill Hospital where "they got these salves and creams and a thing to shove up the penis to clean it out." Hours later, still sweating and unable to sleep, they woke up Joe Kennedy's personal physician for some penicillin. (Horton himself later joined in on a few of Jack's sexual escapades, most notably to a favorite Kennedy brothel in West Palm Beach, The Gypsy Tea Room.)

Having lost their virginity to the same prostitute, it might have been said Jack and Lem experienced the ultimate in heterosexual male bonding. But beyond that first encounter in Harlem—and it is not clear that Lem actually followed through with the prostitute behind closed doors—Billings seemed as doomed to failure with women as Jack was destined to succeed.

Jack's toothsome good looks and self-effacing charm proved irresistible to women, but Billings held no such fascination for members of the opposite sex. Jack could make fun of Lem's pathetic love life—like the time Lem hid quietly in a haystack while

Jack and another friend made love to their dates—and even make light of Billings's insistence that, as a health precaution, Jack be circumcised.

It is not clear when Jack came to the realization that his soulmate was in fact gay. Nor is it clear when he recognized the obvious: that Billings was hopelessly in love with him. "It was more than just a crush," said a family friend, who pointed out that Billings had actually held himself back at Choate to remain with Jack. "It was beyond infatuation. Lem was completely in love with Jack for thirty years. At those boys' schools a lot of experimenting goes on, but I don't think there was anything physical between them. But everyone knew Lem was in love with Jack. Even Jackie."

In those first years at Choate, it must have been incomprehensible to Jack that his strapping giant of a roommate could be homosexual. "That's why he kept trying to set Lem up with women," a classmate said, "and then making fun of him when he flopped with them. Humor was Jack's way of coping with the fact that Lem just wasn't interested in girls."

Professing to have no idea as to why Billings did not have any girlfriends, Jack wrote, "You're certainly not ugly-looking exactly. I guess you are not just cut out to be a ladies' man. Frankly, my son, I'm stumped."

In the long run, Billings unquestionably had a mollifying influence on JFK's attitude toward gays. "He admired intelligence and wit," said Gore Vidal, whose homosexual novel *The City and the Pillar* made him one of the country's most celebrated writers at the age of twenty-two. "He may have been a phenomenal womanizer, but I think he felt quite comfortable in the company of homosexuals, as long as they were smart enough to hold his interest." As a rising young presidential hopeful in 1958, Jack would ask Vidal to introduce him to one of his more prominent gay friends, the playwright Tennessee Williams. After lunching in Palm Beach, Williams pronounced Jack unelectable: "Far too attractive for the American people."

Another friend, Henry James, would suggest that this all reflected a strong feminine side to Jack that, through his macho exploits, he went to considerable lengths to conceal. "He was very narcissistic, which is very characteristic of a gay person—incredibly so," James said. "If you know any homosexuals, you'll know they are constantly looking in mirrors at themselves. Appearance is *very* important to them—and it was to Jack."

———

The illness that had baffled the physicians at the Mayo Clinic disappeared as quickly and mysteriously as it had appeared. Infused with a new energy and optimism, Jack concentrated not on his studies but, tellingly, on school politics. Before long, his personal charisma had fellow students clamoring to get into his renegade Muckers Club.

He also campaigned toward the end of his senior year to get elected "Most Likely to Succeed"—an honor Jack knew was likely to impress his father, who was now head of Franklin Roosevelt's Securities and Exchange Commission. Jack was right. He had shown Joe that he was a natural political gamesman, and that he had inherited the Old Man's burning desire to win. At any cost, it would seem. Jack's innate charm notwithstanding, the vote to elect him "Most Likely to Succeed" was rigged. When they graduated from Choate, Jack gave his partner in crime Rip Horton an autographed picture. "To Boss Tweed from Honest Abe" it read. "Pray we room together at Sing Sing."

Predictably, Joe was determined that Jack follow his older brother to Harvard. But when Lem Billings was accepted at Princeton, Jack proved his devotion to his friend by insisting that he be allowed to join Billings at Princeton. Both schools accepted Jack, but before he could pack up and move to New Jersey, he was literally hijacked by his father.

In September 1935, Joe and Rose took Jack and Kick on their first trip to Europe. They dropped Kick off at a convent school and enrolled Jack for what was to be a year's study at the London School of Economics, the prestigious institution Joe Jr. had also attended the year before.

Jack lasted scarcely a month there. Severely jaundiced, he was hospitalized with what doctors now speculated was a liver ailment, perhaps hepatitis. Once again he bounced back and, against his father's wishes, moved in with Billings and Rip Horton at Princeton. Jack's Princeton sojourn lasted six weeks. Stricken again, he spent two months at the Peter Bent Brigham Hospital in Boston.

In his scatological letters to Billings, Jack portrayed himself as a kind of medical Candide. According to the young patient, he claimed to have been pawed, "goosed," and "necked" by nubile nurses. In one instance, a battery of doctors and nurses were on hand when the attending physician pulled back the sheets of his hospital bed to reveal Jack's erect penis "quivering with life."

Most of the time, however, Jack endured the normal routine of being poked, prodded, and having tubes stuck in every orifice. He was delighted when his chart showed that he had tested negative for syphilis—a lifelong concern—and strangely philosophical when someone jotted down a possible diagnosis of leukemia (which was later retracted).

As he had done so many times in the past, Jack rebounded—but not sufficiently to return to his studies at Princeton. Instead, Jack spent the rest of that academic year recuperating in Palm Beach, on a ranch in Arizona, and with his father in Hollywood. In a letter to Lem Billings, he sounded as if he had recovered completely. "I met this extra in Hollywood that is the best-looking thing I've ever seen," he wrote.

Not yet out of his teens, Jack was doing his best to make his father proud. "Dad told all the boys to get laid as often as possible," Jack later related. "I can't get to sleep unless I've had a lay." Young Kennedy also claimed that, if he went for more than twenty-four hours without an orgasm, he suffered from crippling migraine headaches.

Acquiescing to his father's wishes, Jack enrolled at Harvard in the fall of 1936. Once again, he was in and out of the infirmary on a more or less routine basis. The precarious state of his health, however, did not dissuade Jack from seeking glory on the playing field—or in the pool. "Jack was sick a lot," recalled Charlie Houghton, one of the three campus football stars he chose to be his roommates at Harvard. "I remember the swimming team tryouts. He got very sick and had to go to the infirmary." When the doctors forbade him to return, Jack had a friend sneak him out. Through sheer grit, Jack, who stood over six feet and weighed less than 150 pounds, made it onto the boxing and swimming teams in his freshman year.

His college football career, however, was decidedly short-lived. In October 1937, Joe Sr. motored down to New Jersey to see both his sons play against Princeton—Joe Jr. on the varsity team and Jack as a junior varsity substitute player. Just before the game, the family chauffeur decided to surprise Jack by tackling him from behind.

The resulting back injury sidelined Jack permanently. But it also prompted the coach to give him a varsity letter out of sympathy—the coveted H in football that he never would have earned on the basis of his ability as a player. "He had a bad back when he was at Harvard," Houghton remembered. "He wore a corset all the time to brace it. It was real bad. If I'd been anywhere near the shape he was in, I wouldn't have gone out for football or anything else."

In interviews, Jack never mentioned the fact that his injury was the result of a prank by the family chauffeur. Instead, he claimed the mishap had occurred during practice. "Three big linemen fell on me," he said during a White House interview. "The first thing I remember was that my left leg tingled and didn't seem to be responding when I ran or crouched or moved. The

-40-

next thing I knew, my back started to ache like all hell. I've never been free from pain since that day in practice."

Kennedy's back trouble, alternately blamed on the "Harvard football injury" and his celebrated act of heroism in the Pacific during World War II, was in fact congenital. He had been born, revealed one of the physicians who treated him as a child in Boston, with an "unstable back."

Dr. Janet Travell, who treated Jack when he was a United States senator and in the White House, had an even more startling diagnosis: "What I really thought had happened to his back, what I have never said before, was that he was born with the left side of his body smaller than the right. The left side of his face was smaller. His left shoulder was lower. I have reviewed pictures of him when he was at Harvard and in his childhood and in standing straight it can be seen his left shoulder is always lower and his leg appreciably shorter. This was true all his life."

Jack's physical problems continued to multiply. In addition to his stomach and back difficulties, he began suffering blinding headaches and nosebleeds, the result of a sinus infection. He also decided at the age of twenty-one to be circumcised—a painful procedure that, given the level of Jack's sexual activity, the doctors felt was warranted. Billings, who had urged his friend to undergo the operation, wrote Jack asking for details. "As for your rather unnatural interest in my becoming circumcised," Jack wrote back, "JJ [Kennedy's nickname for his penis] has never been in better shape or doing better service."

Jack's frail physique did not cramp his style when it came to women. On the contrary, it actually enhanced his chances with them. "He had looks, sympathy, *and* money!" one friend said. "What a combination! All the girls wanted to mother him, and Jack wasn't about to stop them."

Even before he enrolled at Harvard, Jack had racked up an impressive number of sexual conquests. But with the exception of Olive Field Cawley, who went on to marry IBM chief Tom Watson,

Jack did not take any of these teenage relationships particularly seriously. Even Cawley, Jack's first serious girlfriend, was not exempt from Jack's sarcasm. After demanding to know whether a mutual friend had "screwed her or not," Jack told Billings, "she had gotten quite a scare when I gave it to her, so I don't think she would try anything. However, she is quite sexy."

Jack's college dates also discovered that he could be astoundingly cheap. "Like a lot of very rich people, he was very offhand about money. He never carried cash, and I never saw him pick up a check," recalled one of his Harvard dates. "If we dined alone, then it was always someplace his father had an account and when he was finished we just got up and left. If we got in a cab, I dug into my purse to pay the fare. He even called me collect a few times. I thought of it as a sort of charming quirk at the time, although if another man had done that to me I'd have been furious. Like all the girls, I was mad for him."

"Jack was always very successful with girls. Very," said James Rousmaniere, one of his classmates. "All he had to do was snap his fingers." In the suite he shared with his three football star roommates at the Winthrop House residence hall, there were wild parties nearly every week. "He had an unending supply [of women]," Rousmaniere said. "Every time he went to New York for a weekend, he returned with ten new names."

Yet during his four years at Harvard, Jack was serious about only two women. As a junior, Jack became infatuated with Frances Ann Cannon, heiress to the Cannon Mills fortune. Their romance heated up to the point where Jack was on the verge of asking her to marry him. Unfortunately, Frances's father made it clear that he did not want his daughter marrying a Catholic. Nevertheless, Jack continued to pursue Frances, and after taking her to dinner at Manhattan's "21" Club (one of the many New York restaurants where Joe Kennedy, Sr., maintained a running tab) accepted an offer to visit her at her mother's apartment the next day. It was there that Frances introduced a stunned Jack to her new fiancé, the novelist John Hersey.

"Jack seems depressed that he let this girl get away," Rose wrote to her husband, who in early 1938 had been appointed United States Ambassador to Great Britain. Yet Jack put on a brave face for Joe Sr. "Cannon and I have cooled a bit," he wrote to the Ambassador, "and am looking around sharply for a substitute."

The substitute was Charlotte McDonnell. "Am taking Kick's friend, Charlotte Macdonald [*sic*] out to the Princeton game," he wrote Joe Sr., "which will be my first taste of a Catholic girl so will be interested to see how it goes." Charlotte, whose sister, Anne, later married Henry Ford II, could hardly have been the first Catholic girl Jack had dated. But what distinguished her from the others was that he briefly considered marrying her.

"He arrived late very often," Charlotte McDonnell recalled, "or he might send one of his friends up to get me, which drove me up the wall. But . . . once you got with him you forgot all that." Jack spoke openly about marrying her, but "when it comes right down to the nitty-gritty, did he ever ask me to marry him?" she asked rhetorically. "No, he did not."

It was not as if he was distracted by his studies. "He was gay, charming, irreverent, good-looking," remembered his Winthrop House tutor, John Kenneth Galbraith, "and far from diligent." During each of his first two years at Harvard, he earned one B, four C's and a D. It was not until his junior year that he buckled down, focusing on a subject that was nothing if not a natural for him: political science.

The following year, Jack produced a senior thesis on what lay behind British Prime Minister Neville Chamberlain's "Peace in our time" complacency leading up to World War II. The Ambassador enlisted the embassy staff to help his son with his research, persuaded Arthur Krock of *The New York Times* to help shape the thesis, and even paid for a small army of stenographers to type up the final manuscript. *Why England Slept* (a takeoff on Winston Churchill's landmark *While England Slept*) rescued Jack's academic career from mediocrity, permitting him to graduate with honors.

Later, Joe pulled all the necessary strings to turn *Why England Slept* into a best-selling book.

In the meantime, Jack's interest in international events was spurred on by his trips abroad. During his four years at Harvard, Jack spent eleven months visiting his father in London or touring Europe. The U.S. ambassador and his lively brood of handsome children were the darlings of Fleet Street, their smiling faces splashed across the London tabloids on an almost daily basis. Joe Sr. needed the boost. His expressed admiration for Hitler and his Irish background made him instantly suspect to most Britons.

Of all the Kennedys, perhaps only Kick was more comfortable in England than Jack. Having spent most of his life at boarding schools and colleges patterned after English schools, it only made sense that he was now both an Anglophile and an unabashed elitist. "He was terrifically snobbish, you know," said the columnist Joseph Alsop, a friend of JFK. "He was terribly old-fashioned, almost like, sort of English Grandee kind of snobbishness. It was a kind of snobbery of style."

With Billings, Jack toured Paris and the Loire Valley, attended a bullfight in Biarritz, gambled in Monte Carlo, climbed Mount Vesuvius, and visited Naples, Capri, Milan, Pisa, Florence, Venice, and Rome. They passed up a chance to see Hitler at a rally in Nuremberg, but they did hear Mussolini speak in Rome. When they returned to London, Jack fell desperately ill with asthma— an allergic reaction to a dog they had brought back from Germany. "He had terrible allergies," Billings said. "We didn't know he had a *dog* allergy." Sighed little brother Bobby, "If a mosquito bit Jack Kennedy, the mosquito would die."

Jack's later tours of Europe were even more extensive—and more hazardous. With some help from the State Department (courtesy of Joe), Jack added Poland, Yugoslavia, The Soviet Union, Turkey, and the Middle East to his list of destinations. In Munich, storm troopers threw stones at the car Jack and his friends were riding in when they realized it had British license plates. Driving down to the Riviera for a party, speed demon Jack missed a curve and flipped his car over. Miraculously, neither he or his passenger was injured.

To his credit, Jack realized that he had a ringside seat to history. Europe was in turmoil and hurtling toward an inevitable war. Jack wanted to learn all that he could as fast as he could—about fascism, about communism, about the historical, economic, ethnic, and political forces behind the upheaval.

Jack's education continued whenever the Ambassador returned home to the United States for a visit. "I can remember sitting around the dinner table and the whole talk would center on politics and international events," Rip Horton said. "Any of the children could ask him questions in the greatest detail, and no matter how simple or how stupid the questions might seem, he would go to great lengths to explain the answers, the strengths or weaknesses of a particular policy. But if I asked him a question, he'd treat me like a piece of dirt. He'd ignore me. He just didn't want to be bothered with your questions. He was only concerned about educating his own children. Period."

Visitors noticed something else: that behind the façade of a perfect family the reality was quite different. "There was laughter and noise all the time," one frequent houseguest allowed. "There was this constant frenzy as all the kids scrambled to please their father. But aside from the intellectual discussions about 'important' issues, you didn't get the feeling the kids were really connecting with their parents. It's funny, everybody thinks of Hyannis Port as this wonderful all-American home, but when the kids visited home they didn't even have their own rooms to go to! Their personal stuff—books, toys, souvenirs—were packed up and stored in the attic the minute they left for boarding school." Indeed, when Jack visited Hyannis Port or Palm Beach he would walk in the front door with his bags and ask his mother, "What room do I have this time?"

Jack graduated from Harvard cum laude in June 1940. The next month *Why England Slept,* with a foreword by Joe's old friend, Time Inc.'s founder Henry Luce, hit the bookstores. Leaving nothing to chance, Joe secretly bought up forty thousand copies—more than enough at the time to land the book on several best-seller lists.

It was then that Mead Paper scion George Mead, who was later killed at Guadalcanal, took his Yale classmate Chuck Spalding to meet Jack Kennedy at the Kennedy home in Hyannis Port, on Cape Cod. "As we got out of the car, all the windows flew open, and everybody was yelling at us, 'Go home! We don't want to see you!'—all jokingly directed at George, who I gathered was a frequent guest. So we boldly just kept going, right in the front door and into a bedroom. And there was Jack Kennedy, sitting on the floor, completely naked. He was autographing copies of *Why England Slept*. I asked him how sales were going, and he looked up and said, 'Great. Dad's taken care of that.'"

With his newfound fame, Jack was less likely than ever to follow his elder brother into law school. Moreover, he was suddenly hospitalized once again—this time with what appeared to be ulcers. It was suggested that Jack take a year off to rebuild his stamina. Toward that end, he headed for California, where he audited classes at the Stanford School of Business Administration.

Jack lasted just ninety days at Stanford. Given the distractions, it was amazing that he lasted that long. Young Kennedy's reputation had preceded him. "Here he was, the ambassador's son from Harvard—rich, handsome, charming, and a best-selling author to boot," said one of Jack's Stanford classmates. "He had his pick of any girl he wanted."

He spent weekends at William Randolph Hearst's fabled castle in San Simeon, and attended premieres with starlets in Hollywood. Robert Stack, who shared an apartment with Jack while pursuing his own movie career, was "utterly dumbfounded" by Jack's success with women. "He'd just look at them and they'd tumble."

They also quickly learned that his back at times rendered him virtually immobile. It was not uncommon for Kennedy to turn the wheel of his dark green Buick convertible over to his date so he could lie down in the back. One of his dates at the time, Harriet Price, recalled "driving pretty fast" with Jack in the backseat and suddenly having to slam on the brakes. Jack was hurled to the floor and "cursed a blue streak." He could hardly complain about anyone else's driving. More than one girl who dated him during this period remembered his recklessness behind the wheel; one said she came close to being killed when he failed to negotiate a turn and nearly flipped the car over as he had done in France.

Of the women he dated during his Stanford interlude, Jack took none seriously. "Jack was never in love," said Henry James, whom he met at Stanford. "He liked women. He needed women, but he didn't want a commitment to a relationship."

Jack returned to Boston in early December 1940 and promptly landed back in the hospital with severe stomach pains—and, according to Jack's urologist, Dr. William P. Herbst, a case of gonorrhea. Sulfonamide drugs cleared up the gonorrhea, but for the rest of his life Jack would suffer from acute postgonococcal urethritis, a persistent, drug-resistant disease that caused inflammation of the genitals, an occasional discharge from the penis, and a burning sensation on urination. Added to this was another related condition, acute prostatitis for which he would receive large doses of erythromycin, penicillin, and tetracycline. Needless to say, Jack's venereal disease and its legacy, which would ultimately have marital repercussions, was kept under wraps.

While doctors treated his gastrointestinal problems and his gonorrhea, Jack monitored world events from his hospital bed. The news was not good: War was engulfing Europe as Japan tightened its stranglehold on China. Even to the son of an ardent isolationist, it was becoming clear that America would eventually be pulled into the conflict.

Jack's draft number—2748—had already come up, but his student deferment kept him out of the service until 1941. Besides, given the precarious state of his health, there was only a microscopic chance that he would ever be accepted by any branch of the military.

But then, other potential 4-Fs did not have the powerful Joseph P. Kennedy for a father. The former ambassador pressured the head of Naval Intelligence, his former naval attaché at the embassy in London, to arrange for both his sons (Joe Jr. had some undisclosed minor health problem) to pass their navy physicals. They did, and in September 1941, Jack, with a myriad of serious health problems and no military training whatsoever, was commissioned as an ensign.

As Joe had been promised by his contacts in the War Department, Jack was assigned to the Office of Naval Intelligence in Washington. With his favorite sister, Kick, working as a reporter at the Washington *Times-Herald,* Jack's life was as sybaritic as ever. He was still, observed Frank Waldrop, Kick's editor at the *Times-Herald,* "a typical Don Juan. You could almost imagine him checking off names in a book."

One of the names would stand out among all the others: Inga Arvad. The twice-married Danish beauty also worked as a reporter for the *Times-Herald* and on November 27, 1941, devoted her entire "Did You Happen to See?" column to Jack. "An old Scandinavian proverb says the apple doesn't fall far from the tree," the piece began. "If former Ambassador Joe Kennedy has a brilliant mind (not even his political enemies will deny the fact), charm galore, and a certain way of walking into the hearts of people . . . then son No. 2 has inherited more than his due. The 24 years of Jack's existence on our planet have proved that here is really a boy with a future."

Jack was instantly smitten with the blond, blue-eyed former beauty queen from Copenhagen, whom he alternately referred to as "Inga Binga," "Bingo," and "the Scandalous Scandinavian." She was four years older than Jack, worldly and fun-loving. Jack did not realize that even before they met she was under surveillance by the FBI, suspected of being a Nazi spy.

In the 1930s, Arvad had journeyed to Berlin to interview Hermann Göring for a Copenhagen newspaper and so charmed him she was invited back to Germany for his wedding. The best man was Adolf Hitler. She asked him if he wore a bulletproof vest. "Frisk me," replied the führer. And she did.

Hitler later invited Arvad to be his personal guest at the 1936 Olympic Games. Hitler's remark that she was "a perfect example of Nordic beauty" was widely reported in the German press.

After Nazi Foreign Minister Joachim von Ribbentrop tried unsuccessfully to recruit her as a spy, she returned to Denmark to make a low-budget movie and wound up marrying the film's Hungarian director, Paul Fejos. On a trip with her husband to Singapore, Arvad began an affair with Axel Wenner-Gren, a Swedish industrialist with strong ties to the Hitler regime.

The fact that she was still married to Fejos did not prevent Inga from embarking on a torrid affair with Jack. For a time, they lived together—until Naval Intelligence learned of the FBI investigation and threatened Jack with a dishonorable discharge. Instead, they got the Ambassador's son out of harm's way by transferring him to Charleston, South Carolina.

Their affair continued as the two shuttled back and forth between Charleston and Washington. Once they got together, the drill was pretty much the same: Jack stripped, took a shower, and wandered about in a towel. " 'If he wanted to make love,' " Inga later told her son, " 'you'd make love—now.' They'd have fifteen minutes to get to a party and she'd say she didn't want to. He'd look at his watch and say, 'We've got ten minutes. Let's go.' "

The intensity of their relationship is borne out by FBI recordings of their lovemaking sessions in her apartment in Washington and at Charleston's Fort Sumter Hotel. According to one FBI report, surveillance discovered that Ensign Kennedy "spent each night with her in her room, engaging in sexual intercourse on numerous occasions." The FBI report also noted that in the course of lovemaking "she called him 'Honey,' 'Darling,' 'Honeysuckle,' 'Honey Child Wilder,' and said, 'I love you.' "

The couple's phones also were tapped:

Jack: I heard you had a big orgy up in New York.

Inga: I'll tell you about it. I'll tell you about it for a whole weekend if you'd like to hear about it. My husband has spies all over the place.

Jack: Really?

Inga: No, he doesn't. But he told me all sorts of things about you, none of which were flattering. He knew every word you had said to your father about me. It made me look like shit, it amused me very much.

Jack: What does he mean by "every word I said to my father about you?"

Inga: Somebody who knows you very well . . . The person has known you since you were a child and I think they live in New York.

Jack: What about it?

Inga: He said, "Jack Kennedy shrugged his shoulders and said, 'I wouldn't dream of marrying her, in fact I don't care two bits about her. She's just something I picked up on the road.' " It's very amusing, darling . . .

In truth, they both fully intended to marry each other. For Jack, that meant disobeying his father. Joe saw her as a ticking time bomb that could blow up his own dreams of a political dynasty. That did not stop the Ambassador, of course, from making a pass at Inga himself when she visited Hyannis Port with Jack.

According to Inga's son, the product of her later marriage to cowboy star Tim McCoy, she thought "Joe was awfully hard—a really mean man. He could be very charming when she and Jack were with him but if she left the room he'd come down on Jack about her and if Jack left the room, he'd try and hop in the sack with her."

In Joe's eyes, Inga—or rather Jack's infatuation with Inga—presented a very real threat to the family fortunes. FDR had replaced the senior Kennedy as Ambassador to Great Britain because of his isolationist beliefs, and his patriotism was being questioned in the press. All the Kennedys needed now was for Jack to marry a suspected Nazi spy.

No one was more delighted with the results of the FBI surveillance operation than J. Edgar Hoover. He sat for hours listening to the tapes of the young naval officer and the "perfect example of Nordic beauty" in flagrante delicto. More significantly, he knew that this was a valuable bargaining chip in his future dealings with the powerful Joe Kennedy. He could not imagine that it would also give him leverage with a future president of the United States.

At first, Jack stood his ground, forcing Joe to explore ways in which Inga's marriage to Paul Fejos could be annulled. On March 2, 1942, it appeared Jack had finally caved in to pressure from his father when he visited Inga in Washington and called off their romance.

Four days later, he changed his mind yet again.

Jack: Why don't you come down this weekend?

Inga: What a question. Don't you remember that we talked it over Sunday?

Jack: I know it.

Inga: Oh, you don't think it's going to stay?

Jack: Life's too short.

Inga: Oh, Kennedy! You're not giving up what we promised last Sunday, are you?

Jack: No, not till the next time I see you. I'm not too good, am I?

Inga: I think you're perfect dear . . . I still love you as much as always and always will.

Once again, Joe played Wizard of Oz, pulling the strings necessary to get Jack assigned to active duty in the Pacific. In scores of letters to Jack before and after the war, Inga's love for Jack leaps from the page. "Loving—knowing it, being helpless about it, and yet not feeling anything but complete happiness . . ." she wrote in one letter. In another: "My love to you. Take plenty, there is an unending lot where it came from." And another: "I will be seeing you—here or there or somewhere in the world, and it will be the best, or rather second best moment in a lifetime. The best was when I met you."

3

Jacqueline Bouvier was only thirteen when Jack Kennedy shipped out for duty aboard a PT boat in the Pacific. But she had already experienced major upheaval in her life, namely her parents' bitter divorce. Many rightly felt that the marriage of the social-climbing Janet Lee and the infamous Black Jack Bouvier was doomed from the start. Black Jack's principal appeal was that his family was listed in the *Social Register,* a distinction that her family, despite its superior wealth, was unable to achieve. But the Bouviers' claim to social prominence was based largely upon a bogus family tree concocted by Black Jack's father, John V. Bouvier, Jr.

"The Major," as he preferred to be called in recognition of his World War I service as Major Judge Advocate for the U.S. Army, wrote a genealogy entitled *Our Forebears,* in which he claimed the family counted a seventeenth-century member of the French parliament and several nobles among its ancestors. He even concocted a coat of arms and family crest, which he proudly displayed at Lasata, his estate in East Hampton, Long Island. In truth, the Bouviers from which Black Jack and Jacqueline descended were not royal—far from it. Having no connection to the aristocratic Bouviers from the French province of Dauphiné, the Bouviers of Savoy were tailors, farmers, and suppliers of kitchenware.

Michel Bouvier (French for "cowherd") emigrated to the United States in 1815 and was said to be a wealthy importer and manufacturer of veneers. The Major neglected to mention that his grandfather was a poor, uneducated, part-time handyman and cabinetmaker. The Major also frequently boasted of Michel's friendship with Joseph Bonaparte; the relationship between Michel Bouvier and Bonaparte, forced to flee Europe after his younger brother's defeat at Waterloo, was strictly that of employer and employee. After purchasing furniture at Michel's cramped little shop in Philadelphia, Bonaparte hired Bouvier to do some odd carpentry jobs, then to supervise the reconstruction of his house.

Jackie, like the other Bouviers, was raised believing that she was a bona fide blue blood. It was not until she came under intense scrutiny as first lady that historians began to cast doubt on her pedigree. The Major's vivid imagination did not negate the fact that, like the Kennedys, the Bouviers started out as poor, uneducated immigrants and went on to amass great wealth.

Michel the cabinetmaker began manufacturing marble and veneer tabletops, then used the profits from that business to make a killing in real estate. His daughter married a Drexel, one of the wealthy Philadelphia Drexels, and *her* sons bought seats on the New York Stock Exchange. By the 1890s, the Bouviers counted Vanderbilts, Morgans, and Harrimans among their business partners.

When he wasn't polishing the family image—a process that required joining nearly every prestigious club in New York—the Major practiced trial law as the senior partner of Bouvier & Warren. His son, Jack, after a lackluster academic career, graduated from Yale in 1914. Instead of following his father into the legal profession, he joined the Wall Street brokerage house of Henry Hentz & Company. Three years later Black Jack, as he was already known, struck out on his own, amassing a personal fortune in excess of $1 million.

And it wasn't enough. He employed a full-time chauffeur who drove him around in any one of four cars, including a maroon Stutz. He had all of his clothes imported from London. He vacationed on the Riviera with other members of the Lost Generation. The parties he threw at his Park Avenue apartment were legendary. A friend put it succinctly: "He gambled, he drank, he pissed it away on women." Not just women, some said. There was a widely rumored romance between Jackie's father and Cole Porter, though Black Jack later insisted their friendship was only that—a friendship.

Despite a then-substantial yearly income of $100,000, Black Jack was seriously in debt. Yet he was not considered the black sheep of the family. That distinction fell to his younger brother William Sergeant Bouvier, known as Bud. Both brothers were hard drinkers, but Bud's addiction to alcohol ultimately proved fatal.

It was the sensitive, self-destructive Bud who first attracted the attention of Janet Lee. Like the Bouviers, the Lees belonged to East Hampton's Maidstone Club, and it was there that the daughter of millionaire banker James Thomas Lee first encountered the dashing Bouvier brothers.

Socially, the Lees were not in the same league as the Bouviers. But they were not about to let Janet marry a divorced alcoholic. The son of poor Irish immigrants, James T. Lee had put himself through Columbia University Law School and quickly rose to become president and chairman of the New York Central Savings Bank—a position he held for forty years. Janet's mother, whose parents had also immigrated from Ireland, devoted herself to her husband and children.

Far more affluent than the Bouviers, the Lees owned several apartment buildings in Manhattan, where Janet attended Miss Spence's School before enrolling at Sweet Briar College and then transferring to Barnard. She was an accomplished horsewoman— a passion she would pass on to her own daughters.

Such impeccable breeding masked the kind of chronic family dysfunction that runs throughout the saga of Jackie and Jack. Janet was still a teenager when her parents ceased living together; after learning that his wife had been carrying on a longtime affair with a well-known attorney, James T. stayed in the building (which he owned) but moved into an apartment on another floor. All the involved parties were devout Catholics, and divorce was out of the question. So Janet's parents simply ignored each other, leaving Janet the onerous task of carrying messages back and forth. The emotional scars would be deep and lasting, and ultimately would influence the marriage of an American president.

Their nouveau riche parents were unable to crack East Hampton society, but Janet and her sisters, Marion and Winifred, were embraced instantly. And while the brooding Bud Bouvier may have been Janet's first choice, the fact remained that he was a divorced man—something the Lees could not countenance.

When the perennially eligible Black Jack, then thirty-eight, announced that he wished to marry twenty-two-year-old Janet, the crowd at the Maidstone Club was stunned. Diminutive, with a narrow, angular face, she seemed almost birdlike—a far cry from the statuesque beauties Jack had always seemed to prefer. And wasn't he a bit wild for James T. Lee's tastes? Curiously, Black Jack's out-of-control spending habits and equally wild sexual exploits, including a string of broken engagements, were not enough for James T. to veto him as a son-in-law. He was, after all, a Bouvier of the *Social Register* Bouviers.

On the morning of Saturday, July 7, 1928, Janet Lee and Black Jack (also known among his legion of feminine admirers as "the Sheik") were wed at St. Philomena's Church in East Hampton. Jack's brother, Bud, fresh from Connecticut's Silver Hill sanitarium, managed to pull himself together long enough to perform his duties as best man. The bridesmaids wore yellow chiffon dresses and green straw hats, and the church was decorated with yellow snapdragons. The bride wore a satin and lace gown trimmed in silver.

After the ceremony, there was an outdoor reception for five hundred. While guests danced to the music of the same Meyer Davis who would play at their daughter's wedding a quarter century later, Black Jack and James T. quarreled loudly—a sign of things to come.

Black Jack and his bride spent their wedding night at New York's Savoy Plaza, the same hotel where Joe Kennedy had met Gloria Swanson. The next day the newlyweds sailed for Europe aboard the *Aquitania*. At sea Jack quickly reverted to his old habits, flirting with a fellow passenger, the heiress Doris Duke, then only sixteen. When she found out about it, Janet flew into a rage. This would, with only intermittent exceptions, last for the duration of their marriage.

Temperamentally, it would be hard to find two people more ill-suited. Black Jack was flighty, self-indulgent, fun-loving, and affectionate, but unable to cope with adversity. He was interested in style, image, the art of living. He generally avoided unpleasantness of any kind, and could be counted on to crumble in a crisis.

Janet, on the other hand, was the toughest of cookies. A disciplined perfectionist, controlling to the point of being dictatorial, Jackie's mother was a realist who always kept her eye on the bottom line. As a young child, she had seen her father go from poor to rich, and as a result she would always live in fear of losing it all. She was also socially ambitious, and would not be content for long with existing on the periphery of New York society as a Bouvier.

A year after their wedding ceremony, on July 28, 1929, Jacqueline Lee Bouvier arrived at Southampton Hospital—six weeks late. She weighed eight pounds and, with her dark full hair and wide-set dark eyes, already bore a striking physical resemblance to her father.

Jackie was three months old when her privileged world was shaken to its foundations by the stock market crash of October 29, 1929. Black Jack, his cash reserves virtually depleted, was forced to turn to his hated father-in-law for financial support. James T. Lee loaned Black Jack a substantial sum, and allowed him to live in one of his buildings rent-free—with the proviso that Bouvier stop his womanizing and rein in his ostentatious lifestyle. As soon as he moved into the huge, eleven-room duplex at 740

Park Avenue, Black Jack responded to his father-in-law's generosity by going on a spending spree.

Jackie was only two when she made the papers for the first time, thanks to her mother. "Little Jackie Bouvier, daughter of Jack Bouvier and the former Janet Lee, will not make her bow to society for another sixteen years or more," the *Easthampton Star* reported when she celebrated her second birthday at the summer home on Long Island. "But she was a charming hostess at her second birthday party given at the home of her parents."

From then on, she appeared routinely in the social columns—entering her Scottie in the local dog show, giving a tea party for the small children of other monied families, competing at an equestrian event. Jackie got her start as a horsewoman early; when Jackie was one year old, Janet, who had been a junior master of the Suffolk Fox Hounds, sat her up on a horse and led her around the ring. By the time she entered kindergarten, Jackie was a regular competitor at horse shows, arriving with her nanny at each event in her grandfather's Duesenberg. "I can still see Jackie in her pigtails and riding outfit—top hat, Ascot tie, long leather boots," remembered Samuel Lester, who exercised horses at the East Hampton Riding Club. "She was soon bringing home blue ribbons by the box load." Jackie was so competitive, in fact, that she would scowl whenever she failed to trounce her opponents. "You could always tell from the expression on Jackie's face whether she'd won or not," said a childhood friend. "Her mouth and jaw would pull as tight as a rope. She wasn't happy unless she won, unless she beat all the other little kids."

She would soon have to share the spotlight. When Jackie was three and a half, her baby sister, Caroline Lee, was born. The "Caroline" quickly fell by the wayside. Several months later, Jackie, Lee, and their English nanny were taking a stroll through Central Park when Jackie vanished. A police officer found her hours later, walking along a path. "My nurse and baby sister," she told the officer sternly, "seem to be lost."

Even as toddlers, the Bouvier girls clearly were two distinct types. Prettier, daintier, more congenial and diplomatic than her sister, Lee was regarded as the China doll of the family. Jackie, on the other hand, was boisterous, headstrong, and precocious. During summers in the Hamptons, she climbed trees and rough-housed with the boys. Yet she was not quite the typical tomboy. In childhood games, Jackie always took on the role of queen or princess while her sister, Lee, was a lady-in-waiting. Jackie even kept a crown on hand, part of a circus costume her father had brought her. According to her cousin Edie Beale, Jackie was always "an odd mixture of tomboy and princess." She never, added Beale, "outgrew the princess role."

And Lee, who preferred her bicycle to horses, never outgrew the lady-in-waiting role. "She had a complex about Jackie because Jackie won all those prizes at horse shows. Jacqueline, even as a teenager, dominated over Lee. People paid more attention to Jackie than they did to her . . . Her father was in love with Jackie."

Not everyone, though, was in love with Jackie. At the Chapin School on Manhattan's East Side, she was so disruptive that she spent much of each week being scolded by Miss Stringfellow, the headmistress. It was not until Miss Stringfellow, at her wit's end, compared the unruly student to a thoroughbred horse in need of discipline that Jackie got the message and buckled down.

Black Jack was another matter. Janet's efforts to put him on a tight leash failed miserably. Priscilla McMillan grew up on the North Shore of Long Island, the so-called Gold Coast, and first encountered Jackie when they were both still teenagers. "My mother often came in contact with Jackie's father," Priscilla recalled. "He was very dashing, and about as dark as you could be, and Jackie inherited his looks. Black Jack's modus operandi was to just stare women down until they surrendered. Not terribly subtle. He was such a preening peacock, so convinced that no woman could resist his charms—a very smooth character, or so he thought. My mother was one of those women who thought he was loathsome. She just *dreaded* dancing with him."

That opinion was apparently not shared by most of the females who came in contact with Black Jack, however. He continued to have affairs—often with the young wives of his friends. In the summer of 1934, Janet and Black Jack invited his sometime golf partner, Virginia Kernochan, to watch Janet compete in a horse show. After the competition, the two women posed together sitting on a fence while Jack stood beside them. It wasn't until the photograph was published in the next morning's New York *Daily News* that Janet saw that, while she smiled for the camera, her husband and his "golf partner" were holding hands behind her back. ("Jackie thought that picture was hysterically funny," George Smathers said later. "In the White House, she would haul it out and point at it and just double over laughing. She had a randy streak of her own, and thought her father's womanizing was sort of comical.")

Unlike Rose Kennedy, Janet was not willing to quietly accept her husband's infidelities. She was constantly confronting him, threatening divorce. Their heated arguments lasted well into the night, often jarring their children awake. While her timid sister merely hid under the covers, Jackie got out of bed and crept into the hallway. There, cross-legged on the floor in her nightgown, she heard her parents rain down a torrent of accusations and cruel epithets upon one another.

"All the fighting had an impact on both girls, of course," said Truman Capote, who knew both sisters but grew especially close to Lee. "It made them both terribly cautious, a little afraid of people and relationships in general. But Lee was probably too young to really understand what was going on. Jackie, on the other hand, understood much more. Even at that age, I think she could appreciate that her mother was this sort of hideous control freak, a cold fish with social ambitions, and her father was a naughty, naughty boy who kept getting caught with his hand in the cookie jar. Of course, both girls loved him more. Who wouldn't, given the choice?" Black Jack called Jackie "Jacks" and Lee "Pekes." Janet had no nicknames for her children, but insisted they call her Mummy.

As the marriage continued to disintegrate, Jackie began exhibiting the signs of what her adult friends later described as a distinct "split personality." One moment, she was exuberant, outgoing, to all appearances the quintessential happy child. The next moment a dark mood would descend, and a brooding Jackie would retreat to her room and her books, shunning all contact with others. "You never knew when it was going to happen," one of Jackie's teachers at Chapin said. "She would turn on and off like a light bulb. But when the light was on, it was blindingly bright."

After a trial separation and failed reconciliation, the Bouviers separated for the last time in 1937. Locked in a struggle with his wife for their daughters' affections, Black Jack pulled out the stops. During his weekend visits over the next three years, he took Jackie and Lee to the movies, to Rumpelmeyers for ice cream, and on hansom cab rides through Central Park. There were visits to the Museum of Natural History and the Metropolitan Museum, to the Bronx Zoo, Coney Island, and a favorite hangout, Belmont Park.

Black Jack took them on shopping sprees at such Fifth Avenue emporiums as Saks, Bergdorf Goodman, Bonwit Teller, and Lord & Taylor. He also began imparting to them his sense of style and flair for the dramatic. Speaking from firsthand experience, over the years he taught them not only how to hold themselves, how to walk, and how to talk, but also the vital importance of maintaining a mystique. The key to a woman's allure, he told Jackie, was not to give too much of herself, to hold something back. "The wide-eyed look, the breathy little voice—she learned that from her father," said Jack Kennedy's close friend Chuck Spalding, who knew Jackie's father. "Jackie's mother was very different. I never got the feeling of any warmth between Jackie and her mother. None at all." Truman Capote put it more bluntly: "Jackie resented her mother, but that doesn't mean she didn't grow up to be in some ways like her."

Janet knew from the beginning that she could not compete

with her soon-to-be-ex-husband on his turf. So she used fear in the war for their children's souls. She made certain that, under her watch, their lives were strictly regimented. Out of frustration and jealousy as much as a misguided sense of perfectionism, she routinely exploded at the children over the smallest infraction. She spanked both girls, but willful Jackie got the brunt of the beatings. As Jackie grew older, Janet stopped the spankings and began slapping her across the face. Janet "was much tougher on Jackie" than on Lee, said Capote. Today, Jackie might well have been considered an abused child.

The issue of Janet's cruel indifference toward the children surfaced in depositions given for the pending divorce. Berthe Kimmerle, the girls' governess in 1937 and 1938, testified that Mrs. Bouvier was an absentee mother who spent most of her time traveling with any number of male acquaintances. One of Janet's maids, Bernice Anderson, also stated under oath that when she was at home, Jackie's mother took sleeping pills, drank heavily, and was an emotional wreck with an uncontrollable temper.

According to Kimmerle, Janet spanked Jacqueline when she was "too noisy in her play" or "for no reasons that I was able to see." Conversely, Kimmerle claimed Black Jack spent a great deal of time with his daughters. "His love for the children, and their very joyous love for him, I could easily see. Both were devoted to him . . ."

There was no question where Jackie's loyalties lay. Once when Janet and James T. were lambasting Black Jack, Jackie raced up the stairs to Kimmerle and said, in tears, "Look what they are doing to my daddy!" As soon as their mother headed out the door, Jackie and Lee pleaded with Kimmerle to let them call their father. But, according to Kimmerle's testimony, Mummy left strict orders that Jackie and Lee be spanked if they so much as mentioned their father.

In June 1940, Janet packed up Jackie and Lee and headed for Reno. After six weeks of horseback riding at the Lazy-A-Ranch,

Mrs. Bouvier had fulfilled the residency requirement for a divorce. It took twenty minutes for the judge to hand down a final decree.

Jackie, who had grown more sullen and aloof as the demise of her parents' marriage approached, coped by plunging into her various projects. She took ballet lessons. She wrote poems and illustrated them with her own sketches:

> *Christmas is coming*
> *Santa Claus is near*
> *Reindeer hooves will soon be drumming*
> *On the roof tops loud and clear*
> *The shops are filled with people*
> *Snow is coming down*
> *And every one is merry*
> *In such a busy town.*

Jackie also continued to make a name for herself on the riding circuit. At age twelve, she rode away from the National Championships at Madison Square Garden with two trophies in the junior division.

Neither Black Jack nor Janet wasted much time on remorse; they left that to their shell-shocked daughters. At the Maidstone Club, Black Jack met the vacationing wife of a British army officer stationed in Washington. "Soon she became virtually a member of the family," said Jackie's cousin John Davis. "They walked arm in arm, they held hands, they hugged and kissed unabashedly, they made love wherever they found themselves: in the Bouvier cabana, at Jack's house, behind the dunes."

The officer's wife did not return home without mementos of her visit. Six months after arriving back in England, she gave birth to twins, a boy and a girl. She told her husband that Black Jack was the father, but the young major gallantly agreed to raise them as his own.

In 1949, Jackie visited her two half-siblings in England and, according to Davis, reported back to Black Jack that the family resemblance was nothing short of striking. Both youngsters possessed the wide-set eyes, broad cheekbones, and dark good looks shared by Black Jack and Jackie. At first Jackie warmed to the idea of having these two additions to her family, but after she married Jack Kennedy she worried that such a scandal might wreck his career. She never breathed a word about the existence of Black Jack's other two children to anyone. By the 1980s it was academic: Both were dead, the girl mysteriously murdered and the boy killed in a car crash.

Following the divorce, Janet lived in fear of going broke. She received only a thousand dollars a month in alimony payments from Black Jack, and her father's bursts of largess were sporadic at best. She wanted to—*needed* to—marry well, and in the summer of 1942 she did better than that. That June, Janet became the third wife of Hugh Dudley Auchincloss, Jr.

Indeed, Hugh D. "Hughdie" Auchincloss's Scottish-American ancestors accrued their wealth in the same fashion. Through marriage, they forged alliances with DuPonts, Vanderbilts, Rockefellers, Tiffanys, Burdens, Winthrops, and Saltonstalls, to name a few. Most of Hughdie's fortune came not from his father but from his mother, Emma Brewster Jennings. She was the daughter of Oliver B. Jennings, who founded the Standard Oil Company with the Rockefellers. A product of Groton, Yale, and Columbia Law School, Hughdie took a low-level position in the Herbert Hoover administration before establishing his own Washington-based investment banking firm in 1931.

With their mother's remarriage, Jackie and Lee suddenly found themselves adjusting to life with a new set of stepsiblings. There was Hugh Dudley III, Auchincloss's son by his first wife Maria Chrapovitsky, the daughter of a Russian naval officer. His nickname, "Yusha," was the Russian equivalent of Hugh. Hughdie also had two children with Nina Gore, whose father was the blind senator from Oklahoma, Thomas Gore: Nina ("Nini," to distinguish her from her mother) and Thomas. Their half-brother,

Nina's son by an earlier marriage, Eugene Vidal, Jr., so worshipped his grandfather the senator that he changed his name to Gore Vidal. And after the spur-of-the-moment wedding of Janet and Hughdie ("My father had no intention of marrying anyone until the day before the ceremony," Yusha said), Jackie seemed happy with her new family.

Bearlike, ruddy-faced, and easygoing, Hughdie was the antithesis of the exotic-looking, debonair, and devil-may-care Black Jack Bouvier. What Auchincloss did share with Jackie's father, unfortunately, was a streak of prejudice. "Hugh Auchincloss was an old-fashioned Republican Club anti-Semite," said his stepson Gore Vidal. "The first question he'd always ask when he met someone was 'Do you know what Kirk Douglas's real name is?' But Hughdie was an anti-Semite of the reflex variety. He told stories about Jews the same way he told stories about blacks and so on."

It was not his only vice. Jackie's "Uncle Hughdie" was a connoisseur of pornography. Although his second wife, Nina, had made him throw much of the material into the Potomac, he secretly withheld a few items for posterity. So long as he kept his few remaining books and French postcards to himself, Janet was more than willing to look the other way.

According to Vidal, it was his own mother, Nina, who actually engineered Janet's marriage to Hugh. "A financially desperate social climber with two small daughters to raise, she was eager to marry someone just like . . . just like poor Hughdie, which Nina suggested that she do," Vidal said.

Vidal also claimed that Hughdie suffered from a form of impotence, which had required his mother to artificially inseminate herself with a spoon to create Vidal's half-siblings. Presumably Janet used the same technique to conceive Jackie's half-sister, Janet, and half-brother, Jamie.

There were compensations, not the least of which were Merrywood, the family's palatial estate outside Washington, and Hammersmith Farm in Newport. Merrywood, which provided the setting for Vidal's 1967 novel *Washington D.C.*, was an imposing brick mansion set on forty-six acres overlooking the Potomac, complete with a baronial dining hall, indoor badminton court, Olympic-size swimming pool, and stables. Riding trails wound throughout the property.

Jackie was given the third-floor bedroom that not long before had been occupied by Vidal, who vacated the premises when he was sixteen. He described it as "not much larger than a closet. To the right, twin beds. To the left, the door to a small bathroom with a white tile floor. Directly ahead, a single large window with a view of lawn, woods, river . . ." In the closet, Jackie found several white shirts with Vidal's name sewn in the collar. She wore them while horseback riding.

Summers were spent at Hammersmith Farm, with its twenty-eight rooms, fourteen fireplaces, seventeen bathrooms, and a resident staff of sixteen. Downstairs the hallways were carpeted in crimson. Already mindful of such things, Jackie decreed that henceforth all Auchincloss dogs should be black to provide suitable contrast. In time, their menagerie included a Scottie, a poodle, a cocker spaniel, and Caprice, Jackie's own Bouvier des Flandres—all black.

The focal point of the house was not the formal living room, but the hotel lobby–sized deck room with its dramatic green-tiled fireplace, wraparound view of the water, and nautical motif—including a stuffed pelican suspended from the ceiling and framed photographs of yachts once owned by the family.

The noted interior designer Elisabeth Draper, who had been hired by the peripatetic Janet to redo Merrywood and Hammersmith Farm, transformed Jackie's third-floor room overlooking Narragansett Bay into a light-filled aerie. The walls were pale yellow, and a classical frieze chosen by Jackie ran along the border of the oddly pitched ceiling. The furniture—two twin beds, mirrored dressing table, and writing desk—were all white.

At first Jackie wrote to her father saying she was lonely and missed New York. It was what Black Jack wanted to hear. For him, the marriage of Hughdie and Janet had been particularly traumatic: Black Jack continued paying for their schooling—Jackie now attended Holton-Arms, a Washington, D.C., day school—but he saw little of his cherished daughters.

Determined that she not be embarrassed by her gangly daughter, Janet followed the lead of Washington's finest families and enrolled Jackie in Miss Shippen's dance class. ("I was a tomboy," Jackie later recalled. "I decided to learn to dance and I became feminine."). At the school's 1942 Christmas party, Jackie wore a blue dress with puff sleeves—her very first adult evening gown. She was self-conscious about the gold kid slippers that accentuated her big feet. When she got home, she drew a cartoon caricature of herself with the caption, "Jacqueline's first evening dress. This was lovely blue taffeta and I had a pair of gold track shoes and a really chic feather cut."

Like children of more modest means, Jackie, Lee, and their stepsiblings were assigned chores at Hammersmith Farm. "During the war we supplied eggs and milk to the local naval base," Yusha said. "Jackie took care of the chickens and I milked the cows. Well, she always got up a little earlier than I did so I told her to just wake me up when she did. She was a little irritated at this. One morning I felt something pouring over my head and woke up to discover that she had poured peroxide on my hair. She had seen a baby picture of me with blond curly hair and decided I should be blond. She thought I'd look like Alan Ladd! I guess she thought I ought to wake myself up."

Of the Auchincloss children, she was closest to Yusha, two years her senior. "We hit it off instantly. We were friends as well as family. Actually, we were friends *before* becoming family. We were probably much closer to each other than a real brother and sister. She loved to walk alone, to paint, to read. Even if I were walking with her, we'd go for an hour without saying a word—always completely comfortable, never any pressure.

"Even as an adolescent, Jackie was very much in control, very focused, and very, very bright," Yusha said. "We played this game where she gave you clues and you had to guess who she was describing. It was always someone like Pericles or Blake."

Because of the chaos caused by her parents' endless bickering, Jackie maintained "a highly developed sense of order. All through her teenage years, she was very well organized and highly disciplined—traits she inherited from her mother, no doubt. But she could also be very spontaneous. You'd be walking along quietly when suddenly she'd break into a run and challenge you to a race—once she had a substantial lead, of course. Jackie was like a racehorse. She never lost that . . ."

Another quality of Jackie's—one that she shared with Jack Kennedy—was a rocklike stoicism. "When she was fourteen, she insisted on having all her wisdom teeth taken out on the same day. She wanted it over with, and she didn't go around moaning about it. I never once heard her complain."

Growing up, they also played matchmaker for each other. "I'd introduce her to my friends, and vice versa," Yusha recalled. "If we'd never been brother and sister, we were such good pals we probably still would have done the same. We'd help each other out and spy for each other, find out who liked us and who didn't. We made a very good team."

According to her stepbrother, Jackie could also "be critical and very severe and yet be very supportive. If she thought I was doing something wrong, she let me know it." When Yusha wanted to leave school at sixteen and join the Marine Corps, she confronted him. "Jackie was furious at me. I had to finish school, she said, because the marines didn't want any dumbbells and they didn't want any cowards, and quitting my studies was a cowardly thing to do. 'Finish school,' Jackie told me, 'then you can join the Marines.' "

Jackie also took an interest in the welfare of people she never met. "After Franklin Roosevelt died," Yusha said, "Jackie wrote me a letter at prep school. She said she worried about Eleanor Roosevelt. How was she going to cope? What was she going to do? She said it was 'the end of an era.' There was no way we could have known people would be asking the same questions about her only nineteen years later."

Jackie did not spend all her time immersed in other people's troubles. Her sense of humor shone through, for example, in the poem she wrote to commemorate the birth of her half-sister, Janet Jennings Auchincloss:

> Listen, my children, and you shall hear,
> It was nineteen hundred and forty-five
> When Janet Jennings became alive.
> She made all the headlines far and near
> And became the Baby of the Year!
> Crowds to do her homage came,
> Bringing priceless gifts and rare.
> The flower shops all had a boom
> And Western Union tore its hair.

Jackie doted on Janet as she would her half-brother, Jamie, born two years later. "She was so much older than us," Jamie recalled. "More like an aunt than a sister." But there was one thing that separated Jackie from all her Auchincloss half- and stepsiblings: money. "You must remember that Jackie and I were in the same boat," Vidal recalled. "We were brought up in style, allowed to live in their very comfortable, rather Jamesian world. But the money was *theirs*. We—Jackie, Lee, and I—were penniless, and were made painfully aware of the fact. I went to work, and they went looking for rich husbands."

At age fifteen, Jackie was shipped off to Miss Porter's School in Farmington, Connecticut, one of the finest finishing schools in New England. At Miss Porter's, the financial chasm between Jackie and her well-to-do classmates was obvious. While the other girls were by and large denied nothing, Jackie had to subsist on the fifty-dollar monthly allowance she received from Black Jack. It was only after she pleaded with her grandfather the Major that she was able to afford the twenty-five dollars a month it cost to board Danseuse, the horse her mother had given her, at the Farmington stables.

Jackie generally kept to herself, reading in her dorm room or taking solitary walks around the campus. Viewed as aloof and snobbish even by her born-to-the-purple peers, Jackie spent most of her time in the company of her former Chapin classmate Nancy Tuckerman. "Tucky" became her closest and most trusted friend—male or female.

"To meet her, even during those adolescent years, was never to forget her," recalled Letitia "Tish" Baldrige, who was a year ahead of Jackie at Miss Porter's and then at Vassar, and later served as Jackie's White House social secretary. "She was a natural beauty, wearing none of the teenage cosmetic fashions of the day. There were no globs of neon purple lipstick, no thick eyebrows blackened by strokes of a dark pencil, no thick layer of Pan-Cake makeup. Even more important to me in my earliest impression of this young girl was her voice—unforgettable in its soft, breathy tones. It was a sound that forced you to draw close and listen well."

Farmington was only a few hours' drive from Manhattan, and Black Jack Bouvier took advantage of the close proximity to strengthen his ties with his favorite daughter. During his frequent weekend visits, he would watch Jackie compete in a horse show or act in a school play, then take her and her friends out to lunch at the Elm Tree Inn. "Everybody loved Daddy," she later said of her smitten classmates. "We must have eaten him broke."

Her father's visits—during one he teamed up with her to compete in a father-daughter tennis tournament—took Jackie's mind off the fact that she was not dating. Not that there was much opportunity. Housemothers were responsible for protecting the virtue of all their girls, and making sure that the college boys who did come for tea at 2 P.M. on Saturdays left promptly at 4 P.M. "I think the boys from Yale and Harvard who came by were just terribly intimidated by her," said Baldrige. "She was so striking, and she had this queenly bearing. It really could be overwhelming."

According to Priscilla McMillan, Jackie was a frequent guest at coming-out parties held on the polo-playing North Shore of Long Island, in such gilded communities as Locust Valley and Brookville. "The first time I laid eyes on Jackie she was coming out of the ladies' room at one of these dances," McMillan said. "She was only sixteen—a little bit precocious when all the other girls were a couple of years older. A striking beauty, but you definitely had the sense that she was ambitious, that she was pushing it socially. She was a little too well-dressed, a little too glamorous. There were clusters of boys around her all the time. She was the center of attention even then, and of course it made the other girls quite jealous."

Jackie's oft-expressed fears of spinsterhood seemed somewhat disingenuous. "I just know," she lamented to a friend, "no one will ever marry me and I'll end up as a housemother at Farmington." But when she graduated in June 1947, Jackie seemed less concerned with domestic bliss and more intent on making her own mark. In her yearbook next to "Ambition in Life," she wrote: <u>Not to be a housewife.</u>

At Vassar, Jackie continued to confound those who knew her. Selwa "Lucky" Roosevelt, later to become chief of protocol in the Reagan administration, occupied the dormitory room next to Jackie's. What bothered her most about Jackie was her "two-headed personality. On the one hand, she had this almost starlike quality—when she entered a room you couldn't help but notice her, she was such an exquisite creature. At the same time, she seemed so very private."

Nationally syndicated Hearst society columnist Igor Cassini (brother of designer Oleg Cassini), who wrote under the name Cholly Knickerbocker, recognized this star quality when he spotted Jackie wearing a skintight pink satin "siren dress" she had borrowed from her fashion-plate sister, Lee. Proclaiming Jackie 1947's "Queen Deb of the Year," Cassini gushed: "America is a country of traditions. Every four years we elect a President, every two years our congressmen. And every year a new Queen of Debutantes is Crowned. Queen Deb of the Year is Jacqueline Bouvier, a regal brunette who has classic features and the daintiness of Dresden porcelain. She has poise, is soft-spoken and intelligent, everything the leading debutante should be . . ."

An avalanche of publicity followed. "Jacqueline Bouvier's poise! What a gal!" reported Walter Winchell. "Blessed with the looks of a fairy tale princess, Jacqueline doesn't know the meaning of the word snob!" With the attention, Jackie's social life picked up considerably. Now she was dating virtually every weekend, often traveling to New Haven and Cambridge to go out with Yalies and Harvard men. "I suppose," her father wrote her, "that it won't be long until I lose you to some funny-looking 'gink' who you think is wonderful because he is so romantic-looking in the evening and wears his mother's pearl earrings for dress shirt buttons, because he loves her. However, perhaps you'll use your head and wait until you are at least twenty-one." Later, as she spent more time with boys and less with her father, he wrote increasingly stern letters warning her not to compromise her "reputation." Considering the source, Jackie thought the advice was nothing short of hilarious.

At seventeen, Jackie retained her mischievous streak. "Jackie sometimes tried to make me blush," recalled Yusha, who would go out dancing with his stepsister at Washington's Solgrave Club. "Jackie thought I was too reserved and stuffy, so she purposely danced with me very provocatively, very sexually."

Jackie was not convinced about what to do with her life, but she knew that she was not interested in any of the young men she had met during the endless rounds of parties in Newport and Washington. "I didn't want to marry any of the young men I grew up with" Jackie recalled, "not because of them but because of their life. I didn't know what I wanted. I was still floundering."

In the summer following her freshman year, Jackie and three friends boarded the *Queen Mary* for a rigidly scheduled seven-week tour of Europe. When she returned to Washington she hit the party circuit, brimming with stories about her adventures on the Continent.

One of those most eager to gaze into Jackie's huge, wide-set eyes as she told her stories was Charles Bartlett, Washington correspondent for the *Chattanooga Times*. "I used to see her up in East Hampton when she visited her father, and then down in Washington," Bartlett recalled. "She always had these sort of English beaux and I must say they were not up to her."

Bartlett did know someone he felt was "up to her," and in 1949 he invited them both to his brother David's wedding in East Hampton. "I spent the whole evening," Bartlett recalled, "trying to get Jackie Bouvier across this great crowd to meet John Kennedy."

———

The Jack Kennedy who attended David Bartlett's East Hampton wedding had been transformed by tragedy and triumph since he left Inga Arvad for duty in the Pacific six years earlier. In that time, he had become a bona fide war hero, lost a brother and a sister, nearly died several times, and been twice elected to Congress.

Jack's heroism as the skipper of PT-109 in the Solomon Islands became the stuff of legend. At 2:30 on the morning of August 2, 1943, Captain Kennedy was at the helm of PT-109 steaming through the Blackett Strait when it collided with the Japanese destroyer *Amagiri*. "This is how it feels to be killed," Kennedy thought as the Japanese ship sliced the boat in two. Two of his crew were killed, and three badly burned by the flaming high-octane gasoline that spread across the water. When the wreckage began to sink, the survivors swam for a deserted island three miles away; "Shafty," as Kennedy was known to his fellow officers, swam the breaststroke, pulling along a wounded sailor by clenching the man's life jacket straps in his teeth.

They made it to the beach, and at nightfall Jack stripped and swam naked back into the Blackett Strait in hopes of signaling an American patrol vessel. (He later told his dates that he swam the backstroke so the sharks couldn't get his testicles.) Swimming against the current, he finally gave up and was miraculously washed ashore. He tried again the next day, with no success.

Finally, two men from a neighboring island happened by in a canoe, and Kennedy carved a message on a coconut shell for them to take to an Australian observation post miles away. Five days after the collision with the *Amagiri*, Kennedy and his surviving crew members were rescued.

Kennedy was angry that none of the other PT boats in the vicinity had come to his rescue, and that he and his crew seemed to have been so quickly given up for dead. He also felt a tremendous burden of guilt. Jack was a notorious cutup in the service; later investigations into the PT-109 incident showed that half his crew was either asleep or lying down on the deck at the time of the collision, and that Captain Kennedy had violated any number of Navy procedures. Had he been more vigilant or reacted more quickly, could he have averted disaster?

Back home, there was no second-guessing. The story of PT-109 was splashed across the front page of *The New York Times*. Joe Sr. could not have been more elated and immediately began lobbying for his son to be given a medal. Joe settled, reluctantly, for a Purple Heart.

There were other, unforeseen consequences. Joe Jr., determined to prove to his father that he was every bit as brave as his younger brother, volunteered for what amounted to a suicide mission over German-controlled territory in France. On August 12, 1944, his plane exploded in midair, and he was killed. He was twenty-nine.

Three weeks later Jack's sister Kick, who had been excommunicated after marrying Billy Hartington, Protestant eldest son of the Duke of Devonshire, became a widow when Hartington was shot by a German sniper. (Four years after that in May 1948, Kick perished when the plane she was riding in with her married lover, Peter Fitzwilliam, crashed in France.)

It was young Joe's death, however, that dramatically altered the family dynamic. It was now Jack's responsibility to pick up the torch for his fallen brother. It was up to the sickly, battered war hero to fulfill their father's dreams of power and glory. The surviving Kennedys, led as always by Joe, were galvanized behind Jack—and he dreaded it. "God! There goes the Old Man!" he told his navy pal Red Fay at a family gathering just a few weeks after Joe Jr.'s death. "There he goes, figuring out the next step. I'm it now, you know. It's my turn. I've got to perform."

After his discharge from the Navy, Jack had toyed with the idea of becoming a political columnist. His father helped him land an assignment with Hearst newspapers covering the founding of the United Nations in San Francisco. But this was the briefest of detours on the road to a political career. "I can feel Pappy's eyes on the back of my neck," he told Fay, a native San Franciscan. "When the war is over and you are out there in sunny California . . . I'll be back here with Dad trying to parlay a lost PT boat and a bad back into a political advantage. I tell you Dad is ready right now and can't understand why Johnny Boy isn't all engines ahead full."

When the legendary pol James Curley, who had been elected while serving a jail term for corruption, gave up his Eleventh Congressional District seat to run once again for mayor of Boston, Joe thrust his son into the fray. *Thrust* was the operative word: "I went in one day," recalled a campaign worker, "and found him humping this girl on one of the desks in his office. I said, 'Sorry,' and left!" When he learned the secretary was pregnant, Jack said only two words: "Oh shit!" Whether the girl went ahead and had the baby or a back-room abortion is unclear, but the issue never surfaced publicly during the campaign.

There were the inevitable carpetbagger charges—Jack established residence in the district by taking a suite at Boston's Bellevue Hotel—but they were eclipsed by John Hersey's glowing account of Kennedy's PT-109 heroism that ran in *The New Yorker* and *Reader's Digest.*

An awkward campaigner and lackluster speaker, Jack made up for his lack of charisma by campaigning twice as hard as his opponent. Nor did it hurt to have the combined clout of the Kennedys and the Fitzgeralds behind him—not to mention an old-style, back-room political machine that had been routinely delivering elections to Democratic candidates since the 1800s.

Patrick "Patsy" Mulkern, a streetwise member of Boston's political "Irish Mafia," was brought in to help. "First day I met him he had sneakers on," Mulkern recalled. "I said, 'For the love of Christ, take the sneakers off, Jack. You think you're going to play golf?'"

The grueling campaign took its toll. In greater pain than ever after a second failed operation on his back, Jack often hobbled from one speaking engagement to another. He was emaciated, with dark circles under his eyes. A carefully cultivated tan concealed a jaundiced complexion that doctors in Boston and at the Mayo Clinic were at a loss to explain.

But Jack soldiered on. "We had a hell of a job with him," Mulkern said. "We took him out to taverns; we took him to hotel lobbies; we took him to the South End; we met 'em on street corners; we took him in club rooms. We took him everywhere. The girls went for him. Every girl you met," said Mulkern, "thought she was going to be Mrs. Kennedy."

After marching five miles in Boston's Bunker Hill Day Parade, Jack waited until he was out of the sight of spectators to collapse. "He turned yellow and blue," said Robert Lee, who worked on the campaign. "He appeared to me as a man who had probably had a heart attack." Lee and George Thomas, Jack's ever-present black valet, carried Jack to a second-floor apartment, stripped off his clothes, and sponged him down. "His father asked me if he had his pills," recalled Lee. "He did, and he took some pills." Then Jack's doctor arrived and whisked him away.

Jack's bout with "malaria" was covered in the Boston papers, and he was shown being carried from plane to ambulance on a stretcher. But the sight of the handsome, stricken young man may have earned him the sympathy of women voters.

In the end, it was Joe Kennedy's fortune (which *Forbes* put at $400 million by 1950) and his influence that won the election for his son. To neutralize a popular Boston city councilman, Joseph Russo, Joe simply paid a different Joseph Russo to put his name on the ballot—confusing voters and dividing the Russo vote. To counter candidate Mike Neville, considered the front-runner, Joe's longtime pal William Randolph Hearst ordered his *Boston American* not to print Neville's name or run any of his ads. For Jack, the outcome was never in doubt.

Elected by a landslide, twenty-nine-year-old John Fitzgerald Kennedy, bronzed from three weeks in the Florida sun, arrived at the Capitol in 1947 and struck up a friendship with another promising freshman: Richard Milhous Nixon of California. Along with another young Turk, Florida's George Smathers, they entered into a friendly competition to see who would be the first to get out of the House and into the Senate.

Kennedy and Smathers also shared a keen interest in chasing women—a sport in which they tried to interest Nixon. When the California congressman made his first trip to Europe as part of a fact-finding delegation, Jack slipped him a note containing the names and numbers of women to ring up in Paris. Nixon, already married to Pat, was, according to his secretary, "too embarrassed" to take the numbers with him.

Jack made his own trip to Europe as part of a congressional fact-finding tour in September 1947. But on a stopover in London he collapsed and was taken to a clinic, where doctors finally rendered a diagnosis for the illness that had landed him in and out of hospitals for years: Addison's disease, a degeneration of the adrenal glands that—like AIDS—destroys the immune system and leaves the individual defenseless against infection. Overexertion, scraping one's knee, having a tooth pulled, catching the flu—all these minor health risks can prove fatal for someone with Addison's disease.

Treatment for Addison's, which had given Jack his jaundiced look since adolescence, consisted of daily injections of a synthetic hormone, desoxycorticosterone acetate (DOCA). Later, he removed the need for injections by having time-released DOCA pellets surgically implanted in his thighs. (Two years later, the DOCA injections would be replaced by another breakthrough substance, cortisone.)

Jack's friend Pamela Churchill, who later married Averill Harriman and went on to serve as the Clinton administration's ambassador to France, checked up on young Kennedy in London. "That young American friend of yours," the doctor told her, "he hasn't got a year to live."

Determined that no one get wind of the grim diagnosis, Jack's handlers issued a press release stating that he was recovering from a mild case of malaria originally contracted in the Pacific. The trumped-up malaria story also served to explain Jack's peculiar yellow-orange coloring.

Sailing home in the hospital ward of the *Queen Mary*, Jack barely survived the voyage. When the *Queen Mary* pulled into New York Harbor, "he was given extreme unction and brought off the ship on a stretcher," said the *Times-Herald*'s Frank Waldrop. "It was touch and go." An ambulance took him to a chartered plane at LaGuardia, and from there he flew to Boston where another ambulance took him to the Lahey Clinic.

After several more weeks recuperating at Boston's Lahey Clinic, Jack returned to work in Washington. (By the end of his life, Jack's adrenal glands had virtually disintegrated. To the very end he and those around him flatly denied that he ever suffered from Addison's disease.)

Even many of those who worked closely with Jack believed the carefully concocted story that he suffered from malaria. Patsy Mulkern, the man who had helped Jack campaign, recalled a typical drive from Boston to Hyannis Port when a state trooper would pull them over for speeding. "Dave Powers was driving," Mulkern said, "and Jack was lying on the backseat. Of course, when he got that malaria, he'd get cold. He had to put a blanket on. Oh, he had it bad, malaria."

Occasionally Jack would take the wheel. As a driver, observed Mulkern, Jack was "wicked, wicked, wicked. Fast, very fast. Wild man." When he was with Mulkern, Jack was "pinched three, four times" for speeding. Once they learned who he was, however, "that was the end of it." Mulkern was amazed that Jack never got in a serious automobile accident. "He was very lucky. Very lucky."

Joe Kennedy, despite his obvious concern for his son's health, was not above taunting Jack to impress a young girl. Recalled Chuck Spalding: "We went out to dinner with Jack—I was with my wife, Betty Coxe, and he was with Charlotte McDonnell. Jack was in great pain but very stoic about it. He looked very frail. After we got home it was decided we were going out to the movies. Before we went, Jack said, 'Let's say good-bye to the Old Man.' So we all trooped upstairs to Joe Kennedy's bedroom and there he was standing in front of the mirror, shaving.

" 'We're off to the movies, Dad,' Jack said. Joe just looked up at Charlotte and smirked. 'Why don't you get a live one?' Can you imagine? It was a very cruel remark—it was *meant* to be cruel, but Jack looked at his father and understood him. You have to understand that Jack was totally devoted to his father. He loved Old Joe more than he ever loved any other human being."

As he waited for an opportunity to graduate to the Senate, Jack watched warily as his old friends succumbed one by one to matrimony. In a letter to Red Fay, he ran down the list of their mutual service pals, nickname by nickname, and then wondered if their new wives would object to him: "While I agree that the Coot kid and the Big George and the Rod and Shafty boy etc. will all end up as buddies what do you think about Mrs. Coot Kid and Mrs. Rod and Mrs. Barney Boy and Mrs. K . . . Is there any possibility that they will take a dim view of the old Red head?"

To the news that yet another acquaintance was getting married, Jack commented, "My limited experience has shown a wife can bollix things up quicker than most people." He seemed to feel marriage made no more sense for women than it did for men, at least when the woman in question was young, attractive, and intelligent. When Priscilla McMillan, who was then doing research in foreign affairs, told him of her engagement, she was taken aback by his response. "Why on earth would you want to marry?" he asked. "There are so many unhappy marriages."

"A lot of it had to do with his parents," McMillan said. "The way Rose sort of shriveled into what he called a 'nothing.' Jack always joked about all the women his father had around—it was sort of comical—but he was also very sensitive to the fact that this hurt Rose deeply. He loved his mother on some level, and he resented her at the same time for playing the fool and not standing up for herself. He knew he could never be faithful to one woman, and I don't think he wanted to be the cause of that sort of pain."

There was speculation that Jack was in fact secretly married during this period, and that the "limited experience" he spoke of referred not to his parents but to the Kennedys' Palm Beach neighbor Durie Malcolm. In 1962, it would be reported that Jack and Malcolm had been secretly wed in 1939 and divorced nine years later. Based on an incorrect entry in *The Blauvelt Genealogy* (Malcolm was a Blauvelt descendant), the rumor was to gain enough momentum in the press to force an official White House denial.

In truth, Malcolm had dated Joe Jr. in the late 1930s. Shortly after his election to congress, Jack took Malcolm, who by then had already racked up two failed marriages, to the 1947 Orange Bowl. She married lumber heir Thomas Shevlin, Jr., six months later.

Pursuing his bachelorhood with a vengeance, Jack spent his two terms in Congress bedding scores of women on both coasts. He went to Hollywood, where Inga "Binga" Arvad was now a gossip columnist and tried to rekindle their romance, but to no avail.

There was no shortage of willing candidates to take Inga's place. In the late 1940s, Jack dated Lana Turner, Joan Crawford, Hedy Lamarr, Susan Hayward, and the libidinous ice skater Sonja Henie. He struck out with Joan Fontaine, and with her sister (and archrival), Olivia De Havilland—though Chuck Spalding recalls that in the case of De Havilland Jack refused to take no for an answer. "He thought she was incredible, and was perfectly willing to make a complete fool of himself if that's what it took to win her over," Spalding said. "We went to her house for tea and Jack couldn't take his eyes off Olivia. When we got up to leave, he opened the hall closet door and walked right in. This whole mountain of stuff just came crashing down on him—tennis balls, rackets, boxes. It was hysterical."

De Havilland would not go out with Kennedy. But when he spotted her at a restaurant dining with writer-artist Ludwig Bemelmans of *Madeline* fame, Jack was dumbfounded. "Just look at that guy!" he told Spalding. "I know he's talented, but really! Do you think it was me walking into the closet? Do you think that's what really did it?"

Perhaps understandable for a man whose favorite phrase was "Wham, bam, thank you, ma'am," finesse was not Jack's strong suit. His modus operandi, according to friend Gloria Emerson, was strictly "Up against the wall, Signora, if you have five minutes. That sort of thing."

Jack was merely following his father's advice to get "laid as often as possible." But the sudden deaths of his brother and sister, his persistent illnesses, and his harrowing wartime experiences instilled in Jack a deep fatalism. "He was obsessed with the idea that he only had a short time on the planet," Spalding said. Concurred George Smathers: "He was very fatalistic. When I first knew him, sometimes it seemed that women and death were all he talked about." After a long discussion about the most desirable way to die (he preferred death by poison over drowning, shooting, freezing, fire), Jack said, "The point is you've got to live every day like it's your last day on earth. That's what I'm doing."

Jack's most significant Hollywood affair was with the stunning Gene Tierney, who rocketed to fame in the 1940s whodunit *Laura*. Tierney was in the midst of a divorce from Oleg Cassini. He already knew Jack from their Palm Beach days, and would become Jackie's official designer during her tenure as First Lady.

Tierney was particularly vulnerable when naval officer John Kennedy visited the set of *Dragonwyk* in 1946, and not just because of her breakup with Cassini. Tierney had given birth to a retarded child after an ardent fan with German measles kissed her during her pregnancy. She and Cassini were facing the ordeal of having to place their daughter, Daria, in an institution.

"I turned and found myself staring into the most perfect blue eyes I had ever seen on a man," she recalled of that first encounter on the movie set. "My reaction was right out of a ladies' romance novel. Literally, my heart skipped."

Jack's appreciation of the pain she was going through over Daria drew them closer together. "Jack understood," Tierney recalled. "He told me about his sister Rosemary, who had been born retarded, and how his family had loved and protected her." (Joe Sr. had actually made the unilateral decision to lobotomize Rosemary in the fall of 1941 when she became too rebellious for the family to handle.)

Jack had not yet been sworn in for his first term in Congress when he told Tierney of his plans to occupy the White House. "That was his goal. He talked about it in a way that was unselfconscious, as another might talk about going to work in his father's store."

"I warned Gene that Jack would never marry her," Cassini said he told Tierney when she informed him she wanted a divorce. " 'No Catholic is going to marry a divorced woman,' I said. 'His family won't stand for it. Gene, be sure you know what you are doing.' "

Tierney visited Jack on Cape Cod, where she thought he "looked like Tom Sawyer" in patched blue jeans. The affair continued on the Cape, in Hollywood, and in New York. It was over lunch in Manhattan that, without warning and just as a group of friends were about to descend on their table, Jack turned to Tierney and said, "You know, Gene, I can never marry you." Over the years, Tierney suffered a series of nervous breakdowns that resulted in her being institutionalized—"the result" she said, "of a gradual series of hammer taps." Her affair with Jack was undoubtedly one of these.

Unlike Tierney, not everyone was favorably impressed by Jack. Philanthropist and Democratic party supporter Mary Lasker was first introduced to the upstart congressman by mutual friend Florence Mahoney, whose husband published the *Miami Journal*. "Florence was devoted to him, and said he was surely going to be president some time," Lasker said. "Well, he was this very, very skinny and very young-looking congressman. I thought, Florence is a wonderful girl and I'm very fond of her, but this is a very unlikely candidate for president . . . His arms were too long for his coat, his pants were not fitting—or the bottoms were turned up. He was really very unimpressive looking."

Lasker did, however, find him entertaining. "Florence is very interested in birth control as a public health problem, and so am I. And he was always saying to her, 'Well, have you any new methods?' Or, 'What is the situation?' There would always be some crack about it. Even when he'd see me alone in the halls of Congress he'd say, 'How is Florence, and how is she getting along with birth control?' " It did not occur to Lasker that, while Jack obviously enjoyed tweaking his friend, he might also be looking for some practical new information on the subject.

———

Now, at the 1949 wedding of his brother David in East Hampton, Jack's friend Charlie Bartlett snaked through the crowd, pulling Jackie Bouvier by the hand. In a far corner, he could see Jack, chatting away with an unidentified blonde. Bartlett managed to get Jackie about halfway across the room when they were intercepted by former heavyweight boxing champion Gene Tunney.

"Tunney was a friend of my father's, and she got involved in a conversation with him. By the time I pried Jackie away from Tunney and got her over to the corner where Jack had been standing, he'd vanished!" Bartlett would get a second chance to bring Jackie and Jack together—nearly two years later.

———

In the summer of 1949 Jackie returned to France—this time to spend her junior year studying at the Sorbonne. She and five other students boarded with the Countess de Renty, a former member of the French underground whose husband perished in a Nazi concentration camp. The apartment at 78 avenue Mozart had neither heat nor hot water, and a single bathroom with a tin tub. As winter approached, Jackie would jump into bed and, wearing earmuffs, scarves, and gloves, do her homework under the covers.

She shared none of these grim details with her parents, although she did write Janet frequently. "I have to write Mummy a ream each week," she wrote to Yusha, "or she gets hysterical and thinks I'm dead or married to an Italian."

Janet may have had cause for concern when it came to Jackie's social life. Although she did well in her studies, she also led a hectic social life—sipping coffee at Deux Magots, haunting Left Bank clubs. "Jackie was there allegedly to go to the Sorbonne, but it was really to have a good time," said Gore Vidal.

Jackie also knew many of the American writers working in Paris at the time—George Plimpton and William Styron foremost among them. She became romantically involved with only one of that group, John Phillips Marquand, Jr. John Marquand, Sr., had first achieved fame with a series in *The Saturday Evening Post* about a Japanese detective named Mr. Moto. But he was chiefly known for his 1938 Pulitzer Prize–winning novel *The Late George Apley* and other gently satirical novels examining the lives and habits of socially prominent New Englanders.

When Jackie met Marquand Jr., he was living on the Left Bank and working on his first novel, *The Second Happiest Day*. After a night of club hopping, they returned to his *pension*, and Jackie lost her virginity to Marquand when the lift to his apartment "stalled" between floors, a maneuver Marquand had used before. Jackie's supposed comment at the time: "Oh! Is that all there is to it?"

Marquand denied this story, but Vidal, who was also a longtime friend of the writer, insists it was true. "What he may have said publicly was one thing," Vidal said. "But Jackie did lose her virginity to him in a lift, and they had a very passionate affair."

In the summer of 1950, Jackie went on a whirlwind economy-class tour of Germany and Austria. She then joined Yusha for a three-week jaunt through Scotland and Ireland. "We did everything—went to pubs, kissed the Blarney Stone," Yusha recalled. "Jackie was fascinated by the history, by the castles and the folklore. She wanted to learn everything she could. But that's the way she was about everything. If she went to a museum, she couldn't just look at a painting. She had to know all about the subject matter, the history of the artist, anything she could soak up. In Ireland she walked up to complete strangers on the street and asked them questions. That was something she shared with Jack. They were both wonderful listeners."

Once back in the United States, Jackie transferred from Vassar to George Washington University in Washington, D.C. While studying for her degree in French literature, she entered *Vogue* magazine's prestigious Prix de Paris contest. The centerpiece of the contest was a five-hundred-word essay on "People I Wish I Had Known." Her choices: the ballet impresario Sergey Diaghilev, the French poet Baudelaire, and Oscar Wilde.

Jackie's entry revealed not only a talent for writing, but a self-deprecating sense of humor. Asked to describe herself, Jackie wrote: "I am tall, 5'7" with brown hair, a square face and eyes so unfortunately far apart that it takes three weeks to have a pair of glasses made with a bridge wide enough to fit over my nose. I do not have a sensational figure but can look slim if I pick the right clothes. I flatter myself on being able at times to walk out of the house looking like the poor man's Paris copy, but often my mother will run up to inform me that my left stocking seam is crooked or the right-hand top coat button about to fall off. This, I realize, is the Unforgivable Sin."

As for her choices of Diaghilev, Baudelaire, and Wilde: "If I could be a sort of Overall Art Director of the Twentieth Century, watching everything from a chair hanging in space, it is their theories of art that I would apply to my period, their poems that I would have music and paintings and ballets composed to. And they would make such good stepping-stones if we thought we could climb any higher."

More than twelve hundred women from 225 colleges entered the contest, and on May 15, 1951, Jackie was informed that she had won the grand prize: a one-year stint as a *Vogue* staffer, to be divided between Paris and New York.

Jackie, who was about to graduate from George Washington University, turned down the prize. Hughdie felt she had already spent too much time abroad and might never return. By way of consolation, Jackie's stepfather agreed to finance yet another European vacation—only this time Jackie would take along Lee.

Before embarking aboard the *Queen Elizabeth*, Jackie accepted an invitation in May 1951 to dine at the narrow Georgetown brownstone occupied by Charlie Bartlett and his wife, Martha. Having missed the chance to bring them together two years earlier, this time the Bartletts succeeded in introducing the boyishly handsome Congressman Kennedy to the stunning Jacqueline Bouvier.

Jack, thirty-four at the time, was intrigued by the twenty-one-year-old college senior. Martha Bartlett, determined to match Jackie up with an eligible man so she would no longer prove a temptation to her own husband, made sure they sat across from each other at the table and that their glasses were never empty. (After they were married, Jack told a reporter that that historic evening he had "leaned over the asparagus and asked her for a date." Jackie coolly—and accurately—pointed out that asparagus had not been served that night.)

Following dinner, the Bartletts and their guests went into the backyard and played a spirited game of charades. Having used her skills at pantomime to demolish her classmates at Miss Porter's and Vassar, Jackie promptly trounced the opposing team.

Jack had never met anyone quite like Jackie—something all the more remarkable considering his exposure to the opposite sex. She was mesmerizingly beautiful, to be sure, and highly intelligent. She seemed more substantial than other girls he had known. But he had known plenty of "substantial" women who combined brains with beauty.

What drew them together? "They were two lonely people," Spalding said, "and they instantly recognized that in each other." Once the little girl caught in a tug-of-war between parents hell-bent on destroying each other, she seemed only truly happy when involved in solitary pursuits like reading or horseback riding. "She could be the belle of the ball when it was required—just like Jack," observed another friend. "But that was just an act. Jack was precisely the same way. Before he'd enter a room, he'd say, 'Time to turn on the B.P.'—the Big Personality—but he hated glad-handers. It's ironic that these two people who personified charm and grace for millions of people around the world were really lone wolves."

In Jack, Jackie would later say she recognized beneath the gleaming armor of self-confidence "this lonely sick little boy . . . in bed so much of the time reading history, devouring the Knights of the Round Table."

As Bartlett and Jack walked Jackie to her car that night, Jack asked her out for a drink. Before she could answer, Josie, the Bartletts' fox terrier, leapt into the open door of her black Mercury and onto a man sitting in the backseat. The stranger turned out to be a former boyfriend who had recognized Jackie's car and decided to surprise her. Flustered by the sudden appearance of another man, Jack turned back to the Bartletts' house and Jackie sped off alone.

While Jack immersed himself in his campaign to unseat Massachusetts Senator Henry Cabot Lodge in the next election, Jackie traipsed through Europe with Lee. The sisters put together *One Special Summer,* a scrapbook chronicling their adventure abroad and presented it to their mother on their return. Featuring Lee's commentary and Jackie's illustrations and verse, it left little doubt as to what was on their minds as they made their way through England, France, Italy, and Spain. "Jackie has warned me about the quirks in the sex lives of Near Easterners!" Lee wrote of her encounter with one man from Beirut, a fellow aboard the *Queen Elizabeth.* The rest of *A Special Summer,* which would be published by Delacorte twenty-three years later, duly recorded their brushes with, among others, a pair of French army officers, a Spanish journalist, and an Italian artist.

When they got back home to Merrywood, Jackie faced a dilemma. The pressure was already on for her to marry someone who could keep her living in the grand manner to which she had become accustomed. Either that or go to work. She chose the latter.

Uncle Hughdie suggested that, given her talents, Jackie might be interested in a career in journalism. He asked his (and Joe Kennedy's) friend Arthur Krock of *The New York Times* to see if he couldn't find a suitable position for his stepdaughter.

Krock picked up the phone and called Frank Waldrop, the hard-bitten editor of the Washington *Times-Herald.* (Waldrop had hired both Kick Kennedy and Inga Arvad before the war.)

"Are you still hiring little girls?" Krock asked.

"Why?"

"Well," said Krock, "because I have a wonder for you. She's round-eyed, clever, and wants to go into journalism. Will you see her?"

It didn't hurt, of course, that she was the stepdaughter of the wealthy and influential Hugh Auchincloss. Waldrop met Jackie the first week of December 1951 and asked her point-blank if she was serious about a journalism career or just biding time until she found a husband. When she assured him she had no intention of getting engaged any time soon, Waldrop told her to return after the Christmas holidays and he would have a job for her.

By the time she returned to Waldrop's office in January, Jackie had a confession to make. She had become engaged to a man she had just met, she told Waldrop, and would understand if that precluded her being given a job on the paper. Impressed by Jackie's candor—and confident that she would not go through with the marriage after knowing the potential groom for such a short time—Waldrop gave her a job as an office gofer anyway.

Jackie's engagement to John Husted had come as a shock to everyone who knew her. A Yale-educated investment banker, Husted was tall and good-looking and from a respected New York family. His father had been friends with Hughdie, his mother knew Janet, and both his sisters had attended Miss Porter's when Jackie was there. "I had met her father, Black Jack," Husted recalled, "and years earlier I had seen Jackie playing tennis with him during a father-daughter tournament at Farmington. But it wasn't until my aunt, Helen Husted, asked me to attend a party at the Solgrave Club in Washington that I actually met her."

For Husted, it was love at first sight. "I thought she was heavenly-looking," he recalled. "She was not aloof at all. She was very giggly, and bright as well. She had a devastating, cutting wit, and an innate sense of style that was obvious even then." There was one drawback: "Her voice was unfortunate. Very breathy, gushing—strangely at odds with her personality and her intellect. But I had fallen totally, completely in love with her."

Within weeks, said Husted, "we had sort of declared our love for each other. I phoned her up at Merrywood and asked her to marry me. I had been going down to Washington to see her and was rather tired of making the trip, so before she could answer I said, 'Well, if you love me, prove it. This time, you come up to

New York and tell me your answer.' I told her to meet me in the Polo Bar of the Westbury Hotel at noon on Saturday." He showed up at the bar a few minutes early. "It was snowing, and I sat there waiting for three hours. I paid the check and was just getting up to leave when Jackie breezed in. Everything was sweetness and light. She said yes."

There was an engagement party at Merrywood, and a sizable announcement in the January 20, 1952, *New York Times* accompanied by a photo of Jackie. The wedding was set for some time in June.

Early on, though, there were signs that Jackie was not wholly committed to the idea. When Husted's mother offered her a baby picture of her fiancé, Jackie declined. "If I want a picture of John," she said, "I'll take my own."

"We were all very surprised," Yusha Auchincloss recalled. "John Husted was a very nice fellow from a very nice family. But he didn't have the same interests that Jackie had. He was a broker, he belonged to all the right clubs, but that was about it. I couldn't imagine what it was they had in common to talk about."

Charlie and Martha Bartlett agreed. Martha particularly "didn't think too much of the fellow Jackie was engaged to," according to Bartlett. "He was nice, but somewhat lackluster. Certainly not worthy of Jackie's hand in marriage." So the Bartletts tried again to match Jackie with the man she was destined for.

Meanwhile, Jackie continued her long-distance relationship with Husted, shuttling back and forth between Washington and New York. She also landed a more interesting job at the *Times-Herald* as the paper's "Inquiring Camera Girl." When Waldrop asked her if she knew how to operate a bulky Speed Graflex camera, she nodded—then dashed out to take a crash course in newspaper photography.

As the Inquiring Camera Girl (at a weekly salary of $56.75), Jackie approached Washington personalities or people on the street, asked them the question of the day, and then snapped a photo to accompany their answer. "She would stop people coming out of the supermarket," Husted said, "and ask them 'Should men wear wedding rings?' or 'Are men braver than women in the dentist's chair?' " Some of Jackie's questions were whimsical: "Noël Coward said, 'Some women should be struck regularly, like gongs.' Do you agree?" "How do you feel when you get a wolf whistle?" Other questions revealed a lot about her state of mind: "Do you think a wife should let her husband think he's smarter than she is?" "Do the rich enjoy life more than the poor?" "Chaucer said that what women most desire is power over men. What do you think women desire most?"

Some of the other questions asked by the Inquiring Camera Girl seemed eerily prophetic: "Should a candidate's wife campaign with her husband?" "Would you like your son to grow up to be president?" "Which first lady would you most like to have been?" "If you had a date with Marilyn Monroe, what would you talk about?" "What prominent person's death affected you most?"

Jackie was particularly fond of interviewing children "because they make the best stories." Not long after Richard Nixon was elected vice president in 1952, she asked his six-year-old daughter Tricia what she thought of her father then. "He's always away," the little girl answered. "If he's famous why can't he stay home?" In a few years Jackie would understand exactly what Tricia Nixon meant.

Jackie's engagement to John Husted was scarcely a month old when Janet Auchincloss pointed out a sobering fact to her daughter. After doing a little digging, Janet discovered that John Husted earned seventeen thousand dollars a year—a decent income for a middle-class couple at the time, but at least a decimal point shy of what she had in mind for her daughter.

Her fiancé aside, Jackie, who stated that her only requirement in a suitor was that he "weigh more and have bigger feet than I do," was seeing other men by March. Most notable among them were newspaperman-turned-State-Department-official John White and *Time* correspondent William Walton, who was about to give up journalism to become an artist. Walton soon joined their tight circle of friends that included Lem Billings, Chuck Spalding, and Charlie Bartlett.

Early on, White realized that what Jackie wanted in a man he couldn't give her. "Jackie wanted to be the confidante of an important man," White said. "Power and charisma seemed to override all other qualities in her estimation of people."

—

Jack Kennedy, of course, had everything she was looking for. But he was busy sharing these qualities with a number of other women. According to FBI files, which continued to track Kennedy's love life after he broke up with the suspected Nazi spy Inga Arvad, Jack was secretly engaged in 1951 to Alicja Darr, later the wife of actor Edmund Purdom. (Coincidentally Purdom would become best known for his role opposite Jean Simmons, who allegedly resisted Jack's persistent advances, and Gene Tierney, who didn't, in the 1954 biblical epic *The Egyptian*.)

The FBI report went on to say that Joe Kennedy forced his son to end the engagement because of Alicja's Polish-Jewish background. But, again according to the report, she had become pregnant by Jack. Years later, Bobby delivered five hundred thousand dollars to Alicja Purdom to settle a threatened breach-of-promise suit. In 1960, she filed for divorce, and in his countersuit Edmund Purdom named John F. Kennedy as a corespondent. Once again, Bobby leapt into action, convincing Alicja to settle with Purdom and get a quiet Mexican divorce. Although Purdom said his wife liked to "wave a check around with a Kennedy signature on it," she denied ever having received cash from any member of Jack's family. Over the years, too, Alicja always stuck to the implausible story that she and Kennedy were never intimate. "He used to say to me 'I love you,' " she conceded, "and I used to say to him 'I love you too, but what does it mean?' "

Jackie was blissfully unaware of Jack's reputed engagement to

Alicja Purdom, or for that matter his simultaneous involvement with model Pamela Farrington and television newswoman Nancy Dickerson. "Women loved being around Jack, and I loved being around him too," said Dickerson, who "gave him hell" when Jack honked instead of walking to her door on their first date. "He was just so gosh-darn physically, animalistically attractive that it was hard to imagine. And of course power is the ultimate aphrodisiac and with that combination he was really something. But to Jack, sex *was* just like a cup of coffee—no more or less important than that."

In a phenomenal lapse of discretion, Jack once explained his mechanical approach to sex for reporters he could trust not to print the remark. "I'm never finished with a girl," he said with a wink, "until I've had her three ways."

——

Again, thanks to the persistent Martha Bartlett, Jackie would get a third chance to connect with the man who could make her dream come true. Ironically, it resulted in Jackie asking Jack out on their first official date. "We were giving another one of our little dinner parties, and Jackie's fiancé couldn't come down, so Martha urged her to invite Jack," Charlie Bartlett said. "Martha really put the pressure on for her to ask him, and I'm sure everyone is grateful that she did. Jack was in the middle of his Senate campaign, but apparently he jumped at Jackie's invitation. They really hit it off just like before, only this time he finally got the chance to ask her out at the end of the evening." Jackie later thanked the Bartletts for their "shameless matchmaking . . . Usually that doesn't work out, but this time it did, so I am very grateful to them."

There were distractions—principally Jack's senatorial campaign. "At that point Jack did not pursue the relationship with Jackie very hard. He was mainly interested in getting elected to the Senate," Bartlett said. "That was his main preoccupation. Not Jackie."

———

Jack was motivated, as always, by a desire to please his father. "When you've beaten Lodge, you've beaten the best," Joe had told him. "Why try for something less?" The name Henry Cabot Lodge embodied everything about the Beacon Hill Brahmins that Joe Kennedy both admired and detested. This was, after all, "the home of the bean and the cod, where the Lowells talk to the Cabots, and the Cabots talk only to God." Winning was not only a big step on the road to the White House, it was a way of wreaking revenge on the New England WASPs who had snubbed him.

No one was more impressed with Jack's grit on the campaign trail than the Ambassador. Watching him shake hands with hundreds of longshoremen in East Boston, Joe admitted, "I would have given odds of five thousand to one that this thing could never have happened. I never thought Jack had it in him."

Kennedy foot soldier Patsy Mulkern claimed Jack was more determined to win than any candidate he'd seen. "Kennedy was a touchy guy—didn't want anybody to say anything bad against him. You'd be walking with him, he'd wave to a guy, and he'd say, 'Is he with us?' He was on everybody. The family's that way. They're tough losers. They hate to lose. Oh, they hate to lose." So much so, Mulkern said, that "if he lost the Senate fight, he'd have been writing books. Because I know Jack. He would never have run again. Jack could never take a defeat and come back. Had to be first in everything. 'Seconds don't count,' he used to tell me."

Preoccupied with managing Dwight D. Eisenhower's presidential race, Lodge started campaigning for election too late; by the time he returned home to Massachusetts, Jack was well on the way to winning over the voters. At thirty-three formal receptions held at the best hotels in Massachusetts, Jack and the rest of his family met with tens of thousands of voters. The events, said *Life* magazine, made "royalty of the Kennedys."

—

After his landslide victory, Jack was able to focus more attention on Jackie. In the beginning, Jackie and the Senator-elect shied away from venturing out in public together, preferring instead to catch a movie with Jack's brother Bobby and his wife Ethel, or to dine at the homes of a few close friends. These included Kentucky Senator John Sherman Cooper and his future wife, Lorraine, and of course the Bartletts. "We played Chinese checkers, Monopoly, bridge," recalled Bartlett. "Somebody said Jack played Monopoly like the property was real, and they were right. He loved winning, and he hated to lose even more. Jackie was the same way—very competitive, a born game player. There was always a great deal of laughter, and everybody always had a great time."

As their affair warmed up, they spent most of their time alone tooling around Washington in Kennedy's convertible and then parking to, in the words of one friend, "make out like a couple of teenagers." Jack later told Lem Billings that, while they were parked in a residential area of Arlington, a patrolman pulled up and peered into the backseat with a flashlight. Catching a glimpse of the half-naked senator and his topless date, the officer apologized and left. "But Jack had visions," Billings told author C. David Heymann, "of possible headlines: U.S. SENATOR MAULS TOPLESS INQUIRING PHOTOGRAPHER. CAMERA GIRL BUSTED WITH TOP DOWN!"

After these steamy encounters, often in the shadow of various Washington monuments, Jack would drive Jackie back to Merrywood. Jackie later recalled the evening that Jack's car broke down as he was leaving and she lent him the keys to Uncle Hughdie's royal blue Bentley. Auchincloss awoke the next morning thinking his Bentley had been stolen—until he recognized the Senator's battered car stalled in the driveway.

Jackie, who was still technically engaged to John Husted, remained coy on the subject of the Senator. When her cousin John H. Davis got wind of the rumors shortly after the 1952 elections, Jackie laughed them off. "You know, he goes to a hairdresser almost every day to have his hair done," she said in mock amazement, "so it'll always look bushy and fluffy? And you know, if, when we go out to some party or reception or something where nobody recognizes him, or no photographer takes his picture, he sulks afterward for hours . . . Really, he's so vain you can't believe it."

Davis suggested that perhaps Jack was just ambitious. "Oh sure, he's ambitious all right," she replied. "He even told me he intends to be president some day." Then she burst out laughing. Davis walked away convinced that she did not take the young man from Massachusetts seriously.

Jackie also wondered aloud how Jack would react to their eccentric Aunt Edie and her forty cats: "You know, I doubt if he'd survive it. The Kennedys are terribly bourgeois." As for his allergies: "Imagine me with someone allergic to horses!"

Jack was equally enigmatic. During the campaign, Jackie recalled, "He'd call me from some oyster bar up on the Cape with a great clinking of coins, to ask me out to the movies the following Wednesday." From his vantage point at Kennedy's side, Powers remembered that Jack "kept making mysterious phone calls. None of us knew he was in love."

Even Jack's trusted Washington staff was kept in the dark. His personal secretary, Evelyn Lincoln, routinely telephoned girls to arrange dates for her boss. "He was a playboy, all right," Lincoln said. "I never saw anything like it. Women were calling all the time, day and night. I more or less organized the ones he wanted to deal with. I'd call them up, tell them where they were to meet him for dinner, that sort of thing." With one exception. Jack placed his calls to Jackie personally. "When he didn't ask me to call her," Lincoln said, "I knew she had to be someone special."

Perhaps, but the first time Kennedy's long-time secretary met

Jackie, the two hardly behaved like lovebirds. Although he often kept people waiting hours for him and sometimes stood them up altogether, Jack could not abide a lack of punctuality in others. One evening they were supposed to meet at the airport and fly to New York. "He called and he said, 'Where's Jackie?' I said, 'I don't know, she hasn't shown up.' She was out at the [Middleburg, Virginia] Hunt Club horseback riding."

"Hasn't shown up?" he exploded. "Round her up. You call—call anywhere you can find her."

When she finally did locate Jackie, Lincoln told her that Jack was waiting for her at the airport. "She walked into the terminal, and he bawled her out," Lincoln said. "Poor thing. She didn't know him. She didn't know that when he snapped his fingers, you'd better be there."

Throughout what Jackie called their "spasmodic" courtship, Jackie was well aware that Jack in the company of George Smathers still pursued other women. She chose to look the other way, at least for the time being. "After the first year they were together," a friend said, "Jackie was wandering around looking like a survivor of an airplane crash."

Besides, she had been keeping secrets of her own, not the least of which was that she had never broken her engagement to John Husted. "She had told me to ignore all the gossip about her and John Kennedy," Husted recalled. "But then I got this letter in early March saying we should not get married in June, that we should postpone the wedding. It definitely sounded a note of doom."

A few weeks later, Jackie invited Husted to the Auchincloss family home in Virginia. "First I went down to Naples, Florida, to visit my family, and then flew to Washington," Husted said. "If Jack Kennedy was the other man—and I was pretty certain he was—then I knew I faced pretty tough competition. I got to Merrywood before Jackie, and cooled my heels for over an hour with Jackie's younger stepsister, Nina Auchincloss. She was wearing her little school uniform and did her best to keep me amused while we waited. Now I knew I was getting the brush-off." Strangely, when Jackie finally did appear, said Husted, "she was kind of giddy. There was absolutely no indication that anything was wrong. I had dinner with the family and stayed overnight just as I always did. I began to think that I'd been concerned over nothing."

Jackie drove Husted to the airport, and just before he boarded the plane casually removed her engagement ring. "She slipped it into my jacket pocket and waved good-bye."

Husted was not about to go without a fight, however. "I felt *desperate,*" he recalled. "I pleaded with her. Letters went back and forth. But it was too late. I knew he was a playboy, and so did she—but that was probably part of the appeal. Jack had to remind her of her father . . . Back in those days you printed a retraction in the paper—usually a small item announcing that the engagement was off 'by mutual consent.' " Janet Auchincloss, much relieved, took care of that detail.

Hugh Auchincloss, who had been in favor of the marriage, sent a note to Husted offering his sympathies. He ended with the line from Alfred, Lord Tennyson, " 'Tis better to have loved and lost than never to have loved at all." At the bottom of the page was the P.S., "And I ought to know!"

"Jackie was very ambitious," Husted said. "Socially I was fine, but financially I was not a great catch." Husted went on to marry Ann Hagerty Brittain, stepdaughter of yeast heir and *New Yorker* owner Raoul Fleischmann. In 1958, he was rousted out of sleep by a late-night phone call from Jackie asking him to come down to the Westbury Hotel where they had gotten engaged. There Husted met Jack for the first time.

"Jack, this is John Husted," Jackie said as the two men shook hands.

"Oh yes, I've heard a lot about you," Jack replied. At that, Husted recalled, "everyone laughed. He was certainly a very glamorous guy, but he had no conceit. He asked me all about Wall Street and my firm. He was very . . . magnetic. You could not help but like him."

On April 18, 1953, Jackie's sister Lee married Michael Canfield at Georgetown's Holy Trinity Cathedral. The reception was held at Merrywood and Lee tossed her bouquet directly at Jackie. The Inquiring Camera Girl then went to work, photographing the ushers for her column.

Spurred to action by Lee's nuptials, Jackie interviewed Senator Kennedy the next day. She asked him what he thought about Senate pages, photographed him, then covered the same turf with Jack's colleague from across the hall, Vice President Richard Nixon (JFK and Nixon shared many of the same conservative foreign policy beliefs, and became so friendly toward each other that Kennedy actually contributed a thousand dollars to Nixon's 1950 Senate campaign against Democrat Helen Gahagan Douglas).

While the Vice President observed that the pages were all "very quick boys" with a bright future, Jack answered, "I've often thought the country might be better off if we senators and the pages traded jobs." His page Jerry Hoobler, in turn, pointed out that the youthful-looking Kennedy was stopped when he tried to use one of the special phones at the Capitol. "Sorry, mister," the guard told Jack, "but these are reserved for senators."

"I think he might be just the fellow to help me straighten out my relationship with the cops," Kennedy said of his page in his typically wry, self-deprecating manner. "I've often mistaken Jerry for a senator because he looks so old."

With the appearance of the column on April 23, the couple was on the brink of going public. To move things along, Jackie even used the paper to flirt with Jack. Picking up the *Times-Herald,* he burst into laughter when he read that morning's "Inquiring Camera Girl" question. "Can you give me any reason," she asked passersby on the street, "why a contented bachelor should ever get married?"

In May 1953, Jack decided to let his trusted political aide Dave Powers in on the secret romance. "I have never met anyone like her—she's different from any girl I know," he told Powers. "Do you want to see what she looks like?"

"Jack pulled out this strip of four pictures, the kind you get in a penny arcade," Powers said. The snapshots, taken in a photo booth, show Jack in a suit and Jackie in a black dress and pearls, gazing adoringly at each other, then at the camera. Jack, his arm around his date, is beaming. "The pictures," Powers accurately pointed out, "clearly show two people in love."

For their first high-profile date after she interviewed him for the *Times-Herald*, Jack took Jackie dancing at the Blue Room of the Shoreham Hotel. Unfortunately, he also brought Powers along to meet her—and to talk politics.

Except for their stolen moments together, the courtship of Jackie and Jack was devoid of the usual trappings of romance. There were no flowers, no gifts, no Valentines, no love letters— and no touching in public. "It was interesting to watch Jack respond," Red Fay said. "When he wanted to put his arm around her and kiss her, well, he didn't want to do it in front of me. He was madly in love with the girl, but he didn't want to make a display of it."

"Jack was really quite the chauvinist, and not a very thoughtful person when it came to the niceties. He didn't bring you roses and he didn't always hold the door open for you," Nancy Dickerson said. "What he gave you was his time, his attention, his complete focus. He was always asking questions, wanted to know what you thought, how you felt. He gave the impression that he valued what you had to say. He was a superb listener, and that can be very seductive."

Jackie was not the only woman with whom Jack was having a top-secret affair at the time. She was the same age as Jackie—a tall, slim, heart-stoppingly beautiful brunette with sophistication and bearing beyond her years. Unlike Jackie, she was already one of the most famous and admired young women in the world, with an Academy Award and dozens of magazine covers to her credit. Her name was Audrey Hepburn.

———

She had the same emotional blocks and panics
that he had. In their strangulated way they
loved each other.

longtime friend Betty Spalding

———

4

"I remember Audrey Hepburn," said Mary Gallagher, who was a secretary in Senator Kennedy's office at the time, "and I remember how the whole office was impressed when she walked in. She was as graceful as a swan and carried a long, slim, red umbrella."

Hepburn had just won an Oscar for *Roman Holiday* and was about to start filming *Sabrina* with Humphrey Bogart and William Holden. "By then all the rumors were about Jackie Bouvier the Inquiring Camera Girl," a Washington journalist said. "Audrey Hepburn was seen a couple of times leaving his place in George-town very late at night, but it seemed so improbable back in those days for a United States senator and a movie star to be involved— the worlds were just so different back then—that nobody thought much of it. Besides, those of us who thought we knew what was *really* going on knew that Jackie Bouvier was the woman in his life."

Jack's fascination with Hepburn was perfectly understandable. "She out-Jackied Jackie," said one acquaintance. "Like everyone else who ever met her, Jack thought Audrey was simply exquisite. She was also extremely intelligent, well-read, and lots of fun. Audrey had this intoxicating laugh. . . . Pretty much what you saw on the screen, really. But she also had this very sexy, very naughty side that the public never saw. They managed to keep their affair out of the press, and the fact that it was clandestine only made it that much more intense."

But as a foreigner, a non-Catholic, and a show business personality, Hepburn was out of the running as a marriage prospect. And now that Joe Kennedy was intent on seeing his son move into the White House in 1960, Jack was in the market for the ideal political wife. (After the engagement of Jackie and Jack was announced, Hepburn began an affair with the married Bill Holden. But when he told her he had undergone a vasectomy, Hepburn, who wanted children, married Mel Ferrer in 1954.)

Jackie may have had all the makings of the ideal political spouse, but even those who loved Jack realized he could never be a model husband. Lem Billings had taken Jackie aside at Dwight D. Eisenhower's inaugural ball, which she attended with Jack, and explained "the facts of life." He told her about Jack's various illnesses—including the potentially fatal Addison's disease—his women, and the fact that at thirty-five he was "set in his ways" and not likely to change. That said, he also told her she outclassed all the competition, and that her sophistication, intellect, and beauty could only enhance his chances of becoming president.

"I want to tell you something," her editor at the *Times-Herald* warned Jackie when he heard she was dating Kennedy. "He's older than you and he's smarter than you and he's been around and half a dozen women have had their shot at him, so you watch yourself."

Chuck Spalding felt all the warnings "only made her more interested in him. Jackie had this thing about Black Jack. Dangerous men excited her. There was that element of danger in Jack Kennedy, without doubt."

Jackie was not without her dangerous qualities. According to Spalding, Jack actually first laid eyes on her at least two years before the oft-recounted abortive first meeting at the Bartletts' Georgetown home. "Jack and I were visiting a friend of mine who played a lot of polo," Spalding said, "and there this guy was with Jackie, just knocking the ball around the field. Even then she was an accomplished horsewoman. Trouble was, Jack couldn't ride and neither could I. But he was already clearly intrigued by her and game for just about anything, so he said, 'Sure, why not?' and hopped on a horse. So there we were riding around this polo field, trying to keep up with this girl and hanging on for dear life! Jack laughed his head off."

Thrills aside, there is little disagreement that there was one overriding factor in Jackie's pursuit of Jack: money. "They were not a logical match, really," said Kennedy friend Priscilla McMillan, who in the spring of 1953 was working in Jack's Senate office. Kennedy, who had taken a special interest in Southeast Asia, was about to make his maiden foreign policy speech on the floor of the Senate and had hired McMillan to do research on Indonesia. "Jackie was far more cosmopolitan than he was, very European in her style and in her tastes. I envisioned her marrying some international playboy type, frankly. Jack Kennedy was not her type at all. He was good-looking and witty, but he didn't really have much time to pay attention to her. She was clearly the kind of young woman who was accustomed to having a great deal of attention paid to her, and that made it a very unlikely union.

"Socially, Jackie was marrying beneath her," McMillan continued. "Financially she was marrying what she was raised to marry. She was brought up with a father who lost his money and a mother who had to marry for security, and it was drummed into her that she had to go out and find a rich man of her own. Years later, they'd say her spending habits were out of scale but eventually, no amount of money would really be enough."

"Her prime motivation in marrying Jack was money," Nancy Dickerson agreed. "Jack was exciting, there was that raw sexuality of his. But you've got to remember that at that time nobody was thinking of him as presidential material. As handsome and charming as he was, there were plenty of other attractive, powerful men in Washington. There just weren't any with as much money as Jack."

"She was a very gracious, wonderful woman," Spalding said. "But she wouldn't have given Jack a second look if he hadn't had the money. Jack grew up knowing that was part of his appeal to women. It didn't bother him a bit. He *enjoyed* being rich."

Gore Vidal is right to the point: "Jackie married Jack for money. Purely. There weren't that many other openings for her. Actually, if she hadn't married Jack she would have married someone else with money, although it wasn't likely she would have gotten someone as exciting as Jack in the bargain. When given a choice of glory or money, most people choose glory. But not Jackie. She also wound up with plenty of the latter, of course, but she didn't need that like she needed to be rich."

In a sense, Jackie was programmed by her mother to seek out a mate who would provide her with more than just a comfortable lifestyle. Vidal recalled that as president, Jack once compared the Auchinclosses to the money-crazed, fratricidal schemers in Lillian Hellman's play *The Little Foxes*. One evening at Hyannis Port, according to Vidal, "Jack denounced all the children and stepchildren of Hughdie Auchincloss without mentioning us, of course. 'So,' said Jackie grimly, 'go on.' "

"Well, you know what I mean," Jack replied sheepishly. Vidal tried to rescue him. "If we are all the disasters that you say we are, then the one thing that we have in common is that our mothers married Hughdie for his money and we all knew it and that casts, perhaps, a shadow."

"You mean for security," Jack said, startled by Vidal's admission.

"No, for money." Vidal shrugged in reply. "Big money."

"Jackie nodded," Vidal recalled, "and said with a radiant smile, 'Yes. *Big* money.' "

"Jackie," giggled Truman Capote, who knew both Bouvier sisters well, "was always a cash 'n carry kinda gal."

Not so her beau, who had little appreciation for what he was worth (at least $10 million in 1953), the size of the family fortune ($400 million, according to *Forbes*), or how his personal finances worked. "I knew more about Jack's finances than he did," Smathers said. Added Spalding: "I used to say that trying to tell Jack about money was like trying to teach a nun about sex."

For Jackie, as with all other women in his life, going out with

Jack often meant her picking up the check. When he did pay, Jack invariably put the meal on his tab—and then at restaurants where Joe had an interest. "But if ever they took a cab or went to the movies," said a friend, "he'd say, 'Could you take care of that?' and leave Jackie fishing in her purse for her wallet. He wouldn't even pay for the popcorn!" At church, it was Jackie who scrounged up a few dollars for the collection plate.

"Jack never carried cash, and I mean *never*," said Smathers. "He didn't even have a dime to make a phone call. One day I told Joe that people were getting pretty fed up picking up lunch tabs and cabs and the like, so he just told me to send him the bill and he'd take care of it."

Belatedly, the elder Kennedy came to the realization that, in an effort to shield his son from petty business matters, he had turned Jack into a fiscal ignoramus. To compensate for his ignorance of how one handles personal finances, Jack was overtly penurious. He did not have to look far for a role model. Although they spent lavishly on their wardrobes, on travel, and on entertainment, Rose and Joe preferred to bundle up in sweaters and blankets rather than turn on the heat. (In this regard they may not have been as cheap as Hugh Auchincloss, who had his servants put food on the porch during the winter months rather than pay to have it refrigerated.)

Still, even Joe was impressed by his son's naïveté. After listening to Jack tell a staffer with four children to be grateful for his five-thousand-dollar salary, Joe angrily informed his son that he was spending fifty thousand dollars a year on "incidentals."

The admonition fell on deaf ears. "Jack just shrugged his shoulders," Smathers said. "Even when Jack was in the White House, it was the Old Man who handled all his bills."

It was ultimately the Old Man who forced Jack to pick a bride and at least give the appearance of settling down and becoming a family man. "It's not what you are that counts," Joe liked to tell his children, "it's what people *think* you are." The patriarch of the Kennedy clan was also worried that despite his son's reputation as a raging heterosexual other assumptions might be drawn. "Old Joe told him he'd better get married," Evelyn Lincoln said, "or people would think he was gay."

However reluctant Jack was to give up his bachelor status, by late May 1953 the identity of the bride was not in question. "I think he understood that the two of them were alike," Lem Billings said of Jack. "They had both taken circumstances that weren't the best in the world when they were younger and learned to make themselves up as they went along." Billings added, "They were so much alike. Even the names—Jack and Jackie: two halves of a single whole. They were both actors and they appreciated each other's performance."

As indispensable as Joe was, Jack was not about to mention his father's name to Black Jack Bouvier. Jackie's father had detested Joe ever since the elder Kennedy had taken charge of the SEC back in the 1930s, imposing rules and restrictions that had a devastating impact on Wall Street specialists like Bouvier. "If anyone had told him in 1934 that his daughter would one day marry Joe Kennedy's son," wrote society chronicler Stephen Birmingham, "he would have knocked that person to the floor and kicked him."

Fortunately, the two Jacks turned out to have much in common. "They were very much alike," Jackie later said. "They talked about sports, politics, and women—what all red-blooded men like to talk about." Not only did they also share an appreciation of the finer things and a decidedly randy sense of humor, but they spent endless hours discussing how to rid themselves of back pain. One evening, they both got tipsy watching a boxing match on television.

Jackie's mother was another matter. Her own rise notwithstanding, Janet considered herself an Auchincloss and as such head and shoulders above the Kennedys socially. "Mummy and Dad had always talked about 'those Kennedys,' so even at the age of six I knew I should be suspicious of them," Jackie's half-brother Jamie Auchincloss said. "When Jack Kennedy first came to visit us, I remember walking down the red-carpeted grand staircase just as he walked in the front door. I cocked my head and said, 'Hello, *Kennedy*.' And he stared at me seriously and said, 'Hello, *Auchincloss*.' That won me over. Then he proceeded to play six games of Chinese checkers with me and beat me in all six games."

Jamie also noticed Jack's deep tan (as much a result of his Addison's disease as of exposure to the sun) and "the odd color of his hair. Or rather, *colors*. Once I counted fifteen distinctly different colors in his hair, ranging from silver to orange. Later I learned that was another symptom of Addison's disease."

Hughdie Auchincloss presented no challenge whatsoever for Jack. Affable and uncomplicated, he had no problem with the idea of Jack becoming his stepson-in-law. One evening Jack walked into the deck room at Hammersmith Farm while Hughdie played his nightly solitary game of chess. It was one of the few games Jack did not know how to play, and after staring at the board for a few minutes he asked Auchincloss to teach him. To Auchincloss's astonishment, Jack mastered the moves almost instantly. "It was a perfectly extraordinary thing," said Janet, who was there at the time, "that anybody could learn enough about chess in half an hour to sit down and play. Hugh D. was very impressed . . ."

Once he'd won over Hughdie and Jamie, Jack concentrated on Janet. "He called her 'Mummy,' but he called his own mother 'Mother,' " Jamie said. "From the very beginning, he seemed to be extraordinarily comfortable around all of us. He made himself right at home at Merrywood, and at Hammersmith Farm."

Janet, who had actually met Jack at a dinner party before he became serious about Jackie, was somewhat ambivalent on the subject. "He used to call me 'Mrs. Auchincloss,' but sometimes he would call me 'Mummy,' in quotes, you know. For some reason, this always seemed very funny to him, that anybody should be called 'Mummy.' "

Jackie reveled in the fact that Jack, unlike Black Jack and Hughdie, knew how to handle her mother. "I'm the luckiest girl in the world," she said. "Mummy is terrified of Jack because she can't push him around at all."

The same week that the engagement was announced, Jack dropped a note to his friend Red Fay inviting him to be an usher at the September 12 wedding. "I need you to walk down the aisle with me," Jack scrawled. "Your special project is the bride's mother—one fine girl—who has a tendency when excited to think I am not good enough for her daughter—and to talk too much. I am both too young and too old for this . . ."

The question of age—specifically the twelve-year difference in their ages—was also of pressing concern to Jack. Dave Powers began to suspect Jack was serious about Jackie when he asked, "Do you think there is really much of a problem in getting married to a girl twelve years younger than you are?" When Powers pointed out that his wife, Jo, was exactly twelve years younger, Kennedy smiled. "You two get along fine, don't you?" he asked.

Step-relation Gore Vidal, who was then close to both Jackie and Jack, insists that the difference in the couple's ages in large part defined the nature of their relationship. "Jackie thought of Jack as an *older man*," Vidal said. "Everybody today thinks of them as this beautiful young couple, perfectly matched. But that was not the case. From the standpoint of a girl in her early twenties, somebody pushing forty is *old*. That, along with the fact that she hated politics, gave her more pause than anything else. But then there was the money, and the prospect of an exciting life."

Oleg Cassini, who knew Jack before he met Jackie, felt they were well suited to each other mainly because Jackie was mature beyond her years. He first met Jack's intended at El Morocco, a few weeks before they were married. "She was a well-read, cultured person. She had quick wit. She spoke several languages—Jack didn't. They had much to offer each other. Besides, the whole age thing is so American. In Europe, the ideal age of a wife is supposed to be half the man's age plus seven years."

Cassini sensed another vital quality that made Jackie the perfect match for Jack. "All eyes seemed to gravitate toward her," said the designer, who was at the famous New York nightclub with Babe Cushing's husband, Stanley Mortimer. (Cushing later married CBS founder William S. Paley.)

"What a shame you're getting married when there are fellows like Mortimer and me to get involved with," Cassini quipped.

"And what," Jackie said matter-of-factly, "sort of fellows are you?"

For Jackie, winning over the Kennedys was at best a daunting proposition. Jack's sisters, given to worshipping their oldest surviving brother, viewed Jackie as an intruder. To make matters worse, "Jackie could not have been more unlike the Kennedys," said Spalding. "They were loud, boisterous roughnecks—even the girls. They looked at her like some hothouse flower. They made fun of her wispy little-girl voice. They called her 'the Debutante.' "

Realizing full well that with the exception of her horsemanship, Jackie was no athlete, Eunice, Pat, and Bobby's wife Ethel (described by Lem Billings as being "more Kennedy than thou") lured her into as many games of their contact sports as possible. For Jack's sake, she tried to compete at touch football, but the family burst out laughing when she asked which way she should run if she got the ball.

They also paired up for furious tennis matches ("It is enough for me to enjoy the sport—it isn't necessary to be the best," she told them), ran foot races, swam relay races, competed in sailboat races, and, if there was nothing else to do, jumped up and down on a trampoline in the yard. "Just watching them," Jackie said of the frenzy, "wears me out."

Ethel was particularly adroit at needling Jackie. When Jackie mentioned in passing that she once aspired to be a ballet dancer, Ethel doubled over with laughter. "With those clodhoppers of yours?" Ethel hooted. "You'd be better off going in for soccer, kid." Jackie felt every bit as warmly toward them. She called the sisters "the Rah-Rah Girls," and told her sister Lee how they "would fall all over each other like a pack of gorillas." It was not long before Jackie broke her ankle during one of their scrimmages. "They'll kill me before I ever get to marry him," she told Lee. "I swear they will."

When it came to playing party games, however, it was an entirely different matter. Jackie's flair for pantomime, honed at Miss Porter's and at Vassar, ensured that she won every game of charades, and as a tournament Scrabble player her victory over the less erudite Kennedys at that game was a foregone conclusion. She was also such a whiz at a game called Categories, a sort of high-brow Trivial Pursuit, that Jack eventually asked her to stop embarrassing him by winning every game. "Jackie just looked at him," recalled one of the players, Father John Cavanaugh of Notre Dame, "and said, 'Why Jack! I thought all of the Kennedys like competition.' "

Dining with the whole family for the first time in Hyannis Port in the summer of 1952, Jackie showed up in an evening gown. "I was more dressed up than his sisters were," Jackie recalled, "and so Jack teased me about it, in an affectionate way, but he said something like, 'Where do you think you're going?' Mrs. Kennedy [Rose] said, 'Oh don't be mean to her, dear. She looks lovely.' Anyway, I liked her enormously. I saw that this woman did everything to put one at one's ease."

But Jack's sisters carried their resentment from the playing field to the dinner table. After being told that their guest's name was technically pronounced "Jock-leen," Eunice muttered, sotto voce, "rhymes with 'queen.' "

"Over dinner, Jackie was put through her paces," said Kennedy family friend Dinah Bridge, "and she stood up extremely well to the Kennedy barrage of questions." Jackie was also struck by the fact that, even at mealtimes, they seemed to be in competition over "who can say the most and talk the loudest."

One of the most telling incidents occurred later that year, when Jackie spent her first Christmas as Mrs. John F. Kennedy with the family in Palm Beach. Jackie's present to Jack was an expensive set of oil paints, which was instantly cannibalized by the others. They each grabbed tubes and brushes and attacked their individual canvases in a ferocious race to see who could finish painting first. Once she saw oils smeared on the carpets and the upholstery, Rose ordered them to the bathrooms where they continued the "race" for several more hours. Jackie, said Lem Billings, stood looking at what they had done to the gift she had given her husband "with her mouth hanging open, ready to explode."

"How can I explain these people?" Jackie later reflected. "They were like carbonated water, and other families might be flat. They'd be talking about so many things with so much enthusiasm. Or they'd be playing games. At dinner or in the living room, anywhere, everybody would be talking about something. They had so much interest in life—it was so stimulating. And so gay and so open and accepting."

That was not the way others remembered it. "God, they were an overbearing bunch," said Betty Spalding, who was married to Chuck at the time, "always chasing around, bursting into the room constantly, interrupting you, dropping in unannounced, having their own private jokes, ganging up to make fun of someone . . ." Smathers concurred: "They could be, well, obnoxious. It was awfully hard for someone like Jackie to take. You couldn't blame her for giving them the cold shoulder."

Even Rose, who had come to Jackie's defense when she overdressed for dinner at her first Hyannis Port dinner, soon fell out with Jackie when she realized her son's intended was not about to toe the Kennedy line. She made fun of Jackie's habit of turning on the tap in the bathroom so that no one could hear her using the toilet, and chided her for not getting enough exercise. "It's about time somebody around here started exercising his mind rather than his muscles," Jackie remarked. It was not long before Jackie came to regard Rose, whom she would wiltingly call "Belle Mère" (just as Jack referred to Janet as "Mummy"), as haughty and self-absorbed.

The final breaking point would come at the Palm Beach estate in the months after Jack was elected president. Late one morning

Rose approached Mary Gallagher, who by then was working as Jackie's personal secretary, and asked if "Jackie is getting out of bed today." When Gallagher said she didn't know, Rose fumed, "Well, you might remind her that we're having some important guests for lunch. It would be nice if she would join us." Once the message was relayed to her, Jackie launched into an unflattering if dead-on impersonation of Rose's distinctive cackle: "You might remind her we're having important guests for lunch." Not unexpectedly, the strong-willed Jackie never left her room that day. "I felt the relationship," recalled Gallagher, "was strained from then on."

Ultimately, Jackie would develop a grudging respect for her mother-in-law. "It's the upbringing," she said of Rose's seeming inability to connect with anyone emotionally. "You see those pictures of her mother with the whalebone corset and the high collar—you're brought up like that and you don't reveal yourself. To reveal yourself is almost dangerous for people like that. I'd say Jack didn't want to reveal himself at all." Then there was Joe, "whose life was like a roller coaster zooming, accelerating, going up and down . . . it almost took her breath away."

Jackie was, in fact, only completely comfortable around one Kennedy—Joe. "Next to my husband, and my own father," she was to say a few years later, I love Joe Kennedy more than anybody in the world."

Setting out to conquer Joe, the one person who mattered most, Jackie stressed all those factors that so aggravated the "Rah-Rah Girls"—her supposedly aristocratic French pedigree, her days at Miss Porter's, Vassar, and the Sorbonne, her Debutante of the Year and Prix de Paris honors, and her family ties to the blue-blooded Auchinclosses. (She downplayed her less-than-prestigious job as the *Times-Herald*'s Inquiring Camera Girl, and of course never hinted at the fact that, unlike her half-siblings Janet and Jamie, she was virtually without funds.) Among all the girls Jack had dated, including the marriageable Catholic ones, Jackie was far and away the most intelligent, easily the most polished.

Jackie's campaign to win Joe's backing got off to a rocky start. Fed up with the debate society atmosphere that prevailed at dinner, Jackie interrupted a loud conversation between Bobby and his father on how to battle air pollution. "I have a solution," Jackie said. "Call out the Air Force and let them spray congested urban areas with Chanel No. 5." No one was amused.

When she and Jack visited the Palm Beach estate, Jackie made the grievous mistake of showing up fifteen minutes late for lunch. "That sort of tardiness could be fatal with the Ambassador when he was in one of his Emperor Augustus moods," recalled a Palm Beach neighbor who was at the table. "So when Jackie came in he started to give her the needle—and she gave it right back.

"Old Joe had a lot of old-fashioned slang phrases, so Jackie told him: 'You ought to write a series of grandfather stories for children, like "The Duck with Moxie," and "The Donkey Who Couldn't Fight His Way Out of a Telephone Booth." ' " There was a moment of stunned silence before Joe exploded with laughter. "By God, that girl's got zipperoo," the Ambassador said. "She's got a mind of her own." Beneath the finishing school gloss was a streak of fierce independence that Joe had not bargained on—perhaps inherited from the side of her family she kept hidden from Joe, the Irish side. From that point on, Joe seemed to look forward to a good-natured ribbing from Jackie.

"It was the first time anybody talked back to him," Spalding said. "He got a big kick out of it." When Joe boasted, as he often did, that he gave each of his children $1 million when they reached twenty-one "so if they wanted they could tell me to go to hell," Jackie thought for a moment.

"Do you know what I would tell you if you gave me a million dollars?"

"No."

"I would tell you to give me another million."

During another Kennedy family dinner, Jack said to Jackie, "A penny for your thoughts."

"But they're my thoughts, Jack," she replied, "and they

wouldn't be my thoughts anymore if I told them. Now would they?"

"A girl with a mind of her own," laughed Joe, "just like us."

While the rest of the family, including Jack, played football or raced sailboats, Jackie and Joe sat on the porch "talking about everything from classical music to the movies . . . I used to tell him he had no nuances," Jackie said, "that everything with him was either black or white, while life was so much more compli-cated than that. But he never got angry with me for talking straight to him; on the contrary, he seemed to enjoy it."

One birthday Joe unwrapped his gift from Jackie—a watercolor that depicted a flock of young Kennedys looking out to sea. "YOU CAN'T TAKE IT WITH YOU," the caption read, "DAD'S GOT IT ALL."

Eventually, they would be the family's odd couple, cooking up pranks together that mystified the others. One evening in Palm Beach, the longtime Kennedy housekeeper Evelyn Jones was pass-ing through the dining room when Joe and Jackie bet who could hit Jones with his lamb chop before she reached the pantry door.

Joe did not merely sanction Jack's marriage to Jackie, he de-manded that it take place—and soon. "Jackie was very intelligent, arch, and clever," McMillan said, "and she knew how to play down her intelligence. She seemed very upper-class, and the Kennedys thought that she was good first lady material for them."

By mid-May of 1953 Jack had still not proposed. "I couldn't visualize him actually saying 'I love you' to somebody and asking her to marry him," Lem Billings told Kennedy family biographers Peter Collier and David Horowitz. "It was the sort of thing he would have liked to have happen without having to talk about it."

That problem evaporated when Aileen Bowdoin, whose younger sisters had accompanied Jackie on her earlier trip to Eu-rope, called with the news that she was going to London to attend the coronation of Queen Elizabeth. Perhaps, Janet Auchincloss suggested, Jackie could wrangle an assignment from Waldrop at the *Times-Herald* to join the team covering the event. "She didn't want to go at all at first," Jackie's mother recalled. "She didn't want to leave Jack Kennedy. Then I said to her, 'If you're so much in love with Jack Kennedy that you don't want to leave him, I should think he would be much more likely to find out how he felt about you if you were seeing exciting people and doing exciting things instead of sitting here waiting for the telephone to ring."

Jackie's articles—ranging from man-in-the-street interviews about the new monarch to a description of a celebrity-crammed ball thrown by "Hostess with the Mostest" Perle Mesta—ran on the front page of the *Times-Herald,* accompanied by her own cunning sketches in pen and ink. Jack Kennedy did not miss an installment.

While she was gone, Jack celebrated his thirty-sixth birthday with his family and attended his sister Eunice's marriage to Sargent Shriver in New York's St. Patrick's Cathedral. She had been gone a week when she received a telegram from Jack: ARTICLES EXCELLENT, BUT YOU ARE MISSED. They talked on the phone briefly, and during this transatlantic call John Fitzgerald Kennedy finally asked Jacqueline Lee Bouvier to marry him.

Now that the moment had finally arrived, Jackie began to have doubts. "How can you live with a husband who is bound to be unfaithful but whom one loves?" she asked a friend in a rare unguarded moment. She also worried about Jack's exhausting family and the daunting prospect of becoming a politician's wife. Not just any politician, but one whose presidential aspirations were beginning to seem less and less preposterous.

Without giving Jack an immediate answer, she made a quick side trip to Paris, where she met her old lover John Marquand, Jr. Gore Vidal quotes Marquand as saying they "resumed their affair" and that "this time he proposed but she turned him down. Jackie told him she was going to marry Jack Kennedy."

Marquand was appalled. "You can't marry that . . . that *mick*," he blurted.

She was coolly to the point: 'He has money, and you don't.'"

According to Vidal, Marquand was well aware of the fact that

Jackie, having grown up on the fringes of Washington, "had no illusions about the breed." "What on earth is going to become of you in that awful world?" Marquand asked.

She smiled. "Read the newspapers."

On the plane ride back to New York, Jackie grilled fellow passenger Zsa Zsa Gabor about what ointments and creams she used to keep her skin beautiful. Zsa Zsa figured the young woman, who did not identify herself, had good reason to ask. "She wasn't the most glamorous or the most beautiful woman. She had kinky hair and bad skin." Almost in passing, Jackie mentioned that a young man had proposed to her and might be waiting for her at the airport. Once the plane touched down, Zsa Zsa breezed straight into the arms of a handsome young man who was leaning against a counter—Jack Kennedy. Gabor had been one of Jack's Hollywood "companions" during his days as a libidinous young congressman.

"So Jack Kennedy said to me, 'I want you to meet Miss Bouvier.' He didn't say 'my future wife.' And I said, 'Oh my God! She's a lovely girl. Don't dare corrupt her, Jack.' "

Jackie looked squarely into Gabor's eyes and said wistfully, "But he already has."

Were they in love at the time of their engagement? According to Evelyn Lincoln, the marriage was forced on Jack Kennedy by his father. "He was a politician who wanted to be president and for that he needed a wife. I am absolutely certain they were not in love. At least not at the time."

Even then, however, there was no denying that a certain indefinable chemistry existed between Jackie and Jack. "There was always an intensity, a sort of electrical current between them," said Jamie Auchincloss. "I think they became attached to each other in time."

"She was no innocent," said a friend. "She knew all about the women, and she could see firsthand what that kind of fooling around did to Rose. But Jackie was only twenty-three, and she was convinced that she could change him."

Jackie called her father's sister, Maud Davis, with the news. "Auntie Maudie," she said, "I just want you to know that I'm engaged to Jack Kennedy. But you can't tell anyone for a while because it wouldn't be fair to *The Saturday Evening Post.*" Maud wanted to know what the magazine had to do with her impending marriage. "The *Post* is coming out tomorrow with an article on Jack, and the title is on the cover. It's 'Jack Kennedy—the Senate's Gay Young Bachelor.' "

Even though he obviously knew long before the magazine hit the stands what the headline was going to be, Jack was unhappy when he saw the "Senate's Gay Young Bachelor" line in print. It was not exactly the statesmanlike image he had hoped to convey. "Christ," he said, slapping the issue on his desk, "it makes me look like a complete asshole."

Jack's political friends and advisors were not exactly sanguine about the prospects for the marriage's success. "I made the mistake of telling Jack, 'I don't think she's quite old enough for you,' " George Smathers said. "Not that he was old, but as far as Washington was concerned, I didn't think she was sophisticated enough. So naturally, he runs to Jackie and says, 'Some of my friends don't think I should marry you. George Smathers thinks you're not sufficiently sophisticated to be my wife!'

"So of course, right up until she passed away, Jackie would never let me forget. We'd be dancing at the White House, and she'd say, '*I remember* what you told Jack, that I wasn't good enough for him.' And I'd say, 'Oh, Jackie, for God's sake. I was just *testing* him. I just wanted to see if he really loved you!' She didn't buy it, but she was nice enough to make a running joke out of it. I'm not so sure she thought it was so funny at the time."

Smathers echoed the sentiments of several of Jack's colleagues and friends. "I didn't think he would ever get married," said Larry Newman, who still lives across the street from the Kennedy compound in Hyannis Port. "I used to have drinks with him at the Monkey Bar in New York and he'd be flirting with every pretty woman in the room. It was just automatic. I think he did love

Jackie, but it was never in his makeup to be monogamous. If he had to marry anyone, though, and of course if he wanted to be president he *did* have to be married, he could not have done better than Jackie."

"Jackie was beautiful, quick, funny, and cultured, but nobody had any illusions about Jack's chances of sticking to his vows," Spalding said. "Jack was no Boy Scout, but then a Boy Scout would have bored her senseless."

"I just had the feeling that Jack wasn't ready to get married," Smathers mused. "But I don't know that he would have ever gotten *more* ready to get married than he was at the time. Look, he was just one of those guys . . . His disposition was such that he liked lots of girls. He inherited that from his father. I just told him to be damn sure that he was ready to give up his rather meandering ways and settle down to being a good husband— which up to that point he had given no indication of wanting to do. His reaction? He just laughed.

"I think of him being many great things," Smathers said. "A great politician, a great author, a great social guy, a great friend. But you never thought of him as a great husband or a great father."

"Well," longtime Kennedy advisor and intimate Langdon "Don" Marvin said when told of the planned marriage, "I suppose it *could* work."

Their engagement was announced on June 23, 1953, and the news was splashed across the front pages of newspapers across the country the next day. The story in the New York *Daily News*, accompanied by a photo of Jackie holding her press camera and headlined SENATOR LOSES BACHELORHOOD TO CAMERA GAL, was typical. "Come September, the Senate's gay young bachelor will be no more," the story began. "Hopeful debutantes from Washington to Boston, from Palm Beach to Hollywood, can begin unpacking their hope chests. Those thousands of Boston teenagers who squealed like Sinatra fans every time young millionaire John Kennedy campaigned at their high schools will get the bad news officially this Friday . . ."

The same day that the word went out to the press, Jack had scribbled down his invitation to Red Fay in San Francisco. It revealed much about his ambivalent state of mind. In the note, he makes a telling reference to "Alice Odds & Ends"—a nickname for his old flame Alicja Purdom: "After the breakup with the bad and the beautiful—Alice Odds & ends—one fine girl, I gave every thing [sic] a good deal of thought—so am getting married this fall. This means the end of a promising political career as it has been based up to now almost completely on the old sex appeal."

Jack then kiddingly asked Fay, who had been married earlier in the year, for some marital advice: "I hope you and the bride will be able to come . . . Will need several long talks on how to conduct myself during the first six months based on your actual real-life experiences." Always mindful of any public relations fallout, he concluded by asking Fay if getting engaged helped or hurt him in San Francisco: "Let me know the general reaction to this in the Bay Area. Yours truly, Jack."

Not one to overlook any opportunity for self-promotion, Jack agreed to a *Life* cover story on his impending marriage. When Jackie arrived to spend her first weekend at Hyannis Port as the future Mrs. John Kennedy, she was surprised to find *Life* photographer Hy Peskin waiting to shoot the happy couple—skipping pebbles over the surf, playing football *and* baseball with the other Kennedys, strolling on the beach. In one shot, Jackie sits at the senator's feet; in another, wearing shorts, she strikes a leggy cheesecake pose reminiscent of Marilyn Monroe. For the cover of *Life*—there were ultimately forty-eight *Life* covers featuring the Kennedys—the editors chose a shot of them sailing.

If the wedding was ever to come off, and at least one of Jackie's friends bet her that she would never go through with it, Jackie knew she would have to close ranks with the family. "The day you become engaged to one of them," she told the press, "is the day they start saying how fantastic you are, and the same loyalty they show to each other they show to their in-laws. They seem proud if I read more books, and of the things I do differently. The very things you would think would alienate them bring you closer to them."

The Auchinclosses threw an engagement party for the couple in Newport; it was followed by another at the home of Kennedy family friends in Hyannis Port. At the second bash, Jack delighted guests by slipping the square-cut emerald-and-diamond ring from Van Cleef & Arpels on Jackie's finger. At Jack's insistence, the guests embarked on a scavenger hunt—an assignment not lightly undertaken by the win-at-all-costs Kennedys. When it was over, one of Jack's sisters had absconded with a bus and Teddy showed up with a hat snatched off the head of a policeman.

In July, Janet invited Rose to Hammersmith Farm to work out the details of the September 12 nuptials. It was then that Jackie caught a revealing glimpse of Jack's lingering resentment toward his mother. To break up the tense negotiations between Janet and Rose, they decided to take a drive to Newport's Bailey Beach. "The two mothers were in the front of the car," Jackie recalled, "and we were sitting in the backseat, sort of like two bad children. Anyway, Jack and I went swimming. I came out of the water earlier; it was time to go for lunch, but Jack dawdled. And I remember Rose stood on the walk and called to her son in the water, 'Jack! . . . Ja-a-ack!' and it was just like the little ones who won't come out and pretend not to hear their mothers calling 'Ja-a-ack,' but he wouldn't come out of the water. I can't remember whether she started on down or I went down to get him, but he started coming up, saying, 'Yes, Mother.' "

There was, however, not even grudging obedience when it came to Jack's personal habits. Unlike his orderly older brother, Jack was unrepentantly sloppy. Contrary to the image that later took hold of John F. Kennedy as the cynosure of elegance, Jack paid little attention to what he wore before wedding Jackie. His shirts were often wrinkled and frayed at the collar, his suits rumpled and ill-fitting; often his socks and sometimes even his shoes were mismatched. "Jack was most comfortable in a T-shirt, shorts, and sneakers," Spalding said, "or nothing at all. You'd be talking to him and suddenly he'd just strip down to his briefs."

The temporary Georgetown quarters he shared with his sister Eunice reflected their mutual disdain for neatness. Papers were piled everywhere. Clothes and towels were strewn on the floors. Dishes piled up in the sink, or worse; it was not unusual for visitors to reach for a book in the library and retrieve a half-eaten sandwich that had been left there weeks before. Jackie did not shrink from the challenge. "What I want more than anything else in the world," she told a friend, "is to be married to him."

There was an impasse in the negotiations between Janet and Rose, so Joe flew down to convince Jackie's mother that while the wedding could take place on Auchincloss turf, he would run the show. The minute she saw Joe get off the plane in Newport, Jackie thought to herself, "Mummy, you don't have a chance."

By way of one last bachelor fling, Jack flew to Europe with his old college friend Torby MacDonald. Janet was outraged. "What kind of man does this sort of thing?" she demanded. "A man who is about to be married wants to be with the woman he loves."

Aware that she had no power to stop Jack, Jackie told herself that perhaps he would "get it out of his system" once and for all. Indeed, Jack behaved as if this was a romantic "farewell tour" of the Continent. He was halfway through his list of former flames when by chance he bumped into his old love Gene Tierney at Maxim's in Paris.

"Isn't it time we started to see each other again?" he asked.

"No, not for me," replied Tierney, who was unaware of his engagement. Later she explained that she was "too crazy about him to risk renewing something that could only end by hurting us both." Tierney was philosophical when she read about his marriage a few months later. Jacqueline Bouvier, she concedes, was "a bride I felt sure his parents approved of."

The prewedding festivities began several days before the ceremony with a rambunctious sixty-fifth birthday party for Joe in Hyannis Port, followed by a bachelor dinner at Newport's Clambake Club. After toasting his future bride, Jack urged all eighteen men in attendance to hurl their glasses—which happened to be Auchincloss family heirlooms—into the fireplace. Twice. Uncle Hughdie, Fay later said, "appeared badly shaken."

The Clambake Club was also the site for the bridal dinner on the eve of the wedding. At the dinner, members of the wedding party were given their gifts—initialed silver picture frames for the bridesmaids and Brooks Brothers umbrellas for the grooms-men. While everyone was eating, Jack quietly slipped Jackie a slender box. In it was his wedding gift to her—the ten-thousand-dollar diamond bracelet she later wore as they embarked on their honeymoon.

"Jack stood up and joked that he was marrying Jackie just to remove her as a member of the press," Yusha Auchincloss said. Then it was Jackie's turn to say a few words about her fiancé. "She pointed out that he wasn't exactly the Great Romantic, that in all the time they'd known each other Jack had never written her a single love letter but that he had once sent her a postcard from Bermuda." With a flourish, Jackie held up the card, took a deep breath and read it to the assembled bridal party: "Wish you were here, Jack."

In the course of the next decade, Jack and Jackie were to become the planet's most celebrated couple. Along the way, they would share the greatest public triumphs as well as the most soul-crushing personal losses imaginable. "As worldly as they both were when they got married," said their friend Chuck Spalding, "they clearly had no idea what they were in for. But then, who on earth could have imagined it?"

———

Comparing their problems to another couple's is like comparing a Duesenberg to a Chevy.

Paul "Red" Fay

———

5

"That honeymoon was so short,"
Jackie later said of their two weeks in Acapulco. "It all went so
fast." After the chaos of their Newport wedding and the high
drama surrounding Black Jack's vanishing act, Jackie was looking
forward to a romantic idyll away from the pressured worlds of
politics and high society.

What she got was the standard dose of Kennedy hyperkinesis.
The newlyweds played fierce matches of mixed doubles at the
local tennis club, water-skied, and chartered a boat to go deep-
sea fishing. Ignoring his back pain, Jack battled a nine-foot sailfish
for three hours before reeling it in. Jackie, who explained that
her shipboard assignment was to "pour water on him—Jack, not
the fish," had Jack's prize catch stuffed and mounted. (Years later
when asked by an NBC interviewer if he did a lot of fishing, Jack
replied, "I have done a lot of fishing off and on through the years.
During our honeymoon we went to Mexico and I f-f . . . ished down
there . . ." and broke up on the word *fished*. Jack waved for the
camera to stop filming and told the crew, "That's the dirtiest
laugh. We better change that." The footage was never broadcast.)

In the midst of all this activity, Jack still found time to cable
his secretary daily and phone instructions back to the office. "It
was as if," Evelyn Lincoln joked, "he'd never left."

Nights in Acapulco were spent attending dinner parties where
Jack was invariably encircled by admiring young senoritas, the
wives and daughters of some of Mexico's most prominent families.
Jackie, meanwhile, chatted away with their husbands and fathers

in fluent Spanish. "People always talk about Jack flirting with other women," a friend said, "but they forget that Jackie was no shrinking violet. She'd toss her head back and laugh at a man's jokes, dance close to him—whatever it took to get Jack's attention. And it worked, sometimes."

What Jackie could not abide was being ignored. From Mexico, they flew to Los Angeles where they spent a few days in the Beverly Hills mansion of the former actress Marion Davies. Better known as William Randolph Hearst's mistress, Davies had often hosted Jack at San Simeon, Hearst's fabulous castle north of Santa Barbara.

Jackie and Jack then drove north to San Francisco, where they visited PT-109's resident cutup, Red Fay. They had been married less than fourteen days—a period during which they were never alone for more than a few hours—and already Jack was eager for time away from his wife.

Their last day in California, instead of taking his bride for lunch atop the Mark Hopkins on Nob Hill or for a stroll along Fisherman's Wharf, Jack accompanied Fay to a 49ers football game and left Jackie behind with Fay's wife, Anita. While Anita drove Jackie across the Golden Gate Bridge to Marin County, Jackie fumed in the passenger seat. "I'm sure this didn't seem a particularly unusual arrangement to Jack," Fay said, acknowledging Jackie's resentment. "The pressures of public life—not to mention those of an old shipmate and his wife—too often intruded on the kind of honeymoon any young bride anticipates."

Chuck Spalding speculated that the whole concept of a honeymoon was probably anathema to Jack. "All your time spent focusing on one woman—the woman you will now spend the rest of your life with. Anyone who knew Jack at all knew this was not his style." Nor did he believe in advertising that he was, technically at least, no longer in circulation. Before he had left the church in which they were married, Jack had removed his wedding ring.

The separation continued after the honeymoon was over. For the first month of their marriage, Jack mended fences in Washington while Jackie spent the work week at Hyannis Port with her in-laws. On weekends, he flew up to the Cape to join her. Hardly, allowed Fay, "the top choice for a bride."

Jackie used this time to write a poem—an ode to Jack in the manner of Stephen Vincent Benét's "John Brown's Body":

Meanwhile in Massachusetts Jack Kennedy dreamed
Walking the shore by the Cape Cod Sea
Of all the things he was going to be.
He breathed in the tang of the New England Fall
And back in his mind he pictured it all
The burnished New England countryside
Names that patriot says with pride
Concord and Lexington, Bunker Hill
Plymouth and Falmouth and Marston's Mill
Winthrop and Salem, Lowell, Revere,
Quincy and Cambridge, Louisburg Square
This was his heritage—this his share
Of dreams that a young man harks in the air.
The past reached out and tracked him now
He would heed that touch; he didn't know how.
For he must serve, a part he must lead
Both were his calling, both were his need.
Part he was of New England stock
As stubborn, close guarded as Plymouth Rock
He thought with his feet most firm on the ground
But his heart and his dreams were not earth-bound
He would call New England his place and his
*   creed*
But part he was of an alien breed
Of a breed that had laughed on Irish hills
And heard the voices of Irish rills.
The lilt of that green land danced in his blood
Tara Killarney, a magical flood
That surged in the depth of his too proud heart

And spiked the punch of New England so tart
Men would call him thoughtful, sincere
They would not see through to the Last Cavalier.
He turned on the beach and looked toward his house
On a green lawn his white house stands
And the wind blows the sea grass low on the sands
There his brothers and sisters have laughed and
    played
And thrown themselves to rest in the shade.
The lights glowed inside, soon supper would ring
And he would go home where his father was King
But now he was there with the wind and the sea
And all the things he was going to be.
He would build empires
And he would have sons
Others would fall
Where the current runs
He would find love
He would never find peace
For he must go seeking
The Golden Fleece
All of the things he was going to be
All of the things in the wind and the sea.

Rose was won over, albeit temporarily, by "that marvelous poem" and its fawning sentiment. Not at all embarrassed by the gushing verse, Jack urged Jackie to get it published. Deeming "Meanwhile in Massachusetts Jack Kennedy Dreamed" too personal for public consumption, Jackie refused.

A month after their wedding, the newlyweds appeared on Edward R. Murrow's popular prime-time television program *Person to Person.* Sitting bolt upright next to her comparatively relaxed-looking husband, Jackie stumbled nervously through the interview while Jack finished her sentences and Murrow puffed on his trademark cigarette. "Now which requires more diplomacy,"

Murrow asked, "to interview a senator or to be married to one?"

Jackie looked dazed. "Well, um, I sup—"

"To be married to one, I guess," Jack jumped in.

They divided their time between Hyannis Port and Merrywood while they hunted for a permanent residence of their own. Shortly before the marriage, Jackie had described her dream house to *The Boston Globe:* "I'm dying to get a place of our own, so I can fix it up myself and get our wedding gifts out of storage. What I hope we'll find is some little Georgetown house. I'd love to have a little cozy house you can really run yourself. Then to furnish it, I'd like some lovely comfortable things mixed in with some nice old pieces of furniture."

While they searched for their "little Georgetown house," Jackie wrote and illustrated a book for her eight-year-old half-sister. *A Book for Janet: In Case You Are Ever Thinking of Getting Married This Is a Story to Tell You What It's Like* started off with a drawing of Jackie waving good-bye to Jack in the morning, and went on to depict their life together. One drawing showed the dome of the Capitol building at night, completely dark except for a single light. "If he isn't home and that single light is on," the caption read, at least "you know the country is safe." Janet Auchincloss, Sr., would describe *A Book for Janet* as "deeply touching in a beautiful way."

By Thanksgiving, 1953, they had found a narrow "cozy" nineteenth-century townhouse to rent at 3321 Dent Place in Georgetown. Twenty years younger than most of the other Senate wives, Jackie soon found that she did not fit in. "They'd talk about their children and grandchildren," she said, "and I would talk about my little half-brother."

Jackie also worried that she was losing intellectual ground to her husband. To charges that he was a glamour boy, she replied, "Nonsense. Jack has almost no time anymore for sailboats and silly things. He has this curious, inquiring mind that is always at work. If I were drawing him, I would draw a tiny body and an enormous head."

Jackie felt most inadequate when the subject turned to American government, so she enrolled in an American history class at Georgetown University. "The more I hear Jack talk about such intricate and vast problems," she complained, "the more I feel like a complete moron. If he'd only change to European history, I'd have a chance."

Amazingly Jackie, who had grown up on the outskirts of Washington, worked as a member of its press corps, and been involved with Jack Kennedy for two years, was unprepared for the task of being a senator's wife. "She hated politics and politicians. Jackie was accustomed to politics," Gore Vidal observed. "After all, she was brought up there. Jackie saw there was nothing glamorous about that world. To her it was just sleazy. And boring."

Ignoring the promise she had made to herself "not to become a housewife," Jackie decided the best contribution she could make was on the domestic front. "I brought a certain amount of order to his life," she said of their first months as a married couple. "We had good food in our house—not merely the bare staples that he used to have. He no longer went out in the morning with one brown shoe and one black shoe on. His clothes got pressed and he got to the airport without a mad rush because I packed for him. I can be helpful packing suitcases, laying out clothes, rescuing lost coats and luggage. It's those little things that make you tired." Her efforts at reforming her husband were not entirely successful; Jack Kennedy still had no qualms about answering the front door wearing nothing but his white Jockey briefs.

With no parental model to imitate, Jackie plunged headlong into the role of loyal wife and helpmate. When it was required, she sat in the gallery and gazed down adoringly as her husband addressed his fellow senators. She rolled bandages for the Red Cross with other Senate wives and joined a bridge club to perfect her game (like Jack, she was described by other players as an amazingly quick study). And while both she and Jack tried to avoid the Embassy Row cocktail parties that were the social lifeblood of Washington, Mrs. Kennedy shook hands with diplomats, lobbyists, and government officials when called upon to do so.

Jackie also took golf lessons, in the hope of spending more time with her husband on the links. After an afternoon spent watching Jackie struggle along, Jack politely suggested that she stick to horseback riding.

For the most part, Jackie now chose to emulate Donna Reed and June Cleaver. "The main thing for me was to do whatever my husband wanted," she later explained. "He couldn't—and wouldn't—be married to a woman who tried to share the spotlight with him. I thought the best thing I could do was to be a distraction. Jack lived and breathed politics all day long. If he came home to more table thumping, how could he ever relax?" She did not stop there. "I'm an old-fashioned wife . . . Housekeeping is a joy to me," she told a reporter. "When it all runs smoothly, when the food is good and the flowers look fresh, I have much satisfaction. I like cooking, but I'm not very good at it. I care terribly about food, but I'm not much of a cook."

To rectify that, she signed up for cooking classes. The day she graduated, Jackie decided to put what she had learned to the test. She asked Evelyn Lincoln to warn her when Jack left the office for home, then swept into action. "I'd heard those silly stories about the bride burning things and I just knew everything was going right when suddenly, I don't know what went wrong, you couldn't see the place for smoke." As she pulled the lamb chops from the stove, the oven collapsed. "The pan slid out and the fat splattered. One of the chops fell, but I put it on the plate anyway. The chocolate sauce was burning and exploding. What a smell! I couldn't get the spoon out of the chocolate. It was like a rock. The coffee had all boiled away. I burned my arm, and it turned purple. It looked horrible. Then Jack arrived and took me out to dinner."

No matter. As soon as they had moved into their little townhouse, Jack and Jackie had secured the services of a full-time cook and a maid—this in addition to Jack's loyal valet George Thomas. Jackie's efforts in the kitchen were nothing more than an attempt to see if she could make do on cook's night off. As for housekeeping, Evelyn Lincoln claimed Jackie "never did manual labor. She would not know how to clean a house." They hurried to the spacious splendors of Merrywood whenever the Auchinclosses were out of town.

Even with a household staff of three in Georgetown, Jackie could only pull herself together enough to hold two dinner parties during the first six months of their marriage. The first and most unnerving of these was a get-together for ten including Senator John Sherman Cooper and his wife Lorraine, Bobby and Ethel, and Hugh and Janet Auchincloss. "I think I could entertain a king or queen with less apprehension," she said, "than my mother." From the food to the ambience to the conversation, it seemed in every respect to be a flawless evening.

Until, that is, Janet abruptly interrupted the dinner table chatter to accuse her daughter of an unpardonable faux pas. "Jackie," she said haughtily, "isn't the record player broken?"

"Oh no, Mummy," Jackie replied. "It's just Fred Astaire tap dancing."

Over the years Lorraine Cooper, who became one of Jackie's closest friends in Washington, reminded Jackie of the record player incident. "She thought it was very funny," said Jackie, who nevertheless understood her mother's apprehension. "She was quite nervous about me, you know . . . I'm not sure I had it all together then," Jackie conceded.

She had it together enough to spring into action when, at eleven in the morning, Jack called from the office to ask what she was planning to serve their forty guests for lunch. "No one had told me anything about it," she later recalled. "I was in a panic. As soon as I could gather myself, I tore up to a little Greek place that made wonderful casseroles." When the guests arrived at one, they were served a salad, the casseroles, and raspberries for dessert. "I vowed never again," she said disingenuously, "to be disturbed when Jack brought home unexpected guests."

In reality, Jackie's efforts at creating an Ozzie and Harriet home life were for naught. The life of a young senator with his eye on the White House was a blur of working lunches, late-night meetings, and out-of-town trips. "My God," she told Lorraine Cooper. "You told me what it would be like, but you really didn't tell me everything. You only told me half."

To make matters worse, tweedy advisors recruited from the Ivy League as well as rank-and-file members of Kennedy's "Irish Mafia"—which Jackie acidly labeled the "Murphia"—tramped in and out of the house at will, soiling the carpets, leaving toilet seats up, behaving as if Jack were still their favorite unkempt bachelor. "They sprawled all over her furniture," recalled Tish Baldrige, "broke her Sevres ashtrays, dropped their cigarette butts in her vases and, most of all, took up her husband's time."

Publicly, Jackie resolutely fostered her image as the Senator's true-blue suburban wife. "The most important thing a wife needs is to really love her husband," she would say repeatedly. "Then any sacrifices or adjustments she has to make are only a joy." Privately, she railed against Jack. "I felt like we were running a boardinghouse, and he didn't understand." And, as is the case with many young marrieds, this period was marred by pitched battles as they tried to adjust to each other's idiosyncrasies. While they were careful not to argue in front of their friends, neighbors heard yelling and the sound of slamming doors emanating from 3321 Dent Place.

It was not long before Jackie hit upon what would become the secret weapon in her marital arsenal: the sulk. "Jack hated it when people sulked," Spalding said. "He had a hell of a temper, no doubt about it, but after he blew up it was all over. He didn't hold grudges, and he couldn't stand it when somebody gave him the silent treatment." Jackie, on the other hand, was by all accounts the moodier of the two. She could sulk for days, wearing

Jack down until, as one friend put it, "Jack would do anything to make her happy, just to make her stop."

That ploy worked, of course, only if Jack was actually on the premises. "During our first year of marriage," she later admitted, "we were like gypsies living in and out of a suitcase. It was turbulent. Jack made speeches all over the country and was never home more than two nights at a time."

After their lease was up in June, they again bounced from Merrywood to Hyannis Port to a series of hotels. Later, from the vantage point of the White House, Jackie said this period in her marriage was "hectic, but I rather enjoyed it. You don't really long for a home of your own unless you have children."

In more candid moments, she conceded that was far from the case. "The first year I longed for a home of our own," she said. "I hoped it would give our lives some roots, some stability. My ideal at that time was a normal life with my husband coming home from work every day at five. I wanted him to spend weekends with me and the children I hoped we would have." Instead, Jackie found herself "alone almost every weekend. It was all wrong. Politics was sort of my enemy, and we had no home life whatsoever."

The stress took its toll. Growing tired of her solitary horseback rides at Merrywood whenever Jack was out of town, Jackie now fully indulged the fondness for cigarettes she had developed during her days at Miss Porter's. She was chain-smoking two packs a day—a habit that Jack, who smoked the occasional Upmann Havana cigar, firmly instructed her to keep out of the public eye.

As much as she resented the intrusive "Murphia" led by Jack's key advisors Dave Powers and Kenneth O'Donnell, Jackie suspected that Jack might be up to more than just political business on the road. Priscilla McMillan wrote to Jack in the spring of 1954 about the research she had done for him on French Indochina. "I told him it had been great fun working for him, but that he'd forgotten to pay me. He never answered my letter. But after Jack gave the Indochina speech in the summer of 1954 he called me up and said that I would be paid by Joe. He was very thankful for my work on the speech, and credited me with its success. 'Thank you,' he said, 'Oh, I owe it all to you.' I took it with a grain of salt—you know, politicians . . ."

Thanking McMillan for her work on the speech wasn't the only reason for Jack's call. "He told me he was coming to New York and would like to have a drink with me. I wore my best black suit and waited, but he never showed, he never called. He stood me up."

The next day, McMillan was having lunch with a young man at Manhattan's legendary Le Pavillon, a restaurant in which Joe Kennedy had an ownership interest. "Who should sidle up next to us on the dark red banquette but Senator and Mrs. Kennedy, dressed in a navy blue suit. Jack didn't skip a beat, he introduced us but said nothing about standing me up the day before. When Jackie got up to go to the ladies' room, he reached over and took my hand and said hello. Then he got up and left without paying. He *never* had to pay. Wherever he dined, he treated each restaurant like his personal five-and-dime."

"Jackie was not naïve about Jack," Smathers said. "Every once in a while she would tag along when Jack least expected it. She knew the score. She knew he liked pretty girls, and he wasn't about to stop chasing them."

One Sunday several weeks later, McMillan flew to Washington for a dinner at the F Street Club celebrating Kennedy friend Don Marvin's birthday. "Jack came in on crutches first. Then Jackie made a separate entrance, wearing a black V-neck dress very much like mine and carrying a bottle of champagne for Don Marvin. She gave the crutches to George Thomas, Jack's valet, and made it all seem very charming, even dramatic. Then Jack sat down next to me, with Jackie across from us. I wasn't very sophisticated, but of course later I figured out that Jack had arranged it this way.

"Jack didn't drink anything and he just sort of toyed with his food. But he spent the whole evening talking to me. At one point, he looked across the table at Jackie and said, 'You know, I only got married because I was thirty-six and people would think I was queer if I didn't.' The whole time he was saying this to me, he didn't take his eyes off Jackie. The entire time he was looking at her, literally drinking her in with his eyes, *absorbing* her. She was bewitching, of course—sitting there, immersed in conversation with the man next to her. But what Jack was saying was at such variance with the way he was looking at Jackie, I was stunned. He was obviously proud. It made his ego even bigger because he had in some incredible way assimilated her."

McMillan was also surprised that Jack "didn't even lower his voice. He knew how to pitch his words just so she couldn't hear. Still," McMillan continued, "there was a *separateness* about her. She made a separate entrance. There was the sense of a person here, not some docile wife in his wake. These were not warring camps, but definitely two totally separate and distinct people. But even back then, *she* was the high point of the evening, not Jack." McMillan remembered that when she got up to get her coat, she turned to see Jackie "coming down the marble steps toward me. 'Could we give you a ride to the airport, Priscilla?' she asked. I told her thanks, but that I'd be fine. I was confused enough as it was.

"I have no idea what she thought of me. Jack's flirting was rather obvious, and I wasn't sure whether or not she'd heard what he said to me about marrying just because he didn't want people to think he was 'queer.' But she was very thoughtful. I did not entirely expect her to be quite so . . . nice."

Jackie's public show of confidence masked a deep insecurity over what role she was to play in her husband's life. When asked by a reporter to share her secrets for a successful marriage, she sighed, "I can't say I have any yet."

Jackie did, however, make a conscious decision to change her approach. Rather than casting herself exclusively as the dutiful spouse, she would find ways to insinuate herself into her husband's working life. She started coming into the office to help with the mail. She translated directly from the writings of Voltaire and Talleyrand so that Jack could quote these and other historical figures in his speeches.

Jackie also proved instrumental in transforming him from an uninspired, even irritating public speaker to a spellbinding orator—something the Emerson School of Oratory in Boston had failed to do. Jackie worked with him to replace his nasal New England twang ("Sometimes he sounds like Bugs Bunny. Ehhhh, what's up, Doc?" she once said) with deeper, more resonant tones. She also got him to slow down—his rapid-fire delivery was scarcely intelligible to many of his southern colleagues—and to effectively punctuate whatever points he was trying to make with air-slicing hand gestures (up to this point they were usually plunged deep into his pockets, jingling change). Most of all, she succeeded in getting Jack to calm down, to appear less frenetic and more self-composed. Jack's inventory of nervous ticks included tapping his front teeth with his forefinger and a nervous leg that, according to one friend, "would be going a mile a minute underneath the banquet table or behind the lectern."

These mannerisms, which Jackie worked diligently to bring under control, stemmed directly from an excess of nervous energy and an impatience with the gentlemanly pace of the Senate. "Legislative life," Charlie Bartlett said, "was not his idea of bliss." Jack often complained to Smathers that he felt he was accomplishing little in the Senate. "Jack didn't like being a congressman, and he didn't like being a senator," Smathers said. "It bored the hell out of him. In that sense, he was not a thirsting politician."

Boredom would soon be the least of Jack's problems. Throughout the first year of their marriage, Jack's excruciating back condition grew steadily worse. He always wore a baby blue back brace under his shirt, and by May he was hobbling around on crutches. "Jackie was suddenly confronted with the fact that her husband was practically an invalid," Vidal said. "Jack *was* decrepit. He spent most of his time in hospitals suffering from one thing or another. Jack was dying most of the time. He was in constant pain, always sick. Nobody knew why . . ."

In the Senate, Jack tried to conceal the severity of his condition from all but a few close friends. One of these was George Smathers. "He was so sick that if they would ring the bell for a quorum call, I would have to go to his office and say, 'Come on,' and lift him up out of his chair. He would lean on me, and I would literally almost carry him down to the underground train that led to the chambers. It wasn't very difficult. He was six feet tall and weighed about 125 pounds." Once they arrived, "Jack summoned all his strength and walked on his own to the Senate floor. Afterward, he'd duck into a corridor or a stairwell and lean up against the wall. He never said anything, but you could see the pain etched in his face."

By October 1954, the pain had become unbearable even for Jack. It had been a decade since his last back surgery, and doctors were still unsure about the precise nature of his ailment. To determine whether surgery was an option, he checked into New York's Hospital for Special Surgery (formerly the Hospital for the Ruptured and Crippled) for tests.

The night before, Jack and Jackie attended a rally for congressional candidate Anthony Akers, another PT boat commander he had served with during World War II. "Jack was on crutches, and Jackie was wearing a black dress that went up to her neck in front but was very naked, very low-cut down the back," said Priscilla McMillan, who was working on Akers's campaign at the time. "When she turned around, there was this gasp from the crowd."

From her brother-in-law, who was a physician at the hospital, McMillan learned what few others knew—that Jack suffered from Addison's disease, and that major surgery of any kind would likely kill him. "Here he was in great pain and here she was waiting to learn if she might lose her husband, but standing up there on the stage they radiated youth and vigor. They really should have gotten an Academy Award."

McMillan visited him in the hospital a few days later. "I called his room and he told me to come up, but to tell everybody that I was his sister," McMillan remembered. "Later one of the nurses told me that he was not allowed to have any guests except immediate family, but that he received so many phone calls the hospital had to install a special switchboard. 'And,' the nurse exclaimed, 'Senator Kennedy has so many sisters!'

"When I walked into Jack's hospital room for the first time it was hard to believe what I was seeing," she recalled. "There was a life-size poster of Marilyn Monroe in dark blue shorts and a white tennis shirt hanging on the door—upside down. Her legs were up in the air, in other words. At the foot of his bed was a tank full of tropical fish. He was lying in bed and under the sheets beside him was a Howdy Doody doll that was just as big as he was."

———

In 1954, the Monroe poster represented a bit of wishful thinking on Jack's part. They had met briefly in the 1940s, when he was rooming with Robert Stack and she was a struggling contract player. But there were no signs of a possible romance between them until a party Jack and Jackie attended early in 1954 at the Beverly Hills home of Hollywood agent Charles Feldman. Among the guests were Marilyn and her husband, former Yankee slugger Joe DiMaggio. Jack did not attempt to conceal his interest in the voluptuous star. "He can't take his eyes off me," said Marilyn, who slipped the senator her phone number.

As for Jackie: "She wasn't bothered, not at all," said Peter Lawford. "Every man in the room was drooling over Marilyn. Jackie would have thought something was wrong if Jack *hadn't* stared at her." The next day he dialed Marilyn's number but hung up when DiMaggio answered the phone. JFK and Monroe, who spent that year making the hit film *The Seven-Year Itch*, had not seen each other since. As for the poster: "It wasn't as if Jack was hiding it from her—it was right there in the open for everyone to see."

———

Dreaming of Marilyn in his hospital bed, before long Jack went stir-crazy. "He would be lying on his stomach having the doctors poke and prod his back, and at the same time be on the phone asking what the latest political joke was in New Hampshire," said McMillan, who began visiting him almost daily. "He asked me to bring him books, so I brought him the ones I'd liked. He'd call me up at three A.M. and say, 'I've never heard of Nietzsche and Hegel, and you've got me reading them!'

"Jack had trouble sleeping. He'd read all night, then start pacing the corridors," McMillan said. It was not long before he started sneaking out for nights on the town. "He was probably the most difficult patient they'd had. The nurses would take his temperature and say good night, and then he'd get up, slip down the back stairs, and meet some girls at the Stork Club or '21.'"

One Saturday afternoon, McMillan was with Jack in his hospital room when Jackie, wearing a tailored black suit, walked in with her stepbrother Yusha. "Jackie was very playful and kittenish—frolicking on Jack's bed, jumping up and down on her knees. She ate Jack's dinner even though she was going out to some dinner party. This was obviously all for our benefit. It struck me then that Jackie was a superb actress. She was very good at putting on a performance. It didn't occur to me until much later that the objective was to keep him *interested*—and she did, even though he was unfaithful to her."

During another of McMillan's hospital visits, Jack was engrossed in deep conversation with two teenage girls from New Jersey. "He introduced them to me as his cousins! I guess he ran out of 'sisters,' " said McMillan. "He asked them to stay, but they left, and none too soon. Just moments later, Jackie walked in with a young man. 'Priscilla,' she said, 'Have you met Teddy? He's the real politician in the family.' "

McMillan ran into Jackie not long after, at a children's bookstore on Madison Avenue in New York. She was wearing a heavy kelly green wool winter coat and buying books for Jamie. "Jackie was *very* friendly, so much so that I became sort of suspicious. It was if she was encouraging me to see her husband. I wasn't a threat to Jackie. I guess she could tell I wasn't the type to sleep with a guy I scarcely knew—particularly a married man—and that made me valuable. I took up the time he could be spending with someone who *would* sleep with him—and there were plenty of those. Although, I have to say that at the time I had no idea of the *extent* of his shenanigans."

It wasn't that Jack didn't try to seduce McMillan. He did, repeatedly. "When Jack was ambulatory, Jack was very intense. He would swoop down on you, and to be perfectly honest, to see him once every few months was all you could take. The pace was too much, too hectic. He certainly more or less attacked you, followed by an evening of hand-to-hand combat! I owe all the strength in my arms to pushing him away."

Once the results of the exhaustive battery of tests were in, the doctors at Cornell rendered their verdict: The only hope of relieving his pain significantly, they told Jack, was a double fusion of the spine. The metal disc that had been placed in his spine by Navy surgeons in 1944 would have to be removed, and the separated vertebrae fused.

Jack's doctors at the Lahey Clinic back in Boston were foursquare against the delicate procedure. They pointed out that the operation, risky enough for a patient with no other serious medical problems, was unthinkable for someone suffering from Addison's disease. There was only a fifty-fifty chance for survival; if infection set in, they said, he would almost certainly die. "We were not sold on the *need* for the operation," said the Lahey Clinic's Dr. Elmer C. Bartels. "We simply wouldn't do the operation in Boston."

Jack, left with no other options, argued furiously on behalf of surgery. He had stared death squarely in the face several times before and was not afraid to do it again. Joe Kennedy begged his son repeatedly not to have the surgery. According to Rose, Joe "tried to convince Jack that even confined to a wheelchair he could lead a full and rich life. After all, he argued one needed only look at the incredible life FDR had managed to lead despite his physical incapacity."

Jack was adamant. Unable to budge his son, the Ambassador asked Jackie to intervene. She shared her father-in-law's concern, but she felt it was Jack's decision to make; she refused to try to talk him out of it. "I'd rather be dead," he told them both, "than spend the rest of my life on crutches." Turning to Joe, he said, "Don't worry, Dad. I'll make it through." Jack was more candid with Dave Powers. "This is the one," Jack said of the operation, "that kills you or cures you."

Dr. Philip D. Wilson led the team of four surgeons who operated on Jack on October 21, 1954. The night of the operation, Joe could not sleep. He wandered into the library at Hyannis Port around 1 A.M. and sat for hours staring at the last letter Joe Jr. had sent him just before he was killed. "The memory was so painful," Rose recalled, "that Joe actually cried out in the darkness with a sound so loud that I was awakened from sleep."

As predicted, a staph infection of the urinary tract set in, and three days after the operation Jack was placed on the critical list. He lapsed into a coma, and was administered the last rites of the Catholic Church. Doctors told Evelyn Lincoln that they did not expect her boss to survive the night.

For nearly a month, Jack hovered between life and death. Joe kept up a good front, reassuring inquiring Senate colleagues like Stuart Symington and Lyndon Johnson that Jack was on the mend. But he was devastated by the possibility that he might lose Jack. During a visit to Arthur Krock's office at *The New York Times,* he broke down. "He told me he thought Jack was dying and he wept sitting in the chair opposite me in the office." Rose later said that it was "inconceivable" to Joe that he "could once again be losing his eldest son, and his entire body shook with anger and sorrow . . . he was heartbroken."

Faced with the looming prospect of widowhood at twenty-five, Jackie surprised everyone by swinging into action. While he lay in a coma, she squeezed his hand and read poetry to him. Once he regained consciousness, she spoon-fed him, helped him with his robe, plumped his pillows, summoned nurses when he needed pain medication, smuggled in the candy to which he had long been addicted, played their usual parlor games, and brought friends in to visit.

"It was a very grim time for Jack, obviously," Charlie Bartlett said. "Jackie was always looking for ways to lift his spirits." This was particularly difficult at night, when senior staff members replaced the young nurses who hovered over him during the day. While attending an intimate Park Avenue soirée, Jackie asked one of the guests to return with her and pay a surprise call on Jack.

After the party, she went with Jackie to Jack's room, tapped gently at the door, and poked her head in. "I'm the new night nurse!" announced Grace Kelly, whom Jackie had even talked into donning a nurse's uniform. "When Jack opened his eyes," Jackie recalled, "he thought he was dreaming. He was hardly strong enough to shake hands with her. He couldn't even talk." Kelly was rattled at Jack's feeble response. "I must be losing it," she said as she left the room.

"During the time Jack was in the hospital, Jackie was the Rock of Gibraltar," Chuck Spalding said. "She stepped right in and did everything humanly possible to see that he'd pull through. People who thought she was some flighty society girl realized they'd made a big mistake. Jackie was far from helpless." She could always count on Joe, but now Jackie also enjoyed a newfound measure of respect from Rose and the sisters. "There is no doubt that Jackie came through for Jack," Vidal agreed. "She did everything she had to do when it came to nursing him. She lived up to her end of the marriage contract."

One of Jackie's most important contributions to Jack's recovery were the snippets of gossip she was able to glean from her sources in Washington and New York. Unfortunately, much of this chatter revolved around him. Not only was there rampant speculation about the state of his health—there was talk that he suffered from Parkinson's disease, and that cancer was the cause of his stick-figure physique.

There was political fallout, as well. The Senate was on the verge of censuring Joseph McCarthy, and there was pressure from both sides for Jack to take a stand. But Joe McCarthy had long been an ally of the Kennedys (Joe Kennedy had been a major contributor to McCarthy's campaigns), and Jack's sisters Pat and Eunice had even dated the rabidly anti-Communist senator from Wisconsin. It was likely that one Irish Catholic voting to bring down another would not sit well with the staunchly pro-McCarthy Catholics back home in Massachusetts.

Jackie was sitting on the edge of Jack's hospital bed in early December 1954 when the Senate voted to censure McCarthy. Jack had prepared two speeches, one explaining why he was voting for McCarthy's censure, the other explaining why he was not. In the end, he delivered neither. John F. Kennedy was the only senator who sidestepped the issue completely, refusing to cast an absentee vote. "There's going to be about ninety-five faces bent over me with great concern," he told Spalding, "and every one is going to say, 'Now, Senator, what about McCarthy?' Do you know what I'm going to do? I'm going to reach for my back and I'm just going to yell 'Ow!' and then I'm going to pull the sheet over my head."

Jack knew he could count on his colleague Richard Nixon not to be one of these. Although they eventually became mortal enemies, for the time being they seemed to harbor a genuine respect, even affection, for one another. On the drive home from the Capitol just a few days after the operation, Secret Service agent Rex Scouten listened to Vice President Nixon express grave concern for Kennedy. "Poor brave Jack is going to die," Nixon said. "O God," he went on, his voice cracking with emotion, "don't let him die."

During Jack's eight-month absence from the Senate, Nixon frequently checked in on his friend's progress. Before the November 1954 elections, Nixon went so far as to send a message via Jack's assistant Ted Sorensen. Nixon pledged that he would not use his vice presidential power as President of the Senate to break a tie until Jack returned. Whether or not he ever would have followed through on his promise, Nixon clearly hoped to ease his friend's mind.

In her December 5, 1954, letter to Nixon, Jackie wrote, "I could never describe to you how touched and appreciative Jack was at the message you sent him.

"If you could only know the load you took off his mind. He has been feeling so much better since then—and I can never thank you enough for being so kind and generous and thoughtful. He was having such a difficult time, and I know one of the reasons was he just felt so frustrated and hopeless—cooped up in the hospital and wondering if it would affect everything in Washington.

"I don't think there is anyone in the world he thinks more highly of than he does you—and this is just another proof of how incredible you are."

Nixon was not the only high-ranking official Mrs. Kennedy contacted on behalf of her ailing husband. While he lay in bed fighting for his life, she wrote to a number of luminaries thanking them for their concern. "You did more for him," she wrote to President Eisenhower, who had sent him a get-well note, "than any doctor could possibly do." When Jackie learned that Bernard Baruch had come by but was barred from visiting Jack because he was not an immediate relative, Jackie sat down and dashed off a note: "If you only knew how crushed we are to have missed you—I know Jack is miserable—because he would have adored to have seen you—but I am sure I am much more—because I would rather meet you than anyone in the world—and now I feel that you are a ship that has passed in the night." She told Adlai Stevenson, the party's standard-bearer in the last presidential election, that his phone call had "transformed" her husband.

Two months after the operation, Jack remained in poor condition. Believing that a warm climate and familiar surroundings might speed up his recovery, doctors suggested that he move into the Palm Beach house. Jack was loaded into the ambulance on a stretcher and taken to LaGuardia Airport, where a private jet waited to take him to the West Palm Beach airport. Jackie never left his side.

A wing of the estate in Palm Beach was made over into a hospital suite complete with a round-the-clock staff of nurses and aides. But lying there day after day, he began to doubt if he would ever walk at all, even with crutches. Sapped of strength and still in unrelenting pain, Jack began to undergo a transformation in his personality. No longer the ebullient, upbeat survivor, he was becoming an embittered man. "We came close to losing him," Lem Billings said. "I don't mean losing his life. I mean losing him as a *person*."

"I think convalescence is harder to bear than great pain," Jackie observed of her husband's declining state of mind. This time, seeing how desperately unhappy his son was in this condition, it was Joe who pressed for a second operation. Jack flew back to New York and went under the surgeon's knife a second time, on February 15, 1955. He came so close to dying that a priest was called in to administer the last rites again, and again he rallied.

A week later, Jack returned to Palm Beach, and this time began to heal. Jackie was once again indispensable in speeding his recovery, reading constantly to him, relaying messages from colleagues and well-wishers, keeping him abreast of the latest gossip. "She seldom left his bedside," said Dave Powers, who stayed with him at the Kennedy estate for five weeks while his boss recuperated. She also learned to change the bandages that covered the grisly eight-inch-long incision in his back.

"He was in constant pain," Powers said, "all the time I was there, he was unable to sleep for more than an hour or two at a time, but he never complained about the pain, never mentioned it."

On March 1, 1955, Jack eased himself out of bed and, with Jackie's help, walked without crutches for the first time in six months. The next day, clad in shorts and a baseball cap, he got as far as the beach with Jackie and Powers taking turns steadying him. "He stood there," Powers recalled, "feeling the warm salt water on his bare feet, and broke into a big smile."

Joe had been watching Jack's walk on the beach from an upstairs window. "I know nothing can happen to him now," the senior Kennedy told Powers, "because I've stood by his deathbed three times and each time I said good-bye to him, and each time he came back stronger."

A few days later, George Smathers paid him a visit and brought his older brother Frank along. "We were standing in the vestibule, and Jack said, 'Frank, I want you to change my dressing.' So Jack handed my brother the bandages and forceps and the iodine and some antibiotic jelly, lay down on this bench, and said, 'Now, Frank, I've got to change these bandages every four hours, so . . . '

"Frank used the forceps to peel back the bandages, and it was gruesome. It was a gash—a hole, really—big enough to put your fist into. It was all infected and full of green stuff. It smelled horrible . . . You could see right down into the wound and actually see his backbone! So Frank pulled the bloody bandages off and let them drop to the floor, then he applied the antibiotic jelly. All the time Frank is doing this, Jack is *talking* to us about what's happening in Washington, cracking jokes. When it was over, he got up and said, 'Okay, Frank, we've got to get you a damn medical degree. You did a good job.'

"When you think Jackie did this and a hell of a lot more several times a day, well, I was sort of ashamed of myself for telling him not to marry her. She was every bit as tough as he was. They were battling this thing together, and there was something *gallant* about them. Whatever the other problems were in their marriage, they made one hell of a team."

That April 1955, however, Joe feared that one particular man-about-town posed a serious threat to the partnership, or at least the public perception of it. Oleg Cassini, who had known both Jack and Jackie for years, had stepped in to escort Jackie to various social events while Jack was indisposed. Joe might have had reason to suspect that Cassini was pursuing Jackie. Not only had Jack dealt the final blow to Cassini's marriage to Gene Tierney, but Old Joe had had the audacity to make moves on his fiancée Grace Kelly, and then convince Kelly not to go through with marrying the designer.

One evening while they were watching the sunset from the porch of the Palm Beach mansion, Joe cautioned Cassini to be discreet. "Look, Oleg," he said. "I wouldn't be surprised if you have some ideas about Jackie. If the situation were different, I might have some ideas about her myself. But the question is: essence versus perception. I don't care what you do, but it must not be perceived. The worst thing, to my mind, would be to have the perception but not the reality—that would be silly, a real donkey's game. You understand?"

"Jackie was a fascinating woman and we were great friends," Cassini said, "but I was a friend of Jack's. Besides, she did not show any signs of being interested in me romantically."

While Jack had been in the hospital contemplating his own decision, deemed expedient by many of his colleagues, to abstain from voting on the McCarthy issue, he began compiling material for an article on the lives of American political figures—John Quincy Adams, George W. Norris, Daniel Webster, and Robert Taft among them—who had taken unpopular but morally correct stands. Now that he was in Palm Beach, he filled his sleepless hours expanding the article into a book.

Profiles in Courage, as the book was called, went on to become a best-seller and to win a Pulitzer Prize for biography. Once again,

Jack was assisted in this endeavor by a small army of researchers and editors—most notably his young assistant Ted Sorensen, who evidently did much of the actual writing.

In fairness, though, Jack did write large portions of the initial draft after he moved north to continue his period of recuperation at Merrywood. "I can remember him lying in that room, on that board of his, writing almost upside down," Bartlett said. "I got so damned angry when people said he didn't write the book." Jack even began telling friends that he was a writer at heart, and that he would "rather win a Pulitzer" than be elected president.

Next to Sorensen, Jack leaned most heavily on Jackie to bring the book to fruition. She helped assemble some of the research material, read passages to him, and scribbled down passages of the book as he dictated them to her.

Jackie even took on the formidable task of finding a publisher for her husband's book. Not surprisingly, she took the manuscript to Harper and Brothers' Cass Canfield, her sister Lee's father-in-law. Canfield in turn assigned Evan Thomas, who happened to be the son of Socialist icon Norman Thomas, to edit the book.

On May 24, 1955, Jack was greeted warmly by the leaders of both parties when he returned to the floor of the Senate, sans crutches. Although he could walk without assistance, he continued to suffer severe shooting pains down his lower back and left leg.

Two days after his triumphant return to the Capitol, Jack visited physician-pharmacologist Janet Travell at her offices on New York's West Sixteenth Street. "He could walk on the level, but he couldn't step up or down," Dr. Travell said. "We could hardly get him into the office, which had two steps to navigate." He, according to Travell, "greatly resented the fact that he had had three back operations . . . and that they had seemed to only make him worse." Travell prescribed hot baths, massages, and an exercise regimen to strengthen his back muscles—which, amazingly, none of the other physicians had done. She also provided him with a firmer cattletail-hair mattress to sleep on, a new, state-of-the-art back brace (again in baby blue), and a lift to wear in his left shoe to correct the fact that his left leg was a quarter of an inch shorter than the other.

Above and beyond his obvious back problems, his Addison's and venereal diseases, and his severe allergies to horses, dogs, and house dust, Travell's tests revealed new medical problems. Jack, it turned out, was lactose intolerant, had an underactive thyroid—and a startlingly high cholesterol count of 350.

Jack also worried about his fertility, even though he believed he had impregnated at least two women in the past. Out of Jackie's presence, he asked if either Addison's disease or the lingering effects of the genital diseases he contracted in college might have rendered him sterile. He was assured by Travell that he was perfectly capable of becoming a father.

The one thing Jack would not mention was the one thing that plagued him every waking hour: pain. "He was the opposite of a hypochondriac," Travell said. "It was difficult to get him to state his complaints."

That is where Jackie stepped in, asking Travell directly if there was anything she could do to alleviate his pain. Travell said there was an injection she could give him that would eliminate the pain altogether, but that it would leave him numb from the waist down. "Well," Jack laughed, "we can't have that, can we, Jackie?"

There was also a less drastic alternative. Travell began injecting Jack directly in the back with Novocain, providing instant if temporary relief. This was in addition to the cortisone injections for the Addison's disease Jack was giving himself twice a day. Watching Jack give himself one of the shots in the upper thigh without so much as wincing, Red Fay said, "Jack, the way you jab that in looks like it doesn't even hurt."

Without warning, Jack plunged the needle into his friend's leg. Fay shrieked in pain. "It feels," Jack said nonchalantly, "the same way to me."

Stories abound concerning Jack's stoicism during this period. "We were talking together at a party," said Jack's friend Kay Halle. "He was leaning against the top of a high-backed chair.

Suddenly the girl who was sitting in the chair got up, and Jack slid down and fell straight on the floor on the bottom of his spine. He turned white as a sheet, and I remember saying to him, 'Look, Jack, take both of my hands.' He rose, righted himself, and went right on talking to me. I knew that he must have been in desperate pain, but he just went straight on with the conversation—a remarkable demonstration of his iron courage and power to dominate the physical with his will."

Often, he seemed to have an almost reckless disregard for his own health. After he tried out and liked a rocking chair in Dr. Travell's office, Jackie bought him two: one for home and one for work. At his Senate office, he was so intent on convincing one colleague he was in robust good health that he sat in his new chair and rocked so furiously that he flipped over. Again, he was described as turning "white as a sheet." Again, he behaved as if nothing had happened.

Swinging into action on the home front, Jack invited the entire Massachusetts state legislature to Hyannis Port for a clambake. Jackie, without whom Jack might never have survived his life-threatening surgeries, hated it. "She *loathed* politics and politicians," their neighbor Larry Newman said. According to Spalding, "you could see this desperate 'get me out of here' look in her eyes whenever the pols came into view." Usually she would do just that whenever possible, disappear into an upstairs room. On those occasions when she had to meet and greet the wives of state officials and party operatives, she learned to grin and bear it.

In July, Jackie returned to her element, departing with Jack on a seven-week working vacation in Europe. During both their private audience with Pope Pius XII and French Premier Georges Bidault, Jackie served as interpreter. Bidault was dazzled. He later wrote that in meeting her he had "never encountered so much wisdom invested with so much charm."

The burden of the presidency and its attendant foreign policy concerns were still years away. But it was during this trip that Jack got his first faint glimmer of Jackie's potential value in dealing with world leaders. "She had all the wit and the seductive charms of an eighteenth-century courtesan," Clare Booth Luce observed. "Men just *melted* when she gazed at them with those gigantic eyes. The Europeans were not immune to this. In fact, I think if anything they appreciated her style far more than the Americans."

In the course of their vacation, Jack was also treated to a healthy dose of Jackie's patented brand of sarcasm. Greek shipping tycoon Aristotle Onassis invited the Kennedys to a party aboard his yacht *Christina* anchored off the Côte d'Azur. The guest of honor was Winston Churchill. In awe of the Man of the Century since childhood, Jack, wearing a white dinner jacket, hovered about Churchill for much of the evening. But the great man preferred instead to talk to Jackie and his host Mr. Onassis. As they walked down the gangplank at the end of the evening, the Senator was crestfallen. "Maybe," Jackie said, pointing to her husband's tuxedo, "he thought you were the waiter, Jack."

Churchill's behavior was, in fact, a deliberate snub. Britain's wartime prime minister still held a grudge against the Kennedys for Joe's isolationist stand. "Jack admired Churchill tremendously, but who didn't?" said Chuck Spalding. "I can remember sitting with him, his back bandaged and still in great pain, listening to Churchill address Parliament. But Churchill shunned him. Even after Jack was president they never became friends, in part because of his resentment of Joe but also because of Jack's womanizing ways. Running around with women the way he did . . . Churchill knew all about Jack's personal life and did not approve."

Jack chalked up Churchill's chilly reception to the statesman's age and irascible nature. He was less philosophical after he strained his back in Poland, "furious" (in Powers's words) that he had to appear in public on crutches. As much as he feared that photos of him on crutches might hobble him politically, Jack was horrified when he learned that his doctors at Cornell had published an article about his surgery in the *Journal of the American Medical Association*. Although the patient was never named, it seemed to him that anyone who had heard the rumors of his having Addison's disease and who had followed the course of his surgeries in the papers could figure it out:

> A man 37 years of age had Addison's disease for seven years. He had been managed fairly successfully for several years on a program of desoxycorticosterone acetate pellets of 150 mg daily orally. Owing to a back injury, he had a great deal of pain which interfered with his daily routine. Orthopedic consultation suggested that he might be helped by a lumbosacral fusion together with a sacroiliac fusion. Because of the severe degree of trauma involved in these operations, and because of the patient's adrenocortical insufficiency due to Addison's disease, it was deemed dangerous to proceed with these operations. However, since this young man would become incapacitated without surgical intervention, it was decided, reluctantly, to perform the operations by doing the two different procedures at different times if necessary . . .

The article went on to state the dates of both the first and second operations. Fortunately for Jack, no reporter made the connection between him and the *JAMA* article until 1961, after he was firmly ensconced in the White House. And by then, President Kennedy's love affair with an indulgent White House press corps was in full bloom.

By the time they arrived back in Washington, Jackie was pregnant. She convinced Jack that their narrow little house on Dent Place was too cramped for a growing family. "Jack never stopped flirting, not even when he was at death's door," a friend said. "But after all they had been through with his surgery, and working together on the book, and then the trip to Europe and the baby, she convinced herself that he could be faithful to her."

She was wrong. Jack was more acutely aware of his own mortality than ever ("I don't have much time," he often said) and determined to prove that he was his old, fully ambulatory, lusty self. Just before his marriage, Jack had shared an apartment in Washington's Fairfax Hotel with George Smathers. The Fairfax suite was owned by railroad lobbyist Bill Thompson, who also represented the DuPont interests in Florida. It was the site of the senators' trysts with starlets, stewardesses, congressional staff members, and even the occasional hooker. "Nobody ever knew about Bill, but he got along better than anybody with Jack," Smathers said. "Bill was a very intimate friend of the Kennedys, particularly when they occupied the White House."

At the time Jackie was house-hunting, Jack replaced his suite in the Fairfax with suite 812 in the Mayflower Hotel. There he again hosted big parties for the likes of Judy Garland and Frank Sinatra, as well as intimate get-togethers and room service dinners for two. Audrey Hepburn was a guest in suite 812, as were actress Lee Remick and statuesque stripper Tempest Storm.

On October 15, 1955, Jack and Jackie paid the then-impressive sum of $125,000 for Hickory Hill, a historic property complete with stables and swimming pool not far from Merrywood in McLean, Virginia. They were in their new home only a matter of days before Jackie suffered a miscarriage three months into her pregnancy.

"Of course they were both upset," Yusha Auchincloss said, "but they really didn't share their feelings with anyone. They both had entirely too much dignity for that. It wasn't their style at all." In fact, few questions were asked; in their discretion, Jackie and Jack had informed only their immediate families that they were expecting. By January 1956, she was pregnant again.

That month there was another birth of sorts, the publication of *Profiles in Courage*. True to form, Joe Sr. left nothing to chance. He leaned on his powerful friends in the press for favorable reviews, and spent in excess of $100,000 on advertising and promotion to guarantee *Profiles* a spot on the best-seller lists. Joe again approached Arthur Krock, who had helped Jack with the manuscript, to lobby for a Pulitzer. *Profiles in Courage* was not even nominated by the Pulitzer jury for biography, but at Krock's urging the advisory board overruled the jury and gave the prize to Jack. Ironically, historian James MacGregor Burns, another Kennedy pal who had helped with the book, had been the inside favorite to win for his *Roosevelt: The Lion and the Fox.*

It is doubtful that *Profiles in Courage* would have become the enormous best-seller it did—and certain that it would never have won the Pulitzer—had Joe not intervened. It is equally certain that Jack fully appreciated his father's Machiavellian string pulling. Even before the advisory board met to render its verdict, Jack was calling friends with the news that he had been awarded the Pulitzer.

Back-room deals were such an integral part of the Kennedys' world that they seemed blithely unaware of the moral questions raised. For the benefit of Robert Coughlan, who worked with her on her memoirs, Rose Kennedy pointed to Joe's credo that "things don't just happen, they are made to happen." She then proudly fired off some examples: "As for instance when Jack got the Pulitzer Prize for his book, or when he or Bob were chosen as Outstanding Young Man of the Year. All of this was a result of their own ability plus careful spadework on their father's part as to who was on the committee and how to reach such and such a person through such and such a friend. However, Joe was lucky because his sons were good material to work with."

Profiles in Courage marked another watershed in Jack's career, for it succeeded in separating him from the rest of the senatorial pack. The dashing young senator from Massachusetts was now seen as somehow being above the fray, reflecting on the true meaning of democracy and bringing his upbeat message directly to the people in a compelling way.

Jackie, having shared in her husband's remarkable recovery and in his publishing triumph, had proven to herself and to her in-laws that she was as full of grit and determination as any Kennedy. Beneath the often helpless-looking exterior was a will of tempered steel—a will to match her husband's. No one was more impressed with Jackie's mettle than Jack, and he gave her full credit in print: "This book would not have been possible," he wrote in the acknowledgments, "without the encouragement, assistance and criticisms offered from the very beginning by my wife, Jacqueline, whose help during all the days of my convalescence I cannot ever adequately acknowledge."

In the wake of his brush with mortality, Jack's sexual recidivism had already cast a pall over their marriage. Soon, it would threaten to end it altogether. But for the moment Jackie could bask in her husband's newfound respect, and pray that 1956 would bring the one thing to end Jack's wandering ways and cement their bond forever: a child.

Jack Kennedy kept his personal affairs,
his various friendships, his political
activities, and other interests in separate
compartments. Getting to know him intimately
was not easy. There were many parts of him
. . . that he never revealed to anybody.

Kenneth O'Donnell,
JFK aide and confidant

You get used to the pressure that never lets
up, and you learn to live with it as a fish
lives in water.

Jackie

$\mathbf{F}$or Jack 1956 was a critical year, the year in which he began to establish a national power base for himself. It also marked the beginning of the ambitious senator's four-year seduction of the American electorate.

There was no hope, of course, of wresting the Democratic nomination from party favorite Adlai Stevenson, who had run unsuccessfully against Dwight D. Eisenhower in 1952. But it was anyone's guess who the former Illinois governor might pick as his running mate. Joe had contributed twenty-five thousand dollars to Stevenson's first presidential campaign, and would obviously ante up considerably more with his son on the ticket.

Jack officially endorsed Stevenson on March 8 and took the opportunity to tell the press that he was not interested in being Stevenson's running mate. In reality, Jack and his advisors worked feverishly to make it happen. Tennessee Senator Albert Gore, father of the future vice president, spoke before forty thousand people at two Boston rallies for Jack and actually endorsed him for both the presidential and vice presidential nominations.

Meanwhile, autographed copies of *Profiles in Courage* were sent to party leaders around the country along with a letter urging them to watch a televised reenactment of the PT-109 saga. Jack also agreed to narrate Hollywood producer Dore Schary's *Pursuit of Happiness,* a twenty-minute film trumpeting the achievements of the Democratic party that was to be shown at the convention in August.

Since Eisenhower's 1955 heart attack was still fresh in the

minds of voters, it seemed only logical that Jack's poor health would become an issue. Amazingly, the subject never came up in 1956. The principal objections raised to a Kennedy candidacy were Jack's youth (venerated House Speaker Sam Rayburn called him "that little piss-ant Kennedy") and his religion. To battle the conventional wisdom that the country was not yet ready for a Catholic as president or even vice president, the indispensable Ted Sorensen urged journalist-author Fletcher Knebel to address the issue two months before the convention in *Look* magazine. In "Can a Catholic Become Vice President?" Fletcher Knebel used Sorensen's research to conclude that not only could a Catholic hold national office, but that it would be good for the nation.

On July 1, Jack declared flatly on CBS's *Face the Nation* that he was not a candidate for vice president even as new allies like Connecticut Governor Abraham Ribicoff and Stevenson advisor Arthur Schlesinger, Jr. scrambled behind the scenes to sway delegates. One of Schlesinger's assignments was to win over Eleanor Roosevelt, who disliked Jack for lacking moral backbone. Alluding none too subtly to Joe's influence over his son, FDR's widow said her party should not nominate for national office "someone who understands what courage is and admires it, but has not quite the independence to have it."

While Jack jockeyed for position in the months before the convention in Chicago, Jackie, whose baby was due in September, tried to remain above the fray. "Instead of most young brides who have a husband with a nine-to-five job," she told a reporter, "I married a whirlwind and I found it rather hard."

Unable to tame her "whirlwind" and not entirely willing to be carried off by it, she threw herself into redecorating Hickory Hill, tearing down drapes, repainting rooms, replacing the Eisenhower-era contemporary furnishings with blue-and-white-satin period pieces more suited to a stately Virginia home. Janet Auchincloss remembered "all the effort Jackie went to for Jack's bathroom and dressing room. The shoe shelves had to be in just the right place to reach and the drawers had to be so he wouldn't have to lean over and open them—so that it wouldn't hurt his back. I remember the endless trouble she took over that."

No room got as much attention as the nursery. "Jackie was very excited about the baby, and worried, too, because of the miscarriage," a friend said. "She didn't come out and say it, but it seemed she was quite miffed at Jack's total preoccupation with the upcoming convention." Being stranded in the Virginia countryside only heightened Jackie's sense of isolation from her husband. "It was a difficult place for Jackie to live," her mother said. "When you are married to a busy senator . . . She was alone very much out in the country, because Jack would not get home until very late. It really had been too lonely for her out there."

Even though she was eight months into her pregnancy and worried that she might again miscarry, Jackie decided to join Jack in Chicago for the August 13 opening day of the Democratic National Convention. At Jack's suggestion, she stayed with his sister Eunice and her husband Sargent Shriver, who ran the Kennedy-owned Merchandise Mart, and Jack operated out of the Conrad Hilton. (Ethel, who was also eight months pregnant, attended the convention as well but Pat Lawford, married to the film actor Peter Lawford, used her advanced pregnancy as an excuse not to make the trip from California.)

Once again, Jack, heading up his state's delegation, insisted publicly that he was not running for anything. The first day of the convention, a national television audience joined the delegates in watching *The Pursuit of Happiness,* and overnight Jack was proclaimed a leading voice of the party. He made a personal appeal for support to Eleanor Roosevelt. But instead of endorsing Jack, according to Ken O'Donnell, she "berated him before a room full of people for not taking a firmer stand against Joe McCarthy." As a last-ditch effort, Jack went directly to Stevenson, who asked the Massachusetts senator to place his name in nomination—a distinct honor but also a clear signal that he had no intention of choosing Jack as his running mate.

Stevenson won the nomination, as expected, on the first ballot.

But rather than pick his running mate, he shocked delegates by throwing the vice presidential nomination open to the convention. All the leading candidates—Senator Estes Kefauver of Tennessee, Minnesota's Hubert Humphrey, Senator Albert Gore, Sr., and Kennedy—were left to fight it out.

All the available Kennedys were pressed into service, corralling delegate votes on the floor and in hotel corridors. One Kennedy who did not approve was Joe, who was staying out of sight in a rented villa on the French Riviera. Jack had instructed Bobby to call their father with the news, and Joe's reaction was predictable. In a blistering tirade, Joe warned them once again that Stevenson was bound to lose to the beloved Ike, and that if Jack was on the ticket the loss would be blamed on Jack's Catholicism. "It will ruin you," Joe said. "Whew!" Bobby told Jack as he hung up the phone. "Is he mad!" But Jack was too caught up in the drama to turn back, and for the first time in his life had set a course for himself in direct defiance of his father's orders.

Jackie, uncomfortable at the end of her pregnancy but desperate to please her husband, gamely did what was asked of her. She attended a breakfast for New England delegates as well as a party for campaign wives thrown by Perle Mesta, and was photographed enthusiastically waving a Stevenson placard at the convention. She drew the line at giving interviews, however, and literally sprinted through a basement garage to avoid *Washington Post* reporter Maxine Cheshire. Pregnancy or no pregnancy, Cheshire recalled that as soon as Jackie spotted her "she hiked up her dress and broke into a run."

Jack confided in friends later that she never would have made the trip to Chicago had she known her husband would spend the entire time on the convention floor and in smoke-filled hotel rooms. She later claimed that she did not speak to him once during the entire convention, and that she saw him only once, when he strolled past their mezzanine box at the convention the night he nominated Stevenson. Once again, it seemed to Jackie as if her husband had frozen her out of an important part of his life.

"She detested politics," Spalding observed, "but at the same time she wanted to be included in Jack's world. She wanted to share the experience of the convention, but Jack was too busy doing what he felt he had to do, and nothing was going to get in the way of that."

After a second-ballot surge in his favor, Jack lost the vice presidential spot on the third ballot. As soon as it became clear he could not win, Jack took to the podium and called upon the delegates to nominate Kefauver by acclamation. One of those who had rallied his delegation behind JFK was Lyndon Johnson, who proudly cast Texas's vote "for the fighting sailor who wears the scars of battle."

Privately, Johnson was amazed at Jack's sudden rise to prominence: "It was the goddamnedest thing, here was a young whippersnapper, malaria-ridden and yellah, sickly, sickly. He never said a word of importance in the Senate and he never did a thing. But somehow with his books and Pulitzer prizes he managed to create the image of himself as a shining intellectual, a youthful leader who would change the face of the country. Now, I will admit that he had a good sense of humor and that he looked awfully good on the goddamn television screen . . . but his growing hold on the American people was simply a mystery to me."

Unaccustomed to losing, Jack took the defeat hard. "He was very bitter about it, and particularly angry at Stevenson," said Smathers, who had placed Jack's name in nomination as vice president. "He stayed angry at Stevenson for the rest of his life."

The night of his defeat, Jack stood on the bed in his Conrad Hilton Hotel suite and thanked his team for their valiant efforts. "He was emotional," recalled Smathers, "which really surprised me. It had all been such a spur-of-the-moment thing, but here he was taking it all very much to heart. The whole time Jack was talking, Jackie was standing next to him, crying. She had never been in the thick of it like that before, and I think she was just completely exhausted, drained. It was very hard on her, but it wasn't until later that we realized just *how* hard."

Charles Bartlett, who was part of the Kennedy team in Chicago, was also unprepared for Jack's reaction. "I was amazed that he seemed to be extremely disappointed afterward," he said. "I was really amazed because I hadn't been aware that he really wanted it that much. It was never quite clear to me why he felt so badly. I never really understood that . . ."

On August 16, 1956, the nation was treated to another glimpse of the young senator and his attractive wife, this time on the NBC program *Outlook* hosted by Chet Huntley. Jackie, wearing her customary triple strand of pearls, sat primly in the living room at Hickory Hill and breathlessly answered the interviewer's questions.

What viewers never saw was a revealing exchange that was edited out of the final broadcast. At one point in the discussion, when she was asked if she wanted to be with her husband, she answered with the expected yes. But when the interviewer went on to say, "You're pretty much in love with him, aren't you?" Jackie's answer was anything but expected.

"Ohh *no*," she said, tossing back her head. She then stared into the camera, smiling, for what seemed an interminable length of time. Finally, as if realizing that she had made a potentially fatal Freudian slip, she said, "I said no, didn't I?"

Giving her a moment to recover, the questioner continued, "I was hoping you wouldn't say anything because your reaction was wonderful."

Jackie, still smiling, said nothing.

"Great . . . you *are* pretty much in love with him, aren't you?"

Rather than jump at the chance to correct herself, Jackie paused yet again before answering, tentatively, "I suppose so . . ." The entire segment was cut from the final broadcast.

The day after the convention Jack and Jackie returned to New York. From there, Jack was to fly off alone to see his parents on the Riviera, and then cruise the Mediterranean with George Smathers and his brother Teddy. Jackie, feeling tired and vulnerable, was hurt that he would consider leaving her this late in her pregnancy, particularly after she had stood by him in Chicago. She pleaded with him not to go, but he was not accustomed to being told by any woman what to do. No sooner did they arrive at LaGuardia than Jack boarded a flight for France.

Jackie, meantime, headed for Newport alone to recuperate from her grueling week of politicking on her husband's behalf. When Jackie arrived at Hammersmith Farm, her mother demanded to know how she could allow Jack to abandon her in her time of need. Janet told her daughter that such callousness on the part of a husband toward his pregnant wife was simply unacceptable, and that perhaps she should consider leaving him. "I'm sure it was obvious to Jackie that he was going to have his share of female company on the trip," said Smathers. "She didn't want him to go and she let him know it, but in the end there just wasn't anything she could do about it. Jack just didn't have it in him to be monogamous."

Even more important than Jack's rapacious sexual appetites was his desire—his *need* to consult with his father as soon as possible. He had disregarded Joe's advice for the first time, choosing at the last minute to go all-out in his drive for the vice presidential nomination. This independent act marked Jack's political coming of age, but it did not mean that he respected his father any less. In the future, as before, the Ambassador would be the guiding force behind his son's career. Jack felt he needed to explain this to the paterfamilias.

After conferring with his father, Jack boarded a chartered forty-foot sailing vessel and struck out for a full week at sea. On board was a full crew and several female guests ("Jack called and begged me to go, but it was pretty obvious what they were up to," McMillan recalled). Among those who accepted Jack's invitation was a stunning blond Manhattan socialite who had previously been keeping Jack company in New York. She spoke of herself only in the third person and called herself "Pooh." Even Pooh could not escape Jack's compulsive need to bestow nicknames. He referred to her as "P."

Jackie awoke the morning of August 23, 1956—one week after she told a television reporter that she did not love her husband and a month before her baby's expected arrival—and cried out for help. Janet rushed to her daughter's room and found her doubled over on the floor. Bleeding internally, Jackie was rushed to Newport Hospital where doctors performed an emergency cesarean section in a desperate attempt to save the baby. The stillborn infant, a girl, was not named.

Jackie's life also hung in the balance. In the course of the hemorrhaging and the cesarean section, she had lost a considerable amount of blood and required several transfusions. She was listed in critical condition, and a priest arrived in the event it became necessary to bestow absolution. When she awoke several hours later, it was Jack's brother Bobby who was sitting at her bedside. He broke the news of the baby's death to her, but did not mention that he had also quietly made arrangements to have the baby girl buried. Officially, the stillbirth was blamed on "exhaustion and nervous tensions following the Democratic National Convention."

Jackie dealt with her loss alone while friends and family tried in vain to contact the dead baby's father. Cruising at sea with brother Teddy and Pooh, he never saw the front-page story in *The Washington Post* under the headline SENATOR KENNEDY ON MEDITERRANEAN TRIP UNAWARE THAT HIS WIFE HAS LOST BABY. While the search went on for Jack, Pat Lawford gave birth to her daughter Sydney just forty-eight hours after the death of Jackie's baby. Two weeks later, Ethel gave birth to her fifth child, Mary Courtney, making Jackie feel her loss all the more keenly.

It was three days after their baby died that Jack's boat finally anchored at Genoa. He called home and heard the tragic news from Jackie. Whether he was in shock or just unimaginably callous—most likely a little of both—Jack told his wife that he did not intend to cut short his cruise. Jackie was hurt, and angry. When he told Smathers about the conversation, the Florida Senator had one piece of advice: "I told him, 'You better get your ass back there right away if you plan on staying married—or on getting to the White House.' We drove like a bat out of hell to get to the airport," Smathers said. "I can't say he was the best or most thoughtful husband. And it's a shame that he didn't sympathize with Jackie more when she first told him. But he was concerned. He was concerned."

Lem Billings claimed that the Kennedy men were "all oriented toward their kids far more than toward their wives." And Joe wrote to his friend Michael Morrissey that the loss of the baby had more profoundly depressed Jack than even the dark days surrounding his failed back surgeries. JFK did later prove himself to be a doting father who reveled in the company of his children, and a man capable of experiencing great pain over the loss of a newborn.

So why did Jack now seem so devoid of compassion, unwilling or unable to appreciate the depth of Jackie's distress? Jack had never seen himself as a husband, much less a family man. Once again, he followed the lead of his own father, who was also not present at the birth of his children. Jack had never expressed an interest in becoming a father, and like many men would not fully appreciate the child-parent bond until he had children of his own.

By the time Jack joined Jackie in Newport, the damage had been done. She felt abandoned and betrayed, and blamed her failed pregnancies on the Kennedys' frantic approach to life in general and Jack's hectic political existence in particular. She refused to move back to Hickory Hill with its empty nursery. "Without the awaited child," a close friend said, "it was sad and lonely for Jacqueline."

Although they would never admit it to each other, the loss of this second baby raised grave doubts in their minds as to whether or not they would ever be able to have children together. Once again, Jack quietly approached his doctors for reassurance that neither his Addison's disease nor the venereal disease he had contracted in college were in any way responsible.

Jackie bore the brunt of the blame from the Kennedys, who speculated behind her back that the highborn Miss Bouvier was of too delicate a constitution to bear a child. By contrast, Ethel would bear eleven children in a seventeen-year period. Ethel, Jackie said, "drops kids like rabbits . . . She's the baby-making machine—wind her up and she becomes pregnant."

Fittingly, just four months after returning from Chicago, Jack and Jackie sold Hickory Hill to Bobby and Ethel. Jackie later gave Ethel a caricature she had drawn of Hickory Hill literally crawling with kids.

Rather than attempt to compensate for his initial thoughtlessness by spending more time at home, Jack plunged back into work. Understandably, Jackie grew even more upset. Sulks and long silences would no longer suffice; Jackie now augmented her passive-aggressiveness by withdrawing completely. While her husband was in Washington fielding reporters' questions as the new spokesman for his party, Jackie was conspicuous by her absence. She spent much of her time at Hammersmith Farm and in New York, where she commiserated with Lee, who was having her own marital difficulties. Randolph Churchill had a nickname for them: "the Whispering Sisters."

It was not the first time Jackie contemplated divorce. During their trip to Europe in the summer of 1955, Jackie had been so upset about Jack's indiscriminate womanizing that she told friends she was leaving him. "Jackie left Jack Kennedy at that time," said Peter Ward, an English friend who joined them in Antibes. "They were split. She said, 'I'm never going back' in my presence several times." However, within days the Kennedys and the Canfields were dining together in Monaco. "That was because," Ward said, "Jack persuaded her to come back."

Amazingly, Jack may have chosen to cheat on Jackie with her own sister. According to Vidal, Michael Canfield claimed "there were times when I think she [Lee] went perhaps too far, you know? Like going to bed with Jack in the room next to mine in the South of France and then boasting about it." Jackie's response to JFK's philandering, said Vidal, was to embark on a brief affair with William Holden.

This time, rumors of a divorce brewing in the Kennedy household made it into print. First Drew Pearson reported it in his syndicated column. Then *Time* printed a story that Joe had met with Jackie and offered her $1 million not to divorce Jack.

The Kennedy camp laughed off the rumors. When she read the story in *Time*, Jackie supposedly phoned Joe and called him a "cheapskate. Only one million? Why not ten million?" Joking aside, Joe, convinced that a divorce would shatter Jack's chances of ever occupying the White House, did step in to broker a peace between his son and daughter-in-law. He flew to New York from Hyannis and pleaded with Jackie not to divorce Jack.

Although she would never admit it to them, Jackie shared her sisters-in-law's doubts about her ability to bear children. But she knew that she did not stand a chance of carrying a baby full-term as long as she was under constant pressure to conform to the Kennedys' crazed pace. She agreed not to leave Jack, but only with the understanding that she could keep her distance from the raucous Kennedy clan. That meant dining with them no more than once a week, and never being pressured into participating in their nerve-wracking, teeth-rattling activities.

As part of the deal, she also asked him for a new car—a Thunderbird, to be precise. "I mean, what could be more *American?*" she said. But Joe would have none of it. "Kennedys," he told her, "drive Buicks."

"So," Jackie sighed to a friend, "I drive a Buick."

"Joe told us that he did offer Jackie a million dollars not to divorce Jack, absolutely," said Clare Booth Luce, who along with her husband, Henry, was a close friend of Joe Kennedy. "*Time* would never have printed the story otherwise."

Jackie was forthcoming on the matter with Gore Vidal. "Yes," Vidal said, "Joe did offer Jackie the money to stay with Jack and she took it. Happily."

It seems doubtful that, for all her pouting and posturing, Jackie would have actually sued for divorce at this juncture. There were few men richer than Jack, and none more exciting. She had already invested too much in the relationship to admit defeat, particularly now that he was on the verge of seeking the presidency. And she needed to prove to the Kennedys and to herself that she could bear children.

What made the resolution of this crisis stand out was Jack's deferral to Joe as chief negotiator in things matrimonial. Where another injured wife might extract some favor from her husband as compensation for her distress, Jackie extracted concessions from her father-in-law. When Joe sought to smooth things over with money—his money—it would have seemed, in the words of one friend, "nothing short of stupid" to turn the offer down.

Thus, as part of the deal, Joe also agreed to rent a house for Jack and Jackie at 2808 P Street in Georgetown while they searched for a permanent residence. However, Jackie spent much of that fall of 1956 in New York, frequently lunching at the Plaza Hotel in the company of Vidal.

One afternoon Vidal took Jackie, whom he described as being "fascinated by Hollywood and movie stars," to a rehearsal of his television drama *Honor*. She was "very much taken" with Dick York (later the star of the comedy series *Bewitched*) and tried to stay out of the way of assistant director Dominick Dunne, who scurried about the set. (Dunne later became a writer for *Vanity Fair* and a best-selling novelist.)

Vidal remembers that they were drinking coffee and watching the rehearsal when suddenly Jackie blurted, "I'd love to act." When Vidal asked if Jack's political stardom wasn't more interesting, she replied, "For Jack it is. Not for me. I never see him."

When Jackie pressed the acting issue, Vidal told her he was sure a studio would cast her for the novelty alone. At her insistence, he took Jackie to Downey's, a hangout for New York actors. Whenever he was asked by other patrons who his glamorous date was, Vidal replied, "It's the new girl at Warner's." This, he added, "seemed to satisfy them."

Jackie returned to Georgetown and this time made no effort to participate as her husband stumped on behalf of Adlai Stevenson and Estes Kefauver. Vidal recalled when visiting them at their P Street house Jack suddenly appeared wearing a loosely tied bathrobe that kept parting to reveal he wore nothing underneath. His face was swollen from an impacted wisdom tooth.

"How can I speak tonight in Baltimore," Jack complained, "looking like this?"

Jackie almost seemed to enjoy her husband's predicament. "Isn't," she said as she poured a drink for Vidal, "he vain?"

In November Jackie paid a call on Lee in London, where Lee's husband, Michael Canfield, was working at the U.S. embassy. Lee had invited Jackie, still depressed over the death of her child and the sorry state of her marriage, to boost her spirits. What Jackie got instead was a desperate plea from Canfield to help him save his marriage. He told Jackie that he had done everything in his power to please Lee, but Jackie appeared unmoved. Her single piece of advice reflected the solution she had reached in her own negotiations with Joe. "Get more money, Michael," she told her brother-in-law. When Canfield reminded her that he received money from a trust fund and salaries from both his father's company, Harper & Brothers, and the embassy, Jackie smiled. "No, Michael, I mean *real* money."

That Thanksgiving weekend, all the Kennedys, their families, and a few close friends gathered in Hyannis Port. While Jackie held her new nieces for the first time and did her best to conceal her hurt feelings, Jack repaired with his father to a small study off the living room. There they debated the pros and cons of Jack's seeking the presidency in 1960. When it was over, Jack beamed. "Well, Dad, I guess there's only one question left. When do we start?" Then the two men threw their arms around each other.

Jack emerged and told Dave Powers that he had decided to run. The senator pointed out that he had managed to come within thirty-three and a half votes of winning the vice presidential nomination after a last-minute effort. "If I work hard for four years," he told Powers, "I ought to be able to pick up all the marbles."

Jackie was not consulted before her husband announced his

decision to the family. Had she been, it is doubtful she would have offered any advice. "I wouldn't dream," she said, "of telling him what to do." But for all her complaining about the cigar smoke, the back-room "Murphia," and the boring rubber chicken dinners, Jackie harbored ambitions of her own. "She basically lived for money and position," Vidal said. "There was no way she was going to try and talk Jack out of becoming president."

Jack and Jackie rendezvoused with Lee and Michael Canfield for a week of sun in Jamaica before spending Christmas all together at Merrywood. Slowly, Jack regained some of Jackie's trust and affection. That did not mean, however, that she was any less adamant about keeping the rest of the Kennedys at arm's length.

In March, Jackie's mood took a decided upturn when she learned that she was again pregnant. This time, she announced her intention to pamper herself. Avoiding the stress and strains of politics, she would concentrate on decorating the new redbrick Federal house they purchased late that spring in Georgetown at 3307 N Street NW.

Jackie used Joe's money to hire interior designer Sister Parish, but there was little doubt who was in charge of the decorating effort. With the same military precision her mother used to redecorate Merrywood and Hammersmith Farm, Jackie took measurements, made drawings, and inspected every carpet sample and fabric swatch.

Jackie painted the wood-plank floors with a white and pale green–diamond design, then carried that color scheme throughout the N Street house (as it would be known to a generation of Kennedy-watching journalists). The rooms were filled with eighteenth-century French furnishings: ornate gold wall sconces, Louis XV armchairs in the high-ceilinged drawing room, Louis XVI cane chairs in the rose-carpeted dining room, blond-wood marquetry tables, gilded and silver-plated lamps with chinoiserie shades, Italian fruitwood bouillotte tables, mahogany end tables, gilt-framed watercolors, tapestries, and copper pots overflowing with fresh-cut flowers. Undeterred by her sad experience at

Hickory Hill, she paid special attention to one room: the third-floor nursery.

She did not have to worry about her husband being underfoot. That year Jack received more than 2,500 speaking invitations from around the country and accepted 144 of them. In its cover story on him (Jack's first), *Time* gushed that the young senator had left "panting politicians and swooning women" in his wake.

Jack was not the only Kennedy achieving a kind of media stardom. As chief counsel of Senator John L. McClellan's select committee on racketeering that spring, Bobby took on Teamster Boss Jimmy Hoffa before a television audience of millions. Less-polished and more boyish than his urbane brother, tousled-haired Bobby nonetheless began receiving his share of fan mail. *Look* magazine devoted sixteen pages to "The Rise of the Brothers Kennedy," followed by a *Saturday Evening Post* article on the entire family entitled "The Amazing Kennedys."

Kennedymania was just beginning that June 1957 when Jackie's nineteen-year-old stepsister (and Gore Vidal's half-sister) Nini Auchincloss married Newton Steers in St. John's Church in Washington. Jackie, having helped Nini shop for her first training bra, earned her place at the head of the bridal party as matron of honor.

During the reception at Merrywood, Jackie once again provided Nini with a bit of womanly advice that Janet was incapable or unwilling to provide. While guests strolled about the meticulously landscaped grounds, Jackie was in a bathroom with the bride demonstrating the proper way to douche. Before she left, Jackie shared one slightly skewed observation with the bride: "The great thing about marriage," she said, "is that you can have lunch with men."

Less than a month later, Jackie got a call from her stepbrother Yusha. He had dropped in on Black Jack in New York and was disturbed at what he saw. Black Jack had been on a steady downhill slide since he had sold his seat on the New York Stock Exchange in 1950 for a paltry ninety thousand dollars—seven times less than what it was worth in 1929 and a dozen times less than it would cost today. A recluse living on the interest from two hundred thousand dollars in savings, he seemed content to spend weeks on end drinking alone in his apartment and railing against his venal ex-wife. There was seldom anyone on hand to hear his complaints. Lee lived in London, and the demands of Jackie's own hectic schedule made it impossible for her to visit. That did not explain why Jackie hadn't sent her father a single card or letter in over a year. When he read in *The New York Times* that Jackie was expecting again, he was deeply hurt; she had not bothered to tell him personally.

This time, Yusha noted that Black Jack was jaundiced and gaunt. Jackie, who had been summering in Hyannis Port, flew immediately to New York, but when she walked into his apartment her father let fly with a scathing attack on ungrateful children. How could his daughters neglect him like this? Why hadn't they written or called in over a year? He had paid for their educations, even instructed them on the ways to capture and hold a man's attention. Obviously, they no longer felt they needed their father. Not now that they had wealthy father figures like Hughdie Auchincloss, Joe Kennedy, and publishing giant Cass Canfield to watch over their interests.

Giving Jackie the full measure of his rage, Black Jack showed no signs of illness. On the contrary, he appeared to be his own forceful self—particularly when sharing his less-than-charitable feelings toward his ex-wife. Her heartfelt apologies falling on deaf ears, Jackie returned to Hyannis Port.

When the pain radiating from his abdomen could no longer be masked by alcohol, Black Jack entered New York's Lenox Hill Hospital to undergo a series of tests on July 27, the eve of Jackie's twenty-eighth birthday. Assured that her father was resting comfortably and that her presence was not needed, Jackie celebrated her birthday with Janet at Hammersmith Farm. Five days later, Black Jack was in a coma. For the first time, she was told that her father had been suffering from liver cancer. Jackie rushed to the hospital at breakneck speed with Jack at her side, but did not make it in time. Her father had died less than an hour earlier. He was sixty-six.

She was angry that no one had told her of her father's dire condition. But even more, Jackie was angry with herself for being too busy poring over wallpaper samples for the N Street house to even pick up the phone and call her father. In his hour of need, she simply was not there for him. What made the pangs of guilt and regret all the more acute was the fact that he had always been there for them. Despite his excesses and his indiscretions, Black Jack provided them with the unconditional love that Janet was congenitally incapable of giving.

Jack, for whom public displays of affection required a supreme effort, put his arm around his wife to comfort her in the hospital corridor. As they turned to leave, a nurse who had been there when he died described Black Jack's final moments, and the final word to leave his lips: "Jackie."

—

*Jackie was a woman full of love and full of hurt.
They were two private people, two cocoons married
to each other, trying to reach into each other. I
think she felt that since he was so much older than
she was, that it was up to him to reach more than
he did. But he couldn't.*

Lindy Boggs

—

Devastated by her father's un-
expected death, Jackie calmly took it upon herself to make the
funeral arrangements. Her top priority was to make sure that
Black Jack was given a proper send-off and not just the minor
mention he otherwise would have been accorded on the obituary
page of *The New York Times*.

Perhaps justifying her father's claim that he had been all but
abandoned by his immediate kin, Jackie had to go outside the family—to one of Black Jack's many former paramours—to find a suitable photograph of him. She wrote the obituary notice herself,
paying particular tribute to her father's questionable business acu-
men, and dispatched Jack with the copy and the photo to the *Times*
with instructions for the esteemed United States senator to personally place the package in the managing editor's hands.

At the funeral home, she unfastened the gold bracelet her father had given her when she had graduated from Vassar and
placed it in the coffin. On the morning of August 6, about two
dozen family members and friends—including a brace of former
mistresses—attended the funeral service in the chapel at St. Patrick's Cathedral. Eschewing the traditional lilies of the valley, red
carnations, and horseshoe-shaped funeral wreaths, Jackie wanted
the altar to reflect her father's overwhelming *joie de vivre*. The
coffin was surrounded by white wicker baskets overflowing with
daisies and bright yellow tulips. To celebrate his perennially un-
wed status, a blanket of bachelor buttons covered the casket itself.

Lee was among the handful of family members who made the trip with Jack and Jackie out to St. Philomena's Cemetery in East Hampton. The plaintive sound of a distant train whistle stirred up childhood memories. "We were his life," Lee acknowledged, and after his children "grew up and went their ways, he became more and more of a recluse. My father always felt he was a failure in some way. In the end he was a heartbreaking figure."

Jackie kissed the coffin before it was lowered into the ground, but shed no tears. "There was a quiet dignity about her that she could draw on in times of crisis," Yusha said. "She just didn't think it was right to bear your soul in public. I know she cried a great deal when her father died. It took her completely by surprise, and she was terribly, terribly hurt."

Black Jack left a hundred and sixty thousand dollars to be divided equally between his daughters—a not inconsiderable bequest in 1957—as well as some antiques and artworks from his apartment. Knowing how much Jackie loved horses, he left her a painting of Arabian stallions that had once hung at Lasata. Unfortunately, Jackie did not believe it fit the decor of the N Street house and sold the painting two months later.

With her trademark efficiency, Jackie unearthed all the letters her father had written to her at Miss Porter's, Vassar, and the Sorbonne, had them typed up and copies sent to Lee in London. Jack and the rest of the Kennedys were concerned about the effect all this would have on Jackie's five months' pregnancy. They worried that the stress of her father's death, like the stress she experienced at the convention, might trigger another miscarriage.

There was even more cause for concern when Jack suddenly developed a fever and back pain that did not respond to his regular Novocain injections. Doctors found a virulent staphylococcus abscess had developed along one of his surgical scars and immediately admitted him to New York Hospital. Jack was released from the hospital two days later, but remained on heavy doses of antibiotics until the spiking fevers and chills finally passed.

Once again, Jack fell into a deep depression as he recuperated on Cape Cod. "This was the only time I knew him to be really discouraged," Dr. Janet Travell recalled. "I was at my wit's end to know what to do. I said, 'You know, what you need is a real good hot bath.' "

"You know I haven't been in a bathtub since I entered New York Hospital because of the wound in my back," he said angrily, then he added, "I can't go on with another great big gaping hole."

It was then that Travell told him that the bandages on his back covered only a slight scar, and not a gaping wound like before. "He looked at me as if he didn't believe me," Travell said. She got Preston Wade, the doctor who actually performed the procedure, on the phone to reassure the patient that he could take a bath. "His eyes brightened," she said, "and he said, 'Ask him if I couldn't use soap, too, could I?' So I put him on the line and Dr. Wade said yes he could get into a tub and could use all the soap he wanted."

The minor medical crisis, yet another reminder of Jack's fragile health, frightened Jackie. "She had buried her father just a few weeks before all this happened," said a friend. "Of course the strain on her was enormous. Everyone, including Jack, was worried about the baby."

Those worries proved unfounded when at 8:30 in the morning on November 27, 1957—the day before Thanksgiving—Jackie gave birth by cesarean section to a seven-pound two-ounce girl at New York's Lying-in Hospital, Cornell University Medical Center. "I'll always remember Jack's face," Jackie's mother said, "when the doctor came into the waiting room and told him that the baby had arrived and that it was a girl and that Jackie was fine and the baby was fine. I will always remember the sweet expression on his face and the way he smiled. And the doctor said, 'She's very pretty.' We had been talking before the doctor came in about did he care whether it was a boy or a girl, and . . . he said anything would be all right with him."

When the anesthesia wore off and Jackie came to, it was Jack who brought the baby in to see her. It was the first time Jackie laid eyes on Caroline (after Jackie's sister, Caroline Lee) Bouvier Kennedy. "He seemed perfectly at home with babies," Janet observed. "I don't ever remember his having that stiffness or that being afraid to touch them that Hugh D. seems to have always had."

Jack's old friend Lem Billings was one of the first visitors at the hospital. Jack took him to the nursery to see his new daughter. "Now, Lem," he said, "tell me, which one of the babies in the window is the prettiest." Billings drew a deep breath and pointed—to someone else's baby. Jack didn't speak to him for two days. "Jack," Billings later reflected, "was more emotional about Caroline's birth than he was about anything else."

Jackie later told friends that November 27, 1957, was "the very happiest day of my life." She had proven to herself and to the skeptical Kennedys that she was not too fragile to give birth— that she was more than just first lady material. She was also mother material.

Given his heartless response to the loss of their stillborn daughter just fourteen months earlier, Jackie was also surprised at how naturally Jack took to fatherhood. Even Janet Auchincloss was impressed by "the sheer, unadulterated delight he took in Caroline from that first day on. The look on his face, which I had never seen before, really, was . . . radiant."

Three weeks after Caroline's birth, the Kennedys moved into the N Street house, along with Maud Shaw, the new British nanny hired to care for the baby. Caroline was just eleven days old and still in the hospital with Jackie when Maud began caring for the newest Kennedy. The new father, according to Shaw, "wanted to give her her bottle and he asked me to stand quite near him in case he dropped her." After a few moments, the perennially fidgety JFK said, "Miss Shaw, how have you got the patience to feed the child all this bottle? You take the bottle and finish her."

"But he really loved her," Shaw said, "and when he came into the house he always came straight upstairs to the nursery. That child always smiled for him when she never did for anybody else.

Right from the very beginning, he loved her and she adored him. There was nobody like him, her father to her."

Betty Spalding told journalists Joan and Clay Blair that the first person Jack opened himself up to emotionally was Caroline. "That was a marvelous relationship," she said. "He was able to release some of his emotions to her and it freed him from the fear of it and he was able to exchange better with Jackie and she with him. Until he had Caroline, he never really learned how to deal with people. It was fascinating to watch him grow in this capacity."

The arrival of a child breathed new life into their marriage, and provided a much-needed boost for Jackie's self-esteem. For the first time, she felt as if she had found a permanent home, a home where she, not Rose Kennedy or Janet Auchincloss, was in charge. Like Rose and Janet, Jackie never lifted a finger to do household chores. She leaned heavily on her personal maid Providencia "Provi" Parades, and there were other maids to assist, as well as a laundress, a cook to prepare the meals, Jack's valet, a full-time chauffeur, and even someone (in this case, Evelyn Lincoln) to fill out her diary for her each day.

Of course, no member of the staff was more important than the nanny. When Caroline awoke crying at 2 A.M., it was Maud Shaw who shuffled down two narrow flights of stairs to the kitchen, heated up a bottle of formula, and brought it to the nursery. Neither Rose nor Janet (and, for that matter, neither Joe nor Black Jack) had ever been troubled by such mundane child-rearing matters, and Jack and Jackie saw no reason to break with tradition.

In fairness, Maud Shaw recalled Jackie would "do a lot of little things for Caroline—dress her, and take her out, and play with her in the garden." In the summer months, they put an inflatable pool in the backyard. "We spent a number of hours playing in the swimming pool and having these little afternoon teas and lunches together . . ."

But for the most part, visitors noted that 3307 N Street was oddly devoid of the joyful sounds one would expect to find in a house occupied by a young family. In what may have been a form of rebellion against the boisterous Kennedys, Jackie forbade the playing of stereos, radios, or television during the daytime. "Never have I ever heard Jackie as much as *hum* a little tune as she went about her daily business, or indulge in a really hearty laugh," said her secretary, Mary Gallagher.

Caroline was kept out of sight until Daddy came home looking to dandle her on his knee. It was not as if Jackie preferred adult company. She seldom called up friends or had any visitors, preferring instead to spend hours going over the mail with Gallagher in the study off the second-floor master bedroom. Jackie always found time for an hour-long nap in the afternoon, presumably in preparation for entertaining her husband's political friends at dinner. "Aside from entertaining in the evening," Gallagher said, "her days were strangely lonely."

Oddly, even when Jack was home she did not seem interested in breaking her routine to spend time with him. According to Gallagher, JFK ate breakfast alone in the downstairs library while perusing the papers. As he left, he called, "Bye, Jackie," and waited, usually in vain, for a response. "I used to wish that Jackie would eat breakfast downstairs with the Senator," said Gallagher, who watched Jack leave from her office window each morning, "or at least come down to see him off at the door."

Whatever time she had available Jackie devoted to her twin obsessions: chain-smoking and redecorating. While she encouraged Jack's cigar smoking to mask the smell of her cigarettes, there was little she could do to conceal the fact that she was spending tens of thousands of Joe Kennedy's dollars on compulsive remodeling.

In the first four months, Jackie redid the living room "at least three times," according to her mother. "You could go there one day and there would be two beautiful needlepoint rugs, one in the little front drawing room and one in the back one toward the garden. The next week they would both be gone. The curtains were apt to be red chintz one week, and something else the next." The wallpaper in the study was changed at least three times in as many months, including a very costly design imported from London.

The Auchinclosses had been invited for dinner one evening and arrived to find that everything had again been changed. "At that moment the room was entirely beige. The walls had been repainted a week or so before, and the furniture had all been done in soft beige, and there was a vicuña rug over the sofa . . . And let's see, carpets, curtains, upholstery, everything was suddenly turned lovely different shades of beige. I knew how wildly expensive it is to paint things and upholster things and have curtains made but I can remember Jack saying to me, 'Mrs. Auchincloss, do you think we're prisoners of beige?' "

More often than not, Jack was frustrated by the impermanence of his surroundings. Once, while trying to find a comfortable, familiar place to read, he bellowed, "Dammit, Jackie, why is it that the rooms in this house are never completely livable all at the same time?"

Jackie was oblivious to her husband's complaints. "I have filled the house with eighteenth-century furniture, which I love, and my pictures—drawings I collect," Jackie allowed. But she felt she had made quite a few concessions. "I haven't made it completely my own because I don't want a house where you have to say to children, 'Don't touch,' or where your husband is uncomfortable . . ."

Not only was Jackie's obsessive redecorating costing Jack's father a small fortune, she had developed a passion for clothes to rival Rose Kennedy's. Society friends like Bunny Mellon and Letizia Mowinckel scouted out the latest designs in New York, Paris, and Rome that they felt would be most becoming to Jackie. Long before her exorbitant clothing bills in the White House made headlines, Jackie was splurging upward of twenty thousand dollars a year on clothes—the equivalent of spending over two hundred thousand in today's dollars.

"Jack was livid when it came to her spending," Smathers said.

"He'd wave the bills in the air and yell, 'Goddammit, she's breaking my ass!' He'd get really worked up about it, turn purple with rage. But of course, he had no idea what constituted a lot of money, really. He was just going through the motions. Let's face it, no matter what she spent on clothes and furniture, it was a drop in the bucket as far as the Kennedys were concerned."

"I have to dress well, Jack, so I won't embarrass you," she would argue. "As a public figure, you'd be humiliated if I was photographed in some saggy old housedress. Everyone would say your wife is a slob and refuse to vote for you."

Not that Jackie didn't engage in her share of false economies. Occasionally, she would go through her closets and weed out items she no longer wanted. Most of these were consigned to Encore, a New York resale outlet, where to throw off the press they were resold under Mary Gallagher's name. At other times, she would allow staff members to pick over her blouses, skirts, shoes, and dresses to see if there was anything they might like. Once she reached into her closet and pulled out a red dress and told Gallagher, "You may not have any need for this, Mary, but it's just your color." Gallagher thanked her boss, agreeing that it was indeed a lovely color. But she also wondered why Jackie was giving her a maternity dress.

That December, Jackie and Lee posed together for a fashion spread in the *Ladies' Home Journal*. "I don't like to buy a lot of clothes," she told the magazine, "and have my closets full." Then "the Whispering Sisters" demanded they be given the outfits they had modeled—or no story.

For Christmas, Jackie dipped into her inheritance from Black Jack to buy Jack a white Jaguar. Deeming the luxury sports car far too extravagant, Jack followed his father's advice and traded the Jaguar in for one of those cars "Kennedys drive"—another Buick.

His wife's compulsive behavior disturbed Jack, as did her violent mood swings. "Jackie could be absolutely giddy and enchanting one moment," Jamie Auchincloss said, "and then you'd turn around, and for no apparent reason, she'd just turn off as if someone had flipped a switch." Concurred the Kennedys' photographer and friend Jacques Lowe: "She could be very moody, and there were times when everybody walked on eggshells around her— including Jack."

To describe the way their characters meshed, Jack drew a straight horizontal line to represent himself. Then he drew a wavy line through the straight line to represent Jackie. When asked to describe her, he paused for moment and then uttered a single word: fey. While the term primarily means "enchanted," it also implies being "touched," "unstable."

As 1957 drew to a close, John F. Kennedy led all the 1960 Democratic presidential hopefuls in the polls. Still, he was the same old randy Jack as far as Lem Billings was concerned. That is until he visited the Kennedys' Palm Beach estate in the fall of 1957. The former Choate roommates were conjuring up some lurid scene from Jack's sexual past and laughing hysterically when suddenly Joe exploded. "You're not to speak like that anymore," he shouted at Billings. "There are things that you just can't bring up anymore, private things. You've got to forget them. Forget the 'Jack' you once knew." He went on to instruct Jack's friend in no uncertain terms that "from now on you've got to watch everything you say." Soon, Joe said without a trace of humor, even he would be calling his oldest surviving son not Jack but "Mr. President."

Shirley MacLaine's comment that it is preferable to have "a president who screws women than a president who screws the country" notwithstanding, Joe knew that Jack's wild past could destroy his presidential prospects. "It seemed rather odd that after encouraging his sons to indulge every schoolboy's sexual fantasy to the hilt, Joe suddenly became concerned that the public would find out," observed Clare Boothe Luce. "He was panic-stricken that a friend would say something about one of Jack's exploits to a reporter and that it would find its way into Drew Pearson's column. Of course the press wasn't as aggressive about digging up dirt on public figures back then. But he still had to overcome his Catholicism, and any hint of scandal coupled with that would have proved *catastrophic*."

Once again, Joe's emphasis was on appearance, not substance. He did not mention to Jack that he should abandon his stewardess-filled suite at the Mayflower, or that he should simply remain faithful to Jackie—at least until he was elected president. "Given Joe's record as a husband," Spalding said, "he was in no position to tell Jack to clean up his act, and he knew it."

"Nobody is going to hand me the nomination," Jack said. "When the time is ripe, I'll have to work for it. If I were governor of a large state, Protestant, and fifty-five, I could sit back and let it come to me." There was never any doubt that Jack would be reelected to his Senate seat in 1958. Even Massachusetts's most optimistic Republicans conceded that much. But the incumbent needed to win big to maintain his momentum. It was agreed that if Jack could rack up a margin of half a million votes, it would be difficult for his party to deny him the nomination.

His opponent in the senatorial race was the same man Jack had defeated in his 1950 congressional campaign: Vincent J. Celeste. The feisty thirty-four-year-old from Boston's working-class Italian neighborhood wasted no time attacking the Kennedys and Joe in particular. Citing Jack's unpopular vote in favor of building the St. Lawrence seaway, Celeste added that "it starts right at the front door of the Merchandise Mart in Chicago, which is owned by old Joe Kennedy."

With Bobby busy in Washington, twenty-six-year-old Teddy took the reins as campaign manager. There was no effort made to conceal the family's dynastic ambitions. "Just as I went into politics because Joe died," Kennedy told journalist Bob Considine, "if anything happened to me tomorrow, my brother Bobby would run for my seat in the Senate. And if Bobby died Teddy would take over for him." Still, as long as Joe was healthy he continued in his role as a political Wizard of Oz, manipulating events but seldom venturing from behind the velvet curtain.

As efforts were under way on the home front, Jack crisscrossed the country honoring speaking engagements designed to spread his message nationally. In this endeavor, he appreciated the important new weapon he had in his campaign arsenal: Caroline. Some of Jack's closest friends felt that this was the only reason he wanted children in the first place: "Jack's desire was," as Charlie Bartlett put it, "to get the bountiful positive publicity only a child might yield."

Even before Caroline's arrival, the editors of *Life, Look, The Saturday Evening Post*, and several other national periodicals scrambled to get the first candid baby pictures of her. When Jack gave the green light to *Life*, Jackie "hit the ceiling," Spalding said. "No pictures of the baby, Jack. That's final," she told him. "I'm not going to let our child be used like some campaign mascot. I don't care how many votes it costs you."

Eventually, Jackie agreed to the *Life* spread, but only after Jack promised to take a break in his campaign that summer to spend time with her in Paris. That April, photographer Ed Clark arrived at the Georgetown house and snapped a series of family photographs. The most memorable of these was Caroline lifting her head up from her lace-trimmed bassinet to play peekaboo with Dad.

Another photographer who played a large part in building the Kennedy image, Jacques Lowe, also became a close friend. A political refugee from Nazi Germany, Lowe was twenty-four years old when he befriended Bobby Kennedy. After Lowe shot the "perpetual bedlam" known as life at Hyannis Port, Bobby was so impressed that he gave an album containing 124 of Lowe's Hyannis Port photos to his father as a birthday present. When a "slightly tipsy" Joe called Lowe at midnight to thank him, Lowe replied, " 'Joe Kennedy? Sure, and I'm Santa Claus.' You've got to remember, Joe Kennedy was a rather mystical figure in those days."

The senior Kennedy asked Lowe to photograph his "other son," but when Lowe arrived in Hyannis Port in August 1958 Jack was "grumpy, awkward, and preoccupied. He was very tired. But,"

Lowe added, "he perked up whenever I asked him to sit with Caroline."

Several weeks later, Lowe was summoned a little after midnight to the Margery, a Park Avenue apartment building owned by Joe. "Jack opened the door wearing nothing but a towel around his waist. Jackie called out hello from the bathroom, where I could hear her still splashing in the tub." Kennedy was "thrilled" with the photos, which were spread out on a coffee table. "He sat down on the couch, and I got on the floor next to the coffee table so we could both go over the contact sheets. He wasn't wearing anything under the towel, so from my vantage point everything was completely visible ... I had to sort of look at the contact sheets and then awkwardly up past the towel at his face. I was embarrassed, but he couldn't have cared less. He was the most unselfconscious person I have ever met. He picked out a photo of the three of them for that year's Christmas card, then we had a drink. In that bath towel at 1:30 in the morning, he was totally at ease, and the entire time he managed to appear nothing less than dignified."

Lowe believed the way Jackie and Jack looked at pictures said much about their personalities. "Jack looked at my photographs as documents. Why did he pick me? Because he liked the way I worked, he liked what he saw. It had documentary power. To Jackie, a photograph was light and shadow and design and composition. She was creatively involved in a way Jack never was."

The Norman Rockwell images recorded by Ed Clark, Jacques Lowe, and other photographers belied the fact that Jack, in spite of a rigorous campaign schedule ("Weekends when most people are relaxing, Jack works hardest," Jackie complained), somehow found time to be unfaithful. Ever since his affair with suspected Nazi spy Inga Arvad, the FBI had continued to monitor Jack's personal life, and the agency's reports to J. Edgar Hoover indicated that the two years before the 1960 presidential election were among the most active of JFK's sexual career.

Even by Joe's standards, the pace of Jack's womanizing at this time appears nothing short of frenetic. There may have been a medical reason for this. The prescription for the time-released DOCA pellets in his thighs had been increased from 150 to 300 mg, and cortisone tablets replaced the twice-daily injections he had been receiving. These elevated levels of cortisone in the bloodstream typically produce feelings of euphoria, increased energy, muscular strength, mental concentration—and a dramatically heightened sex drive.

For Jack, the cortisone had one other highly beneficial side effect in the dawning age of TV campaigning: It filled out the hollows in his cheeks and fleshed out his jawline, making him look solidly handsome. "Overnight," one reporter said, "he sort of became Clark Gable, Cary Grant, and Errol Flynn all rolled into one."

In addition to the parade of stewardesses, models, and political groupies made available to him on the road, Jack set out to conquer several of Hollywood's biggest stars that summer of 1958. The classically beautiful, British-born Jean Simmons was filming *Home Before Dark* in Boston when she claimed Jack "practically broke down" her hotel bedroom door to get to her.

Another glamorous actress, this one with roots firmly planted in Yankee soil, was more obliging. The daughter of a wealthy Massachusetts department store owner, Quincy-born Lee Remick first got to know Jack when she was still a teenager and he was a young unmarried senator. She also had been a guest in the Mayflower suite. Anything but *A Face in the Crowd* after playing a drum majorette in that 1957 film, the striking blond star resumed her affair with Jack in Los Angeles. Remick, who played floozies and boozers to perfection in such films as *Anatomy of a Murder* and *Days of Wine and Roses,* exuded intelligence and sophistication off-screen. "Lee," producer Joseph E. Levine said, "was the epitome of class." She was also just twenty-two—six years younger than Jackie—and "drop-dead gorgeous."

On the rebound from Jack, Remick would later become involved with Peter Lawford, whose marriage to Patricia Kennedy in 1954 inexorably linked Jack to Frank Sinatra's infamous "Rat Pack." (Dubbed "Brother-in-Lawford" by Old Blue Eyes, Lawford would also become a chief procurer of eager females for Jack during the White House years.)

Although Jack's relationship with Remick was characteristically fleeting, Lawford would at one point consider leaving Pat Kennedy for her. The affair with Lawford, which Remick later denied, took place in New York and Los Angeles, and was apparently so obvious that columnist Hedda Hopper ran a thinly disguised item about "Hollywood's most hush-hush romance" and warned that if the unnamed British star wasn't careful "he may lose his million-dollar baby." At one point Lawford invited Remick and her husband, producer Bill Colleran, to a party at his beach house. When Pat answered the door, Lawford's lover stuck out her hand. "Hello, Pat. I'm Lee Remick." Pat replied with a knowing smile, ". . . and I'm the million-dollar baby."

Jack struck gold closer to home when, while Jackie made one of her periodic shopping trips to New York, he attended a party at the Italian Embassy in Washington with George Smathers. Among the guests was the lushly beautiful Sophia Loren, who at twenty-four had just turned down a marriage proposal from her *Houseboat* costar Cary Grant to marry producer Carlo Ponti. Rather than approach Loren himself and risk exposure, Kennedy dispatched his bachelor friend Smathers to invite Loren to the N Street house for a champagne supper. Loren declined. Smathers persisted on his friend's behalf, but to no avail.

Finally, Jack cornered Loren and extended the invitation personally. According to Smathers, Loren finally accepted. "I never saw Jack strike out with anybody if he really wanted to get together with them," he said. "He just would not take no for an answer, and he just kept at it until he wore them down. Miss Loren was no exception. She went with Jack, all right, and I understand they had a wonderful time."

This was also about the time Jack began in earnest his two-and-a-half-year affair with Marilyn Monroe. A year after divorcing

Joe DiMaggio, Marilyn married the playwright Arthur Miller. The couple settled in bucolic Roxbury, Connecticut, but there was soon trouble in paradise. Within months Monroe, who maintained her own apartment on Manhattan's East Fifty-Seventh Street, was meeting Jack secretly in his suite at the Carlyle Hotel. Jack, however, was only a diversion; Marilyn soon embarked on a more serious affair with her costar in the bomb *Let's Make Love,* French heartthrob Yves Montand.

One of the more durable relationships Jack forged during this period was not with a celebrity, but with a receptionist at the Belgian Embassy. A graduate of the tony Mt. Vernon Seminary, Pamela Turnure had first attracted Jack's attention at Nini Auchincloss's wedding. Dark-haired, green-eyed, and slim, Turnure, who had briefly dated the notorious playboy Aly Khan, was petite but in all other respects bore a striking resemblance to the senator's wife in both appearance and bearing. "She was," a friend said, "Jackie in miniature."

Jack hired Turnure as a receptionist in his Senate office right away. By the spring of 1958 he was a frequent guest at her Georgetown apartment. Her landlords, Florence and Leonard Kater, became aware of Turnure's nocturnal visitor when they heard someone tossing pebbles at her second-floor window around 1 A.M. "We looked out," Florence Kater said, "and saw Senator Kennedy standing in our garden yelling, 'If you don't come down, I'll climb up by your balcony.' So she let him in."

The Katers, both strict Catholics, placed recording devices in the building "to pick up the sounds from the bedroom" and were shocked at what they heard. "I can assure you," Kater said, "that he was not a very loquacious lover." From then on, the Katers launched a campaign to discredit JFK with evidence of his adultery. To Jack's horror, they photographed him coming out of Turnure's apartment at 1 A.M. on July 11, 1958, and sent the picture to newspapers, magazines, and television stations.

When only the *Washington Star* ran a small item, even Jack was astonished. At his suggestion, she moved into the Georgetown home of Jackie's artist-friend Mary Pinchot Meyer. An heir to the Pinchot dry goods fortune who had also known Jack since his days at Choate, Mary Meyer was the sister of Tony Bradlee and sister-in-law to journalist Ben Bradlee. After Jack became president, the Bradlees became close friends of the Kennedys—and Mary became far more.

Meanwhile, the Katers continued their quixotic crusade—waving placards denouncing JFK at campaign rallies, taking their case to Cardinal Cushing, and after JFK's inauguration, parading in front of the Executive Mansion with a sign asking "DO YOU WANT AN ADULTERER IN THE WHITE HOUSE?"

After returning from the Parisian holiday she had been promised for cooperating with *Life*'s photographers, Jackie was determined to keep a closer eye on her husband. She spent more time helping him out with his correspondence as she had done earlier in their marriage, working at a large secretary's desk beneath the sailfish that now hung in his Senate office. For the first time, she joined her husband on the hustings, obligingly posing for pictures, smiling benignly, staring worshipfully at the candidate whenever he gave a speech at a Rotary Club luncheon or on the stage of a high school auditorium, answering phones with Jack's sisters as part of a televised "Ask Senator Kennedy" program—even marching alongside him in East Boston's Columbus Day Parade.

More than once, her naïveté showed through. When Jack and several politico cronies tossed about the names of cities that might be chosen to host the Democratic convention, Jackie suggested Acapulco.

Careful not to appear "too New York," she wore little makeup and toned down the jewelry. But even with her white gloves and housewifely shirtwaist dresses, Jackie was still singled out among political wives for her flawless sense of style. "The women, as always, came out to see Jack and shake his hand," said one campaign operative. "But they'd seen all those photos in the magazines saying Jackie was such a fashion plate, and they were just as interested in what she was wearing as what the candidate had to say." At every campaign stop in the state, Jack could expect twice the turnout if Jackie was with him.

"He was never intentionally rude to her," said Jacques Lowe. "But Jack was very focused on what he was doing and not always paying that much attention to her. He could be walking out into a crowd and she'd be about a half mile behind him, just trying to keep up." Betty Spalding chalked this up to Jack's "terrible manners. He didn't have any manners, in the sense of letting women go through the door first or opening doors for them or standing up when older women came into the room. He was nice to people, but heedless of people . . ."

"People forget that before Jack was considered the front-runner for the nomination in 1959, people *ignored* Jackie," Lowe said. "She was accustomed to being the center of attention in her world, and the politicians who milled around Jack treated her as if she wasn't there. It was terribly hard for her to just be more or less invisible while all this adulation was lavished on her husband."

"People saw in Jack whatever they wanted—son, brother, war hero, matinee idol," said a reporter who covered Kennedy throughout his Senate and subsequent presidential campaigns. "To a lot of people, especially from Massachusetts, he was enormously accessible. Strangers would walk up and talk to him, if he didn't talk to them first.

"But they never felt that way about Jackie. They never connected with her the way they did with Jack. I never once saw a civilian—by that I mean someone who wasn't involved in the campaign or the member of a welcoming committee or something—go up to her and start a conversation. I never saw anyone ask her a question. Not once. They just stared at her. You couldn't blame them. She had built this invisible wall around herself. But it couldn't have been much fun for her to be treated like, well, like something other than a human being."

Jackie made a concerted effort to defuse any notion that she was anything but your average housewife. She even, the press was told, packed a hot lunch for her husband so that he would no longer rely on "a candy bar or a saltine" to get him through the day. Jackie also claimed the baby food she fed Caroline was one of Jack's favorite dishes, and that soon she was preparing it not just for the Senator, but for several of his staff members as well. Jackie failed to mention, however, that these lunches were actually whipped up by her cook and then ferried over to Capitol Hill by Jack's chauffeur, Mugsy O'Leary.

Publicly, at least, Jackie did not mind being portrayed as the helpless hausfrau if it somehow bolstered Jack's stature. "He is a rock," she said of her husband, "and I lean on him in everything. He is so kind—ask anyone who works for him! And he's never irritable or sulky. He would do anything I wanted or give me anything I wanted."

Over time, Jackie grew more comfortable on the campaign trail. She gave her first campaign speech to the Worcester Cercle Français, explaining that giving the speech in French was "not as frightening as it would have been in English." She drew cheers when she spoke a few Italian phrases to crowds in Boston's North End.

"I'm so glad Jack comes from Massachusetts because it's the state with the most history," she said. "Driving from one rally to another, we'd pass John Quincy Adams's house or Harvard—or Plymouth. I think I know every corner of Massachusetts." But as Jackie was loosening up, her husband was growing more and more tense worrying that he would not achieve his half-million-vote margin of victory.

While they were having lunch in a back booth at a restaurant in Haverhill, Massachusetts, Kenny O'Donnell was furiously taking down notes as Jack reeled off a series of things he wanted done. "You're always writing things down," Jackie said to O'Donnell with a wry smile, "but I never see you looking at the pad after we leave the restaurant. Do you ever do anything about all these things he tells you to do?"

"Never," answered O'Donnell. "I wait until he calms down, and then I rip these notes off the pad and throw them away."

Jackie laughed, but the candidate was not amused. "You son of a bitch," Jack said, fixing his eyes on O'Donnell, "I bet that's exactly what you do."

As it turned out, Jack need not have worried. He received 73.6 percent of the vote—a victory margin of 874,608 votes. It was the largest number of votes ever cast for a single candidate in the history of Massachusetts. It was also the biggest majority racked up by any candidate for the Senate that year. Nobody in the Kennedy camp, including Jack and Jackie, was especially thrilled. "We were already thinking," said O'Donnell, "about the next ball game."

That Election Day, Jack's sister Pat Lawford gave birth to her third child, a girl, in California. She and Peter named her Victoria Francis—Victoria in honor of her uncle Jack's reelection and Francis after Francis Albert Sinatra.

The following Sunday, Jack appeared on NBC's *Meet the Press* and flatly denied that he had plans to run for president. But at the wedding of Ted Kennedy to Joan Bennett that November, little else was talked about. An outsider like Jackie, Joan was unassuming, soft-spoken, and temperamentally ill-suited to her boisterous in-laws. Jackie took an instant liking to Joan, and Joan looked to her for advice about how to deal with the Hyannis Port tribe.

"In the beginning, Joan was so happy with Ted," Jackie later recalled. "Whenever we were all in Hyannis Port, you could see the pride on Ted's face when she walked in the room with her great figure and her leopard-skin outfits. If only she had realized her own strengths instead of looking at herself in comparison with the Kennedys. Why worry if you're not as good at tennis as Eunice or Ethel when men are attracted by the feminine way you play tennis? Why court Ethel's tennis elbow?"

When Joan worried about Ted's wandering eye, Jackie explained, "Kennedy men are like that. They'll go after anything in skirts. It doesn't mean a thing." Those who knew them both agreed that Jackie had no reason to take Jack's affairs seriously. "Nobody gets involved with that many girls," Spalding said, "on anything but a superficial basis."

Jackie's seemingly lassez-faire attitude toward infidelity surfaced at a 1958 Christmas charity ball at the Plaza Hotel in New York. Gore Vidal was among the guests. "I've put you at Jack's table," she told Vidal. "There's a new import from England, wonderfully stupid but very beautiful, and she'll sit between you and Jack and you two can talk across her."

"In their world, infidelity simply doesn't matter. For the great masses of people, marriage is the center of the earth," Vidal observed. "Heterosexuality is the great god and children are all-important. At a certain level this may be true. But not for Jack and Jackie. People try to make them into John and Jane Smith of Dayton, Ohio. You know, 'Dear, you left a wet towel on the floor again.' But theirs was the world of money and power, and to the rich and powerful quaint things like fidelity and domestic bliss simply don't matter. They lived in a world where sex is something you do like tennis. It can become quite competitive. Who can sleep with the most Hollywood stars, for example. You can't tell the American public this, though. They would never believe it. They've been too propagandized.

"So long as she was not held up to public ridicule, Jackie accepted Jack's womanizing as a fact of life. It's not that they didn't care about each other. I think she eventually grew quite fond of Jack, and he took a certain pride in her . . ."

At that same charity ball, Jack was more candid about his career aspirations than he had been with the panel on *Meet the Press*. One of the Kennedys' Hyannis Port neighbors, Nancy Tenney Coleman, was dancing with Charlie Bartlett when they spotted the senator on the sidelines. "Nancy sort of tickled him," Bartlett recalled. "She said, 'Now, Jack, you don't want to be president.' And he looked at her rather coldly and said, 'Nancy, I not only want to be, but I am going to be.' And he meant it."

Jackie was no less convinced. During a visit to Hyannis Port in the summer of 1959, Vidal asked what she planned to do "when—not if" Jack was elected president. "I've kept a book. With names," she replied. "Who was it who said, 'Revenge is more sweet than love?'"

Jack still had to beat six other Democratic candidates in the primaries to secure the nomination. The prospect of the upcoming primary and election campaigns stretched out before Jackie like a two-year prison sentence. As a result, she was smoking more than ever, biting her fingernails, and spending feverishly on clothes. In preparation, she gamely sought the advice of veteran campaign spouses like Senator John Sherman Cooper's wife, Lorraine. "I remember she told me that she carried little cards with her," Jackie said, "and that whenever she left a town she'd write a little note, 'Dear so and so, thank you for this.' Because otherwise everything piles up and you don't remember . . . but I was too tired to ever do it."

Beginning in September 1959, Jackie sportingly joined her husband as he continued to lay the groundwork for his campaign across the country. Typical of these forays was a trip to Oregon, where only three supporters, including Congresswoman Edith Green, showed up to greet the couple when their plane touched down in Portland. That night in Coos Bay, only a handful of surly longshoremen turned up to hear him speak at the local union hall; afterward Jackie, decked out in a checked Chanel suit, tried without success to make small talk with the men.

The candidate and his wife spent that night at the Let 'Er Buck Motel, then breakfasted the next morning at the local greasy spoon. No one recognized them. "In some towns it was difficult to find anybody who was willing to shake hands," Kenny O'Donnell conceded, "and most of the people who did talk to Kennedy were schoolchildren too young to vote."

Jack persisted. He spoke in high school auditoriums, visited supermarkets and factories, even ran up to cars at stoplights to shove his hand at the driver and introduce himself. Jackie was often with him, doing her best to seem like the housewife next door. "It's not easy, this traveling," she said, "but we are together and he tells me how much it helps him just for me to be there. And I try to be natural with people. I think if you aren't, then they see it immediately."

Jackie remembered being awakened early one morning by Jack in Ashland, Wisconsin. Within moments Steve Smith, the husband of Jack's sister Jean and one of Jack's key campaign strategists, knocked at the door. "While they were talking about the news stories and things like that, I packed my bag and got dressed. Neither of us is very talkative so early in the morning, especially me. But I remember something in the car going to the airport in Ashland. I saw a crow and I told Jack we must see another crow, and I told him the jingle I learned as a little girl: 'One crow sorrow, two crows joy, three crows a girl, four a boy.' And you should have seen Jack looking for crows until he found more. He would have liked to find four crows. I guess every man wants a boy. But that was a tender thing, I thought."

Tender was not the word to describe his feelings toward his Democratic rivals, all of whom he deemed unworthy. "Jack told me something I'll never forget," said Charles Bartlett, who with his wife Martha joined Jack and Jackie for dinner at the N Street house on New Year's Eve. "Jack told me that if the Democrats didn't give him the nomination, then he was going to vote for Nixon. He wasn't joking."

By the time Jack stepped before the press in the Senate Caucus Room and formally declared his candidacy on January 20, 1960, he had already logged tens of thousands of miles aboard his campaign plane the *Caroline*. A ten-passenger DC-3 purchased for Jack by his father, the *Caroline* was luxuriously appointed with sofas, reclining chairs, a curtained-off sleeping area, a dining area, and a galley that was always stocked with Jack's favorite, New England clam chowder.

The *Caroline* became the campaign's flying nerve center. While Jack held strategy sessions with O'Donnell and Powers, or worked

on a speech with Sorensen, Jackie wiled away the time doing needlepoint or reading Jack Kerouac. "She was this island of serenity
amid the chaos," Lowe said. "But you always knew she'd rather
be someplace else."

As the campaign picked up speed, the *Caroline* would often
touch down in six or seven cities a day. In between, reporters and
local politicians would board the plane for in-flight meetings with
the candidate, then be deposited at the next town so they could
drive home.

"We'd start at 6 A.M. in New York, then go to Boston, Chicago,
and a couple of other cities and end up in California at 2 A.M. the
next day," Jacques Lowe recalled. "We'd have gone to three
lunches and three dinners where Jack made speeches, but never
get around to eating. You'd just fall into bed, totally exhausted.
The amazing thing was, I'd be struggling to get out of bed and
Jack would already be up, shaved and showered, and answering
some reporter's questions. His stamina was amazing."

The hectic pace did not seem to faze Jackie, who shared her
husband's stoicism when it came to air travel. "We flew in any
kind of weather," said Lowe, who began the campaign as a white-
knuckle flier. "Blizzards, thunderstorms, terrible fog. Even when
the pilots were reluctant to take the chance, Jack really pushed
the envelope. We'd be tossed around and I'd be turning green,
and I'd look over at Jack and Jackie and they would both just be
sitting there reading, calm as could be."

Lowe was equally impressed by Jack's total self-confidence as
he entered the first of seven presidential primaries. "Jack never
had any mixed feelings," Lowe said. "There was no doubt in his
mind regarding the presidency. He just walked in and took it."

As expected, Jack (with the help of Rose, who made as many
campaign appearances as her son did) handily won the New
Hampshire primary. But the first real test of his political strength
came in Wisconsin, where he was pitted against the popular senator from the neighboring state of Minnesota, Hubert Humphrey.
"Jackie didn't want to go, and she came only after Jack pressured

her to," Chuck Spalding recalled. "It was pure torture for Jackie. She hated it, she really hated it. Wisconsin was not her favorite spot, I don't guess, because it was a windy, snowbound winter . . .

"At our hotel in Green Bay, Jackie would be in her room up on the third floor while Jack was down in the bar trying to round up votes. He got pretty impatient, and so he would send me up to get her. Well, there was this 'Name the Horse' contest in *Look* magazine, where the grand prize was a new Buick. And Jackie was sitting on the bed surrounded with lists of horse's names she'd thought up. She absolutely had her heart set on winning that Buick. I'd say, 'Come on, Jackie, we've got to go down there. We've *got* to, Jackie. Jack's waiting for you.' And she'd stall and say, 'Oh, do I have to?' But she always went down, eventually."

Even when she did face the crowds, Jackie often chose, in the words of Ben Bradlee, "to pull some invisible shade down across her face, and cut out spiritually. She was physically present, but intellectually long gone."

Pierre Salinger, who had come aboard as JFK's campaign press secretary, believed "Jackie did a credible job concealing her natural distaste for politics from the voters." No one appreciated the effort more than Jack. "She breathes all the political gases that flow around us," he said, "but she never seems to inhale them." As for his using her to help achieve his political ends: "Since I am completely committed, and she is committed to me, that commits her."

At that early stage in his declared candidacy, Jack was, despite appearances to the contrary, also wary of all the glad-handing. Newsman Peter Lisagor was interviewing him on his way to a supermarket on the outskirts of Milwaukee when the subject came up. "I was sitting in the back with Jackie, and he was sitting in the front seat," Lisagor said. "I leaned forward as we approached the supermarket and said to him, 'Do you like these crowds and this sort of thing?' He turned back and said, 'I hate it.' Whereupon we pulled up and he got out, and you'd think this man loved the crowds above all other things. He lit up. He signed autographs on the brown shopping bags of these ladies who came pouring in to him. But I remember the intensity with which he told me that he hated this sort of thing."

Jackie trudged on, shaking hundreds of hands in the afternoon and hundreds more at night. "You get so tired you catch yourself laughing and crying at the same time," she said. "But you pace yourself and you get through it. You just look at it as something you have to do. You knew it would come and you knew it was worth it.

"The places blur after a while, they really do," Jackie said, adding that she was surprised to find most people "as shy as I am. Sometimes we just stand there smiling at each other and just don't say anything."

Jackie overcame her shyness to get across her husband's message. At a Kenosha supermarket, the manager was announcing the day's sale items when Jackie asked to borrow the loudspeaker. "Just keep on shopping while I tell you about my husband, John F. Kennedy." After reciting his credentials, she finished with a simple "Please vote for him." But when Jack paid an impromptu Saint Patrick's Day visit to a convent, Jackie shook her head in disbelief. "Nuns," Jack replied, "vote too, you know."

The mounting tension of the campaign was already being felt by Jackie. After asking Jack some tough questions on *Face the Nation,* Lisagor ran into Jackie in the green room. "She was quite obviously cool," he said, "so I asked her if she was angry with me."

"Oh well, I was," Jackie replied. "Because I thought you were asking mean, nasty questions. But Jack says that you were doing your job and you're really a nice fellow. If I seem to be angry, why I'm sorry. I'm just getting a little tense. The thing is building up now, and I'm a little tense . . ."

Actually, Jackie did not always live by her husband's famous "Don't get mad, get even" maxim. "Even though Jack had a hell of a temper, he never held a grudge," Smathers said. "It wasn't his style. Now Jackie was something else entirely." When Jack praised a political rival in Massachusetts, Jackie snapped, "Why are you saying nice things about that rat? I've been hating him for three weeks now."

Kennedy's marginal win in Wisconsin, with its large Catholic population, made the next primary in predominantly Protestant West Virginia all the more important. The jury was still out on Jackie's impact in Wisconsin; Spalding felt she had been a "big hit" there while others claimed a photo of Jackie sneaking a cigarette between campaign stops cost him votes.

Over one of their breakfast strategy sessions at Charleston's Kanawha Hotel, campaign organizer Charles Peters decided he "had to speak up" about Jackie. "I felt she was going to lose us votes. I feared she would be a disaster. She seemed to me to be pretty high-toned for West Virginia, and people there were going to be offended by someone in all these fancy designer clothes.

"Well, I was dead wrong," Peters admitted. "It turned out that the voters loved her. She was perceived as the princess, and they basked in her glamour rather than being offended by it."

West Virginian Clarence Petry remembered one revealing incident at a rally when he noticed that one young woman in the audience was not wearing shoes. "Nobody noticed until a short while after that that *Jackie* didn't have no shoes on. She'd done kicked them off too. People in West Virginia liked that. They liked Jacqueline Kennedy. Sure did."

Of course, Jack was his own best advertisement. Climbing atop station wagons and tractors to address small crowds, kibitzing with coal miners between shifts, and going door-to-door among their tar-paper shacks, Kennedy convinced residents of the impoverished state that he was a man of the people. He also got some important backing from Franklin D. Roosevelt, Jr., whose father was still revered as a saint by most West Virginians.

The landslide victory over Humphrey in West Virginia buried the Catholic issue and all but clinched the nomination for Jack. It also proved that in Jackie he had a valuable political asset. "Until then," Spalding said, "I'm not sure any of us really knew which way she would jump—or how average people would react to her." Jack went on to sweep all the primaries.

Now five months pregnant, Jackie wanted at all costs to avoid a repeat of the 1956 tragedy. This time she decided not to accompany Jack to the convention in Los Angeles. He concurred wholly in the decision, undoubtedly in part because it would allow him to cavort freely, but mainly out of concern for the baby. "After they had Caroline he understood what it was to be a parent," a friend said. "He already saw this baby as a human being, and not a thing. I think he felt guilty for the way he acted in 1956— wanting to stay in Europe even after he got word of the stillbirth. A lot of us felt that was unforgivable. But he was a changed man in 1960. If something like that had happened then, he would have been devastated."

Caroline had already been imprinted with the stamp of a political family. Her first spoken words: "Good-bye," "New Hampshire," "Wisconsin," and "West Virginia." Jackie professed to being "very sorry so few states have primaries, or we would have a daughter with the greatest vocabulary of any two-year-old in the country."

Given the unique circumstances of her early years, Caroline was, and would remain, remarkably unspoiled. And she adored her father. On one of his increasingly rare weekends home, Jack was taking a bath when Caroline rushed in shouting, "Daddy!" and tossed a copy of *Newsweek* with her father on the cover into the tub.

That July Jackie stayed behind in Hyannis Port, where she watched the convention on a small rented TV. She was the only Kennedy not to make the trip to Los Angeles. It seemed inconceivable then, but Jackie was asked what it would be like if the convention nominated someone other than Jack. "I guess it would be like a racing car driver who's way ahead and winning the race," she said, "and then someone tells him there is no more gas for his car."

Jack, Bobby, and the rest of the campaign team set up headquarters in room 8315 of the Biltmore Hotel, while Joe and Rose moved into Marion Davies's Beverly Hills "bungalow." From the beginning, there were charges that Joe had essentially "bought and paid for" the delegates, wheeling and dealing with bosses behind the scenes, softening up rank-and-file Democrats with liquor, women, and cash. "Joe was in that election up to his eyebrows," Charlie Bartlett said. "He did everything within his power to get Jack the nomination, and then to get him elected. And his power was considerable."

Wisely choosing to stay out of sight, Joe worked the phones and spent evenings with friends like Henry and Clare Boothe Luce while Rose and the others courted delegates. "Jack and Bobby run the show" went one of the more popular lines at the convention, "while Ted's in charge of hiding Joe."

Before the convention, Harry Truman had resigned as a delegate rather than participate in "a prearranged affair." At the same time, Truman attacked Jack's youth and inexperience, though by "accidentally" referring to him as "Joseph," the former president made it clear that his main objection was to Joe's influence. With a beaming Jackie at his side, Jack had held a press conference in Washington at which he skillfully refuted Truman's charges.

The next day, however, Lyndon Johnson—who had cast Texas's votes on Kennedy's behalf as vice president in 1956—declared his candidacy. By this time, Johnson had developed an intense hatred for all the Kennedys, particularly Bobby. LBJ echoed Truman's charges of youth and inexperience, adding that he, too, believed "Joe would run the country" if his son were elected.

The Johnson forces fought dirty. Journalist Theodore White remembered receiving a call from someone who later occupied a high post in the Johnson administration. "I think you should know that John Kennedy and Bobby Kennedy are fags," the Johnson operative said. "We have pictures of them in women's dresses at Las Vegas this spring at a big fag party. This should be made public." The source promised to give the pictures to White "within twenty-four hours." But they never materialized.

At the same time, the offices of Dr. Janet Travell and another of Jack's physicians, Dr. Eugene Cohen, were broken into and ransacked. Within days, Johnson supporter John B. Connally held a press conference to announce that Jack had Addison's disease. Connally, who later was shot along with the President as they rode through Dallas, said Kennedy might not live out even one term. (The autopsy of John F. Kennedy did show that his adrenal glands had been destroyed by Addison's disease, and that they in fact had been entirely supplanted by his daily dose of cortisone.)

Johnson, who himself had survived a serious heart attack in 1955, publicly tried to distance himself from this particular charge. But privately, he derided Jack as "that spavined hunchback," "that scrawny fellow with rickets," and "that sickly little shit."

On July 10, the eve of the convention, twenty-eight hundred people attended a hundred-dollar-a-plate Democratic party fundraiser at the Beverly Hilton Hotel. At the head table, Judy Garland sat in place of the absent Jackie on JFK's right. Frank Sinatra was also honored with a place at the head table, along with Jack's fellow presidential hopefuls Lyndon Johnson, Missouri's Stuart Symington, and sentimental favorite Adlai Stevenson.

The next day Sinatra, Dean Martin, Sammy Davis, Jr., Peter Lawford, Tony Curtis, and Janet Leigh—all ardent Kennedy supporters—opened the convention with the national anthem. Then they spread out among the delegates, using their undeniable star power to sway delegates toward their candidate.

Amid all the convention pandemonium, Jack still found time for extracurricular activities. On July 11, Jack repaired to Lawford's suite at the Beverly Hilton to spend the night in the company of a blue-eyed, twenty-six-year-old divorcée with a slender figure and jet black hair. Passed along to Jack by Sinatra, Judy Campbell (who later married golf pro Dan Exner) had slept with the senator for the first time back in March, the night before the New Hampshire primary, at New York's Plaza Hotel.

Jack and Campbell had already managed several trysts from Chicago to Las Vegas to Palm Springs. But that night, on the eve of the convention, she claims he asked for something special: a ménage à trois with what Campbell later described as a "tall, thin secretarial type in her late twenties." She had once turned down a similar proposition from Sinatra, and did so again. "I know you," Jack persisted without success. "I know you'll like it."

Over the next several days, Marilyn Monroe replaced Campbell as Jack's chief source of "entertainment." Crushed by Yves Montand's decision not to leave his wife, Academy Award–winning French actress Simone Signoret, for her, Marilyn now made herself completely available to the nominee. Some of their stolen moments were spent at Jack's secret hideaway in an apartment house owned by Kennedy family friend Jack Haley, who is best remembered as the Tin Man in *The Wizard of Oz*.

On July 12, Marilyn dined openly with Jack, Kenny O'Donnell, and Peter Lawford at a Sinatra hangout called Puccini's. She told the future president's brother-in-law that during their private times together, she found Jack to be "very penetrating." She later told her maid that, while everyone was engaged in polite dinner conversation, Jack slid his hand up her dress to discover she wasn't wearing underwear. At which point, he withdrew his hand and blushed.

The next day, Jackie sat in her Hyannis Port living room watching the convention coverage. She began nervously puffing on a cigarette when a last-minute surge by supporters of Adlai Stevenson momentarily threatened to derail the Kennedy Express. She breathed a sigh of relief when Wyoming put her Jack over the top on the first ballot.

The first phone call Jack placed was to his father, who was still hiding out in Beverly Hills. The second was to Jackie. She congratulated him, but the conversation was strained. "She was no dumbbell," Smathers said. "Jackie knew all about Marilyn and what they were up to at the convention."

One of her chief sources of information was her sister, Lee, who had attended the convention with her second husband, Polish Prince Stanislas Radziwill. Lee had married "Stas" (pronounced "Stash") the previous year, after her marriage to Michael Canfield was annulled. Everyone who had known their father marveled at how closely the perpetually tanned, mustachioed, worldly Radziwill resembled Black Jack. Twenty years her senior, Lee's new husband also shared some of Black Jack's unfortunate habits. From their suite at the Beverly Hilton, Lee called Jackie with all the gossip of the convention, including regular bulletins on Jack's whereabouts.

"Jackie was not threatened," Clare Boothe Luce said. "Not even by Marilyn Monroe. But if somehow word had gotten out, it would have upset her terribly. She could not bear the thought of being publicly humiliated."

Jackie did not have to rely on Lee for all her information. Reporters tracked the Democrats' top contender to his secret hideaway. When Jack tried to make his getaway by climbing down a fire escape, they chased him over a neighbor's fence and finally caught up with him as he got into a waiting car. Jack's explanation was that he was on his way to see Joe.

None of this appeared to faze Jackie, who spent much of this time working on her husband's homecoming present—a drawing of Jack, clad in a Napoleonic tunic, making his victorious return to the Cape aboard his sailboat *Victura*. Waiting at the pier to greet him was a mob waving a placard that read "Welcome Back, Mr. Jack."

In fact, the stories that had filtered back from the convention had left Jackie shaken. She confided in Walter Sohier, a Georgetown bachelor she had grown particularly close to, that she felt the nomination might have altered their relationship forever. "She hid it from the press, from the cameras, the public," said their Hyannis Port neighbor Larry Newman. "But I saw her practically every day, and there were plenty of moments when there was this look in her eyes—something between sadness and panic."

Jackie intimate Walter Sohier may have actually been privy to her innermost confidences. "Jackie spent hours with Walter at his townhouse in Georgetown, unburdening herself to him," said a friend. Certainly their relationship was grist for the gossip mill. "The press never got wind of it, or at least they didn't print anything," Priscilla McMillan added, "but a lot of people were wondering . . ."

"I heard many rumors about the Kennedy marriage," PT-109 friend Red Fay conceded. Following a round of golf, Fay confronted JFK with one of them. "The sister of the wife of one of my closest friends, who supposedly travels in the same set in New York as Jacqueline and Lee, has circulated the story that Jacqueline is staying with you only until you are nominated or the election is over, and then is going to divorce you," Fay told Jack. "She claims she got the information from one of Jackie's closest friends. I want the rebuttal directly from you, so I can kill the story at its source."

Jack, according to Fay, looked at him as if his friend "had just told him his shoe was untied." "Red," he said, without a flicker, "the story is false, but I wouldn't feel at all confident about killing it if I were you. People who spread stories like that don't want to accept a denial. I think I know the girl in New York who is spreading that report. She and Jackie go to some of the same parties and amazingly enough, Jackie says she is always very friendly. You can never tell who is going to try to stick it to you."

Later aboard the *Caroline*, the Kennedys and Fays were chatting about some innocuous topic when Jack abruptly raised the rumor issue. "Jackie, out on the golf course today Red asked me if there was any truth to the rumor that you were going to divorce me after the campaign," Jack said calmly. "Your good friend who married the fellow with the Russian name in New York is spreading the story."

1

*Daddy's girl. Already a ribbon-winning equestrienne
at age five in 1934, Jackie is led off the course by her father after an event.
It was the dashing, womanizing Black Jack Bouvier who, by example, taught
his elder daughter and her sister, Lee, what to expect of men.*

*The Kennedy clan in 1934, minus Joe Jr., who was away at school. In the front row
(left to right): Patricia, Rose, Joe with Teddy, Rosemary, Eunice, and Kathleen. John, Jean,
and Robert brought up the rear. Powerful, philandering Joe Sr. was Jack's role model.*

The Washington Times-Herald's intrepid Inquiring Camera Girl at work shooting a friend feeding goldfish in 1952. Jackie was twenty-three.

4

5

The Massachusetts senator and his bride-to-be prepare to set sail from the Kennedy family compound in Hyannis Port.

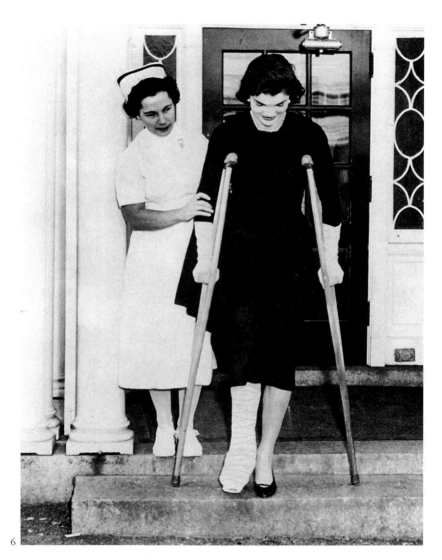

6

*"They'll kill me before I ever get to marry him," Jackie said
after breaking her right foot during a touch football game at the Kennedy
family compound in Hyannis Port. "I know they will."*

7

*Wedding Album. On September 12, 1953, the bride and groom
exchanged vows at St. Mary's Church in Newport, Rhode Island, then
headed for the reception at Hammersmith Farm (see following pages).*

8

9

10

While her husband of seven months looks on, Jackie leaves their town house for classes at Georgetown University's School of Foreign Service.

11

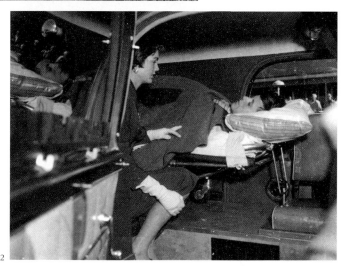

12

After spinal surgery in New York that nearly cost him his life, Jack was flown to Palm Beach to celebrate Christmas 1954 with the rest of the Kennedys. Jackie stayed at her husband's side during the ambulance ride to the Kennedy estate.

13

In a rare public display of affection, Jack kisses his wife good-bye at the Hyannis airport before he heads back to Washington.

14

15

Mom and Dad enjoy some quality time with two-year-old Caroline.

Two weeks before the 1960 presidential election, Jack and Jackie share the excitement of a New York ticker tape parade in their honor.

16

Carrying three-year-old Caroline in his arms, the President-elect fields reporters' questions in Hyannis Port while his very pregnant wife strolls off, virtually unnoticed.

17

18

*Although he was suffering from excruciating back pain and she
had not yet recovered from John Jr.'s birth by cesarean section, the First Couple
looked radiant as they arrived at the inaugural gala.*

19

*The President brushes the hair off the face of his beaming First Lady
after an open-air motorcade through the streets of Washington in May 1961. JFK took
increasing pride in his wife's newfound status as a global trendsetter.*

*During an official
White House visit,
Princess Grace of
Monaco gazes
adoringly at her host.*

20

*The former Jacqueline
Bouvier and her
husband arrive for
dinner at the Élysée
Palace in May 1961
and are greeted by
Charles de Gaulle.
Jackie so charmed De
Gaulle and the French
people that JFK
remarked, "I'm proud
to say I am the man
who accompanied
Jacqueline Kennedy to
Paris."*

21

23

24

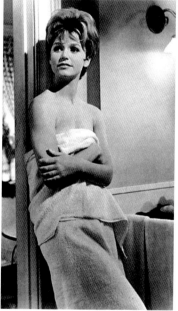

22

25

Affairs of the heart—and otherwise (clockwise from bottom left): *Frank Sinatra introduced JFK to Judith Campbell, and at one inaugural ball the new President slipped out with Angie Dickinson. Jack's dalliances with Sophia Loren and fellow Yankee Lee Remick were also kept out of the press, as was his romance with the stunning Audrey Hepburn* (opposite page).

After JFK, Hepburn came close to marrying actor William Holden (right). *In a strange twist, according to Kennedy intimate Gore Vidal (Jackie's stepfather Hugh Auchincloss had been Vidal's stepfather), Jackie sought revenge for Jack's infidelities by briefly becoming involved with Holden.*

Like FDR, JFK went to great lengths to conceal his disabilities from the voting public. Kennedy frequently used crutches, but photographs like this one, taken in the summer of 1961 and never before released, are rare.

28

29

The President congratulates Pablo Casals after the cellist's historic return to the White House. He had last performed there for Teddy Roosevelt in 1904.

Described as "an incurable speed demon" by one close friend, JFK piloted his golf cart around the grounds of the Hyannis Port compound with reckless abandon. He and Jackie often took several Kennedy cousins along for the wild ride.

30

Jack is clearly delighted to be sharing the Palm Beach sunshine with (from left) Jackie, Ted, Ethel, Joe, Bobby, Eunice, and Stephan and Jean Smith.

31

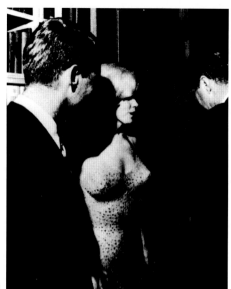

Following her famously breathless rendition of "Happy Birthday, Mr. President" on May 19, 1962, Marilyn Monroe linked up with Bobby and Jack at a private party afterward.

32

33

Both insatiable gossips, the President gets an earful from Jackie at the 1962 America's Cup dinner.

*Jackie whispers a
confidence to the
President as they
watch the America's
Cup races from the
deck of the USS*
Joseph P. Kennedy, Jr.

*On a weekend sail off Cape
Cod, Jackie is engrossed in a
copy of William Manchester's*
Portrait of a President:
John F. Kennedy in Profile.

36

*December 25, 1962. In Palm Beach, Jackie, Jack, and the Radziwills
share the pandemonium of Christmas morning with the kids.*

37

*Always the fearless
horsewoman, Jackie
jumps fences at Glen
Ora, their weekend
getaway in Virginia.*

38

*At a rally in Miami, JFK looks on proudly as his wife charms
Cuban refugees in their native Spanish.*

39

*A bemused Jackie poses
with Nina Khrushchev,
her plump Russian
counterpart, while their
husbands confer in Vienna.*

40

The Bouvier sisters gamely ride an elephant during Jackie's much-publicized tour of India.

41

Relaxing with U.S. Ambassador to India John Kenneth Galbraith, the former
Inquiring Camera Girl turns her camera on the press corps.

42

*Ben and Tony Bradlee were one of only a few couples
with whom the Kennedys socialized regularly. Jackie
had her short skirt, which rode up to her thigh, inked
in before giving the Bradlees a copy of this photo.*

43

*JFK calls on the Pinchot women—matriarch Ruth
and daughters Tony Pinchot Bradlee (left) and Mary
Pinchot Mayer—in Virginia. The Bradlees claim to
have been unaware that Mary, later murdered, had
been having an affair with the President.*

44

45

46

*John-John's favorite pastime was surprising Daddy by crawling
through the secret panel in his Oval Office desk.*

47

*Only days before going into premature labor with Patrick,
Jackie relaxes aboard the* Sequoia.

*The anguish still shows
on their faces as the
President and First
Lady leave the hospital
at Cape Cod's Otis Air
Base so she can
recuperate after the
death of their infant
son, Patrick.*

48

49

Puppies seemed just the thing to keep up the children's spirits after Patrick's death.

*Aristotle Onassis plays
host to his future wife
and Franklin Roosevelt,
Jr., as they cruise the
Mediterranean aboard
his yacht* Christina.
*JFK stayed behind in
Washington.*

50

51

*Jackie suspected that JFK was having an affair with Pam Turnure, at right.
Here White House usher J. B. West looks on as they celebrate the birthday
of Jackie's closest friend, Nancy Tuckerman* (center).

52

*More loving and attentive toward his family than ever, Jack was undone
by his two goblins when they visited him on Halloween 1963.*

53

Nine days before JFK's assassination, the family was photographed together one last time, listening to the legendary bagpipes of the Black Watch Regiment.

54

*Seconds before the assassination, JFK smiled at the enthusiastic crowds
and Jackie squinted into the blinding Texas sun.*

55

A widow's anguish: *Dazed, her face swollen from crying, Jackie waits
with John-John and Caroline as Jack's body is carried from the north portico of the White
House. "I consider," she told friends, "that my life is over."*

"That little bitch," Jackie said. "And she always acts like such a dear friend."

There was certainly no substance to that particular rumor. As a child of divorce herself, there was no way that Jackie would subject Caroline to the kind of wrenching emotional pain she had endured. But there is little question that, hearing of Jack's escapades in Los Angeles, Jackie sought some sort of comfort and reassurance in the company of the obliging Sohier.

As soon as Jack clinched the nomination, talk turned to who the nominee would pick as his running mate. The leading candidates were Missouri Senator Stuart Symington, Senator Henry "Scoop" Jackson of Washington, and Lyndon Johnson.

While Jack pondered the question in his Los Angeles hotel room the next morning, across the country the press had already descended on Jackie in Hyannis Port. "I'm so excited," she told them. How did she feel about being "ordered" by her husband to stay home? "He's very strict, but very affectionate." She smiled.

Jackie was contrite about her decision to stay home during her pregnancy. "I suppose I won't be able to play much part in the campaign," she told the reporters, "but I'll do what I can. I feel I should be with Jack when he's engaged in such a struggle, and if it weren't for the baby, I'd campaign even more vigorously than Mrs. Nixon. I can't be so presumptuous as to think I could have any effect on the outcome, but it would be so tragic if my husband lost by a few votes merely because I wasn't at his side and because people had met Mrs. Nixon and liked her."

One reporter asked if the baby was due before or after Inauguration Day. She gave him a quizzical look before asking, "When's Inauguration Day?"

On a more serious note, Jackie sidestepped the issue of her husband's potential running mate. "I like everyone," she answered brightly.

That morning following his nomination, Jack summoned Lyndon Johnson to the Biltmore. The only other person in the room when Jack offered LBJ the vice presidency was Jacques Lowe. "It was 10:15 in the morning, and Johnson was knocking back these tall glasses of straight bourbon," Lowe recalled. "He was very nervous. He knew he'd be giving up his powerful position as Senate majority leader to accept one of the lousiest jobs in government. Remember, John Nance Garner, who was vice president under Roosevelt, said being V.P. 'wasn't worth a pitcher of warm spit.'"

The selection of Johnson ignited a firestorm of protest within the party, and even LBJ's wife, Lady Bird, implored him not to accept the second spot on the ticket. So why, finally, did Johnson accept? "I looked it up," he told Clare Boothe Luce. "One out of every four presidents has died in office. I'm a gamblin' man, darlin', and this is the only chance I got."

Marilyn joined Sinatra's Rat Pack and a hundred thousand others who jammed into the Sports Arena on July 15 to hear Jack's stirring acceptance speech. They also heard Symington, Stevenson, Humphrey, Jackson, Johnson, and even Eleanor Roosevelt (who only days before had chided Jack for showing "too much profile and not enough courage") join the chorus of praise for their young champion. Marilyn was satisfied that she had made her contribution. "I think," she told Lawford, "I made his back feel better."

Later that night, Jack, Bobby, and Marilyn attended a victory celebration at the home of Pat and Peter Lawford. Several of the guests, including Monroe, went skinny-dipping. When neighbors called police to complain about the noise, it took Jack's personal intervention to keep police from breaking up the party and hauling several of the famous celebrants off to jail.

Back in Hyannis, Jackie waited patiently on the tarmac at the Barnstable Airport. She did not want to be there. Earlier, Larry Newman had had to go upstairs to Jackie's bedroom to fetch her after she told Kennedy advance man Frank Morrissey to "get the hell out! I'm staying right here!"

"She was sitting on the edge of the bed with this wistful look on her face and she was shaking her head," Newman said. "She said she was not going to go to the airport because she knew exactly what was going to happen: She was going to join Jack on the *Caroline* as soon as it landed and then, as planned, she would reemerge with Jack to the roar of the crowd. Then somebody would shove a bunch of roses in her arms and he would desert her to shake hands with the crowd. 'Then I'll be left standing there completely alone as always,' she told me. 'I hate it.' "

Newman promised to stand by her if that happened, so she went. "In the car, she didn't say a word," Newman recalled. "As we got closer to the airport and you could see the people waiting to greet Jack, she became very tense. Jackie looked like a frightened deer. She just hated crowds."

After Jack arrived at the airport, events unfolded just as Jackie had predicted. As they left the plane, photographers shouted, "Kiss him, Jackie," but before she could he peeled off and headed for the screaming fans who pressed against the chain-link fence. Jackie turned to Newman and sighed, "What did I tell you?"

For the next two weeks, before Jack plunged into the campaign against his old friend Richard Nixon, he and Jackie managed to squeeze in some moments of relaxation at Hyannis Port. There was snorkeling, sailing, and, of course, touch football. Jack sped around the grounds at the wheel of a golf cart, Caroline and her cousins hanging on for dear life. At Hyannis Port as well as in Georgetown and in the White House, all Jack had to do was clap his hands twice and call for "Buttons," his pet name for Caroline. The instant she heard her father's clapping, Caroline "took off like a rocket," Salinger said.

One afternoon Lowe snapped away while Jackie, clad in a one-piece bathing suit and flowered bathing cap, cavorted in the surf with Jack. In one playful moment, she tried to steady him in a bathtub-sized boat before tipping it over, sending the Democratic presidential nominee into the drink.

It was not all fun and games. Lowe recalled a morning in Hyannis Port when "I saw Jackie coming down for breakfast and the house was full of people who had come to curry favor with Jack.

She went into the living room, and there was a meeting of immigrant groups and people were shouting at each other in Polish and Hungarian. Then Jackie went out on the porch, and it was filled with beefy, red-faced Irish pols and their big wives. You could cut the cigar smoke with a knife. When she tried the dining room, Jack, in the middle of an important meeting, waved her away. She pushed the door into the kitchen, and Pierre Salinger was surrounded by reporters, giving a press conference. With nowhere to go, Jackie just turned around and went right back upstairs. I felt sorry for her."

It was during this hiatus that Lowe found himself in the middle of a spat between Mr. and Mrs. Kennedy. Since the early primaries, when Jack changed his schedule to eliminate what Jackie called the "silly zigzagging back and forth," she felt confident enough to make periodic suggestions to the staff. When it came to family photographs and how they would be used, Jack usually deferred to her wishes. "*Modern Screen* wanted to do a twelve-page layout on the family," Lowe remembered, "but Jackie wanted me to give the pictures to *Vogue*. At the time, *Modern Screen* had ten times as many readers as *Vogue,* and I knew *Vogue*'s readers were probably mostly wealthy Republican women in mink coats, anyway. But Jackie insisted, so I took my case to Jack."

The senator instantly agreed with Lowe and instructed him to give the photographs to *Modern Screen*. Lowe asked him to explain his decision to Jackie, but his boss grew impatient. "You tell Jackie," the candidate said, "that there isn't a single vote for me among that bunch of rich bitches."

Jack's personal photographer later learned, as did all those who worked in the White House, that his employer never confronted Jackie himself on such matters. "He'd tell us to do something Jackie expressly didn't want done," Lowe said, "and then play dumb. You know, 'What? Who, me?' He didn't like any unpleasantness with Jackie. Jack would do anything to avoid an argument with her. He genuinely cared about her feelings, and tried his best, even with all the distractions and incredible pressures involved in running for the presidency, to keep her happy."

By mid-August, the campaign was again in full swing, and would not let up for the next eleven weeks. The turning point came on September 26, 1960, when CBS bumped *The Andy Griffith Show* to air the first of four historic presidential debates between John Kennedy and Richard Nixon.

It was then that Jack stumbled upon a secret weapon—one that would not only play a key role in vanquishing his opponent, but also enable him to set a superhuman pace as president. "I was working at the J. Walter Thompson advertising agency in New York and going through a messy divorce that left me just exhausted," Chuck Spalding recalled. "A family friend suggested that I see a doctor named Max Jacobson, so I went. Well, I walked into his New York office and *everybody* was sitting in the waiting room—Eddie Fisher, Alan Jay Lerner, Zero Mostel, Johnny Mathis, and several actresses. They were all patients of his, plus half of Hollywood!

"Max was a strange man—loud, arrogant, kind of a mad scientist type. But I was desperate, and so I let him give me a shot. Well, I went over the top of the building! I felt wonderful, full of energy—capable of doing just about anything. I didn't know exactly what he was giving me, but it was a magic potion as far as I was concerned."

Jacobson, better known as the notorious "Dr. Feelgood," was actually injecting Spalding and the rest of his patients—including photographer and Kennedy friend Mark Shaw—with amphetamine "cocktails" containing mostly Dexedrine. The stimulant imbues the user with a sense of power and well-being. But the highly addictive drug can also lead to depression and even trigger symptoms of paranoid schizophrenia.

Not long after that first memorable session, Spalding went out of town on a political errand and returned "raring to go. Jack and I had both been to a party the night before, and he was pooped.

'Where do you get all this energy?' he asked me, and when I told him he said he wanted some.

"That made me nervous," Spalding continued. "I told him, 'If you're thinking of doing it, I'm going to tell Bobby. I can't be responsible.' He said, 'Fine,' and I did. So Bobby knew all about it."

From that point on, Spalding said, "of course we were *all* taking injections. Jack, Jackie, Bobby, *everybody*. At least twice a week. I thought, this doesn't make any sense. It's so simple. It wasn't until much later I found out it wasn't so simple after all."

Spalding called ahead one afternoon just days before the scheduled debates, and Jacobson agreed to clear the waiting room of his East Seventy-second Street office. Jack, meanwhile, gave his Secret Service detail the slip and appeared in Jacobson's office late that afternoon.

"The demands of his political campaign were so great he felt fatigued," Jacobson recalled. "His muscles felt weak. It interfered with his concentration and affected his speech. I was not at all surprised. These constituted the most common symptoms of stress." After the first injection of a mixture that was 15 percent vitamins and 85 percent speed, Jack felt rejuvenated. "He told me his muscle weakness had disappeared," Jacobson said. "He felt cool, calm, and very alert."

Right up until the morning of the debate, Nixon campaigned hard in Chicago. Jack, looking tanned and relaxed after several days in the Palm Beach sun, spent some of the previous evening listening to Peggy Lee records in his room at the Ambassador East Hotel. Jack "unwound" even more when, an hour before the debate, he rendezvoused at the Palmer House Hotel with a local call girl who had been hired by his advisor Don Marvin.

Nixon, whose knee was infected from an earlier injury, turned sheet-white when he bumped it getting out of his car at the studio. He then made the mistake of declining makeup. Jack, in contrast, needed none. "He looked," said Don Hewitt, who produced the debate, "like a young Adonis."

Those who listened to the debate on the radio came away believing that Nixon had scored a decisive victory. Lyndon Johnson agreed with them. "I was with LBJ the night of the first debate," Nancy Dickerson said. "We were listening on a car radio. Johnson was distressed that Kennedy had blown it. 'The Boy didn't win,' he kept saying. That's how LBJ referred to Jack, you know, 'The Boy.'"

But for those who watched, Kennedy's almost blasé self-assurance and calm demeanor contrasted sharply with Nixon's darting eyes and five o'clock shadow. Nixon used Pan-Cake makeup for the subsequent three debates, but it was too late. Jackie had watched the debates at home, but for the final face-off she and Lee accompanied Jack to the ABC studios in New York. "The Whispering Sisters" watched from one of two private screening rooms built especially for the candidates' guests. Aside from casting the knowing Mona Lisa smile she had perfected over the seven years of her marriage, the very pregnant Jackie made no comment other than "I think my husband did very well."

After the debates, Kennedy's crowds swelled from ten thousand to as much as a hundred thousand. On the stump Jack electrified audiences, sparking a kind of mass hysteria unprecedented in American politics. Dickerson remembered "all those screamers that turned up at every stop. Jack had this incredible sexual pull. It is hard to imagine, hard to explain the hold he had on these young women. But it was as strong as any rock star's. At the time, Jack was second only to Elvis. Make that a tie."

Illinois Democratic Senator Paul Douglas divided Jack's female supporters into various categories: "jumpers, shriekers, huggers, lopers, and touchers." To this, *Life* magazine added "gaspers, gogglers, swooners, and collapsers." Stuart Symington remembered one woman screaming to her friend, "Touch him for me, Gladys!"

"You could practically smell the excitement in the air, the reaction of the women," Lowe recalled. "It was *orgasmic*."

The campaign schedule as drawn up by Bobby, O'Donnell, Powers, and Jack's other handlers called for Jack to deliver speeches and shake hands a minimum of eighteen hours a day. "Every time I get in the middle of a day," he complained, "I look down at the schedule and there's five minutes allotted for the candidate to eat and rest." But for all his chronic physical problems, Jack continued to be the tireless dynamo he was during the primaries.

On the home front, Jackie apologized for not campaigning with her husband the way Pat Nixon campaigned for Dick. "It's the most important time of Jack's whole life," she said, "and I should be with him."

To a few close friends, she expressed her true feelings. Railing against the "crushing handshakes" and "boring politicians," she breathed a sigh of relief. "Thank God, I get out of those dreadful chicken dinners," she said. "Sitting at head tables where I can't have a cigarette and have to wear those silly corsages and listen to some gassy old windbag drive me up the wall. Poor Jack." But she worried about the toll campaigning took on him. "One day in a campaign," Jackie said, "can age a person thirty years."

What aged Jack thirty years was the controversy generated by Jackie's spending habits. "A newspaper reported Sunday," Jackie told an interviewer, "that I spent thirty thousand dollars buying Paris clothes and that women hate me for it. I couldn't possibly spend that much unless I wore sable underwear."

The candidate's reaction was predictable. "Good Christ!" Jack boomed when he was shown the quote. "That's the last interview that woman will give until after the election!"

Once he calmed down, Jack appreciated his wife's efforts to counter Pat Nixon's more down-to-earth, cloth coat image. In Hyannis Port, Lowe photographed a perfectly coiffed Jackie in full makeup painting a watercolor with Caroline at her side. A *Life* spread showed her poring over mail in the study of the N Street house, then tucking Caroline in for a nap. No reference was made in the piece to Jackie's secretary, who handled all the mail.

As for Caroline's indispensable nanny Maud Shaw, who was also instructed to stay out of the range of press photographers, *Life* told its readers that Jackie raised Caroline without a nurse.

"A big problem in my life," Jackie explained, "has been that campaigning with Jack has taken me away from home. If Jack proved to be the greatest president of the century and his children turned out badly, it would be a tragedy."

They may have been the most photogenic couple in American political history, but Jack and Jackie both actually hated being photographed. "They knew how to relate to the camera, not just pose," photographer Alfred Eisenstaedt said. "They were absolute magicians in this regard. But I think they were never completely comfortable being photographed, not even when they were with the children. Beneath the smiles they were tense. It was a job to them."

Eschewing the role of traditional backslapping politician, Jack refused to be photographed wearing hats, caps, or ceremonial headgear of any kind. With one exception. In Sioux Falls, South Dakota, JFK stood stiffly as tribal leaders performed a ceremony around him that would culminate with Jack putting on a feathered headdress. "The chief was going to put it on his head," *Look* photographer Stanley Tretick recalled, "and God, Kennedy was so nervous. He knew it was going to happen and it was killing him too, really."

As soon as the chief placed the headdress on, Jack snatched it off—but not quickly enough to avoid being snapped by Tretick. "I nailed it on his head, and it's a silly-looking picture, but he got a big kick out of it." There was one hat he would pose in: "a hard hat, although he would never keep it on very long."

JFK also "just couldn't stand to be photographed eating food," Tretick said. "He had these two hot dogs. He had a funny way of trying to hide things—he'd kind of hold them down close to him like they weren't there." He then got in his car with the hot dogs, but Tretick and the other photographers got a telephoto lens to catch him eating the hot dogs in the car. Kennedy waited until the motorcade began to move and then "slid down under the dash and hid under there and ate the hot dogs that way. He really hated to be shown eating."

Jack also didn't like "pictures of him combing his hair," Tretick recalled. "And he *constantly* combed his hair. One of the sneakiest things he did was when we'd come to a viaduct or underpass or tunnel, he'd comb his hair." When Tretick threatened to wire one of the tunnels with flashbulbs, Jack just smiled. "I hope," he said, "they're all misfires."

Tretick remembered that JFK was not shy when it came to hecklers. In Oregon, a large man passing out Nixon buttons "kept screaming about how Kennedy had screwed the Teamsters. Kennedy was getting very irritated. And the guy got close, about ten feet away. We were all set. We didn't know what was going to happen. When the guy got in real good earshot Kennedy said, 'Get lost, fatso.' The guy didn't know what to say. He just sort of went away."

As the campaign heated up, so did the rhetoric. By October, Nixon and Kennedy despised each other. The Republican candidate called Jack a "bare-faced liar," and Kennedy responded by calling him a "filthy, lying son of a bitch and a very dangerous man."

"I think it's so unfair of people to be against Jack because he's a Catholic," Jackie replied. "He's such a *poor* Catholic. Now, if it were Bobby, I could understand it." Certainly Jack's libertine behavior would have raised eyebrows in the Vatican. At one point in the campaign, when Jack lost his voice he communicated by scratching his thoughts on a notepad. Aboard the *Caroline*, he scrawled a note and handed it to one of his advisors. "I got into the blonde," the note read. "I suppose if I win," read another note, "my poon days are over (*poon* being a derogatory term for female genitalia). These and other notes were saved for posterity by the *Caroline*'s lone stewardess Janet Des Rosiers, whose other responsibilities included massaging Jack's neck and combing his hair.

Jackie rarely saw her husband that fall, so she was thrilled when Jack stole a few moments to spend time in Palm Beach. But instead of spending time with her, he wanted to play golf. "She wanted to be with him and she didn't want him to go," recalled Chuck Spalding, who was Jack's partner that day. "Jack said, 'Chuck, go back to the house and see her.' So I went up to her and she *flew* at me in a rage. I had never seen her so angry. She really went off the deep end, yelling and screaming at me."

Spalding tried to calm her down. "I said, 'Hey, hey. We've been friends a long time. You and I are family. It's just a golf game. Why don't you come with us?' She just looked at me, absolutely fuming, then turned on her heels and left."

On another occasion, a friend watched as Jack headed for the golf course with Betsy Finkenstaedt, who lived near the Hyannis Port compound with her husband and children. "Jack liked playing golf with Betsy," said Priscilla McMillan, "and she continued to be a partner of his while he was in the White House." A friend saw Jackie on that day, about a month before she gave birth to their second child, standing on the lawn and watching as Jack and Finkenstaedt headed off to play golf. "She had this melancholy look," she said. "You couldn't help but feel sorry for her."

Jackie was also resisting attempts by others in the campaign to use her in the closing weeks of the campaign. "I'm so afraid of losing this baby," she told friends. "I can't take the chance. I *won't* take the chance."

But Jack pleaded with her to join him for a final campaign push in New York City. Against her doctor's orders, Jackie relented. She had already recorded campaign audiotapes addressed to immigrant groups in their own languages. Now she spoke Italian to crowds in Little Italy and Spanish in Spanish Harlem.

The trip climaxed with a tickertape parade through New York's "Canyon of Heroes," with the candidate and his eight months pregnant wife balancing on the back of an open car as thousands of frenzied New Yorkers reached out to touch them. Several times, they were both nearly yanked from the car by over-zealous fans tugging at their sleeves. At one point, the surging crowd rocked the car so violently it threatened to spill its occupants out onto the street.

By the end of the day, an estimated three million people had turned out to cheer them. "Yeah," sighed Jack over teenage squeals, "but half of them are too young to vote."

On November 8, 1960—Election Day—Jack and Jackie cast their votes at Boston's West End library. (Jackie had actually already voted by absentee ballot, but showed up at the polls for the photo op.) To the dismay of the other Democrats on the ballot who worked hard to elect her husband—especially old ally and future House Speaker Tip O'Neill—Jackie claimed she voted for only one candidate because she didn't want to "dilute" the experience by voting for someone else.

From there they went to Hyannis Port to await the results. Thousands of reporters clogged the Hyannis National Guard Armory while Bobby and Teddy tossed a football around on the front lawn of the compound. That evening they watched the results on television. But not content to rely on TV coverage, the Kennedy camp had installed thirty phone lines on Joe Kennedy's sun porch. Each of the lines was connected to a crucial district. A tickertape machine clattered out up-to-the minute results as they were tabulated in each precinct.

"At first it looked as if we were going to win by a landslide," Salinger said. "But then the tide started turning and everything went to hell. It went right down to the wire." As the evening wore on, Jack appeared occasionally at the armory to chat with Salinger and members of the press, then returned to the compound.

At one point during the long wait, Jack dropped in on Larry Newman. Earlier during the campaign, when Lyndon and Lady Bird Johnson had visited the compound, Jack had brought LBJ over to meet his neighbor. "Jack liked to come over here just to get away from everybody and relax," said Newman, who like a surprising number of Jack's friends voted for Nixon that year. "Jack was a wonderful human. Don't get me wrong, I loved the guy," Newman explained. "But I just thought Nixon would make a better president."

On election night, according to Newman, JFK "sneaked in the

back door, sat down in my kitchen, and asked if I had any beer. He only drank Heineken—unless he was around potential voters and then he'd drink a domestic brand," Newman recalled. "Do you know what he talked about the day he was elected president? Girls. He drank beer and talked about women. I don't think it was out of disrespect for Jackie, I really don't," Newman said. "It was just the way he had been raised by Joe. Jack always had women all over him. None of us in Hyannis Port ever thought he'd get married. We just couldn't imagine it . . . Jack talked about women fifty percent of the time. It was by far his favorite subject."

"The longest night in history" was how Jackie later described the feeling of suspense as everyone awaited the outcome of the election. With the results still seesawing between Nixon and Kennedy at 3 A.M. the following morning, a wan Nixon appeared with a tearful Pat at his side. He allowed that the outcome appeared to be going in the Democrats' direction, but he did not officially concede. When Jack's supporters grumbled at this, JFK sprang to his former colleague's defense. "Why should he concede now? If I were him, I wouldn't."

At 4 A.M., Jack left to join Jackie in bed. "Wake me," he told Salinger, "if anything happens." Dave Powers was flabbergasted. "How will you be able to sleep?" he asked.

He shrugged. "Because it's too late to change another vote."

While they slept, LBJ worked his wonders in Texas, and Chicago's Mayor Richard Daley delivered Illinois, helping Kennedy squeak by Nixon.

That morning, Jack woke around 9 and was in the bathtub when Caroline came racing in to tell him he had won (a bit of information already imparted to him by Ted Sorensen). "Your daddy's upstairs," Maud Shaw had told Caroline. "You can call him 'Mr. President' now."

Jack put on a gray suit and a blue tie with red polka dots, then joined Jackie and Caroline for breakfast. However, at 10:30 that morning after the election, the outcome was uncertain. Minnesota and Illinois remained undecided and Jack held on to only the slimmest of leads. Jack sat glued to the television set for an hour, nervously twirling a pencil in his right hand. Salinger, Bobby, Ethel, Eunice, Teddy, Sargent Shriver, and a score of other family members and aides drifted in and out of the room. Jackie remained upstairs.

At last, they watched Nixon spokesman Herb Klein appear on television to congratulate the winner on his boss's behalf. Out of nearly 69 million votes cast, Jack won by only 118,550—fewer than one fifth of 1 percent. Jack went outside and, oblivious to his back pain, picked up Caroline and gave her a piggyback ride around the compound.

Seizing this historic moment, Lowe scrambled to pull all the Kennedys together for a family portrait. "Jack said fine, he'd do it if I could get everybody to cooperate," Lowe recalled. "But they were spread out all over the compound, and too excited about what had happened to focus on what I was asking them to do."

Lowe managed to get all the Kennedys together in the paneled living room. It marked the first time Joe, in self-imposed exile throughout the campaign, was seen with Jack in public. But Jackie was still nowhere to be found. When no one was looking, she had thrown on a coat and dashed out of the house for a solitary walk on the beach. "Through a window, I caught a glimpse of her rushing down to the sea," Lowe said. "That Wednesday morning when the rest of the family was jubilant and embracing each other and laughing it up, Jackie was deeply shaken. She was clearly in a state of shock. I felt sorry for her.

"At Jack's greatest moment of triumph—the moment they had all worked so hard for—Jackie suddenly seemed full of doubt. She definitely had ambivalent feelings about becoming first lady. She had always lived in a fairyland, in the role of the storybook princess. I'm not sure Jackie ever counted on being queen."

"It's okay," Jack told the photographer, "I'll go get her." He hurried down to the beach, put his arm around her, and brought her back to the house. Jackie changed upstairs into a red scoop-neck dress and a triple strand of pearls—almost identical to what Rose was wearing. At long last she materialized at the door. Jack walked over and gently took her arm. It was then that all the Kennedys—including the sisters who had taunted her and the indomitable Rose—got to their feet and gave Jackie a standing ovation.

―――

*Now my wife and I prepare for a new
administration, and a new baby.*

**JFK's victory speech,
November 9, 1960**

―――

I'm never there when she needs me.

**JFK on the plane to
Palm Beach upon learning
Jackie had begun hemorrhaging**

―――

"Okay, girls," Jack said to Jackie and her equally pregnant friend Tony Bradlee the day after the election. "You can take out the pillows now. We won." He told the Bradlees that after he took the oath of office, it would be best to address him in public as "Mr. President," though for now "Prez" would do. Jackie instructed her friends not to refer to her as the "first lady. It always reminds me of a saddle horse."

Even before Nixon officially conceded defeat through his spokesman, strange men in dark suits and fedoras seemed to be everywhere. "It was amazing," Salinger recalled. "One of the Secret Service guys I had never seen before stopped early that morning, took one look, and said, 'Oh, hello, Mr. Salinger,' and waved me through. They had evidently memorized all our faces, and what our jobs entailed as far as access to the President-elect."

The Secret Service faced one of its earliest tests later when Jack went with Chuck Spalding to see Gore Vidal's Broadway hit *The Best Man*. (The drama, which deals with deceit, duplicity, and behind-the-scenes double-dealing during a national convention, was also the first play Nixon saw after his defeat.) Jack, seated front row–center next to Spalding, periodically got up to shake hands with friends before the curtain went up, vanished down a back staircase during intermission, then—to the Secret Service agents' profound relief—magically reappeared.

From backstage left, Vidal watched the expression on Jack's face when in the course of the play the issue of one presidential candidate's checkered sexual past was raised. "Jack blinked with recognition and then glanced over quickly at Spalding," recalled Vidal. "I'm sure it took him completely by surprise."

Jack and Jackie arrived back in Georgetown that November to find that the Secret Service had already cordoned off the block around the N Street house. The press and crowds of onlookers were now a constant presence. Already hard at work putting together a cabinet, Jack accommodated the faithful whenever he could, periodically crossing the street in front of the house to shake hands.

One morning Mary Gallagher and Jackie were going over mail at their respective desks in the second-floor study when a roar went up from the crowd outside. Gallagher went to the window and saw the President-elect reaching out to shake the hands of people who had come to catch a glimpse of him. Gallagher invited Jackie to the window, but Jackie didn't budge. "Oh, Mary," she replied, never raising her head from her work.

Now that the election was over, Jackie might have expected that Jack could make more time for her and Caroline. But after she had risked her health and that of their unborn child to hit the campaign trail in New York, she still took a backseat to the demands of JFK's insatiable public—a public that she increasingly came to resent.

In fairness, the First Lady–elect did have demands of her own to contend with. To begin with, she had to cope with the flood of baby presents that had poured into the N Street house since the election. Among them were blankets and crocheted caps and coverlets, nearly all blue in obvious anticipation of a boy.

Jackie also took on the added pressure of a book deadline. Oddly, she later claimed to have no interest in writing about her time as first lady. "So many people, you know, hit the White House with their Dictaphone running," she said. "I never even kept a journal. I thought, I want to live my life, not record it."

But she did try, in the words of one publishing executive, to "head everyone else off at the pass" by publishing her memoirs *before* she entered the White House. "It was also," the executive added, "an opportunity Jackie was not about to pass up to make some money of her own"—a hundred and fifty thousand dollars for North American first serial rights alone, gladly paid by *Ladies' Home Journal.*

Family friend Mary Van Rensselaer Thayer was enlisted to work on the manuscript with Jackie. Thayer was credited as the sole author of *Jacqueline Bouvier Kennedy,* but the words were Jackie's, scrawled on yellow legal pads and passed along to anxious editors in New York. The book gave Jackie an opportunity to get her version of events on record first, and to perpetuate her grandfather Bouvier's fabricated family tree.

During the two and a half months between the election and inauguration, the Georgetown house served as home base for the youthful and energetic Kennedy transition team. Luminaries of every political stripe came to pay their respects, seek favors, or sometimes simply offer advice. Jack would call upstairs for Jackie to come down and meet McGeorge Bundy, or Robert McNamara, or Dean Rusk—and after keeping them all waiting a suitable amount of time, she would sweep into the room. She could not hold herself back when a special visitor arrived. Still in her robe, she leaned over the banister and waved down to an early-morning guest. "Hello, Mr. President," she called to a pleasantly surprised Harry Truman.

Frayed nerves soon became a problem in the Kennedy household. "I can't stand this chaos, Jack," Jackie finally said. "It's driving me crazy." Jack shot back, "Oh for God's sake, Jackie. All you have to worry about right now is your inaugural ball gown."

Alternating with the N Street house as "transition central" was the Palm Beach estate, where Jack spent the weeks immediately following the election relaxing by the pool and talking over his cabinet choices with his father. During this time Jack also paid a call on LBJ at his ranch in Texas. Jack even went along with Johnson on an early-morning deer hunt, but grudgingly. "I've got enough on my mind right now," he told O'Donnell, "without getting a guilt complex from shooting a poor dumb animal." After bagging his deer, Kennedy was disgusted when LBJ sent him the animal's head, stuffed and mounted. Ultimately, this sad trophy wound up hanging in the Fish Room of the White House, next to the nine-foot sailfish JFK hooked on his honeymoon.

Jack flew back to Georgetown to spend a quiet Thanksgiving with his wife and daughter; he planned to return to Palm Beach that night. Just three weeks from her due date, Jackie was under strict orders from her doctor not to leave the house. Understandably apprehensive as the date approached, she pleaded with her husband to stay in Washington until the baby arrived. "Why can't you stay here until I have the baby," she asked, "and then we can go down together."

But Jack refused. "For the first time Jack was really torn between Jackie and the job he was elected to do," their friend Bill Walton recalled. To Jack, the three weeks Jackie still had to wait "might as well have been six months to him. Caroline had arrived on time, and he saw no reason to think anything would be different this time around. He was not about to put everything on hold just because Jackie was a little nervous." Said another friend of the couple: "You couldn't really blame Jack. He had a country to run."

Immediately after Thanksgiving dinner, Jack departed for Palm Beach, leaving a wounded Jackie behind. An hour later, she was resting in her room when Maud Shaw heard her cry out. Shaw rushed to the room and found Jackie on the edge of the bed clutching her stomach. Blood stained the bedspread. Shaw called John Walsh, Jackie's obstetrician, and within minutes an ambulance was speeding her to Georgetown University Hospital.

Jack was in an upbeat mood aboard the *Caroline*, talking about his planned cabinet appointments, when word crackled over the radio. He was instantly gripped by fear, "stricken," O'Donnell recalled, "with remorse because he was not with his wife."

At the West Palm Beach airport, Jack contacted Dr. Walsh and was told Jackie was already being prepped for an emergency cesarean. The DC-6 press plane that trailed Kennedy's aircraft was actually capable of flying at much higher speeds than the *Caroline*, so Jack commandeered it and flew straight back to Washington. En route, the grim-faced President-elect clamped the cockpit headphones on and waited for any news.

A little after 1 A.M., JFK removed the headphones and smiled for the first time in hours. Jackie, he had just been told, had given birth by cesarean section to a six-pound three-ounce boy. Both mother and child were healthy and resting comfortably. When Salinger announced the news over the loudspeaker, the reporters cheered. Jack, mightily relieved, took a deep bow.

As soon as she came out from under the anesthesia, Jackie, still very much in pain, demanded to see her son. Despite the glowing reports, both mother and child remained in guarded condition. John Fitzgerald Kennedy, Jr. spent his first six days of life in an incubator. His mother took months to fully recover from her ordeal, suffering a near-fatal setback along the way.

It did not help that the press, so long smitten with the handsome Mr. Kennedy, now shifted its focus to his beautiful wife and their growing brood. "I feel as though I've turned into a piece of public property," Jackie said. "It's really frightening to lose your anonymity at thirty-one." Even as the Kennedy family's private nurse Luella Hennessey wheeled Jackie in to see her son in his incubator, a photographer leapt out of a storage closet and began shooting. A half-dozen flashbulbs popped before Secret Service agents, caught completely off guard, finally wrestled him to the ground and ripped the film out of his camera.

Determined to make up for his absence in her time of need, Jack visited his wife and their newborn son in the hospital three times a day—in the morning, at lunch, and again after dinner. Accompanying her father everywhere, the adorable and precocious Caroline was the new darling of the press. As her father met with those who would occupy the most powerful positions in government, she dashed up and down the stairs at breakneck speed, slid down banisters, and made faces behind the backs of correspondents.

When John Jr. was a week old, Jack and Caroline arrived at the hospital for the baby's christening. As Jack wheeled Jackie and the baby toward the hospital chapel, they spotted press photographers lying in wait at the far end of the hall. "Oh God," Jackie said, "don't stop, Jack. Just keep going." Not wanting to disappoint the press or the American public, Jack paused for a moment, allowing a few photos to be taken of the infant wearing his father's forty-three-year-old baptismal gown before they moved on.

While still recuperating in the hospital, Jackie summoned her old acquaintance Oleg Cassini to talk over plans for her wardrobe. When he walked into her hospital room with twenty designs under his arm, he was startled to see "sketches all around her, by the best American designers—Norell, Sarmi, Andreas of New York's Bergdorf Goodman—the very best of their collections, very pretty dresses. But I was proposing something much more elaborate."

Cassini wanted to create a distinctive look for the new First Lady, one based on her own regal style. "When I thought of Jackie, I saw a hieroglyphic figure: the head in profile, broad shoulders, slim torso, narrow hips, long neck, and regal carriage. With the sphinxlike quality of her eyes, she was a classic Egyptian princess. Nefertiti."

Cassini opened his sketchbook to reveal a simple white full-length evening dress that he told her would be perfect for the inaugural ball. "Absolutely right!" she agreed. What might have influenced her even more was the designer's vision of her as a symbol of what was already being called the New Frontier. "I talked about history," he recalled, "the message her clothes could send—simple, youthful but magisterial elegance—and how she would reinforce the message of her husband's administration through her appearance. You have an opportunity here," he told her, "for an American Versailles."

There was a small problem: Jackie had already ordered an inaugural dress from Bergdorf Goodman. So she worked out a compromise: Cassini would design the clothes and Bergdorf's would make them.

Jackie's choice of Cassini pleased her husband. Despite the fact that they had both once loved the same woman, Gene Tierney, Jack enjoyed the suave Russo-American designer's company. "He was a playboy like me," Cassini said, "but even more because he was wealthier than me."

Jack was also grateful to Cassini for contributing fifteen hundred dollars to his campaign back when he was battling Hubert Humphrey in West Virginia. "One of the great satisfactions of running for president," Jack told Cassini, "is that I found out that all the people who supposedly were for me, my dear friends, disappeared. *Nobody* helped me, nobody voted for me. Just you and a few others."

"He didn't need my check, of course," Cassini said. "To him it was symbolic." Long after taking office, Jack fumed about the "good friends"—including various Auchinclosses, Bouviers, and the Park Avenue crowd, who quietly backed Nixon. Why? "Simple jealousy," Cassini said with a shrug.

The diametric opposite of Jackie—with the exception of a similarly steely will—the incumbent First Lady was more dowager than empress. When Mamie Eisenhower invited her successor for a White House tour the same day Jackie was released from the hospital, she wanted to decline the invitation. "I don't want to go, Jack. I'm not up to it," she told her husband, but he insisted. "For God's sake, Jackie" frequently prefaced Jack's remarks ("I can hear him saying it now," Lowe said), and this was a case in point. "For God's sake, Jackie," Jack said, "you don't want to insult Mrs. Eisenhower. You've got to go."

The President-elect's own powerful sense of duty was legendary. Jackie knew her husband had ignored pain, discomfort, and life-threatening illness to fulfill his obligations. She did not want to disappoint him. To Luella Hennessey's horror, Jackie obeyed her husband and accepted Mamie's invitation. "If you get on your feet now, Mrs. Kennedy," Luella warned her, "you might die." Luella begged her not to go.

But Jackie did, having Dr. Walsh call ahead to the White House and ask that a wheelchair be waiting for her when she got there. When she got word of this, Mamie was not amused. "Oh dear," Mrs. Eisenhower said, scowling to White House Chief usher J. B. West. Mamie had wanted to show Jackie around the house herself. West recalled that the very thought of the imperious Mamie Eisenhower pushing the wife of a political enemy through the corridors of the West Wing was "too much for me."

"I'll tell you what," said Mamie, "we'll get a wheelchair and put it behind a door somewhere, out of sight. It will be available *if she asks for it.*

West was impressed with how pale and drawn Jackie looked when she arrived at the White House at 11:30 that morning. The wheelchair was just out of sight, but Jackie later admitted that she was "too scared of Mrs. Eisenhower to ask." For the next two hours they trekked through every room in the White House. Jackie nearly passed out several times, but managed to steady herself. Her hostess showed no sign of concern as they marched up and down staircases and later posed together for photographers.

After they emerged at precisely 1:30 as planned, Mrs. Eisenhower zoomed off to her weekly card game. Jackie climbed back into her three-year-old station wagon, exhausted and in severe pain.

On December 9, the *Caroline* left for Palm Beach with the First Family–elect aboard. Jack chatted excitedly with his aides about his plans for the administration, spewing cigar smoke around the baby's bassinet. Although Jackie had encouraged her husband's cigar smoking to mask the odor of her cigarettes, she finally put a halt to the conversation and ordered her husband to take his cigar to the other end of the cabin.

Still feeling the effects of her long march with Mamie Eisenhower through the corridors of the Executive Mansion, Jackie spent the next two weeks in bed. At the same time, the baby took a dramatic turn for the worse. "There was, thank God, this brilliant pediatrician in Palm Beach who really saved his life as he was going downhill," she later said.

Two days later, Richard P. Pavlick was parked outside Joe Kennedy's Palm Beach estate waiting for the President-elect to emerge and head for Sunday mass at St. Edward's Church. Pavlick, a would-be suicide bomber armed with seven sticks of dynamite in his car, planned to crash into Jack's car as he left the house.

But before Pavlick could step on the accelerator, Jackie and Caroline came out to say good-bye. Luella Hennessey also appeared, carrying John Jr. Touched, Pavlick did not go through with his grisly plan. Later claiming to police that he "did not wish to harm Mrs. Kennedy or the children," Pavlick said he still planned to "get" Jack "at the church or some other place." A few days later a drunk-driving arrest led police to uncover his assassination plan. Pavlick was charged with attempted murder and eventually sent to prison.

When told of the plot, Jack was fascinated. But he was "not a bit upset or worried by the ugly incident." Jackie, on the other hand, was horrified. "We're nothing but sitting ducks," she said, "in a shooting gallery."

With only a month to go before taking office, Jack could not afford the luxury of worrying. The pace he had set for himself in Georgetown continued beneath Florida's swaying palms. Jackie, still convalescing, once again found the circumstances barely tolerable. "It was so crowded that I could be in the bathroom, in the tub," Jackie went on, "and then find that Pierre Salinger was holding a press conference in my bedroom."

Adding to the confusion, Caroline kept upstaging her father at press conferences. At one briefing she careened between reporters' legs on her tricycle; at another, she hobbled around in her pajamas and Mommy's size ten and a half stiletto heels.

To avoid the chaos, Jackie stayed in bed much of the time,

refusing to join the rest of the boisterous Kennedy clan downstairs for meals. "I couldn't hold food down," she explained.

Throughout it all Jack still managed several rounds of golf (during one of these his ball accidentally struck a Secret Service agent in the head), his mandatory daily swim and nude sunbathing in a walled-off area near the pool called the "Bull Pen." (It was here in the Bull Pen that Joe, nude except for a broad-brimmed hat, ran his business empire by phone.)

Jack also spent time with his old flame Florence Pritchett, now the wife of U.S. Ambassador to Cuba Earl Smith. "He liked to trick the Secret Service guys," Don Marvin said. "He'd duck out the back and stroll down the beach to the Smiths, where he'd spend the afternoon alone with Flo."

Jackie was perhaps too distracted to notice that her husband was still "girling," as he liked to call it. The same day she was told that a man had almost blown up her entire family, Jackie dashed off a lengthy letter to Cassini. Charmingly phrased and Machiavellian in its studied diplomacy, the letter opened with a discussion about the compromise she had worked out between Cassini and Bergdorf Goodman.

> Thank heavens all the furor is over—and done without breaking my word to you or Bergdorf's. Now I know how poor Jack feels when he has told 3 people they can be Secy. of State.
>
> But I do think it turned out nicely for you—no?—and you were charming & gallant & a gentleman & everything you should be and are.

Jackie wrote that the rest of the letter was a

> series of incoherent thoughts that I must get settled so I can spend these next weeks truly recuperating & not have to think about details, otherwise I will be a wreck & not strong enough to do everything I have to do.

1) I wired Bergdorf to send you my measurements so you can go ahead with clothes.

2) For every evening dress I order from you, will you please send a color swatch to a) Mario—at Eugenia of Florence to have evening shoes made—State if shoes should be satin or faille—if necessary send material to make shoes—& tell him to hurry. b) to KORET—some man there makes me matching evening bags, simple envelopes or squares. Send him same material as dress— If you can do these two things you don't know the headaches it will save me. c) also to Marita—Custom Hats at Bergdorf Goodman's—send color swatch. She does my hats and gloves—tell her what color for each.

3) Diana Vreeland will call you about . . .

Jackie went on to say that she wanted Cassini to dress her "as if Jack were President of FRANCE . . . ARE YOU SURE YOU'RE UP TO IT, OLEG? Please say yes." Jackie wrote that she could not devote any more of her time to wardrobe issues: "I will never see my children or do the million things I'll have to do."

Alluding to the charges made during the campaign that she spent thirty thousand dollars a year on clothes and her flip retort about sable underwear, Jackie wrote, "I refuse to have Jack's administration plagued by fashion stories of a sensational nature . . . I don't want to seem to be buying too much."

She also wanted Oleg to "make sure no one has exactly the same dress as I do . . . I want all mine to be original and no fat little women hopping around in the same gown."

Finally, Jackie ended the list of instructions with "some tiny last things to say to you."

1) Forgive me for not coming to you from the very beginning. I am so happy now.

2) Protect me—as I seem so mercilessly exposed & don't know how to cope with it (I read tonight I dye my hair because it is mousy gray!).

3) Be efficient—by getting everything on time and relieving me of worry about detail.

4) Plan to stay for dinner every time you come to D.C. with sketches—& amuse the President & his wife in that dreary *Maison Blanche*—& be discreet about us—though I don't have to tell you that—you have too much tact to be any other way.

5) I always thought if Jack & I went on an official trip to France I would secretly get Givenchy to design my clothes so I wouldn't be ashamed—but now I know I won't have to—yours will be so beautiful—that is *le plus grand* compliment I can give you—as a designer anyway!

XO, Jackie

In less than a week, Cassini had assembled a team to carry out the new First Lady's unambiguous orders. He had three separate mannequins, and a live model, with Jackie's measurements (35½–26–38) on hand at all times. Although Jack continued to erupt like Vesuvius over Jackie's expenditures, Joe, as always, funded the entire enterprise. "Don't bother the kids with the bills," Joe told Cassini. "Just send them to me. I'll take care of it."

Before Jackie wore one Cassini-designed dress in her new capacity as first lady, *Life* was already gushing about her impact on American fashion. "Fashion ads twinkle more mischievously with Jackie's unmistakable wide eyes," the story read. "Her bouffant hairdo is becoming a by-word in beauty salons. All in all, the shy, beautiful First Lady's fashion followers are building up quite a bandwagon . . . despite herself, she is becoming the nation's No. 1 fashion influence."

Before she fled to Palm Beach, Jackie had hired her old friend Letitia Baldrige, who was then working as publicity director for Tiffany, to be her social secretary. A friend of such Washington "newshens" as Maxine Cheshire of *The Washington Post* and Betty Beale of the *Washington Star,* Baldrige got into trouble immediately when asked by the press what she really thought of the incoming First Lady. "She is a woman who has everything," Tish responded, "including the next President of the United States."

Yet it was Tish who got an earful from Jackie after the house tour with Mamie Eisenhower. Jackie thought the Executive Mansion looked like "a Statler Hotel that had been decorated by a wholesale furniture store during a January clearance."

"Oh my God," she told another friend. "It's the worst place in the world. So cold and dreary. A dungeon like the Lubyanka. It looks like it's been furnished by discount stores. I've never seen anything like it. I can't bear the thought of moving in. I hate it, hate it, hate it."

But Jackie had made her decision to put her stamp on the White House long before her tour with Mamie. "The minute I knew that Jack was going to run for president," she confessed to Hugh Sidey, "I knew the White House would be one of my main projects if he won."

In Palm Beach, Jackie studied blueprints and photographs of the White House until she had virtually memorized every room down to the most minute detail. On January 16, just four days before the inauguration, Jackie returned to Georgetown alone. Caroline and the baby remained behind in Palm Beach with their father, Maud Shaw, and Mrs. Philips, the new nanny hired to take care of John Jr.

No sooner did she arrive at the N Street house than she met with Sister Parish, who had decorated her house at the Hyannis Port compound and the Georgetown house. They spread out the carpet swatches, wallpaper, and paint samples on the dining room table and got to work.

"All these people come to see the White House," Jackie later explained of her desire to transform the mansion, "and they see practically nothing that dates back before 1948. Every boy who comes here should see things that develop his sense of history. For the girls, the house should look beautiful and lived-in. They should see what a fire in the fireplace and pretty flowers can do for a house."

She told Parish that "everything in the White House must have a reason for being there. It would be sacrilege merely to 'redecorate' it—a word I hate. It must be restored—and that has nothing to do with decoration. That is a question of scholarship."

Just as she had instructed Cassini on how to deal with her clothes, Jackie assigned Parish the task of coming up with names for a committee to guide the restoration effort. Ultimately, dozens of experts from art historians to horticulturists were involved in the Herculean effort. Jackie oversaw them all.

As the moving cartons began piling up, the N Street house began to look like any other on moving day. Between deciding what was going into storage and what was going to the White House—not to mention wardrobe fittings and the imminent arrival of her hairdresser Jean-Louis—Jackie was overwhelmed. Add to that the presence of Jack's transition team, and for the first time Jackie found it impossible to cope.

"If you think I'm going to move to the White House without any preparation, you're crazy," Jackie told Jack, "and if you stay in this house I cannot move. You have to get out!"

On January 18, the Kennedys' longtime friend and Georgetown neighbor Bill Walton received a call from Alice Roosevelt Longworth. "Say, you're having a visitor tomorrow."

"What do you mean?" Walton asked.

"You don't know?"

"No," Walton answered, incredulous. "I don't know."

"Ha, ha, ha. Well, they've just announced it on TV," Mrs. Longworth said. "He's moving into your house tomorrow." Before he could call the President-elect, the Secret Service was knocking at Walton's front door. "If Jackie said he had to go, then he went. Jack always did what he had to do to make sure she was happy. It made him crazy when she wasn't."

A little before noon the next day, inauguration eve, the first wispy flakes began to drift down on the capital. By nightfall, Washington was in the grip of a full-fledged blizzard. It would be a white inauguration, and the coldest in history.

That night, as snow piled waist-high and city traffic ground to a halt, Frank Sinatra was understandably in a state of panic. All eyes were on him as producer of the star-studded Inaugural Gala, a hundred-dollar-a-plate black tie fund-raiser aimed at raising two million dollars to erase the Democrats' campaign debt.

On N Street, Jack and Jackie behaved in many ways like any young parents getting ready for a night out. By 7:30, Jack was already dressed in his tuxedo and waiting for Jackie, who fussed about her hair and worried about what—if any—jewelry to wear. Clad from collar to toe in shimmering white satin, she was leaning toward wearing no jewelry at all. Jack, on the other hand, wanted her to don an emerald necklace and matching earrings.

Finally, Jack brought in Mary Gallagher as a tiebreaker. Without knowing what either Jack or Jackie thought, she watched the future First Lady model the dress without the jewelry, then with. Gallagher voted for wearing the jewelry, unknowingly siding with the President-elect. Annoyed that Jack was questioning her judgment on such matters, Jackie wore the emeralds anyway.

They then tucked Caroline into bed, and emerged from the N Street house beneath umbrellas held aloft by Secret Service agents. Flashbulbs popped as she lifted the hem of her gown and tiptoed to the waiting Chrysler limousine. After dining at the home of *Washington Post* owner Philip Graham and his wife, Katharine, they were driven to a concert at Convention Hall. Even in the snow, people lined the streets to catch a glimpse of their handsome new president and his glamorous wife. Jack leaned forward and ordered the driver to turn on the lights in the car "so they can see Jackie."

They made it to Convention Hall on time, but many of the musicians were not so fortunate; the concert began with only forty members of the National Symphony in their chairs. From Convention Hall, the First Couple headed for the National Armory. Broadway producer Leland Hayward closed two of his hit shows— *Gypsy* and *Becket*—for one night so Ethel Merman could sing "Everything's Coming Up Roses" and *Becket* stars Laurence Olivier and Anthony Quinn could give dramatic readings. Joey Bishop was master of ceremonies, joined by fellow comics Milton Berle and Alan King. Also appearing that night were Nat King Cole, Harry Belafonte, Ella Fitzgerald, Bette Davis, Juliet Prowse, Shirley MacLaine, Tony Curtis, and Janet Leigh, just to name a few.

"It was a fearful evening," said Leonard Bernstein, who conducted a fanfare he had written especially for the occasion, as well as the "Hallelujah Chorus." "I was stuck in Bette Davis's car. There were about six of us all being asphyxiated in this limousine that couldn't move. Cars had run out of gas and were blocking the streets, and this blizzard kept falling. Somebody in our car knew somebody who lived nearby and we went up there to use the phone. We called the White House to come and rescue us and get us to the armory so we could perform, but all their cars were out picking up other people who had been stranded."

Eventually, police cars picked up Bernstein and Davis and drove to the armory on the sidewalks. "Oh, it was *ghastly*," Bernstein said, trying to capture the mood that night. "We drove between trees on the sidewalk in this insane police car back to the armory, unwashed, unchanged, un-black-tied, and everybody was in kind of a special blizzard festival mood where everybody feels helpless anyway and perfect strangers embrace and sing and jump in the snow . . ."

The armory was only half full when Jack and Jackie arrived shortly before 11—two hours after the show had been scheduled to begin. Everyone jumped to their feet, applauding wildly as Jack and Jackie took their seats, and then the President-elect stood to acknowledge the ovation.

"Jack, as usual, drove the Secret Service guys crazy," said Lowe, who, because he had not been able to get to his hotel, covered the event wearing a sports jacket and a bow tie. "He'd suddenly jump up and then run down an aisle to shake hands with a friend, or duck down the back stairs."

Amazingly, the show itself came off without a glitch. Among the high points: Prowse's rollicking dance number, Academy

Award–winner Frederick March's reading of Lincoln's Inaugural Address, and Frank Sinatra singing his patriotic ballad "The House I Live In," which reduced Jackie to tears. At intermission, she quietly ducked out, returning to Georgetown to collapse in her bedroom.

As the gala drew to a close around 2 A.M., Jack stood to address the capacity crowd of ten thousand. "I know we're all indebted to a great friend—Frank Sinatra," Jack said. "Long before he could sing, he used to pol a Democratic precinct back in New Jersey. That precinct has grown to cover a country . . ." He also thanked his Brother-in-Lawford. "I want Frank and Peter to know we're all indebted to them, and proud to have them with us."

While Jackie spent her last night in the N Street house ("My sweet little house [that] leans slightly to one side") alone, Jack showed no sign of slowing down. He went on to a party thrown by his father at Paul Young's Restaurant. At one point, Jack pulled Red Fay into a pantry and whispered, "Have you ever seen so many attractive people in one room? I'll tell you, Dad knows how to give a party. And here's the paradox of the whole thing. Here I'm President-elect of the United States and if I dance or talk to one girl for more than thirty seconds, somebody tries to read something into it, but here Grand Old Lovable is conducting one of the smoothest operations I've ever seen and is going unnoticed." At 6 A.M., Jack left, arriving on N Street just before dawn.

Three hours later Jack, who had already attended early-morning mass alone, was in the library of the Georgetown house. While Jackie breakfasted in bed, he practiced his inaugural address.

This time, they could not afford to be late. Jack was to assume the mantle of the presidency precisely at noon. He pleaded with Jackie to be on time, but soon hit a snag of his own. In Palm Beach, he had fretted about how puffy his face had become in recent weeks. Grabbing his cheek, he said, "If I don't lose some of this weight, the inauguration is off!" Now he could not manage to fasten the collar of his dress shirt. After several attempts, he dispatched Mugsy to borrow a shirt from his father.

Once again, Jackie kept him waiting as she dressed. She finally appeared, looking like a cross between a schoolgirl and Russian princess in a fawn-colored wool coat with a sable collar and matching muff. Crowning her trademark bouffant coiffure was another fashion item that would forever be associated with Jacqueline Kennedy—a pillbox hat, in beige to match the coat.

The President-elect, in a cutaway and striped pants, cooled his heels in the foyer a while longer while she fetched a compact from her purse and did a last-minute touch-up. "Please hurry," he called to her. No response. Jackie did not like being rushed. "Come *on,* Jackie. For God's sake!" he shouted, the anger in his voice growing. This time it worked.

JFK's preference for going hatless was legendary—the industry never recovered after he took office—but he popped the top hat on anyway. "What do you think?" he asked her.

"Just hold it in your hand, Jack," she said. "That will be fine."

At 11 A.M., Speaker of the House Sam Rayburn and inauguration chairman John Sparkman arrived at the N Street house in the presidential bubbletop Lincoln limousine to escort the Kennedys to the White House. There they were also greeted by the Johnsons and the Nixons. After coffee and strained conversation, the soon-to-be former and future presidents rode together to the swearing-in at the Capitol.

Mamie and Jackie followed in a second car. "Ike looks just like Paddy the Irishman in his top hat," Mrs. Eisenhower joked before suddenly remembering the ethnic background of the man who was about to be sworn into office. The women remained silent for the rest of the trip.

Huddled against the bone-chilling twenty-degree temperatures, spectators watched the eighty-six-year-old poet Robert Frost struggle in the blinding light to read a poem he'd written for the occasion. Jackie, seated between President Eisenhower and Lady Bird, looked on in anguish as Lyndon Johnson gallantly tried to shield Frost's pages with his top hat, but finally the poet gave up the script and recited another of his works from memory. When he was finished, Jack, having shed his overcoat, leapt to his feet and escorted his fellow Yankee back to his seat.

At noon Jackie stood, gazing at Jack in practiced wonder as he placed his hand on the Fitzgerald family bible and took the oath of office from Chief Justice Earl Warren. At that moment forty-three-year-old Jack became the youngest elected president in U.S. history, succeeding the oldest, seventy-year-old Ike. Jack was also the first president born in the twentieth century, and the first Roman Catholic to hold the office.

Jack's inaugural address, with its enduring "Ask not what your country can do for you" message, stirred the nation. But Jackie had no opportunity to congratulate her husband on the dais. He did not follow tradition by kissing his wife immediately after taking the oath. And as soon as Marian Anderson closed the ceremonies with a rousing rendition of the national anthem, Jack—overcome with the excitement of the moment—bounded up the red-carpeted stairs and off the platform, inexplicably leaving Jackie behind.

Moments later, they met in the Capitol rotunda. "I was so proud of Jack," she said. "There was so much I wanted to say. But I could scarcely embrace him in front of all those people, so I remember I just put my hand on his cheek and said, 'Jack, you were so wonderful!' And he was smiling in the most touching and most vulnerable way. He looked so happy."

From there they were hustled off to an inaugural luncheon at the Capitol Building's old Supreme Court chamber. The atmosphere was congenial, even celebratory—in sharp contrast to the early "luncheon" that had been held at the Mayflower Hotel for members of the Kennedy, Fitzgerald, Bouvier, Lee, and Auchincloss families before the swearing-in.

When Joe Kennedy, who was paying for the luncheon, caught a glimpse of the gargantuan buffet table heaped with shrimp, caviar, and lobster—and the open bar—he called Tish Baldrige aside. "Who are all these people?" he demanded of Baldrige, who had arranged the affair.

"Your family, Mr. Ambassador," she replied.

"They are *not*," he insisted. "Just who the hell are all these freeloaders? I want to know exactly why you asked them." Joe then grilled a dozen or so of the assembled guests before apologizing to Baldrige. "They *are* all family," he conceded. "And it's the last time we get 'em all together, too, if I have anything to say about it."

From their luncheon in the Capitol, Jack and Jackie, despite the arctic conditions, led off the inaugural parade, driving in an open car as far as the White House. Before proceeding to the reviewing stand, Jack could not resist trying out his desk in the Oval Office, swiveling in the chair and opening and closing the drawers. When the new President finally joined LBJ and the other dignitaries on the inaugural stand, Joe Kennedy did something he had never done before: He doffed his hat and stood out of deference to his son. Jack, deeply touched by the gesture, shook his father's hand and motioned for him to sit down.

Parading up Pennsylvania Avenue, units of the armed forces, marching bands, and floats all passed in review before the new commander in chief. There was another emotional moment when a float carrying his old PT-109 crew stopped in front of the reviewing stand. As they saluted their old comrade, he waved and hooted back.

Tired, freezing, and facing a long night ahead, Jackie excused herself after an hour. "I'm exhausted, Jack," she said. "I'll see you at home." The President nodded. Clearly intent on not missing a single magical moment, he remained in the cold for the entire three-and-a-half-hour parade.

"Home" for the Kennedys was now 1600 Pennsylvania Avenue. While painters and carpenters put the finishing touches on John Jr.'s nursery and a newly renovated family dining room, Jackie moved into the Queen's Room (so named because five queens had slept there) on the second floor. Jack, meantime, would sleep across the East Hall in the Lincoln Bedroom.

In addition to Tish Baldrige, Jackie was joined that first day in the White House by Pam Turnure. Jack had told Pierre Salinger, now White House press secretary, to "put in Pam and tell her what to do." That meant appointing Kennedy's on-again, off-again mistress as the First Lady's press secretary. "What in the world," Jackie asked chief usher J. B. West, "do I want a press secretary for?"

Strictly for public consumption, Jackie wrote the twenty-three-year-old Turnure, who had no journalism experience, a flowery welcome-aboard letter: "I'm so *glad* you are doing it, the more I think of it—for this very reason that you haven't had previous press experience—but you have sense and good taste enough not to panic, and to say the right thing."

At the very least, Jackie already suspected that Turnure and her husband were still being intimate. "The only indication I ever had that Jackie knew about all of Jack's women," Betty Spalding said, "was when they were in the White House and she asked me if I knew if he was having an affair with Pamela Turnure. I said I didn't know, and even if I did I wouldn't tell her." Spalding speculated that what bothered Jackie more than the possibility of Jack having an affair was the fact that she had to see Turnure daily.

That afternoon, while Jackie rested upstairs, several busloads of family members arrived for a reception in the State Dining Room. Rose, Janet, and Peter Lawford mingled, but the various tribes expressed little interest in interacting. The atmosphere grew more and more strained; all eyes were trained on the doorway as everyone waited for the First Lady to make her entrance.

They were still waiting two hours later when Jack arrived fresh from the parade, plunging into the crowd with smiles and handshakes. He looked around the room before asking, "Where's Jackie?"

"Upstairs, resting," someone replied.

Jack's puzzled look quickly gave way to one of resignation. Janet went upstairs to try to coax her down. "I can't," Jackie replied from her bed. "I just can't." Around 8 P.M., guests began trickling out the door without ever having seen their famous relative. Reactions ranged from disappointment to anger. It seemed unconscionably rude for Jackie to snub her family in such an offhand manner. Surely she could have made the briefest appearance.

No one knew that she had nearly died after her cesarean, or that her recovery had been dealt a major setback by Mamie's grueling White House tour. She did not have Jack's natural reserves of energy, nor did she receive the daily doses of cortisone that at times gave Jack almost superhuman stamina. Facing another long and demanding night—she was determined to look nothing less than regal—Jackie had to set her priorities. Her aunts, uncles, nephews, nieces, and cousins—most of whom she had not seen in years—were not among them.

Jackie was deeply concerned about her sister, Lee, who was in bed in London, too ill to attend the inauguration. In an odd twist of fate, Lee had also been expecting a child in November. But Lee's daughter, Anna Christina, was born three months early, and struggled against all odds to survive in an incubator. Unable to even hold her child, Lee had suffered bouts of severe postpartum depression and anxiety over Anna Christina's delicate condition. Lee's latest relapse, coming at a time when Jackie was still coping with the effects of John Jr.'s birth, only added to a growing sense of helplessness. Jackie decided there was only one way she could possibly fulfill her obligations to Jack, and that was to husband her strength.

"Darling, you've never looked lovelier. Your dress is beautiful," the President said when she finally appeared wearing a white silk crepe gown with a bodice embroidered in silver thread. Over this was a sweeping, floor-length cape with a high mandarin collar. She wore long white opera gloves, and diamond pendant earrings borrowed from Tiffany. Jackie suddenly seemed energized, helped along by a Dexedrine pill she had taken moments earlier.

With Lyndon and Lady Bird in tow, they arrived at the May-flower for the first of the five inaugural balls. A gasp went up from the crowd when they made their entrance to the strains of "Hail to the Chief." Tonight, the men were in white tie and tails. "If men only knew how good they look in their white tie and tails," Jackie told Tish Baldrige, "they'd wear them every night of their lives."

From there, they went to another ball at the Statler Hilton, where Jack ducked out of the presidential box to look in on a star-filled party being thrown by Frank Sinatra. There he saw Angie Dickinson, the striking blond twenty-eight-year-old actress he had allegedly skinny-dipped with at the Lawfords' the night of his nomination. With his wife, Anita, in Europe, Red Fay had unhes-itatingly agreed to be Dickinson's escort for the evening.

"From the moment I met him I was hooked, like everybody else," Dickinson has said of their relationship. "He was the killer type, a devastatingly handsome, charming man—the kind your mother hoped you wouldn't marry." When asked what it was like to have sex with the President, Dickinson allegedly replied: "It was the most exciting seven minutes of my life."

A half hour later, Jack sheepishly slid back into his seat in the presidential box with *The Washington Post* tucked under his arm "as if," Kenny O'Donnell recalled, "he had just gone outside to pick up the newspaper. His knowing wife gave him a rather chilly look."

Their next stop was the largest of the balls, held at the cav-ernous, two-and-a-half-acre Washington armory. The throng broke into applause when Jackie was conducted to her seat. Throughout the evening, all eyes were fixed on the presidential box in a sort of bizarre staring match. Jackie, flanked by her hus-band and LBJ, complained that few people seemed to be dancing. "Just a bunch of people milling around like mesmerized cattle," she observed. Jack disagreed. "I think this is an ideal way to spend an evening," he told the crowd. "You looking at us and we looking at you."

At midnight Jackie began to wilt. "I just crumpled," she later said. "All my strength was finally gone." She made her apologies, and told Jack to go on to the remaining two balls.

Her inexhaustible spouse did not have to be told. After Jackie went home, Jack hooked up again with Red Fay and Angie Dickinson. When he invited them to tag along as he party-hopped, Fay asked if the rest of their foursome—actress Kim Novak and architect Fernando Parra—could join the party. At that point, something clicked. "I can just see the papers tomorrow," Jack told his old war buddy. "The new President concludes his first day speeding into the night with Kim Novak and Angie Dickinson while his wife recuperates from the birth of their first son." With a tone of resignation, he added, "Well, Redhead, for a moment I almost forgot I was President of the United States. It has its advantages and its restrictions, and this is one of the restrictions. Good night."

As his car pulled away from the armory, Kennedy spotted an old friend who had campaigned for him when he first ran for Congress in 1946. At the President's request, he sang a few bars of "Danny Boy." Jack thanked him and, beaming, headed off to the next event. After stopping in on the fifth and last ball, Jack dropped in on a small party at the Georgetown home of Joe Alsop at 2 A.M. and stayed for an hour and a half. "The President was hungry," the columnist recalled, failing to mention that several attractive young women were also in attendance. "So I fed him terrapin."

After the Alsop party, Jack went home to the White House. With Jackie asleep in the Queen's Room across the hall, the new President crawled into Abraham Lincoln's enormous, ornately carved rosewood bed and finally succumbed to sleep.

Less than five hours later, President Kennedy was behind his desk in the Oval Office presiding over a staff meeting. It was then that Jacques Lowe, who had been summoned to record the event, noticed for the first time how much Jack had aged just in the past few months. "He could almost have passed for a college kid when

I first met him just a few years before," Lowe said, "but now he suddenly looked like the middle-aged man that he was. There were lines in his face, his face was fuller, still very handsome but more substantial. Now that he was the leader of the free world, he looked the part."

Jackie needed the weekend to recuperate, but on Monday she attacked her job with similar zeal. Wearing jodhpurs, a white shirt, and riding boots, she sat on the edge of her desk and interviewed all the members of the household staff in groups of three. The staff was shocked to see the famous fashion plate so casually dressed, and with her usually meticulously coiffed hair, in the words of one, "flying in every direction."

But this was the Jackie behind closed doors at the White House. She never wore a dress unless she had company, preferring to knock around in pants and a blouse or sweater. More often than not, she bounded into a room unannounced, kicked off her shoes, and plopped on the floor.

This did not mean, however, that Jackie invited familiarity. From anyone. "She was famous for her elusiveness, her shifting moods," Cassini said. "She might be very warm one day and freeze you out the next; she did this to everyone, even to her closest friends."

To J. B. West, who served every president from Franklin Roosevelt to Richard Nixon, Jackie was "the most complex personality" of all the first ladies he had known. "In public, she was elegant, aloof, dignified, and regal. In private, she was casual, impish, and irreverent. She had a will of iron, with more determination than anyone I have ever met." There was an invisible line over which one dared not cross, but the line, as Jack knew all too well, shifted constantly.

"The Kennedy buildup goes on," wrote longtime Kennedy champion James MacGregor Burns. "The adjectives tumble over one another. He is not only the handsomest, the best-dressed, the most articulate, and graceful as a gazelle. He is omniscient; he swallows and digests whole books in minutes; he confounds experts with his superior knowledge of their field. He is omnipotent."

All of which made Burns and most other Kennedy fans nervous. "The buildup is too indiscriminate. The buildup will not last. The public can be cruel, and, so can the press. Americans build their triumphal arches out of brick, so as to have missiles handy when their heroes have fallen." But, as *Time* pointed out in its issue hitting the newsstands on April 15, 1961, Jack and Jackie were both "plainly unbothered" as they "lit up front pages and the television screens with their tireless activities."

Two days later, on April 17, Jack was dealt his first major foreign policy defeat when twelve hundred Cuban exiles launched their abortive invasion of Cuba. The Bay of Pigs fiasco shook his confidence in his advisors and in his own judgment. Yet it paled in comparison to the unprecedented series of domestic and foreign policy crises that would rock the Republic to its foundations and bring the world to the brink of nuclear war.

While Jack coped with weighty affairs of state, Jackie embarked on the tasks she had chosen for herself: to make the White House "so grand De Gaulle would be ashamed of Versailles in comparison"; to set a standard of beauty and culture that would inspire future generations, and above all else, to make a home for her husband and young children. In these, she would succeed spectacularly.

———

When they got to the White House,
they fell in love all over again.

Oleg Cassini

———

Jackie loved him. Jack loved her.
Maybe for different reasons . . .

Jacques Lowe,
JFK's personal photographer
and friend

———

She went through so much with him,
and still she decided to stand by her man.
I can't think of a better definition
of love than that.

Letitia Baldrige

———

9

The children's toys were the first things to arrive, secretly smuggled into the White House in boxes two weeks before the official transfer of power. "Oh good," Jackie said when told J. B. West had hidden them in his closet, out of sight. "We'll bring them out as soon as the children's rooms are ready."

West, who had sent her photos and blueprints after her disastrous tour with Mamie, quickly discovered that the new First Lady knew every square inch of the Executive Mansion. Moving from room to room that first Monday, she let fly a number of withering observations that West found "hilarious." The cavernous East Room was a "roller-skating rink," the bedroom curtains were "seasick green," and the ground-floor hall a "dentist's office bomb shelter." She railed against the "Pullman car ashtray stands," the "eyesore ornamentation," and the Grand Rapids reproduction furniture that she deemed, simply, "junk."

To Sister Parish, she made clear her intentions: "Let's have lots of chintz and gay up this old dump." Just as she had done with Cassini, Jackie unleashed a blizzard of memos specifying precisely what that entailed: "No Mamie pink on the walls except in Caroline's room." "Something must be done about the window shades throughout the WH. They are enormous and they have pulleys and ropes. After pulling them down I feel like a sailor taking in a sail." "No glass-and-brass ashtrays or trinkets." "If there's anything I can't stand, it's Victorian mirrors—they're hideous—off to the dungeons with them. Have them removed and relegated to the junk heap."

Since Jackie's first priority was her family, the upstairs living quarters were the first to undergo a dramatic change. "I felt like a moth banging on a windowpane when I first moved into this place," Jackie said. "It was terrible . . . They were painting the second story and they moved us way down to the other end. The smell of paint was overpowering and we tried to open the windows in the rooms and we couldn't. They hadn't been opened for years and years. Later, when we tried the fireplaces, they smoked because they hadn't been used.

"Sometimes I wondered, 'How are we going to live as a family in this enormous place?' I'm afraid it will always be a little impossible for the people who live there. It's an office building."

When she felt overwhelmed, which was often, Jackie would "go and sit in the Lincoln Room. It was the one room in the White House with a link to the past. It gave me great comfort . . . When you see that great bed, it's like a cathedral. To touch something I knew he had touched was a real link with him. I used to sit in the Lincoln Room and I could really feel his strength. I'd sort of be talking with him. Jefferson is the president with whom I have the most affinity. But Lincoln is the one I love."

Opposite the Yellow Oval Room, with its doors opening onto the Truman Balcony, were the children's rooms. Jackie erased any trace of the hotel modern decor. Caroline's room was done in pink and white, with matching rosebud bed linens and drapes, a white canopy bed, rocking horses, stuffed animals, a Grandma Moses on the wall—and eventually an elaborate dollhouse from Charles de Gaulle. Her brother's room was blue and white, and between them was the small room strategically occupied by their nanny. "Maud Shaw won't need much," Jackie wrote to J. B. West. "Just find a wicker wastebasket for her banana peels and a little table for her false teeth at night."

Once the children were moved into their rooms, it was the First Couple's turn. Jackie's chandeliered French provincial bedroom was decorated in hues of blue and green, with leopard-skin throws tossed in for drama. Separated from the First Lady's bedroom by a walk-in closet that contained their stereo system, the President's off-white bedroom was dominated by Harry Truman's large mahogany four-poster bed. Jackie picked a blue-and-white design for the bedspread, canopy, and drapes. Everywhere were signs that Jack was still bothered by his back: the extra-firm mattress prescribed by Dr. Travell, a heating pad always kept within reach on the nightstand, a Carolina rocker that Jackie had padded and upholstered. On the wall hung Childe Hassam's *Flag Day*.

Nothing said more about their divergent interests than their choice of reading material, spread out on tables at the foot of their beds. For Jackie: *Le Figaro, Paris Match, Realités, Art à la Mode, Elle, Vogue, Femme Chic.* For Jack: *The New York Times, The Washington Post, Time, Newsweek,* and his favorite, *History Today.*

To her husband's delight, Jackie also turned the family quarters into an art gallery, hanging the walls with Cézanne landscapes, John Singer Sargent watercolors, and twenty portraits of Native Americans by George Catlin.

Like previous occupants, Jackie was unhappy with the cavernous, impersonal "Family" Dining Room on the first floor, and with the fact that meals cooked in the ground-floor kitchen were usually cold by the time they arrived upstairs by dumbwaiter. So she did something about it, designing her own kitchen and dining room in the family quarters on the second floor, within steps from the West Sitting Hall where the family congregated.

There were other practical matters to contend with. No matter was too large (she complained the White House was not heated even as well as "any rattletrap") or small (she shot off a memo to West after noticing one of the cigarette boxes in the Blue Room was empty) for Jackie's attention. But she took particular interest in the staff. "Big problem with WH maids," she wrote to West, "is they are so terrified of First Family that they are rigid with fear & get panicky—even Lucinda who knows me well still apologizes 10 minutes if she drops a pin. I can't teach them anything—nor have time—when they are that scared." Jackie's Georgetown cook, Pearl, had cause to be frightened. Shortly after moving into the White House, Jackie hired a French chef, René Verdon, and assigned West the onerous task of firing the large, forbidding Pearl.

Within three months, Jackie had accomplished all she wanted in the family living quarters. "She wanted to cozy things up with flowers and family photographs and the paintings that she liked," Baldrige said. "She turned this drafty, cold old place into a warm environment for a young family overnight."

Just as quickly, the family settled into a daily routine that would vary little whenever they were in residence over the next thousand days. The President and First Lady almost never saw each other in the morning. Usually up by 8 A.M., the inexhaustible Commander in Chief devoured a huge breakfast—usually two soft-boiled eggs, bacon, toast, orange juice, and a cup of coffee to which he added three or four teaspoons of sugar and cream.

He would then pore over the morning papers and urgent cables in the tub ("It was not at all unusual to get a sheet of paper from him that was soaking wet," said Salinger). Maud Shaw then brought the children in to say good morning. After they kissed Daddy, Caroline turned on the television and sat on the floor watching cartoons. Jack LaLanne came on at 9 A.M., and Jack laughed and clapped as the kids imitated LaLanne's exercise routine.

When he was dressed and ready, Caroline walked her father hand in hand to the Oval Office. Then she went off to the school Jackie had set up on the third floor for her children and the sixteen or so children of several White House staffers and a few close friends.

On the way to school, Caroline popped in to see her mother. Depending on how late she had stayed up the night before, Jackie ate breakfast on a tray in her room any time between eight and noon. After going over the newspapers, she summoned Mary Gallagher to her bedside and for the next hour dictated letters and memos in a nonstop style that would have put any corporate executive to shame.

When she was done giving dictation, Jackie put on casual attire and took a brisk hour-long walk, always alone, around the White House grounds. (Later in the day she would make time to push the baby carriage up and down the circular drive.) Then the First Lady worked at the piece of furniture she regarded as her single most prized possession: the ornate Empire-style ormolu-mounted slant-front desk that had belonged to Black Jack Bouvier.

If she had time, she joined Caroline and John Jr. while they ate lunch—usually a hamburger or hot dog served by a butler on a silver tray. Later, Provi would carry Jackie's favorite lunch—a grilled cheese sandwich—upstairs to her room.

Jack, meanwhile, usually left his office at 1:30, walked to the indoor pool, took off all his clothes at poolside and dove into the eighty-degree water. "He hated to swim alone," Lowe recalled, "so he was always grabbing people by the collar to swim with him." His most frequent partner for his daily nude swim was Dave Powers, whose story-telling ability by then had earned him the sobriquet "Court Jester." (Dave, in turn, was responsible for nicknaming Jack's two Filipino Navy stewards "Quemoy" and "Matsu.")

Thirty minutes later, Jack climbed out of the pool, put on a terry cloth robe, and then exited out a back door through the White House flower shop and the exercise room to the elevators that would take him upstairs to the bedrooms. Once he stepped off the elevator in his robe, still dripping from his swim, there was total tranquillity in the family living quarters. Maud Shaw had tucked Caroline and John Jr. in for their afternoon naps, and Jackie was waiting to have lunch with the President in the living room.

"Mrs. Kennedy dropped everything, no matter how important, to join her husband," West recalled. "If she had visitors in tow, they would be left for me to entertain." For the next two hours or so, the doors to the second floor were sealed. No visitors, phone calls, messages, or servants were allowed. This was the time Jack and Jackie had carved out for themselves to be alone.

They dined, the President still wearing only his bathrobe, in the living room—Jackie on her daily grilled cheese sandwich, Jack usually on a medium-rare hamburger or, since he constantly watched his weight, a glass of the diet drink Metrecal.

After lunch, Jackie would turn on the stereo between their rooms, and music—usually show tunes, jazz, or bossa nova— wafted throughout the corridors. Usually, Jack would go to his bedroom, shut the door, take off his robe and climb into bed. Wearing the reading glasses he was too vain to be seen in in public, he might go over a file if the matter were urgent enough. But once he was finished with his reading, he always napped.

Jackie also preferred to nap alone in her room, though not always. Several times Jack's valet George Thomas, having standing orders to wake him at 3:30, would find the President was not in his room. Tiptoeing into Jackie's bedroom, he would gently wake the President so as not to disturb the First Lady sleeping next to him.

Once she was so engrossed in her work that Jackie forgot Jack was waiting for her. The President sent his valet to fetch her. "Miz Kennedy," George Thomas said gravely as he stood in the doorway. "The President says if you don't hurry, he'll fall asleep." With that, she dropped everything and bolted from the room.

After his nap, Jack showered, dressed in a fresh suit, and returned to the Oval Office while Jackie played outside with Caroline and John Jr. before returning to her mounting pile of correspondence. At this point, the maids descended on the rooms, changing sheets as they were instructed to do every time someone so much as sat on a White House bed. Jackie took some time for herself to relax around 5:30 before spending time with the children as they ate dinner.

The President nearly always managed to leave the office by 5:30 and would then merely repeat his morning ritual—another naked swim with Dave Powers or perhaps Ken O'Donnell (who were admittedly replaced with attractive young women when Jackie was out of town), another trip upstairs in his bathrobe to shower, shave, and change into yet another suit.

For all the attention paid to Jackie's expenditures on clothes, no one noticed that Jack wore three suits—made by the most expensive American and British tailors—every single day. Given all the formal entertaining done by the Kennedys during their short time in office, JFK's formal wardrobe was the most extensive of any American president before or since.

Jackie, who always changed into a dress for dinner, then joined her freshly minted husband for drinks, usually daiquiris, in the Yellow Oval Room. When there were no state functions requiring their presence, they usually dined alone, or with close friends like the Bartletts, the Coopers, or the Bradlees. In keeping with the Kennedy family's Hollywood tradition, they would sometimes screen a film.

Ben Bradlee, who described Jack as "the most urbane man I have ever met," was startled by his host's decidedly lowbrow taste in movies—Westerns, war films, and action-adventure pictures that were short on dialogue and long on gunplay. Even then, he was too restless ever to sit through an entire film, usually leaving after the first twenty minutes.

Not long after JFK's assassination, Caroline's religion teacher, Sister Joanne Frey, asked her students to put their heads on the table and think about Jesus. After a few minutes, she asked the students what it made them think of. Caroline raised her hand. "It made me think of how my mommy always watched cowboy movies with my daddy," she said, "because my daddy always liked cowboy movies. My mommy doesn't like cowboy movies *at all*, but she watched them because she loved my daddy."

Even in front of White House staff members who were around them every day, the new occupants seemed oddly stiff in each other's company. This was an extension of Jack's lifelong dislike of being touched and his oft-expressed disdain for husbands and wives who insisted on "hanging all over each other" in public. But it also reflected Jackie's own studied sense of propriety. "Jackie was a very self-contained person, especially in the White House," said Lowe, who was given carte blanche by JFK to record family life in the White House. "She very much lived her own life, as much as she was allowed to. Jack certainly wasn't jumping into bed with her every night. But when they were both there, they made time for each other . . ."

"Jack and Jackie had a very close, very romantic relationship," Yusha Auchincloss said. "When I was invited to the White House I stayed in the Lincoln Bedroom, and you would see them together all the time. Technically they had separate bedrooms, but they slept together. There was a lot of laughter. They enjoyed each other. They had *fun*."

Tish Baldrige refuted the idea that there were not shared moments of affection. "She used to leave funny little notes all over the White House to cheer him up," Baldrige recalled. "He'd read one of these little notes and burst out laughing. It was their private joke.

"Maybe they weren't always madly 'at' one another," Baldrige insisted, "but there were plenty of tender moments when I'd catch him putting his arm around her waist, or she'd lean her head on his shoulder . . ." At night in his room, when Jack's back was keeping him awake, Jackie braved the cold floor to put on the cast album of Lerner and Loewe's *Camelot*. His favorite line came at the very end of the record and was sung by Richard Burton: "Don't let it be forgot, that once there was a spot, for one brief shining moment . . ."

Yet the public got to see precious few of these moments. As a result, much has been made of the apparent lack of affection between the Kennedys. There would appear to be little mystery involved. Not only were their respective parents calculatedly cold toward one another, but Jack and Jackie grew up in an era where egregious public displays of affection were frowned upon—particularly among wealthy Northeasterners.

There was, undeniably, a yawning emotional chasm that Jack

and Jackie sought to bridge during their brief time in the White House. But if their early afternoons together—hundreds of them in the course of JFK's presidency—were not proof of closeness, they were definitely proof of commitment.

"Jack respected Jackie," Spalding said. "He knew she had helped him get there in the first place." Periodically, friends reminded him just how important a role she had played in winning the election. Toasting his White House hosts, Yusha Auchincloss pointed out that "if it hadn't been for Jack, I wouldn't be sleeping in the White House, and if it hadn't been for Jackie, he wouldn't be either."

Having established a warm family environment and some semblance of a normal routine, Jackie turned her laserlike focus on the business of revamping the rest of the White House. The state interiors, furnished largely with inexpensive reproductions from B. Altman, posed her greatest challenge.

"My mother brought me to Washington one Easter when I was eleven," Jackie recalled. "That was the first time I saw the White House. From the outside I remember the feeling of the place. But inside, there wasn't even a booklet you could buy. Mount Vernon and the National Gallery made a far greater impression. I remember the FBI especially because they fingerprinted me."

Jackie admitted that when she first moved into the White House, she wished "I could be married to Thomas Jefferson because he would know best what should be done to it." Searching for the words to explain why she cared so passionately about the White House, Jackie told Hugh Sidey, "I don't know . . . is it a reverence for beauty or for history? I guess both. I've always cared. My best friends are people who care. I don't know . . . when you read Proust or listen to Jack talk about history or go to Mount Vernon, you understand. I feel strongly about the children who come here. When I think about my son and how to make him turn out like his father, I think of Jack's great sense of history."

In addition to Parish and her old friend, the artist Bill Walton, Jackie brought in a wide range of experts to help. To serve as chairman of the White House Fine Arts Committee, Jackie chose Henry Francis DuPont, one of the leading experts on American antiques and creator of Winterthur, the great museum of American decorative arts in Delaware. The names of the other members resonated with taste and, more pointedly, great wealth. Among them: Mrs. C. Douglas Dillon, Mrs. Charles Engelhard, Mrs. Henry Ford II, Mrs. Albert Lasker, Mrs. Paul Mellon, and Mrs. Charles Wrightsman.

Coordinating the effort to restore America's most treasured home was a Frenchman, Stephane Boudin, the president of the Paris decorating firm Jansen. The most fashionable French decorator from the 1930s until his death in 1967, Boudin numbered among his clients the Duke and Duchess of Windsor.

From the outset, Jackie's pet project was fraught with political peril. "I was warned, begged, and practically threatened not to undertake the renovation," Jackie recalled. Despite Salinger's assurances to the contrary, there was a suspicion among members of the press that Jackie was tinkering unnecessarily with a cherished American institution—more pointedly, that she was trying to make it more . . . *French.* "Nothing was without controversy," Tish Baldrige remarked. "You couldn't even make a peanut butter sandwich in the kitchen without somebody getting upset."

Moreover, Jack, concerned about his image, worried what this all might cost him politically. "For God's sake, Jackie," he said when she had the walls in the Blue Room painted white. "Shouldn't the Blue Room be *blue?*" West observed that JFK "fretted about the color of the walls, the height of the fences, any departure from tradition. He was always entirely serious about the White House."

Behind the scenes, the patrician DuPont, a prickly purist, clashed instantly with the flamboyant Boudin, who was less interested in historical accuracy than flair. DuPont had the scholars on his side, and American manufacturers who saw the use of any Paris-made fabrics or furnishings as tantamount to high treason. More often than not, Jackie, the fervent Francophile, leaned toward Boudin. Preferring to create an atmosphere of ceremonial grandeur, they justified their purchase of Louis XVI and Empire furniture with the argument that the early presidents would have hated anything British.

Still, Jackie tried desperately to smooth down ruffled feathers. When she walked Boudin and DuPont from room to room together for the first time, she realized they must never again meet if the restoration was ever to be completed. Dealing with each separately, she catered to their outsized egos, praising, cajoling, and coaxing until she got both men to agree to what *she* wanted.

Some of the biggest battles were over how paintings should be hung. DuPont wanted them arranged individually, while Boudin wanted them arranged in groups to liven up the Executive Mansion's huge expanses of blank wall. In this, Boudin got his way, while DuPont scored a minor victory in the Green Room, where he mandated fragile eighteenth-century American antique tables and chairs that seemed overwhelmed by the architecture. When Jackie took Boudin to see the room as redone by DuPont, he took one look at the spindly furniture and shouted, "It's full of *legs!*"

The temperamental French designer, however, prevailed nearly everywhere else. "Boudin's schemes for the Blue Room, Red Room, State Dining Room, Treaty Room, and the Oval Office," declared *The New York Times* in 1995, "remain the high-water marks of American ceremonial style." To avoid controversy, however, Jackie downplayed Boudin's contribution. He went along with the deception, claiming to be nothing more than "a family friend."

No one's contribution to the renovation came close to matching Jackie's. On what she called her "spelunking" expeditions rummaging through the White House basement and storage rooms, she unearthed one treasure after another—the James Monroe gold and silver flatware service, the Lincoln china service, a portrait of Andrew Jackson that had been languishing in storage until she moved it to a place of honor in the Cabinet Room. In a men's room, Jackie unearthed busts of Martin Van Buren, Columbus, and Amerigo Vespucci that had been commissioned from some of the finest sculptors of the nineteenth century. "I had a backache every day for three months," she said. "But now I know every corner of the White House. I poked into them all. It was exciting, a new mystery story every day."

Perhaps her biggest find was President Monroe's 1817 Bellange pier table. The historic table had gone unrecognized because in 1924 someone had covered it in gold radiator paint. Jackie finally came across the table in the basement carpenter shop of the White House, being used as a sawhorse.

The basement yielded another discovery: a mammoth desk carved from the timbers of the British warship H.M.S. *Resolute,* a gift from Queen Victoria to President Rutherford B. Hayes in 1878. Woodrow Wilson had used it, and FDR sat behind the desk as he delivered his famous "Fireside Chats" on the radio.

On Jack's first day in the Oval Office, he ordered the "seasick green" walls painted off-white, then personally carried photos of his children and a watercolor painting over from the family quarters to brighten up the room. But over the next few days the room took on a distinctly nautical air. Jack decorated the office with scrimshaw, naval paintings, flags, the coconut shell from the war with his SOS carved in it, and a plaque with an old fisherman's prayer: "O God, Thy sea is great and my boat is so small."

Jackie had the *Resolute* desk refinished and delivered to the Oval Office in February. The President loved the desk so much that he asked if Jackie could get a copy to take with him when he left office. As fond as Jack was of the desk, there was another family member for whom the desk later represented an endless source of fun.

At times presidential advisors, cabinet members, or even visiting heads of state might be locked in serious conversation with JFK when they would suddenly hear a strange scratching sound emanating from the desk. "Is there a rabbit in there?" the President would exclaim in mock horror. Then a hinged door would swing open, and out would pop John Jr., who would proceed to laugh and whoop as he careened around the room. John Jr., whose hide-and-seek games with his father beneath the Oval Office desk were immortalized by *Look*'s Stanley Tretick and others, acquired the nickname "John-John" because whenever the President called his name over and over again, the boy dropped whatever he was doing and came running.

"John-John and JFK quite simply break each other up," Ben Bradlee observed. "Kennedy likes to laugh and likes to make people laugh, and his son is the perfect foil for him." Caroline, though more well-behaved, also had her moments. When the President's dinner guests got off the elevator one evening, they were nearly knocked over by a stark-naked Caroline as she dashed down the main corridor with an abashed Maud Shaw in hot pursuit.

"They were two such different people going into the White House," Jacques Lowe said of Jack and Jackie during this time of adjustment, "but that didn't mean they didn't learn from each other." The President, who had never expressed the slightest interest in furniture, now took early visitors from room to room, opening and shutting doors, pointing to the "nauseous" colors used on the walls. "Look," he said, getting on his hands and knees to examine a table. "It's not even a good *reproduction*."

The Kennedys' high-powered friends weighed in with major contributions. Bunny Mellon sent in a portrait of Thomas Jefferson by Rembrandt Peale. The C. Douglas Dillons donated a roomful of Empire furniture that included Dolley Madison's sofa. Mary Lasker provided an antique Savonnerie rug for the Blue Room, while the Englehards contributed rare Federal furniture for the President's Dining Room.

Unsolicited gifts also flooded in from around the country. Lamps, paintings, tables, quilts, and knickknacks of every imaginable type arrived at the White House. Culling through everything, Jackie came up with some more pleasant surprises. A woman from Des Moines, Iowa, sent a rare nineteenth-century Baltimore desk decorated with three etched-glass panels representing Fame, Temperance, and Justice. Someone else contributed a two-hundred-year-old mahogany high chair for John-John. Another collector sent in a set of Bellangé chairs that had been used in the White House dining room during the administration of James Monroe.

Over the next year, paintings, furniture, even massive crystal chandeliers were shifted from one room to another. A large, brooding portrait of Lincoln was moved from the foyer to the State Dining Room. Harry Truman was given a prominent spot at the head of the main staircase, and William McKinley went from the Red Room to a first-floor hallway.

Even with all the generous gifts, hundreds of thousands of dollars still had to be spent on paintings, furniture, and the experts and craftsmen to restore them. Contributions from wealthy friends and organizations like the DAR took up some of the slack, but in the end it was Jackie's innovative plan to publish the first White House guidebook that saved the day. "She pushed it through," said presidential assistant Arthur Schlesinger. "It was a formidable executive effort, but she carried it out with a perfectionist's attention to detail, steel determination, and lovely command."

The White House guidebook was such a phenomenal success that it did far more than just pay for the White House restoration. Since it was published in the summer of 1962, *The White House: An Historic Guide* has sold more than 4,400,000 copies, making it the best-selling guidebook of all time.

Jack's delight in what Jackie had accomplished was "visible. His eyes brightened," Schlesinger said, "when he talked of her or when she unexpectedly dropped by the office." Tish Baldrige agreed: "He knew she was knowledgeable and that her taste was exquisite, but I think he was surprised at what a superb diplomat she was. He was afraid that there would be a backlash. Don't forget, there was a great hue and cry when Dolley Madison bought a mirror for fifty dollars without the authorization of Congress! It astounded him that she was able to do it, but even more so that she was able to sell the idea of changing the White House so brilliantly."

And sell the idea she did. With veteran CBS broadcaster Charles Collingwood in tow, she took Americans on their first televised tour of the White House on February 14, 1962. "Jack was a master at the medium, of course, but he had to persuade her to do it," recalled Collingwood, who had known the Kennedys for years. "Jackie took me aside and whispered, 'My husband is making me do this, you know.'

"She felt she didn't really come across very well on television. She had a point. It was the first time American audiences saw her for any extended period of time, and her breathless voice and that deer-caught-in-the-headlights look did take some getting used to." Early in the broadcast, Collingwood tried to break the ice with "Oh, this has a very different feeling from the Red Room."

"Yes," Jackie replied without hesitation. "It's blue."

At the end of the broadcast, Jack made a brief walk-on appearance. More than forty-six million viewers had tuned into Jackie's White House tour, at the time making it the most-watched prime-time broadcast in history. It was an unqualified success for Jackie. Not even the lone dissenting voice of Norman Mailer, who wrote that she "walked through the program like a starlet who would never learn to act," bothered her. She shrugged. "He's probably right."

———

He was Lancer. She was Lace. The code names, bestowed upon the President and First Lady by the Secret Service, were piercingly apropos. She and Jack were, much to Jackie's chagrin, not the only White House occupants with Secret Service code names. Caroline was Lyric; John-John was Lark. Even before they set foot in the White House, Jackie worried less about their being harmed than the possibility they might be emotionally scarred, robbed of their childhood.

"I want my children to be brought up in more personal surroundings, not in the state rooms," Jackie insisted. "And I don't want them to be raised by nurses and Secret Service agents." In addition to the school she set up in the third-floor solarium, Jackie designed a play area for Caroline and John outside not far from the Oval Office.

White House carpenters followed the First Lady's sketches precisely, installing a barrel tunnel, a slide, a leather swing, a rabbit hutch, a trampoline surrounded by trees ("All they'll be able to see is my head, sailing above the treetops," Jackie remarked), and—mounted inside the branches of Herbert Hoover's white oak tree—a tree house with a slide. "The slide comes down from the tree just exactly right," Jackie told J. B. West. "In fact, Caroline wants to push her baby brother down, carriage and all."

Eventually, there would be doghouses for the family dogs Charlie and Pushinka ("Get those damned dogs out of here" was the allergic President's usual reaction when encountering them), a stable for the children's ponies Macaroni and Tex, and pens for the lambs, ducks, and guinea pigs. Caroline's hamsters and her favorite pet, a canary named Robin, took up residence in her room.

"Not since Shirley Temple zoomed into international fame," wrote one reporter, about Caroline, "has an American child received so much international coverage in so short a time." It was the kind of statement that sent chills up Jackie's spine. Fiercely protective of the children's privacy, Jackie ordered that trees and shrubs be planted at various strategic spots around the White House to foil gawkers. When Jack objected on the grounds that the American people had a right to see the White House, Jackie backed down a bit. "They're entitled to *some* view of the White House. . . . But I'm sick and tried of starring in everybody's home movies!" This became a familiar refrain. "I can't bear all those people peering over the fence," she would say. "I may abdicate."

"If Mrs. Kennedy had her way," West believed, "the White House would be surrounded by high brick walls. And a moat with crocodiles."

When it came to press coverage of Caroline and John-John, spreads in magazines like *Life* and *Look* were fine—as long as she controlled the access and the circumstances. In the coming months, the public was treated to heartwarming shots of Caroline riding her pony, Macaroni, or sitting in a horse-cart with her mother at bucolic Glen Ora, the family's rented getaway in the Virginia hills; Caroline and John-John dancing a jig in the Oval Office while their beaming daddy clapped; the kids showing off their Halloween costumes to delighted White House staffers. (On Halloween night, 1962, Arthur Schlesinger opened the door of his Georgetown home to find several goblins hopping up and down. "After a moment a masked mother in the background called out that it was time to go to their next house." The voice was unmistakably Jackie's. With the Secret Service lurking in the shadows, she was escorting Caroline and her cousins on their trick-or-treat rounds. "They had just rung Joe Alsop's bell; Dean Acheson was the next stop.")

Controlled glimpses into the lives of the First Family were one thing, unauthorized shots by overzealous photographers were quite another. "Mrs. Kennedy," *Look* photographer Stanley Tretick said, "had a kind of way with her that sort of strikes terror to your heart. She was a very strong-minded girl and very tough. And she's one way about the way she wants it. I think this is one thing that old Joe Kennedy liked about her, that she was a tough babe."

Tretick found out firsthand when he showed up at the Kennedy clan's Fourth of July celebration at Hyannis Port in 1961. Although he was there to shoot pictures for a story on the Shrivers, Tretick, who had been warned by Jackie not to take any photos of Caroline playing with her cousins, could not resist. *Look* held off publishing them for a year, hoping to get a nod of approval from her that never came.

When *Look* finally did use the photos, "Kennedy got very upset because he got the heat from Jackie," Tretick said. "Ted Sorensen told me, 'It's a good thing you weren't here that minute. The President tried to get you on the phone.' He said, 'Get that——— Tretick on the phone.' He used one of his favorite navy expressions. Thank God I was out shopping at the local Safeway . . . But he'd get sore for about two minutes. I don't think he held grudges unless somebody did something really malicious to him. He got mad at that time because I'm sure Jackie called up and raised the devil about it. He just wanted to do whatever it took to keep her happy."

The President did indeed have an explosive temper, but as Jacques Lowe observed, he did not stay mad for long. "I'd pick up the phone and hear '*Jacques!* It's the President!' and then he'd bawl me out about something. *The New York Times Sunday Magazine* ran a picture of him with his glasses on his head, and even though the shot had been used quite a few times before without him saying a word, this time he was really pissed off. Just furious. I just stuttered a few words in response, and wondered what the hell was going on. When the President of the United States yells at you, you know it. But the next day all was completely forgotten."

Tish Baldrige was also a periodic target of the President. "Our first official White House party got me into the hottest of water with the President," she recalled. "In fact, it was boiling." Baldrige had broken tradition and scheduled the reception on a Sunday. There were food tables and bars scattered throughout the first floor, and members of the press were allowed to mingle and were treated just like any other guests.

The next day, Baldrige was called into the Oval Office expecting to be "patted on the back" for the successful affair. "Tish," the President said angrily, "why didn't you tell me there had never been hard liquor at a party like this before? And to make matters nicer, it was on a *Sunday!*" He then handed her one of the morning papers with the front-page headline NEVER ON SUNDAY AT JFK'S HOUSE, SAYS BAPTIST CONGRESSMAN.

"He was mad—and rightfully so," Baldrige said. "I went back to my office to lick my wounds and take an antiulcer pill." That afternoon he called her and apologized for being "a little rough" that morning. "He said that I must understand that he had a lot of things on his mind, and that he didn't mean to be short with me. He was that kind of a man, JFK."

But Jackie was not so quick to apologize, nor quite so concerned about bruising the feelings of White House staffers. "Jackie was just ferociously protective of their privacy," said Salinger, who took most of the heat whenever the lioness felt her cubs were endangered. "From the moment she set foot in the White House, she wanted to keep them out of the spotlight."

"Jackie didn't want Caroline and John-John to be treated like stars," Tish Baldrige said. "But of course they *were* stars. The American people just fell in love with them."

"She became very paranoid about the press," Jacques Lowe said. "But Jack knew the kids were a great asset for his administration. He was proud of them. He wanted to show them off. It got to be a game between the two of them, with me stuck in the middle."

One day Kennedy approached Lowe and said, "Jacques, take some pictures of Caroline and give them to Ben Bradlee." Bradlee was then with *Newsweek*.

"You know I can't do that, Mr. President," he replied. "You know Jackie doesn't want any photos of Caroline running around the White House."

JFK shrugged. "Then don't tell her."

"I took the pictures, and of course when they came out in *Newsweek* Jackie got all upset. Of course, the President played totally innocent. So naturally I took the rap. I frequently found myself caught between them."

Salinger was also a victim of the presidential squeeze play.

When Jackie complained to him that yet another unauthorized photograph of the children had surfaced, he would explain that JFK had requested the photograph be taken. "I don't give a damn," Jackie replied. "He has no right to countermand my order regarding the children."

Not even the President had the courage to face his wife when the subject of the children and the press came up, so much of this subterfuge took place when she was out of town. "As soon as she snuck out," Tretick said, "I snuck in."

Tretick, who had photographed JFK extensively on the campaign trail, was impressed with how affectionate he was with his children—particularly his young son. "His interest in the boy was incredible. It was almost sensual. John-John was sitting on the floor of the Oval Office one night and the President was talking to him. And he was saying something to the President and the President was looking down and talking to him. And then he just kind of reached for him—he reached for the boy and pulled his pajama up—you know, bathrobe and pajama—and he kind of rubbed his bare skin right above his rear end. He wanted to touch him.

"And then another time when he was sitting outside with John-John he put him over his knee like he was going to spank him, but you could see the way he was feeling him and was having fun with him. And you know, it was a genuine thing between the two of them. The boy also sensed his father. I think it would have really grown . . ."

This growing delight JFK (for years the favorite "Uncle Jack" to a score of nieces and nephews) took in both his offspring was apparent to everyone. In the late afternoon, he would throw open the doors to the Rose Garden, clap his hands, and they would come running.

"The children could be playing all over him and he could still be conducting a conference or writing a speech," Baldrige remembered. JFK would also drop in on Caroline and her classmates at the school Jackie had set up in the White House. "He would be up there to see the children constantly. He would go out on the South Lawn and play with them and talk to them and they would all troop into his office at the drop of a hat whenever he gave the signal.

"So the house was full of children morning, noon, and night," Baldrige remembered. "You never knew when an avalanche of young people would come bearing down on you—runny noses, dropped mittens in the hall, bicycles . . ."

Fatherhood opened Jack up to all children, not just his own. In Palm Beach, Chuck Spalding and his twin daughters, Josie and Elizabeth, were swimming when the President joined them. "Jack took Josie on his back and I took Elizabeth on mine, and we got into this wild fight in the water," Spalding recalled. "The object, of course, was for one of the girls to knock the other off. It lasted a long time, really furious. He was so incredibly competitive, there was no way he was going to lose, and sure enough, he and Josie eventually won." Spalding later watched as Jack, wincing in pain, gingerly left the pool and strapped on his back brace.

"Years later," Spalding continued, "I pulled a photo out of my wallet of Jack and me and for the first time noticed that Josie had scribbled something on the back. 'They say awful things about him,' she had written, 'and I don't know if they're true or not, but he was the neatest guy I ever saw. We played war in the swimming pool and I'll never forget him.' "

Like all those in the Kennedys' inner circle, Arthur Schlesinger witnessed Jack telling stories to Caroline and John-John: "Stories about Caroline—he called her 'Buttons'—hunting with the Orange County hounds and winning the Grand National, and about John-John in his PT-boat sinking a Japanese destroyer. He would tell them about Bobo the Lobo, a giant, and about Maybelle, a little girl who hid in the woods, and about the White Shark and the Black Shark. The White Shark lived off people's socks, and one day, when the President and Caroline were sailing with Franklin Roosevelt, Jr., off Newport, Kennedy pretended to see the White Shark and said, 'Franklin, give him your socks, he's hungry.' Franklin promptly threw his socks into the water, which made a great impression on Caroline."

Other guests were not immune to the same request. "We all learned that when Jack began telling Caroline about the White Shark," Lem Billings said, "it was time to move to another part of the yacht."

John-John's favorite game with Daddy was "Going Through the Tunnel," which usually occurred en route to the office. "President Kennedy would have to stand tall," Maud Shaw said, "and John would go through his legs time and time again. John never got tired of this game. I'm sure the President did."

As the boy grew older, Jack took more time to answer his questions. "John had a very inquisitive mind . . . I've seen the President at Camp David go along to the hangar and take John in the helicopter and sit for quite a few moments, just sitting patiently inside the helicopter, putting on the helmet and showing him how things work, moving gadgets for him just like a big boy."

Before the *Look* story on John-John was published, Tretick gave the President a set of the photos. "He ran all over the White House with them, showing people. There again it was like a guy with a wallet full of pictures more than anything else. When Jackie got back, he showed them to her upstairs and she was pleased with them. She wasn't mad at all."

Jackie reveled in Jack's growing need to spend time with their children. "Sometimes they even have lunch with him," she said. "If you told me that would happen, I'd never have believed it. But after all, the one thing that happens to a president is that his ties to the outside world are cut, and the people you really have are each other."

That did not mean, of course, that JFK could even remotely be described as a homebody. "When I start to ask him silly little insignificant questions about whether Caroline should appear at some reception, or whether I should wear a short or long dress, he just snaps his fingers and says, 'That's your province.' And I say, 'Yes, but you're the great decision maker. Why should everyone but me get the benefit of your decisions?' "

The "outside world" was something she clearly feared when it came to her children. Her positive reaction to the Tretick photographs of John-John was the exception that proved the rule. Jackie ordered Secret Service agents to seize film from any photographer who took a picture without first getting her permission. One such picture of Caroline riding Macaroni ran all over the country. Jackie was furious. "I thought you made an arrangement with the fotogs not to take the children playing at WH," she wrote to Salinger. "They have had all the pictures of Macaroni they need. I want no more—*I mean this*—and if you are firm and will take the time, you can stop it. So please do. What is a press secretary for—to help the press, yes—but also to protect *us*."

"Poor Pierre," Baldrige said. "She had him seeing a photographer behind every tree." Neither was Jackie's high-powered social secretary, who like Salinger was much admired by the press, exempt from Jackie's wrath. "Your first responsibility is to the family," she told Tish, "not the White House."

When another picture of Caroline—this time playing on the White House lawn—was splashed across front pages worldwide, Jackie tried to contain herself:

DON'T WORRY—A NICE CALM MEMO!
Pierre—

Your policy of no peep shows has worked marvelously all Fall—now if they get away with this I am afraid they will start up in full force again—so could you berate the fotog—or the AP for buying it—if it was taken by a tourist.

Guards should be told to watch out for people through grilles—The guards at the gate could have stopped this—If necessary one can patrol up & down outside by S.W. gate—I don't think we need one at end of s. lawn yet as its [*sic*] so conspicuous—but the minute any fotos get taken from there lets [*sic*] put a guard out there too—

Do speak to present guard—This must have been taken on

that locked-off street by JFK's office—or out of Old State Dept window—They should watch for people there—climbing on cars to take pictures etc.

Jackie also worried about the privacy of the family pets. A bland newspaper piece about Charlie, the Kennedys' Welsh terrier, sent Jackie storming at the kennel keeper. "Don't you ever give another thing to those damn nosy reporters," she commanded.

The only thing that bothered Jackie more than the press's insatiable appetite for anything concerning the Kennedy kids was their blatant attempts to capitalize on them. In another memo to the put-upon Pierre, she complained,

> they are now selling *Caroline* Christmas dolls—with wardrobe and Jacqueline dolls with STATE wardrobe at F.A.O. Schwartz [*sic*]—which is the first time it has gotten into the really available—rather proper domain—They are in window displays or were—Can you do something about this—John McInerney did some law work on this problem for me once—If a call such as you made to the sunglass people doesn't work will you try Clark Clifford—McInerney or Better Business Bureau—
>
> A company called Ideal Toy Co. is trying to pressure me (through Tom Walsh) into endorsing a Caroline doll that would have our backing & all royalties would go to charity & there would be no other dolls—I would rather have a doll a month than endorse one—
>
> But this is irritating—so please do see what you can do—call F.A.O. Schwartz [*sic*]—N.Y.C. I guess—JFK said to write you this. Jackie.

Any attempt to profit from the White House irked Jackie. "I would very much prefer that you don't use our photograph on the cover of your Inaugural Album," she wrote to society bandleader Meyer Davis, who had played at their wedding, the inauguration, and numerous other Kennedy functions. "Also that you do not reprint my letter. I feel that is commercializing on the Presidency—which is something I will fight against every day of my husband's administration—I should think that if it is written on the back of your album that you played for my mother's wedding and my coming-out party and wedding and husband's inauguration—that would be interesting enough for everyone."

To maintain tranquillity in the White House, Jack was careful not to overtly contradict Jackie when it came to the press. There were exceptions, however. When a photographer shot Jackie at Paul Mellon's Virginia estate being thrown headfirst from her horse, she called JFK and demanded he intervene to stop the picture from being published. That constitutes, she claimed, an invasion of privacy. "I'm sorry, Jackie," Jack replied, "but when the First Lady falls on her ass, that's news." Tellingly, the bay gelding that threw Jackie was named Bit of Irish.

Jackie's own relations with the press were strained from the start; in part because she made it clear she resented the spotlight. "Sometimes," she mused, "I think you become sort of a—there ought to be a nicer word than *freak* but I can't think of one."

"I sympathize with all first ladies when it comes to the press," veteran Washington columnist Betty Beale said, "because you're damned if you do and damned if you don't. What Jackie did, she did well. But there were many times when she really goofed off. She had no intention of going to ladies' luncheons and doing the things a first lady had always been expected to do. And that made some people *mad*."

Jackie dismissed these traditional duties as "boring and a useless waste of my time. Why should I traipse around to hospitals playing Lady Bountiful when I have so much to do here to make this house livable? I'll just send them some fruits and nuts and flowers."

"When the congressional wives gave a luncheon in her honor, Jackie didn't even bother to attend," Betty Beale remembered. "But the President showed up, and apologized. It turned out she had gone to New York to see the ballet instead." Another time, she went fox hunting at Glen Ora rather than greet thousands of foreign students at the White House. And when Beale reported that Jackie had danced the night away doing the Twist with Defense Secretary Robert McNamara, "she hit the roof. Jackie actually banned me from covering all future White House affairs. Of course, the President was much less sensitive and infinitely more practical than that. He had me reinstated as soon as he found out."

At Jack's urging, Jackie did make the occasional friendly overture. In April 1961, Jackie invited two hundred women journalists from around the country to a lavish luncheon in the East Room of the White House. Like visiting heads of state, they were driven in through the Southwest Gate, past the duck pond and the children's playground and tree house.

Despite some grumbling among reporters who found Jackie stiff, the event had the desired effect. "It was exactly the female kind of party that we took up a career to get out of going to," wrote the *New York Herald Tribune*'s Eugenia Sheppard. "But somehow, at the White House, it was different."

Time quaintly described the luncheon as "a gracious gesture toward the nation's newshens," and reported that "Jackie greeted each guest with a warm friendliness." Later, "Jackie stood up to welcome the women in words that women understood" and was "grateful" for their "warm stories."

On rare occasions, she ribbed the press good-naturedly: Asked what the family's new puppy ate, she replied "reporters." But Jackie's resentment of them at times bordered on the obsessive. Unable to bar reporters from official functions entirely, she suggested in a memo to Baldrige after a party honoring astronaut John Glenn that they "be permitted to attend important receptions but be kept out of sight behind the pillars and potted palms because they are too intrusive. They surround our guests and monopolize them. Nobody could get near John Glenn the other night. Also, the minute the photographers have finished shooting they are to be ushered out the front door so the marine band can strike up 'Hail to the Chief.' "

She did not want members of the press hanging around at state dinners, either. "That is when they ask everyone questions and I don't think it is dignified to have them around. It always makes me feel like some social-climbing hostess. Their notebooks also bother me, but perhaps they should be allowed to keep them as, at least, you know they are press, but I think they should be made to wear big badges and be whisked out of there once we all sit down to dinner."

Increasingly, Jackie found the whole business of doing interviews tedious. Turning down a request from one of the leading women's magazines, she wrote, "I wish I could either tell you that I would love to do it—or had just been run over by a bus—and couldn't pose for a month. They are marvelous articles—but if you won't be too angry—I think I would just as soon not do one—revealing my few tragic beauty secrets and disorganized wardrobe!"

After appearing in *Life, Look, Ladies' Home Journal, Redbook,* and *McCall's* in rapid succession, she pleaded with another editor: "I am so tired of all the hard work and confusion that goes into a story—especially one with pictures, and feel pretty stale right now . . . Please no little photographic essays. Jacques Lowe and I have been through about three sessions like that together—changing clothes, fixing lights, driving to find nice scenery, trying to make the baby smile—I'm sure he wants to avoid it as much as I do!"

At the end of 1961, Jackie presented a gift to Salinger: A photograph of the First Lady signed "From the greatest cross you have to bear."

———

There have been some great wives
in the White House—like Abigail Adams
and Dolley Madison—so great you can't
think of their husbands without
thinking of them. It looks like we're having
another one now.

Robert Frost

———

I'm going to keep the White House white.

JFK to Charlie Bartlett,
when asked about his lifestyle

———

10

"Jackie was aloof from the press. No question about it," Tish Baldrige said. "But everyone forgets that she wasn't feeling well that first year. After all, she came very close to dying after John-John was born, and she just didn't want to do anything. Jackie was making this tremendous effort to restore the White House, and she just didn't have the energy to do much of anything else. The President, on the other hand, kept seeing photo ops behind every tree . . ."

Jack was clearly worried about Jackie's health and her state of mind in May 1961 as they prepared to make their first official trip abroad. The trip to Canada was intended as a goodwill gesture to the United States' most important trading partner, as well as a practice run for the European summit with Nikita Khrushchev the following month.

Several days before their scheduled departure, Jack summoned Max Jacobson ("Dr. Feelgood") to Palm Beach, where he and Jackie were renting the palatial oceanfront estate belonging to their friends Charles and Jayne Wrightsman. As soon as he reached his hotel, Jacobson was picked up by Secret Service agents and whisked off to meet "Mr. and Mrs. Dunn," the special code names the doctor had been told to use for the President and the First Lady. Jacobson waited on the porch, where after a few minutes he saw the President walking toward him from the garden.

"He came right to the point," Jacobson recalled. "He was very much concerned about Jackie's condition following her last delivery. She suffered periodic depression and headaches. He wanted to know whether she could endure the strain of a trip to Canada in the near future, but more important, whether she would be able to accompany him to Paris, Vienna, and London for the summit meeting."

Provi, her maid, led Jacobson to Jackie's room. "She seemed unhappy and complained of a severe migraine," Jacobson said. "The least I can do for you is to stop your migraine," Jacobson told Jackie. Then Jacobson opened his medical bag, filled a syringe from a small vial containing speed, and injected it into the unknowing First Lady. "Her mood," Jacobson recalled, "changed completely. After the President saw her, there was no further discussion over the feasibility of a trip." Jacobson also obliged JFK with a "treatment" of his own.

The trip to Ottawa was pivotal for two reasons. "It was the first time Jackie was making a trip abroad as First Lady, and we planned it very carefully," said Cassini, who designed a red wool suit for her to wear when she reviewed the Royal Canadian Mounted Police.

Jackie discovered that her appeal traveled well. "Her charm, beauty, vivacity, and grace of mind," Canada's Senate speaker proclaimed in Parliament, "have captured our hearts." Jackie also distracted the press from JFK and Canadian Prime Minister John Diefenbaker, who did not hold each other in particularly high regard.

Cassini observed that "for the first time Jack recognized she was not just a wife, but a great political tool—a force to be reckoned with and a powerful symbol for the United States. It was a turning point for Jackie, too. She began to realize her own political value, and that boosted her confidence. From that moment on, the relationship between Jack and Jackie changed. They became partners."

The trip was significant for another reason. During a treeplanting ceremony on the grounds of Government House, Jack did not just follow his wife's lead and dig a token shovelful for the cameras. Instead, he burrowed in like a ditchdigger, lifting out ten heavy shovelfuls of Canadian dirt. The macho display cost him dearly. The American President injured his back so severely that for the rest of his life he would never again be entirely free of pain.

It would be one of the most stunning acts of deception ever pulled off by a sitting president, tantamount only to polio-stricken Franklin Roosevelt's success at keeping the general public unaware of his inability to walk. "People don't understand just how bad off Jack was during his presidency," Smathers said. "He could barely stand up much of the time, much less walk. He leaned on Secret Service guys all the time."

Smathers recalled a banquet JFK was to attend in Miami when "he could hardly dress himself. I had to put on his shoes and socks for him. Jack was just like FDR, and he did a great job concealing it." But unlike FDR, JFK managed to accomplish this subterfuge without the press's tacit cooperation. "Jack even managed to hide it from them."

There were times, of course, when JFK appeared the very picture of robust health. But when he was on the golf course, for example, he spent nearly all the time riding around in a cart. "He would seem fine and all of a sudden his face would go absolutely white," Salinger said. "Much of the time he was in pain, but I never heard him complain once."

"Look closely at the photographs," Lowe said. "He tried to avoid it when someone was taking a picture, but occasionally he is caught off guard, leaning. He was always leaning—on tables, on desks, on windowsills, the backs of chairs." Tish Baldrige recalled that "people covered up for him. He had this uncanny knack of leaning up against a wall and going to sleep. He could sleep *standing up*, which always astounded me. Jack had this little trick. He would put on his sunglasses, and people thought he was watching a parade or whatever, and the whole time he'd be sleeping behind those glasses! I'd catch him doing it all the time."

Whether it was also caused by his digging too enthusiastically at the tree-planting ceremony in Ottawa, or was a side effect from the medications he was taking, Jack's hands would sometimes tremble imperceptibly. "To disguise this," Jamie Auchincloss said, "he would slip his hand into his jacket pocket nonchalantly. Naturally, everybody thought this was very suave and began copying the pose. But it was to keep people from seeing him shake."

When he returned home from Ottawa after that first state visit of his administration, an angry and frustrated Jack was unable to walk down the stairs even on crutches. He had to be lifted off Air Force One aboard a cherry picker. On May 23, 1961, Jacobson was summoned to Washington. He was ushered into the family living quarters, where Jackie was waiting for him. After he injected her with his potent amphetamine "cocktail," she said, "Jack wants to see you."

To alleviate his back pain, Dr. Travell had been injecting JFK with Novocain and spraying his back with ethyl chloride, which numbs the skin temporarily by freezing it. Neither of these treatments seemed to be working. Jacobson, who would soon be at loggerheads with Travell, offered to increase the strength and frequency of his "treatments"—but only if Jack swore off alcohol and sedatives of any kind. In combination with the speed, these could have been lethal. Jacobson then gave Jack a stronger dose than he had previously—"not only to relieve his local discomfort," Jacobson rationalized, "but to provide him with additional strength to cope with stress."

The President got up and walked back and forth several times. "I feel very much better," Jack said. "I would like you to come with me to Europe next week." Jacobson agreed, pointing out that he was a Jewish refugee from Nazi Germany and that he felt he owed it to his country to serve the President in his "hour of need."

When he returned to the White House (code name Château) the next morning, Jacobson found Jackie in a mild state of panic. "She showed me a vial of Demerol she had found in the President's bathroom. I told her that I was in principle absolutely opposed to the use of opiates and their derivatives . . . it would interfere with my medication and was highly addictive."

Jacobson asked who prescribed the Demerol, and Jackie began investigating. She found out that a Secret Service man had supplied the controlled substance to the President. The agent was summarily dismissed, but that was not enough for Jacobson. He confronted the President directly. "I emphasized that Demerol would . . . interfere with his ability to function," Jacobson told the President, who made a point of never asking what it was Jacobson was giving him, that he would no longer administer the magic elixir if JFK continued to use Demerol. Kennedy agreed, and over the next several days before the European summit, Jacobson administered a dozen injections to the President and First Lady.

The Demerol incident was not the first time Jack had obtained prescription drugs illegally. "He had been on so many drugs for so long because of his back," Smathers said, "and he didn't trust doctors worth a damn." Added Spalding: "If somebody said a pill worked, he'd try it. He wouldn't bother to tell the doctors. I don't think he worried at all about how these various drugs might interact at the time."

By the time he left on his all-important trip to Europe, Jack was dependent on Jacobson's injections. Jacobson was even rushed at the last minute to meet Air Force One on the tarmac at New York's Idlewild (later John F. Kennedy) Airport. On the flight from Washington to New York, the President's back had been giving him trouble. Before his long transatlantic flight, he wanted Jacobson to give him a shot.

Fearing that suspicion would be aroused if Jacobson traveled aboard Air Force One, the White House arranged to have him fly to Paris via Air France. It was "the strangest flight I ever made," Jacobson said. In his desire to keep their relationship out of the press, Jack had reserved the entire airliner for the doctor and his wife, Nina. "We were," Jacobson said, "the only passengers on the plane."

Charles de Gaulle met the Kennedys at Orly airport with a 101-gun salute, then escorted them to the palatial residence reserved for visiting dignitaries at the Quai d'Orsay. The normally cynical Parisians went wild. More than a million of them waited for hours to catch a glimpse of the world's most glamorous couple, screaming "Jacqui! Jacqui!" as the presidential motorcade passed by. "The First Lady is bursting with youth and beauty," declared *Le Figaro.* "From the moment of her smiling arrival at Orly airport," *Time* concurred, "the radiant young First Lady was the Kennedy who really mattered."

While the two leaders talked about the growing Soviet threat and specifically the future of Berlin, Jackie toured Malmaison, the home of the French Empress Josephine, with the one Frenchman (next to De Gaulle) she most wanted to meet, French Minister of Culture André Malraux.

At lunch, Jackie and De Gaulle chattered away in French about French history. Eventually, he leaned across the table and informed the American President that his First Lady knew more about French history than most French women. "My grandparents were French," she explained. "So were mine," De Gaulle replied.

Jack was delighted. "It was as if," Jack later told a friend, "Madame de Gaulle had sat next to me and asked all about Henry Clay."

Jackie's mischievous streak surfaced in the formal receiving line at the Elysée Palace, where Yusha Auchincloss was among the guests. "Jackie kissed me rather affectionately," Yusha said, "and De Gaulle was clearly taken aback. Then she explained I was her brother, and then he was really confused." Yusha knew "just how much it meant to Jackie to spend time with De Gaulle. After all," he said, "she named her poodle Gaullie."

Wearing a dress of pink-and-white straw lace, Jackie continued to dazzle her hosts at the glittering state dinner in Versailles' Hall of Mirrors. De Gaulle found Jackie "enchanting" and praised her as "the gracious and *charmante* Madame Kennedy." For once, Jack did not mind taking a backseat. "I do not think it entirely inappropriate for me to introduce myself," he said with pride. "I am the man who accompanied Jacqueline Kennedy to Paris. And I have enjoyed it."

Later that night, Jacobson was summoned to the Palais d'Orsay. Everyone in the President's party was overjoyed at their reception. Jacobson found his way to Jackie's cavernous room, where she was chattering animatedly about the day's events. Jacobson, taken aback by Jackie's sudden talkativeness ("in contrast to her usual reserved attitude toward me"), looked around the room and spotted an irregularity in the otherwise flawless molding. "I suspected a microphone," Jacobson said. "I called her attention to it by pointing in its direction, and put my other hand to my lips. She quickly understood."

After giving Jackie an injection of Librium to help her sleep, Jacobson found the President's separate bedroom—not so immense as Jackie's—and did the same for him. Jack then asked the doctor to return early the following morning. "With the change in time plus a strenuous schedule," Jacobson said, "it was most important for him to wake up the next morning rested and ready to face another busy day."

The next morning, Jacobson showed up as promised to give the President his injection. This time Jack invited Jacobson and his wife to accompany him on Air Force One for the remainder of the trip.

"There were two motorcades," Jacobson recalled of their arrival in Vienna. "One followed Jacqueline Kennedy to her engagement with Khrushchev's wife, Nina. Our motorcade followed the President to the private residence of the American ambassador, a beautiful house in the Semmerings, where the summit meeting with Premier Khrushchev was to take place. The route to the mountains was lined three-deep with waving and cheering crowds. It seemed like a national holiday.

"No sooner had we arrived than I was hurried up to the living quarters and into the President's room. He said, 'Khrushchev is supposed to be on his way over. The meeting may last for a long time. See to it that my back won't give me any trouble when I have to get up or move around.' "

The first meeting began pleasantly enough. With Secretary of State Dean Rusk and Soviet Foreign Minister Andrei Gromyko listening quietly, Kennedy and Khrushchev tried to break the ice over cocktails. JFK sipped a Dubonnet, the chairman of the USSR a dry martini.

"You know," Jack said, "my wife, Jacqueline, says that Gromyko looks so kind, so pleasant, that he must be a very nice man."

"You should remember, Mr. President," Khrushchev replied, "that some people say Gromyko looks like Nixon."

Despite the "boost" from Jacobson, the summit itself was something of a disaster. Khrushchev, who expressed a thinly veiled contempt for his much younger counterpart, was the first leader JFK had ever encountered who simply refused to exchange ideas. The experience, Schlesinger observed, "deeply disturbed" him.

Jack may have failed to impress the Soviet leader, but the same could not be said of Jackie. At the state banquet held in Vienna's Schönbrunn Palace, Khrushchev sputtered, "It's beautiful," when he was introduced to Jackie—presumably referring to the shimmering white sheath that clung to her like a second skin.

Khrushchev insisted on sitting next to Jackie all evening, and the two bantered, recalled Schlesinger, "like Abbott and Costello." When he bragged that there were more schoolteachers in the Ukraine under the Soviets than there had been under czarist rule, Jackie said, "Oh, Mr. Chairman, don't bore me with statistics."

"Jackie talked about Dostoevsky, Pushkin, Tolstoy, Chekhov," said Yusha Auchincloss, who accompanied them to Vienna. "She knew a lot more about Russian culture than Jack did. She probably knew more about Russian culture than *Khrushchev* did."

The unlikely pair also chatted about the space program, and Jackie pointed out that one of the Russian dogs who had been sent into orbit had recently given birth to puppies. "Why don't you send me one?" she asked blithely. When a puppy arrived at the White House two months later, she sheepishly explained to Jack, "I'm afraid I asked Khrushchev for it in Vienna. I was running out of things to say." They named the dog Pushinka.

"When Jackie could get Khrushchev's ear, and he would lean close to her," Baldrige said, "the President was proud and pleased. After all, he couldn't get Khrushchev to lean close to *him*. That trip completely changed the way he saw her. One minute she was a wife complaining about his cigar ashes being ground into the carpet. The next she was charming heads of state and entire nations, arising like the queen of the world." Or, as *Life* unfortunately chose to put it, she was undergoing "queenification."

"Europe was great for both of them," Chuck Spalding said. "It showed how truly impressive on the world stage she was to him. It also showed how good he could be if he curbed his appetites. He did not so much as flirt with another woman during that entire trip."

On the way home, Air Force One stopped over in London so that Jack and Jackie could attend the christening of the Radziwills' daughter, Anna Christina. (The ceremony had, in fact, been postponed until the President could make the trip.) No sooner did Max and Nina Jacobson check into their room at Claridge's than the phone rang summoning him to the Radziwills' Georgian townhouse around the corner from Buckingham Palace. "The car took me to the back entrance," Jacobson recalled. "The driver escorted me through the garden to the back door. From there we ascended a very steep and long staircase . . . I walked into Lee Radziwill's bedroom where Jackie, the President, and Lee were informally chatting," he said. "The President and I retired to an anteroom, where I attended him . . ."

That evening, Jack and Jackie attended a state dinner hosted by Queen Elizabeth and Prince Philip at Buckingham Palace. Among the guests were Louis Mountbatten and Prime Minister Harold Macmillan. Directly from the dinner, the President's motorcade drove to Heathrow for the flight back to the United States aboard Air Force One. Jackie, however, stayed behind. While Jack attended to affairs of state at home, she would be touring Greece with Lee and Stas Radziwill.

A few hours later aboard Air Force One, Jacobson was startled when the President emerged from his private quarters in a night-shirt. "He couldn't help but smile at my bewildered expression," said Jacobson. JFK had been trying to nap but couldn't. Again the doctor, who regaled the President with what he called his "Jewish jokes," obliged him with a shot of Librium to help him sleep. "He wanted to be in his best form for the return to the USA," Jacobson recalled.

According to Jacobson, Jack insisted the regular injections, which were now being administered up to four times a week, "never interfered with his public appearances or the long diplomatic discussions with heads of state." In the next two years, Jacobson would make countless trips to the White House, to Hyannis Port, to the Kennedys' weekend retreat in Virginia, to Palm Beach, and to JFK's suite at New York's Carlyle Hotel.

"During one of my visits to the White House," Jacobson recalled, "I was standing at the window in the salon, watching the helicopters take off from the front lawn. All of a sudden, Providencia the maid came running into the salon. She said, very excitedly, 'Dr. Travell has entered the second floor!' The 'doctor' wanted to confront me.

"It is highly improper for anyone to enter the President's private residence unless so requested by him. I therefore avoided the encounter and any possible incident that might have arisen by quietly slipping out a side door and returning to New York City."

The next time they met at the White House, Dr. Max handed the President his letter of resignation. "I have to resign, Mr. President," he said, "I've run out of Jewish jokes." Kennedy "laughed, tore up the letter, and said, 'That's out of the question.'"

Jacobson, who wore a PT-109 tie clip given to him by Jack, refused any compensation for his services. "President Kennedy was concerned over my financial situation. On two occasions, I found an envelope in my jacket pocket en route to the airport. When I opened it, I found several hundred-dollar bills . . . I returned the envelope and its contents [to the President]. He seemed slightly embarrassed and laughed as he accepted them."

Bobby Kennedy and Pierre Salinger—who miraculously managed to conceal Jacobson's identity from the press—joined Dr. Travell in pleading with the President to drop Dr. Max. In his capacity as Attorney General, Bobby asked that all medications Jacobson used on his brother be submitted to the Food and Drug Administration for analysis.

"The President," Jacobson recalled, "after much pressure and with apparent embarrassment, asked me if I would consider complying. Without hesitation I agreed and forwarded to Robert Kennedy fifteen vials of medication for use on the President. A week later the President informed me that the material had been examined, tested, and approved." Dr. Travell never received a promised copy of the report. It showed that the mixture routinely being injected into the President and the First Lady contained not only large amounts of amphetamines, but steroids as well. At the time, neither of these perfectly legal drugs was officially deemed by the FDA to be harmful or addictive.

Jack and Jackie remained patients of "Dr. Feelgood" for the remainder of his presidency. It was not as if they had a choice. Victims of incomprehensible public pressures and private stress, they had found a way to cope. And Jack, burdened by pain his entire life, was experiencing an unprecedented degree of relief. But by any clinical definition, they were now dependent on the medication dispensed by Jacobson. The President of the United States and the First Lady were, unknowingly, addicted to speed.

"I knew Max well," Gore Vidal said. "All of us in Hollywood and in show business knew what he was all about. I'm not one for drugs, but I must say the injections gave you a feeling of total well-being. But then, of course, there is an awful crash when the drug wears off. Max drove several people mad . . .

"When I learned that Jack was getting these shots from Dr.

Max, I told Jackie, 'Watch out. Stay away from him.' I didn't know at the time that she was getting the shots, too."

In September 1961, Jacobson was in Washington giving Jackie an injection when he was called to the phone and instructed to return to New York and the Carlyle Hotel. Earlier in the month, UN Secretary General Dag Hammarskjöld had been killed in a plane crash, and now the Soviets were trying to neutralize the international body by replacing the secretary general with a *troika*—two representing the superpowers, and a third the nonaligned nations.

President Kennedy was scheduled to argue against the Soviet proposal before the General Assembly. But when Jacobson arrived at the Carlyle he found the President still in his pajamas. "Meetings had gone on all night judging from the empty and half-empty glasses and full ashtrays strewn about the room," Jacobson recalled. JFK greeted Dr. Max "with a whisper that was so hoarse I could hardly understand him."

"So, Max—what are you going to do about this?" Jack said, pointing to his throat. Jacobson said he could cure JFK's laryngitis in time for his UN speech, but only by injecting him below the larynx. "Do what's necessary," Jack replied. "I don't give a hoot."

Jacobson opened his black bag to discover there were three dirty shirts inside; someone had switched his bag with someone else's almost identical valise. Max's nurse rushed the short distance from Jacobson's office to the Carlyle with the necessary medication. "I can still see the surprised expression on Kennedy's face," Jacobson said, "when he could again speak with a normal voice."

On another occasion, this time during the Steel Crisis, Dr. Max gave the President a shot just before an important reception in the East Room. "Now I can go downstairs to shake hands with several hundred intimate friends." Jacobson also injected the President during the tense moments when National Guard troops were brought in to desegregate the University of Mississippi

("Wasn't that a ball breaker?" Jack said of the tense standoff), and even during the Cuban Missile Crisis.

Jack did not ask what was in Dr. Max's chemical concoctions, and clearly did not wish to know. "I don't care if there's panther piss in there," he said, "as long as it makes me feel good." He was willing to overlook the fact that Max always appeared disheveled, was constantly dozing off, and that his fingernails were blackened from chemicals (once when Jacobson had fallen asleep in a bathtub, his long-time patient Eddie Fisher had tried without success to scrub them clean). Yet Jack might have felt differently had he known the shiny black medical bag neatly packed with vials was itself a calculated deception.

Jacobson's standards of hygiene left much to be desired. Fisher described the medical bag the doctor usually carried as "a jumble of dirty, unmarked bottles and nameless chemical concoctions which he would just dump out on a table when he began to mix an injection."

For his presidential house calls, he instructed his assistant, Harvey Mann, to "get my black bag polished and filled—we're going to see the Prez." Mann said he "would actually shine up his bag, then put in vials of amphetamines and vitamins I had mixed."

On a half-dozen occasions, Mann went along with Jacobson to the Carlyle. JFK "was especially warm to the doctor, and always called him Max. They were quite fond of each other. Dr. Max would follow JFK into another room and sometimes stay for as long as an hour."

Jacobson and Mann were never searched by the Secret Service during these trips to the Carlyle, nor did anyone ever examine Dr. Max's bag. "Some security!" said Mann. "They never looked at the stuff. Why, I could have killed the President. No one, not even Dr. Max, supervised me when I made up the amphetamine cocktails, so I could have easily slipped in poison."

That might not have been necessary. "Many of Max's patients

ended up with hepatitis," Mann said, "because the office was filthy."

The man who had brought Jacobson and the Kennedys together was among the first to attempt to bail out—literally. "I was driving Jacobson to LaGuardia, and he was putting on quite a performance. He kept saying for me to go ten times faster, and rattling on about all his experiments with cells from elephant hearts and sheep placenta . . . He had obviously swallowed too many of his own pills.

"Finally," Chuck Spalding continued, "I just stopped the car, got out, gave him the keys and said, 'You go to LaGuardia by yourself.' I was really very frightened at that point, the whole thing had gotten so completely out of hand." In retrospect, Spalding admitted that Kennedy's dependence on Jacobson's injections had the potential for disaster. "If you're President, I suppose you should be more careful. But at the time we all needed a boost."

A few months later, JFK came across a letter from then-President Theodore Roosevelt to his Marine Corps Commandant suggesting his men take a periodic fifty-mile hike to stay in shape. "Kennedy thought this was a great idea," Salinger remembered, "and he wanted somebody from the administration to march with the Marines. Unfortunately," said the rotund, cigar-chomping Press Secretary, "he kept staring at *my* waistline. He was dead serious about my going on the fifty-mile hike, and I knew if I went *I* would be dead—serious!"

Once the President's intentions were announced, the press had a field day with the Salinger Affair—until the Press Secretary bowed out, citing health concerns. When Bobby Kennedy managed to complete a fifty-mile hike, JFK bet Stas Radziwill a thousand dollars that he could never equal Bobby's time of eighteen hours. Eunice wagered another thousand that the prince, who with Lee had also joined Dr. Feelgood's list of patients, could not best their brother. If Radziwill won, the money would go to Jacobson's own Constructive Research Foundation.

"Bobby had hiked through the woods, and Jack didn't want to be shown up by his little brother—it was that simple," said Spalding, who joined Radziwill in the hike from Palm Beach south to Miami. "People from all over the country sent us sneakers—it was quite an event. Of course, just to make sure we would win, Jack sent Max down to go along with us. He was giving us shots all over the place," conceded Spalding, who for the purposes of the hike accepted the chemical "boost" Jacobson offered. "So we did the walk in record time—fifteen minutes ahead of Bobby. Jack, Jackie, and Lee met us at the halfway mark and gave us a pep talk as we sprawled on the grass. At the end, Jack had a big buffet waiting for us and champagne, and the jukebox was playing 'Bei Mir Bist Du Schon' by the Andrews Sisters. Jack even pinned paper medals on our chests. The whole thing made front-page news across the country. What people didn't know was that with all that speed we could've walked all the way to Rio, we were so hyped up!"

The last time Dr. Max saw the President was at the Palm Beach estate on November 3, 1963. "He was in the midst of preparing for his trip to Texas," said Jacobson, who was "disappointed" that he had not been invited along. "The atmosphere was tense. Rumor had it that the trip was too risky and would jeopardize his life. The President, himself, was relaxed and in good spirits. I expressed my concern over his upcoming trip. He brushed it laughingly aside and said he was looking forward to it."

After their triumphal first tour of Europe in the spring of 1961, Jackie proved that she also had drawing power as a solo attraction. While Jack unwound in Palm Beach, his First Lady (who had traveled on to Greece when Jack had flown home) sailed the waters of the Aegean aboard the 125-foot yacht *North Wind,* courtesy of the Greek government.

"A tall, handsome young woman stepped from the yacht and walked the length of the pier alone," gushed one reporter, noting that she was all but oblivious to the two hundred spectators on the other side of the rope barrier straining to catch a glimpse of her. "She was tawny with the Aegean sun, bare-legged, dressed casually in a sleeveless beige dress—and it was hard to realize that she was the same Jacqueline Kennedy who had swept like a queen through Paris, Vienna, and London only a few days before."

In the thyme-scented village of Epidaurus, she watched the National Theater of Greece perform a scene from Sophocles' *Electra*. With hundreds of reporters in tow, she visited Apollo's birthplace on the island of Delos, and the ruins of the Temple of Poseidon and Hydra, where she danced the Kalamatianos in a local tavern. When chartered boats full of photographers ventured too close to the villa where she was staying outside Athens, the captain of a naval vessel waved them away, then reenforced his point by crashing into one of the press boats.

———

Jack, his libido sent into overdrive by the combination of cortisone and Dr. Max's regular amphetamine injections, took advantage of Jackie's absences. "The White House doesn't take away a man's physical desires," Smathers said. In addition to Pam Turnure, his distractions at home included two young White House staffers known to everyone as "Fiddle" and "Faddle." Priscilla Weir had acquired the nickname "Fiddle" in college and Jill Cowan became known as "Faddle" after palling around with Weir.

The party-loving twenty-year-olds had been sharing an apartment in Georgetown when they showed up looking for jobs in the Kennedy presidential campaign wearing the same dress. After the election, Fiddle went to work for Evelyn Lincoln and Faddle worked for Salinger in the White House press office.

Gossip concerning the women's relationship with JFK was rampant within the White House, but Jackie took it in stride. When she was showing a member of the foreign press around the Executive Mansion, Jackie stuck her head in one of the offices and told the journalist in French, "And this is one of the young ladies who is supposed to be sleeping with my husband."

When Jack stayed at his penthouse suite in the Carlyle, he would ditch his Secret Service detail and make his way to a town-house several blocks away via a secret underground passageway running beneath the hotel. Terrified, the detail assigned to guard him finally located the door leading to the tunnel and locked it. When JFK returned at 3 A.M., he was forced to enter the hotel through the main entrance. "Okay," the President said sheepishly, "you got me."

From that point on, the Secret Service agents tagged along on their boss's nocturnal excursions through New York's subterranean passageways. "The whole experience was bizarre," Chuck Spalding said. "We'd be walking through this huge tunnel with flashlights in hand, and the Secret Service guys would be looking at their underground maps . . . and every once in a while one of them would stop and say, 'We make a left here, Mr. President.' I think they kind of got a kick out of the cloak-and-dagger aspect of it."

The Secret Service agents were not only apprised of all the President's womanizing, but played the major role in concealing those activities from the press and public. At private parties where the President might be seen in the company of Marilyn Monroe, Angie Dickinson, or even Jayne Mansfield ("She claimed they had an affair, but she seems awfully lowbrow for Jack," commented Vidal), agents warned waitresses, bartenders, busboys, and parking attendants never to disclose what they'd witnessed. "You'll see things but you won't see them," they would tell frightened servers. "You'll hear things but you won't hear them."

Marilyn Monroe still rendezvoused with Jack in New York and in California, and she donned a disguise—usually a black or at times a red wig, bandana, and sunglasses—for their trysts. At one large fund-raising bash in the Palm Springs home of Bing Crosby, California Democrat Philip Watson stumbled upon another, more exclusive party going on inside the President's bungalow. "The

President was wearing a turtleneck sweater, and she was dressed in kind of a robe thing. She had obviously had quite a lot to drink," Watson remembered. "It was obvious they were intimate, that they were staying together for the night."

"I Believe in You" from the then-new Broadway hit *How to Succeed in Business Without Really Trying* became Marilyn's private anthem, and at parties she would sing it to herself into a mirror— just as the lead character does in the musical. At thirty-six, seeing the end of her reign as the planet's leading sex goddess drawing near, she dreamed that Jack would leave Jackie for her. "Can't you just see me," she asked her neighbor and friend Jeanne Carmen, "as first lady?"

Such fantasies were to be expected from Marilyn, whose long-standing psychiatric problems and drug and alcohol abuse left her in a continuous fog. "There were always women throwing themselves at Jack, but now that he was president it was unreal," said Spalding. "Marilyn fell in the girlfriend category. Jack never considered her on a par with Jackie."

Still, wearing her dark wig and sunglasses, she accompanied the President on Air Force One. She also, contrary to popular belief, was a guest of JFK's at the Executive Mansion when Jackie was out of town. "Jack had Marilyn Monroe up at the White House, absolutely," Smathers said. "I know because I saw Marilyn at the White House. She was there. A lot."

Although she had become obsessed with JFK, Monroe still kept him waiting, like she had everyone else in her life. (She worshipped Clark Gable, but kept him waiting on the set of 1961's *The Misfits* for hours. The stress contributed to Gable's fatal heart attack the day after the picture wrapped.)

Marilyn's penchant for tardiness was much in evidence at a fund-raising gala held May 19, 1962, to celebrate the President's upcoming forty-fifth birthday. Some fifteen thousand of the party faithful joined JFK at Madison Square Garden to be entertained by, among others, Jack Benny, Jimmy Durante, Ella Fitzgerald, Peggy Lee, and Maria Callas.

The climax of the evening, however, was to be the appearance of Monroe. Upon learning that Monroe might play some part in the festivities, Jackie opted instead to stay in Virginia and compete in the Loudoun Hunt horse show, taking home a ribbon for third place. She had left it for Rose, Pat, Eunice, and Ethel to surround Jack, thereby discouraging speculation in the press that the event was tantamount to a presidential stag party.

For the occasion, Monroe, the world's reigning sex symbol, had literally been sewn into a flesh-colored Jean-Louis gown shimmering with rhinestones. As usual, she wore no underwear; the dress clung to her like a second skin. Marilyn and Jackie shared the same New York hairdresser, Kenneth, but backstage at the last minute the President's hair stylist, Mickey Song, gave her platinum coif a dramatic flip that would spark a national trend.

Realizing she would be late, Peter Lawford "introduced" Monroe early in the proceedings: "Mr. President, on this occasion of your birthday, this lovely lady is not only pulchritudinous but punctual. Mr. President—Marilyn Monroe!"

The throng thundered its approval, but Monroe, as planned, did not appear. Peter mugged his disapproval, and other entertainers went on instead. An hour later, Lawford made another melodramatic introduction. Still no Marilyn. This time Peter walked offstage. The tension mounted, and moments later Peter returned. "Because, Mr. President, in the history of show business, perhaps there has been no one female who has meant so much . . . who has done more . . . Mr. President, *the late Marilyn Monroe.*"

Suddenly Marilyn, wrapped in white ermine, stood in the spotlight. The crowd, which also included Lyndon Johnson, Adlai Stevenson, and Robert Kennedy, went wild. Groggy from drugs and seized by panic, she minced slowly up to the microphone where Lawford took her fur and vanished into the shadows.

After a long pause, Monroe delivered a sultry, suggestive rendition of "Happy Birthday" that would be parodied for decades: "Happy Birthday, Mr. *Pres-i-dent* . . ." A giant cake was wheeled on stage, and soon Jack was standing next to Marilyn at the microphone. "I can now retire from politics," he said, "after having had 'Happy Birthday' sung to me in such a sweet, wholesome way."

Although perhaps it's not difficult to imagine now, the notion that JFK and Monroe might have been lovers would have been utterly inconceivable to the American people at the time. The scene played out at Madison Square Garden could only have been described as an act of presidential hubris without parallel. Jack was so confident that the world (most importantly Jackie) suspected nothing that he had no qualms about acting out the fantasy in plain view of the unknowing electorate.

After the gala, Marilyn attended a party for Jack in the townhouse of United Artists head Arthur Krim. "She was wearing what she calls skin and beads," Adlai Stevenson remarked. "I didn't see the beads."

Kennedy confidant Bill Walton was also at the party, and recalled Jack telling him, "Go talk to Callas. No one's talking to her. She's pouting." Walton also shared a laugh with Jack at his brother's expense. "I happened to be with him when he was playing a trick on Bobby, who had never met Marilyn Monroe," Walton recalled. "The President and I are on a staircase above, watching. Marilyn started making passes at Bobby and backing him up against the wall. He died of embarrassment. He didn't know what to do or where to look. And we're upstairs rocking with laughter."

Later in the evening, Walton was looking for the men's room when he passed a darkened bedroom and realized someone was inside. He pushed the door open and saw Marilyn. "I caught her standing before a window, doing a naked erotic dance for guards who were on the rooftop of an adjoining building. I had a bursting bladder, and there she was in this bedroom and I couldn't believe it! She was an exhibitionist."

From the Krim party, Marilyn and Jack proceeded to his suite at the Carlyle. It was the last time they would see each other. After learning that their lovemaking sessions at the Lawfords' beach house had been taped by the Mafia, the President abruptly ended the affair. When a distraught Marilyn threatened to go public, JFK sent Bobby to California to "talk some sense into her."

The Attorney General succeeded, perhaps too well. After their brief encounter at the Krim party, Bobby took up with Marilyn where his big brother left off. "The initial relationship was with John," said singer Phyllis McGuire, who at the time was the girlfriend of Chicago mob kingpin Sam Giancana. "And there definitely was a relationship with Bob. And, you know, that's very like the Kennedys, just to pass it down from one to the other—Joe Kennedy to John, John to Bobby, Bobby to Ted. That's just the way they did things."

If anything, Monroe's affair with Bobby was even more intense. In June 1962 she was telling friends that Bobby was going to divorce Ethel and marry her. But by this time the FBI had obtained tapes from private detective Fred Otash and from Jimmy Hoffa's wiretap expert Bernard Spindel—tapes of Marilyn with both Kennedy brothers. The potential for political disaster was too great; in July, Bobby stopped returning her phone calls.

Invited to spend a few days at the ranch of a friend north of Santa Barbara, Bobby, Ethel, and several of their children arrived on August 3. The following day Bobby flew down by helicopter to meet with Marilyn at her Brentwood home. According to wiretap experts who claimed to have heard tapes of the conversation between Bobby and Marilyn that day, he told her they were through and a violent quarrel ensued.

On the morning of August 5, 1962, only hours after her confrontation with Bobby, Marilyn was dead from a drug overdose—an apparent suicide. Disturbing questions still linger decades after Monroe's tragic death. But at the time the American public, stunned by the news, had not the slightest inkling of a connection between Marilyn and the Kennedy brothers. An equally shocked Jackie was asked for her reaction. "Marilyn," said Jackie, "will go on eternally."

At the same time he jettisoned Marilyn, Jack was winding down his affair with Judith Campbell (later to become Judith Campbell Exner). As the girlfriend of both JFK and Sam Giancana, Campbell had been prevailed upon to do a number of favors beyond the sexual. She claimed that, on twenty separate occasions during the 1960 presidential campaign, Jack had given her suitcases full of cash to deliver to the mob boss, presumably in return for helping to deliver votes in the crucial West Virginia primary and in Chicago.

Even more shocking, Judy Campbell claimed that she perched on the edge of a bathtub in Chicago's Ambassador East Hotel on April 28, 1961, while Giancana and JFK were in the next room talking about plans to assassinate Cuban premier Fidel Castro. Campbell also said she carried envelopes containing details about the plot back and forth between the two men. "Jack told me outright," Campbell later told journalist Anthony Summers. "He said the envelopes contained 'intelligence material,' and that it involved the 'elimination of Fidel Castro.' "

In addition to liaisons with Jack in Palm Springs and in New York, Judy visited him at the White House twenty times between May 1961 and April of the following year. When they weren't together, White House telephone logs indicate that Evelyn Lincoln put calls from Judy Campbell through to Jack several times every week during the first year and a half of his administration.

When the truth concerning Judy Campbell's torrid affair with the martyred President surfaced in the late 1970s, JFK's inner circle closed ranks. Dave Powers was among those who suddenly developed a case of amnesia. "The only Campbell I know," he said, "is Campbell's soup."

Powers's response was indicative of the kind of blind, often unthinking loyalty that astonished even JFK. Of his devoted secretary Evelyn Lincoln, Jack said, "If I called her in here and told her that I had just cut off Jackie's head, and then said to her, 'Mrs. Lincoln, would you bring me a nice large box so I can put

Jackie's head in it?' she would say to me, 'Oh, that's lovely, Mr. President, I'll get the box right away.' "

By the spring of 1963, the Kennedys had turned their backs on Giancana. The consequences, some conspiracy theorists believe, would ultimately be felt in Dallas on November 22, 1963. But even if the Mafia was not involved in JFK's assassination, his relationship with a mobster's moll left the President open to blackmail. "I have no interest in their sex lives," Gore Vidal said. "But when Sam Giancana's girlfriend gets involved, you realize something heavy is going on beyond poke-poke. That's serious stuff. I have no doubt who killed Kennedy: the Mob."

Did Jack flaunt his affairs? Or merely hide them in plain sight? Either way, Jack's behavior seemed risky at best. "He was as brave a fellow physically and mentally as I ever knew," Smathers said. "We'd be on his boat and he'd dive in and stay underwater until we'd think is this bastard ever going to come up? Then when we thought he must have drowned, he'd suddenly pop to the surface. He was *fearless*. Well, he was always taking the same chances with his career, with his personal conduct as president. He believed in brinkmanship."

Much has been written about JFK's "Gentleman's Agreement" with the Washington press corps. And with 20/20 hindsight, it seems incomprehensible that the President's philandering was not common knowledge among members of the Washington press corps.

Jack's premarital womanizing was indeed well known. But with the exception of George Smathers and perhaps a few others, even those closest to the Kennedys were unaware of Jack's White House affairs. "If you put me on the witness stand," said Charlie Bartlett, "I would have to tell you that I never saw any evidence of Jack's cheating. He hid his infidelity completely."

Ben and Tony Bradlee have insisted they knew nothing of Jack's womanizing and were shocked when they learned that Tony's sister, Mary Meyer, carried on an affair with Jack for the final two years of his life. In October 1964, Meyer was strolling along the towpath by the canal in Georgetown when she was grabbed from behind and shot, execution style, once under her cheekbone. A young black man was charged and acquitted of the crime. After Meyer's death, the Bradlees discovered a diary in which she described in considerable detail her affair with Jack Kennedy. They turned the diary over to the CIA to be destroyed, but instead it surfaced in 1976. Later that year the original was returned to Tony Bradlee, who burned it.

"To say we were stunned doesn't begin to describe our reactions," Bradlee wrote in his memoir, *A Good Life*. "Like everyone else we had heard reports of presidential infidelity, but we were always able to say we knew of no evidence, none."

Smathers and Chuck Spalding were also "totally unaware" of the Meyer affair. Yusha Auchincloss conceded that Bobby might well have had an affair with Marilyn Monroe, "but not Jack. He and Jackie were too much in love."

"Look, I'm the biggest prude who ever came down the pike," Tish Baldrige said, "but we simply never saw a thing. The President's dalliances were kept hidden. That was just not part of our working lives in the White House."

Pierre Salinger enjoyed what amounted to total access to the President, seeing him virtually every day of his presidency. He conceded, however, that with the exception of the occasional dinner he was not privy to what went on behind closed doors in the family quarters.

"Of course I heard gossip," Salinger recalled, "but I can honestly say I never caught him with another woman—that I never knew of a single specific incident of the President having sex with a specific woman other than Jackie while I worked in the White House. But I did not think he was a totally faithful husband at the time, no. Jack Kennedy was always encouraging me to have affairs, so I took that to mean he was having affairs, too.

"People keep saying it was common knowledge, that the press was protecting him. But only once did a reporter ever even broach the subject. A journalist came into my office one day and said 'I hear Kennedy has got mistresses.' I replied, 'Look, he's the President of the United States. He's busy running the country. He doesn't have *time* for a mistress.' He never mentioned it again, and neither did anyone else."

Columist Betty Beale said that "the press was totally in the dark. I mean *totally*. The idea of the President having an affair with Marilyn Monroe or anyone else . . . well, it was just inconceivable." UPI White House correspondent Helen Thomas agreed. "I was right there every day," Thomas said, "and I didn't know a thing. Period."

"All those people who are now so brilliant and say they knew all about Jack's womanizing are wrong," Nancy Dickerson said. "The public was totally unaware, and so was the press. Ben Bradlee didn't know and Charlie Bartlett didn't know, and if they didn't know—and I surely didn't know—then nobody knew.

"At the time Mary Meyer was having her affair with Jack, I was going out with her ex-husband Cord Meyer. So I was paying attention to those things. I knew Jack was fond of Mary Meyer, but nobody remotely suspected they were having an affair. None of us knew. We knew he was interested in women, but never dreamed he was being unfaithful to Jackie. I never *heard* of Judith Exner or Judith Campbell or whatever her name was. Nobody in the press knew her at the time."

For what remained of his lifetime, then, JFK succeeded in his attempt to keep his Don Juan activities out of the press. Had the more titillating details of JFK's private life been made public, even Ben Bradlee conceded that it would almost certainly have led to Jack's removal from office. "If the American public had learned," Bradlee wrote over thirty years later, "that the President of the United States shared a girlfriend, in the biblical sense, with a top American gangster, and Lord knows who else, I am convinced he would have been impeached. That just seems unforgivably reckless behavior."

But Kennedy appeared to think the precautions he had taken were adequate. "They knock Jack now for being sort of reckless,"

Spalding said. "But he was far wiser than anybody knew. He is now portrayed as being out of control, but that wasn't the case at all. Jack was just the kind of person who had to run free, to a degree. Jackie knew that."

The press corps and even some of his closest friends remained clueless, so Kennedy probably felt he was being sufficiently careful. However half-hearted this attempt at discretion may seem in retrospect, at the time it worked. Without question, JFK's primary goal was to protect his reputation and that of his administration. Had Jackie been forced by embarrassing public disclosures to sue for divorce, his career would have effectively been dealt a death blow.

But there were other, more personal reasons Jack did not actually flaunt his infidelities—or certainly not to the degree that has been erroneously reported in recent years. "Jack wanted to protect Jackie as much as he could," Smathers said. "Jack would never intentionally hurt anyone, most of all Jackie. He was never rude or cruel to her; he respected her too much. He was particularly impressed by her intellect, and of course her style. There is no doubt that she was crazy about him, and there is no doubt that he loved her. I just don't think he was capable of being monogamous, and he handled it the best way he could . . ."

———

My wife is a shy, quiet girl.
But when things get rough, she
can handle herself pretty well.

JFK

———

11

Inspired by the dazzling state dinners in Paris, Vienna, and London—and fueled by Max Jacobson's amphetamine cocktails—Jackie set out to turn Oleg Cassini's vision of an American Versailles into reality. In the span of less than three years, Jack and Jackie played host to seventy-four foreign leaders and hosted no fewer than sixty-six state dinners and receptions.

The first and most ambitious of these was a candlelight state dinner for Pakistan's President Mohammed Ayub Khan on the lawn of Mount Vernon, overlooking the Potomac. It was also the first state dinner held outside the White House.

For Jackie and for Tish Baldrige, it was a logistical nightmare. A bandstand was constructed on the site for the seventy-four-piece National Symphony Orchestra, as was a tent pavilion dripping with flower garlands. Transportable hot and cold kitchens were set up for White House chef René Verdon. Since at the time there was no electricity at Mount Vernon, three large generators were brought in. Army trucks, meanwhile, transported the White House china and silver—not to mention the round tables and gold ballroom chairs usually used in the East Room—to Washington's stately home.

Navy vessels were commandeered to take the 150 guests downriver from Washington. As each boat docked, the passengers passed by rows of Marines in dress uniforms to a fleet of White House limousines that whisked them to the main house. The Colonial Color Guard and a fife-and-drum corps performed an intricate drill, and later the Air Force's "Strolling Strings" serenaded guests while they sipped mint juleps from silver cups.

Jackie, wearing a white organza gown with a silk chartreuse sash, made a grand entrance flanked by a Marine Honor Guard in full-dress uniform. After dining on Avocado and Crabmeat Mimosa, Poulet Chasseur—washed down with a Château Haut-Brion Blanc and Moët et Chandon Imperial Brut—they danced to the music of top-society orchestra leader Lester Lanin.

"The evening went off without a hitch," marveled Baldrige. "It was a magical night. Unforgettable." And the first of many, although the planning took its toll on the First Lady. The next morning, Jackie flew to Hyannis Port for the rest of the summer. "I've just got to relax," she told Jack. "This party took every ounce of energy I had."

From that point on in the administration, the White House itself was the venue for a series of glittering state dinners and receptions that rivaled anything the court of Louis XIV had had to offer. The host and hostess—he tanned and handsome in black tie, she a vision in her shimmering Cassini gowns and elaborate bouffant coifs—set the tone.

"When they appeared at the top of those stairs," Betty Beale recalled, "they were a glorious-looking, stunning couple, almost beyond belief. I don't know if they brought culture to Washington, but they sure brought *glamour* to Washington. No one had ever seen anything like it before. It was more a royal court than an administration."

Even the Europeans, who always prided themselves on their cultural superiority, were envious. "They certainly have acquired something we have lost, a casual sort of grandeur about their evenings, pretty women, music, beautiful clothes, champagne, and all that," British Prime Minister Harold Macmillan conceded.

Robert Frost's appearance at the inauguration had set the tone for the Kennedy administration, which celebrated culture to an unprecedented degree. Shakespearean actors, stars of the Metropolitan Opera, and the world's leading classical musicians were invited to perform at the White House before visiting heads of state.

One of the most memorable of these was a dinner honoring Puerto Rico's Governor Luis Muñoz Marín in November 1961. The evening's entertainment was provided by the legendary Spanish cellist Pablo Casals, who had been living in self-imposed exile in Puerto Rico. Although he had refused to perform in any country that recognized Spanish dictator Francisco Franco, Casals made an exception for Jackie. It was the first time Casals had set foot in the White House since 1904, when he played for Teddy Roosevelt.

Comparing his last state dinner during the Eisenhower administration with the Casals dinner, Leonard Bernstein recalled, "is to compare night and day ... The food was ordinary, and the wines were inferior and you couldn't smoke ... Everything was very different then; it was very stiff and not even very pleasant. Dinner was a huge horseshoe-shaped table at which seventy-five or so people were seated so that nobody could ever really talk to anybody."

In contrast, at the Casals dinner "you were served very good drinks first, and there were ashtrays everywhere just inviting you to poison yourself with cigarettes." Instead of the large horseshoe-shaped table there were "many little tables, seating about ten people apiece, and these tables are in three adjacent rooms so that it's all like having dinner with friends. Fires are roaring in all the fireplaces. The food is marvelous, the wines are delicious, people are laughing, *laughing out loud,* telling stories, jokes, enjoying themselves, glad to be there ... It was a joy to watch it. It was like a different world, utterly like a different planet."

The guest list at these White House soirées came to read like a *Who's Who* of arts and letters. Among those at a May 11, 1962, dinner for André Malraux, for example, were George Balanchine (who arranged for Rudolf Nureyev and Margot Fonteyn to perform a *pas de deux* at the White House), Andrew Wyeth, Arthur Miller, Tennessee Williams, Elia Kazan, and Geraldine Page.

Leonard Bernstein was also a guest at the dinner party for twelve honoring Igor Stravinsky in 1962. As soon as he arrived at the White House, he asked Jackie if she could direct him to a television set so he could watch the first few minutes of one of his famous Young People's Concerts. "Jackie said there was one in Caroline's room," he recalled. "So I sat with Caroline and Maud Shaw watching, and I remember very well Caroline sitting, hypnotized, or so I thought, by this program and just thrilled with every moment. We were sitting holding hands, and she was all wrapped up in the concert, and then she suddenly looked up at me with this marvelous clear face and said, 'I have my own horse.' Now that really brought me down to earth, so at that moment I turned off the set and rejoined the others."

Returning to the party, Bernstein found himself standing in a line waiting to greet Stravinsky. "When he came to me, Stravinsky kissed me on both cheeks in the Russian fashion, and I kissed him on both cheeks. There was all this Russian kissing and embracing going on when I suddenly heard a voice from the other corner of the room saying, 'Hey, how about me?' And it was the President. That's what I mean. It was so endearing and so insanely unpresidential, and at the same time never losing dignity. I can't think of the word—*stateliness* is the only word I can think of. Majestic presence."

At a historic April 1962 dinner honoring forty-nine Nobel laureates, two-time-winner Linus Pauling whirled around the dance floor with his wife while Jack, his arm on Jackie's bare shoulder, chatted with the likes of Pearl Buck and John Steinbeck. At one point JFK stood to praise the group as "the most extraordinary collection of talent, of human knowledge, that has ever been gathered together at the White House, with the possible exception of when Thomas Jefferson dined alone."

Overnight, Washington, which Jack once wryly described as "a city of northern charm and southern efficiency," had become a cultural mecca. Proclaiming the arrival of "a new Augustan age of poetry and power," Arthur Schlesinger gave the lion's share of the credit to Jackie. "The President's curiosity and natural taste," he wrote, "had been stimulated by Jacqueline's informed and exquisite responses: art had become a normal dimension of existence."

Indeed, the cultural renaissance that flowered during the Kennedy years was entirely a reflection of Jackie's tastes, not Jack's. "I always got a kick out of the President with all those longhairs," said Baldrige, who noted that he much preferred show tunes, contemporary music, jazz, even rock and roll. At the time, "The Twist" by Chubby Checker was one of his favorite recordings, and at private parties he requested that it be played repeatedly.

"He had no interest in opera, dozed off at symphony concerts, and," Ted Sorensen said of JFK, "was bored by ballet." At the historic Casals dinner, the President confided to a friend, "Pablo Casals? I didn't know what the hell he played—someone had to tell me."

Wisely, Jack nearly always deferred to Jackie's taste on ceremonial occasions. During one state dinner, however, he called his aide Chester Clifton to his table and whispered in his ear. Clifton took the message over to Jackie. "Mrs. Kennedy," Clifton said, "the President feels the marine band should play something 'livelier.'"

"Oh, he does?" Jackie responded. "What does he suggest?"

"The President has in mind some semiclassical numbers."

"I chose that music myself," Jackie said sweetly. "But, if he insists, have them play 'Hail to the Chief' over and over. That should amuse him." For the remainder of the evening, the Marine Band stuck to Jackie's classical program. (After the Casals dinner, she similarly noted, "the only music Jack really appreciates is 'Hail to the Chief.'")

Always wary of any potential political fallout, the President took note of criticism in certain quarters that—under Jackie's influence—the White House was becoming "too French." When

Tish Baldrige told him it was impossible to eliminate the French in White House menus, he told her to bring him a menu and he would show her how.

"We started out with Potage aux Vermicelles, and he said, 'All right, what the hell is that?' I told him it was 'consommé with little things squiggling in it.' He said, 'Well, we can't very well say that, can we? All right, instead of "potage" call it consommé. Some of the congressmen will understand that.' " By the time they went over the entire menu, JFK managed only one change from French to English. Instead of "Salade Verte, Fromages Assortis," the menu read "Green salad and assorted cheeses."

A number of the criticisms were unfounded. When *Newsweek* reported that three French wines had been served at a state dinner, Jackie called Ben Bradlee to complain. "Almaden Cabernet Sauvignon," she patiently explained, was not three French wines but one California wine.

At state functions, Jack and Jackie were charming to a fault, hospitable, and, to a certain degree, false. When they were not performing in their official capacity they felt increasingly isolated. "Being in the White House does make friendships difficult," Jackie allowed. "Nobody feels the same. Jack's even more isolated than I, so I do try to have a few friends for dinner as often as possible. Mostly it turns out to be the Charlie Bartletts or Bill Walton or someone we know really well, because I hate to call and have people feel they have to come." Her poignant comment to Oleg Cassini: "Come here anytime and keep us company. Because we are so lonely."

It was at the small dinner parties for two or three couples held in the family quarters that the First Couple felt they could really unwind. Leonard Bernstein, who was also invited to one of these intimate get-togethers, recalled how "you dine on Abraham Lincoln's china, with Madison's spoons, and it's just very moving. After dinner we were all in great high spirits, and we were sitting around the drawing room just chatting, and some of us were sitting on the floor. It was that informal."

Jack would usually leave right after dinner at nine, and seldom stayed past ten, but that night he was in a festive mood. At midnight, Bernstein asked Jackie, " 'It's getting very late, shouldn't we go?' She said, 'Don't worry about it. If he wants to stay up, let him stay up, he hasn't done this in ages.' And he was up until two. We weren't doing anything except talking and laughing, and I couldn't tell you *one* thing we talked about the whole night, it was just so delicious an evening."

When they were with their closest friends—the Bartletts, Walton, the Fays, Chuck Spalding, Lem Billings, the Bradlees, George Smathers—Jack and Jackie were at their most uninhibited. Cassini and Jack talked, among other things, about the *Kama Sutra*. "It's not just the eighty-six positions—no one has ever tried all of them successfully and lived—it is a guide to the achievement of happiness," Cassini said, "through the perfect knowledge of another. And this can only be done through love."

JFK and Cassini also liked to "zoomorphize" their friends. Jackie was a fawn, they agreed, and Joe was an owl. Bobby was a basset hound and Cassini a Siamese cat. "I thought he was a fine hunting dog, like a golden retriever or an Irish setter."

Seldom drinking more than a single scotch or daiquiri at these cozy get-togethers, Jack would also take the opportunity to blast political foes and assorted international figures as "bastards" and "total shits." Jawaharlal Nehru was one of those who fit into both categories as far JFK was concerned. "That sanctimonious bastard," he would say of the Indian prime minister. "He is the worst phony you've ever seen."

Jackie, meanwhile, employed her gift for mimicry after state dinners to lampoon many of the guests, including heads of state and American politicians. The Shah of Iran was a favorite target—they also speculated on his sex life with the considerably younger Shabanou Farah Diba—as was venerated postwar German Chancellor Konrad Adenauer, whom Jackie described to André Malraux as *un peu gaga*. On the domestic front, she skewered everyone from cabinet members Dean Rusk and Robert Mc-

Namara to Lyndon and Lady Bird Johnson, whom she dubbed "Colonel Cornpone and his little pork chop."

"Jackie could be just hilarious," Tish Baldrige said. "The way she imitated people's accents, their mannerisms—it was uncannily accurate. These were some of the most respected, revered people in the world, and the imitations she did once they left the room were just withering. Imagine if any of her little performances ever got out at the time. It would have been truly awful if she hadn't been so hysterically funny. She was a natural comic, and if you ever saw Jackie with friends, you'd realize the whole thing about her being 'shy' was nonsense. That was purely an act. Jackie was only shy around people she didn't like."

Vidal in particular enjoyed this side of the Kennedys. "She was very malicious, but in the most enchanting, life-enhancing way. She had a very black humor. She hardly had anything good to say about anyone. Jack was very much the same way, but of course he had to be much more guarded. Alone with friends the two of them were just *devastating* about everyone else, and when you left the room, you knew they'd be doing it to you, too. That was one of the reasons I liked them so much. We got on famously."

That is until a private White House party for Italian auto magnate Gianni Agnelli (whom, incidentally, Jack became jealous of) in November 1961. After quarreling with several of the other guests—notably Lem Billings ("the principal fag at court") and Jackie's mother—Vidal searched for his host and hostess. "In the Blue Room I found a friendly face," he recalled. "Jackie was seated in a straight, armless chair . . ." Vidal squatted beside her to chat, and when he got up he steadied himself by putting his hand on her shoulder. "The other option was her knee, hardly a decorous thing to do. As I started to rise, a hand pulled my hand off her shoulder. I looked up. There was Bobby." Vidal followed Bobby to the door of the Red Room, "blood, as they say, in my eye . . . then I said something like 'What the fuck do you think you're doing?' "

A bitter argument ensued between the two men, after which

it was erroneously reported by Truman Capote that Vidal had been physically thrown out of the White House. In truth Vidal, who later sued Capote for libel and won, left ("I confess, in a rage") with Arthur Schlesinger, John Kenneth Galbraith, and George Plimpton. Nevertheless, it was Vidal's last visit to the Kennedy White House.

In coming years Jackie became expert at severing ties with friends and family, with a minimum of personal discomfort. "She was one of the most emotionally self-sufficient people ever," said Jamie Auchincloss. "You'd be in her life one moment, and out the next. Gone. And it really didn't seem to bother her one bit."

There were only a few people she truly needed in the world: her husband and children, of course. And Joe. "When the President's father came to visit," J. B. West recalled, Jackie "danced down the halls arm in arm with him, laughing uproariously at his teasing." (Joe was no less popular with the other women in the East Wing of the White House; he frequently dropped in on "les girls," as he called them, often bringing gallons of ice cream fresh from an ice cream factory he owned.)

On December 19, 1961, the senior Kennedy was playing golf in Palm Beach with his favorite niece, Ann Gargan, when he suddenly became ill. Gargan brought her uncle home to bed and called Rose, who said he'd be fine after a short nap. After lunch, four hours after he was first stricken, an ambulance was finally called. While it sped away with its sirens blaring, Rose, in a state of shock, numbly went about her routine—golf followed by a swim.

A massive stroke had left the seventy-three-year-old Kennedy family patriarch paralyzed on his right side and unable to speak. Only days before, Jack and Jackie were in the midst of a triumphal whirlwind tour of Puerto Rico, Venezuela, and Colombia. As in Paris, Jackie had once again stolen the show, speaking Spanish to people on the street and embracing children in orphanages and hospitals. Wherever the presidential party went, shouts of "JFK!" blended with "Hi, Beautiful," and "Hey, Miss America!"

The President and First Lady rushed to Joe's side. Jack and Jackie were both crushed by Joe's illness, which left him confined to a wheelchair and capable of uttering only one word: No, which he repeated over and over again in abject frustration.

Although his face was contorted and he drooled, Jackie insisted that he be included at White House functions. At the dinner table, she would always sit next to Joe, talking to him, helping with his food, dabbing his chin with her napkin. She teased him as she had before his stroke, reminding him that if it weren't for him convincing Jack to marry her, she wouldn't be first lady.

"Jackie and Joe were buddies," said Secret Service agent Ham Brown, who was assigned to guard Joe Kennedy. "She loved him and he admired her, respected her." Brown, who was the man behind Joe's wheelchair in Hyannis Port for the next several years, recalled that "everybody—Bobby, Teddy, the President—all thought that I understood what their father was saying. Once the Old Man was saying 'no no no' over and over again, and Jack took me aside and asked what the hell his dad wanted. 'Well,' I said, 'he wants you and Jackie and Bobby and Ethel and Ted and Joan to all come by for dinner tomorrow.' Jack said, 'Oh sure, of course.' Then Jack would turn to Joe and say, 'We'll be here to-morrow at seven,' and he'd light up. Hell, I had no more idea of what Joe was saying than the man in the moon. But of course every father wants to have his family around for dinner. Everybody was very happy with this arrangement."

Jack was resolutely upbeat in his father's presence, always careful to include Joe in the conversation ("Don't you think so, Dad?" "Isn't that right, Dad?"). But privately he agonized over his father's condition. That Jackie felt just as deeply about Joe—that she shared his devotion to the one man who was at the epicenter of the Kennedy cosmos—moved JFK. Whatever their other transgressions and deceits, this unconditional loyalty to the family and to each other was the glue that held them together.

Leaving Hyannis Port by presidential helicopter, Jack watched his father below on the lawn, waving feebly from his wheelchair.

"It's all because of him, everything," he said to Chuck Spalding. "None of this would have happened if it weren't for him. We owe it all to him."

To Jack and Jackie, the antidote for despair was gossip—the more salacious the better—and Spalding was a major source. "One day in 1962 I had just gotten back from New York," Spalding recalled, "and I went straight to the White House. Jack loved to hear what was going on in New York—who was going out with whom, the real gossip. So I'm at the White House sitting on the edge of the bathtub, filling him in on all that's been happening while he shaves.

"All of a sudden, he looks at me and puts his forefinger to his lips. Then he reaches around the door, and who does he pull into the room but Jackie. Then he says, 'We had a deal. We wouldn't open each other's mail, we wouldn't listen in on each other's phone conversations, and we wouldn't eavesdrop on each other!'

"I thought he really had her this time," Spalding said. "But instead of being embarrassed, Jackie just looked at us and said, 'Two excited little schoolboys jabbering away about what's going on in New York. It's pathetic.' Of course, she wanted to hear all the hot gossip, too. But somehow she managed to turn the whole thing around. I was impressed."

Their favorite targets were each other, although more often than not it was Jackie who did the teasing. "She'd start calling him 'Bunny,'" said a friend, "and they'd be off and running."

"She loved to tease him," Jacques Lowe recalled, "and he loved it when she did." One evening she asked, "Where's that famous Kennedy wit I keep hearing so much about? We certainly don't see any of it around here."

One afternoon, while the President and his wife were waiting to be photographed at a champagne reception, Jackie grabbed a floral wreath and put it around his neck like a racehorse. "Damnit, Jackie, take this thing off me, and don't act so stupid. I can't be photographed this way, for Christ's sake." Giggling, Jackie then proceeded to make funny faces at him.

Many of Jackie's more barbed comments hinted at what she knew of her husband's sexual escapades. "She loved to needle him," Smathers said. "He was pretty good at it, too. At the White House parties they used to give, they'd be dancing together and then I'd cut in, and she'd say, 'You can't fool me. I know you two. I'll bet you boys wish you were back ten years ago, when you *really* used to play. Back in the South of France, maybe. You guys would both rather be somewhere else tonight . . .'"

On more than one occasion Jack and Smathers would be discussing the physical endowments of a particular female guest when Jackie suddenly appeared. "We'd change the subject, but she'd laugh and say, 'I know what you were talking about. You guys will never grow up!' "

One of their most private jokes involved a painting that hung in the West Sitting Room of the White House entitled *Arab in Desert Seated on Carpet with Tiger.* On the reverse of the painting was the biblical inscription: "It is better to dwell in the wilderness than with a contentious and angry woman." Either Jack or Jackie would glance knowingly in the direction of the painting, making his or her point without having to utter a word.

Jackie was the soul of discretion, though there were times she intentionally made blistering remarks within earshot of others. In Palm Beach, she came back from the beach and said to Jack, "You'd better get down there fast. I saw two of them you'd really go for."

Another time, Jackie uncovered a pair of panties beneath a pillow in the President's bedroom. "Would you please shop around and see who these belong to?" she asked, dangling the undergarment in front of her husband's face. "They're not my size."

There is consensus among those who knew them best that while Jackie was keenly aware of her husband's faithlessness, she had no desire to know the details. "Under the Napoleonic Code," Oleg Cassini explained, "a man is guilty of adultery only if he commits it in his own home." Describing "old Irish families" like the Kennedys as having held on to "feudal" customs regarding sex, Cassini reasons this enabled Jack to rationalize his woman-izing. It also explains, in part, why Jackie tolerated it. "She un-derstood it," he said. "She may not have liked it, but she understood it."

"Jackie put up with the situation because she loved him, in her way" Gore Vidal observed. "However, she would not accept being humiliated . . . And he was very careful that she *not* be humiliated. But when things started to leak out, when she became threatened, she sent him a message."

There were many such moments when Jackie felt threatened. "It wasn't that she worried about losing Jack," Spalding said. "She could beat anybody, and she knew it. No other woman on earth could compete with her. She loved him, and she was obviously willing to put up with a lot. But she was also very proud, and she could be very angry if her nose was rubbed in it."

Smathers witnessed more than one confrontation between Jack and Jackie on this issue. "The only person who ever fussed at him was Jackie," Smathers said. "She was the only person during the whole time in the White House, to my knowledge, who ever told him off. She would ask him point-blank if the rumors were true, and he would just deny that anything was going on.

"Once he said, 'Jackie, I would never do anything to embarrass myself.' And she just looked at him and said, 'Well, you're em-barrassing *me!*' She didn't like Jack's fooling around. She was damn mad about it. But she was willing to look the other way as long as he was careful. Jackie could not stand the idea of people pitying her or making fun of her. She didn't like being made to look like a fool."

After one of these battles behind closed doors, Jackie usually took her revenge by vanishing (JFK periodically substituted for his suddenly absent wife at ceremonial events). "She simply dis-appeared to Glen Ora and rode horses when she got mad," Bald-rige said.

Other times, she would spend. The forty thousand dollars she was now spending each year on clothes (again, the equivalent of over a half-million dollars in the 1990s) infuriated JFK. A rundown of the bills "had him boiling," recalled Ben Bradlee, who was present for one of their confrontations over money. "Not so much mad, as amazed and indignant. For a man who could afford to take no salary, Kennedy groused more or less constantly if good-naturedly about money. Jackie was spending him into the poorhouse, he would say."

Jackie offered a plausible defense. She pointed out that while an ambassador's wife received a certain amount of money from the government to cover expenses, the first lady per se did not. "She had to make a certain impression when in the White House and when she went abroad," Cassini said, "and that cost money."

And it wasn't just Jackie's costly wardrobe that had him "boiling." Jackie spent thousands to redecorate Glen Ora, their rented country house, to her taste. Unfortunately, she did not bother to consult the owners, who wanted things back the way they were—whatever the cost. Wanting a house of her own, Jackie was now overseeing the construction of Wexford, their new country house in Atoka, Virginia. JFK bet Bradlee a hundred dollars that the house would cost less than fifty thousand dollars to build; Bradlee wagered it would cost at least seventy-five. Wexford, which was not completed until November 1963, "ended up costing more than a hundred thousand dollars," Bradlee said, "and I never got paid."

Jackie's secretary, Mary Gallagher, was "caught smack in the middle" of what she called "the Battle of the Budget." No matter what international crisis was under way, Jack found time every month to go over Jackie's household bills—and explode over her spendthrift ways.

"The president seems more concerned these days with my budget," Jackie said, "than with the budget of the United States." As usual, she resorted to sarcasm when Jack handed Gallagher the onerous assignment of helping to bring Jackie's spending under control. "Oh yes, Mary," she told her secretary, "and from now on, if I ever order anything you think I really don't need, just slap my hand."

Jackie came up with a few cost-cutting ideas of her own: At White House parties, she instructed butlers "to refill those glasses that looked relatively unfinished and didn't have lipstick marks on the edge." The suggestion "really staggered" Gallagher. "Whether she meant it in dead earnest or tongue-in-cheek, I don't know."

They had no qualms about quarreling over money in front of their friends; the Bradlees later said they served as "insulation" for these battles. But for the occasional lapse, they revealed nothing to the outside world about their private life. "They both considered 1600 Pennsylvania sacrosanct," Baldrige said. "She wore a mask."

Cassini attributes Jackie's reluctance to go public with her personal problems to a "natural dignity. She was a woman of great pride. If she and Jack had had a fight ten minutes before, she would have *never* shown it.

"When you see Princess Diana, who is now older than Jackie was when she was in the White House, disemboweling herself in public—Mrs. Kennedy would never have done that," Cassini added. "Jackie was of sterner stuff made."

With the White House restoration complete, Jackie cast about for new projects. At Jack's behest, she set out in March 1962 on her first official solo trip abroad as first lady. First stop: Rome, where Jackie, wearing a full-length black dress by Cassini and a mantilla borrowed from Ethel, had a private audience with Pope John XXIII—the longest he had ever granted. They chatted for over a half hour in French, and when she left she proclaimed that he had "centuries of kindness in his eyes."

From Italy, Jackie—accompanied by her sister, Lee, her maid, Provi, her hairdresser, her favorite Secret Service man, twenty-four security guards, sixty-four pieces of luggage, and sixty reporters and photographers—flew to India on what was billed as a fourteen-day semiofficial cultural goodwill tour. By the time she was greeted at the New Delhi airport by Prime Minister Nehru, she had already upset delicate diplomatic sensibilities by postponing the trip three times, triggering forty-seven separate schedule changes. The postponements had been blamed on sinus trouble, but Jackie was actually summoning the courage to go. "Jack is always so proud of me when I do something like this," she said, "but I can't stand being out in front. I know it sounds trite, but what I really want is to be behind him and be a good wife and mother."

With lanky U.S. Ambassador John Kenneth Galbraith at her side, Jackie saw the Taj Mahal in the morning and in the moonlight, sailed aboard a marigold-decorated boat down the Ganges past water buffalo and Hindi pilgrims, rode a thirty-five-year-old elephant named Bibi ("My first and last ride on an elephant!"), fed pandas, saw a polo match, jumped horses with New Delhi guardsmen, and cringed in Nehru's arms as they watched a mongoose battle a cobra.

"The scene on the Prime Minister's lawn last night would last in anyone's memory," Galbraith wrote in his diary, describing one of several official dinners thrown for Jackie. The lights "flashed on a stunning array of saris—every woman present had . . . spent hours on the choice." The "supreme guests" were enclosed in "a little canopied area, the canopy being made of flower petals. Finally, before all was the stage, dancers, and musicians in vivid or sometimes wild costume, the women being especially sinuous as they turned and twirled."

But Ambassador Galbraith was also impressed with Jackie's grasp of the region's social issues. "She was very interested in the population problem, particularly India's policy regarding birth control," Galbraith said. "I know she expressed her opinion on this and other issues to the President." Did JFK pay attention? "Absolutely," Galbraith said. "When Jackie looked at you with those eyes and spoke, believe me, you paid attention."

Yet, after she had stayed two days at the famous "Pink Palace" as the guest of the Maharaja and Maharani of Jaipur, newspapers criticized her for spending too much time hobnobbing with the upper classes. So the President instructed that more hospitals be hastily added to his wife's packed itinerary. In a gesture of homage toward modern India's founder, she visited the spot where Mahatma Gandhi was cremated and left behind a bouquet of white roses.

It hardly mattered where she went or what she did. From the moment she set foot on the subcontinent, Jackie was revered as something akin to royalty. As she rode in the back of an open car giving her first *namastes*, the traditional Indian palms-together greeting, crowds lined the streets shouting *Jackie Ki Jai! Ameriki Rani!* ("Hail Jackie! Queen of America!") "Nothing else happened while Mrs. Kennedy was here," the *Times of India* reported. Another newspaper simply called her the new "Durga, Goddess of Power."

Among the gifts lavished on the visiting "goddess" were a sari of shimmering gold silk, a golden necklace encrusted with pearls, a silver dagger, ceremonial children's clothes to take home to Caroline and John-John, and twin tiger cubs. The baby tiger cubs, a gift from Air India, died before they could be flown to the United States.

The next stop was Pakistan, where crowds lined the streets as she made her way in an open car with President Ayub Khan from the airport to Lahore. Later, she made her entrance at the Lahore Horse and Cattle Show riding beside the president in a gold-trimmed carriage drawn by six horses and flanked by forty mounted horsemen in crimson uniforms. More than forty thousand cheered Jackie as she watched prize Arabian horses perform intricate equestrian maneuvers, and camels dance.

To show his appreciation for the spectacular state dinner that had been given in his honor at Mount Vernon, the Pakistani leader gave her a magnificent ruby, diamond, and emerald necklace and what would become her most treasured gift from a foreign head of state: Sardar, a prizewinning ten-year-old thoroughbred bay gelding.

Jackie visited Rawalpindi, Karachi, and the Khyber Pass. As thrilled as she was to see the Taj Mahal, built by the Mogul emperor Shah Jahan as a memorial to his wife, Jackie seemed even more enchanted by Pakistan's glistening Shalimar Gardens, which Shah Jahan had built as a memorial to his father. "All my life I've dreamed of coming to the Shalimar Gardens," Jackie said. "It's even lovelier than I'd dreamed. I only wish my husband could be with me."

Jackie was also keenly aware that, at times, she had left her sister in the dust. "Lee was just marvelous," she said somewhat disingenuously. "It must have been trying sometimes. Though we'd often ride together, sometimes I'd go ahead with the most interesting person and Lee would follow along five cars behind, and by the time I got there I couldn't even find her. I was so proud of her—and we would always have such fun laughing about little things when the day was over. Nothing could ever come between us."

After a stopover in London for lunch with Queen Elizabeth at Buckingham Palace, Jackie returned to Washington. Her trip to India had reaped a publicity bonanza for the Administration. Photos of Jackie and Lee atop an elephant and strolling beside the Taj Mahal filled magazines for weeks. "He knew how valuable she was at enhancing American prestige abroad," Teddy White observed. "Franklin and Eleanor Roosevelt were beloved figures, but no one could excite crowds here and abroad like Jack and Jackie Kennedy."

Despite criticism from disgruntled Republican congressmen that military aircraft had been used to transport Sardar, Jackie's horse, from Pakistan to the United States, Jackie greeted her husband with a renewed confidence in her value to him as First Lady. She was also confident, and rightly so, that he had spent nearly all his free time during her absence in the company of other women.

It was around this time that, according to Peter Lawford, Marilyn Monroe allegedly called the White House and told Jackie she was having an affair with her husband and that they were serious. "Marilyn," Jackie reportedly responded, "you'll marry Jack, that's great, and you'll move into the White House and you'll assume the responsibilities of first lady, and I'll move out and you'll have all the problems."

Some dismiss the story as apocryphal. But others are not so sure. "I have no trouble believing it happened, absolutely," said Jamie Auchincloss. "Jackie was my sister, after all, and it sounds just like the kind of gutsy thing she would say."

In truth, Jack was winding down his affairs with both Marilyn and Judy Campbell—and focusing his considerable attentions on Mary Meyer. That affair would take a curious turn when Meyer, according to James Angleton, the top CIA operative who later read her diary, smoked three joints of marijuana with Jack in the White House. Angleton also claimed JFK took LSD—"a mild acid trip together, during which they made love."

Jackie knew nothing of the Mary Meyer affair, and she had little time to dwell on the dimensions of Jack's relationship with Marilyn Monroe. In April, there were the state dinners for the Shah of Iran and the Nobel laureates.

The dinner for the Shah and his Empress presented a special challenge for Jackie. "You'd better watch out, Jackie," JFK teased. "You'd better put on all your jewels." According to Baldrige, Jackie began "borrowing jewels like mad from everyone left and right trying to match Her Royal Highness, Queen Farah. But finally Mrs. Kennedy did a very crafty thing. She took off all her jewels except for one in her hair.

"Of course, Farah arrived with the Shah in a gold embroidered dress glittering with sequins and every jewel in the whole Iranian kingdom on her back, front, and head. And the President just kept laughing at his wife and pointing and saying, 'Are you sure you did the right thing? You know, she's pretty good-looking, Jackie, and the dress is pretty good. I bet her clothes bill is even more than yours.'"

On May 2, she hosted an afternoon diplomatic reception, and the next day attended a luncheon at the Congressional Club. On May 8, she christened the nuclear submarine *Lafayette* in Groton,

Connecticut (*"Je te baptise Lafayette!"*), the following day hosted a luncheon in honor of the Norwegian prime minister, and two days after that hosted the spectacular White House evening for André Malraux. On May 22 she appeared alongside her husband wearing another splendid creation, this one encrusted in crystal beads, at a state dinner for the president of the Ivory Coast. In between were countless photo sessions, meetings, and press conferences. "Their schedule," conceded White, "would have floored lesser mortals."

By the time they embarked on their official visit to Mexico in June, Jack and Jackie both needed their amphetamine injections from Max Jacobson just to function. "Mexican emotions literally exploded at the sight of a young, bareheaded John F. Kennedy," recalled Tish Baldrige, "and the curtain of confetti was so thick for several blocks that the drivers of cars could not see beyond their headlights." Once again, Jackie made the usual rounds of children's charities and won over audiences with her flawless Spanish.

Most of July was spent with the children on Cape Cod, but that brief summer idyll was shattered by word of Marilyn Monroe's death. The news sent shock waves around the world, provoking a flurry of articles condemning the compassionless Hollywood star-making machine and eulogizing Marilyn as its ultimate victim.

Jack's reaction to Monroe's death—not to mention the urgent phone calls ricocheting from Peter Lawford to Bobby to Jack and back again—went far beyond the fact that she had sung "Happy Birthday" to him nine weeks earlier. There was very real concern that the FBI had managed to get hold of the tapes of Marilyn making love to both Kennedy brothers, tapes that would bring down the administration if they were ever leaked.

Jackie did not know all the details, but she recognized damage control when she saw it. In exasperation, she took Caroline and a dozen Secret Service agents to Ravello, the village on Italy's Amalfi coast where the Radziwills had rented a clifftop villa for the summer. "It was her way of telling him," Smathers said, "that he'd gone too far this time. The possibility that she might be humiliated or embarrassed really got to her. She didn't like it, not one damn bit."

Pursued by the relentless paparazzi at every turn, Jackie strolled village streets, shopped, read, went waterskiing, and took Caroline to an ice cream party with local children at the villa of an American friend, Dr. Judith Schoellkopf. But after two weeks passed and Jackie showed not the slightest intention of returning home, the American press began to take notice.

"Jacqueline Kennedy had originally planned to stay at Ravello for two weeks," *Time* reported. "But the two became three, and now they have stretched into four. She was having such a wonderful time that it almost seemed she might yet declare herself a permanent resident."

Halfway through her Italian escapade, an earthquake struck Naples some twenty miles away. Jackie, who felt the tremor, sent a personal message to the quake victims. "I am deeply distressed by the destruction caused by the earthquake in Southern Italy," she wrote. "The past two weeks have reaffirmed my admiration and affection for the people of this part of the world and filled me with gratitude for all their kindness and courtesy. That they, who give so much in heart and spirit, should suffer loss of life and home is truly a calamity. I pray that all who have suffered may speedily be helped in their great need." This unsolicited gesture won *la bella Jackie* the few remaining Italian hearts that were not already hers.

Jack usually enjoyed—even encouraged—his wife's absences. But now there were murmurings that Jackie might have had other reasons for staying on the sun-splashed Amalfi coast. Namely, the attention being lavished on her by another Radziwill houseguest, the dashing Fiat chairman Gianni Agnelli.

There were several transatlantic calls from Jack urging his wife to come home. When photographs of Agnelli and Jackie swimming together off Agnelli's yacht were carried over the Associated Press wire, JFK fired off a cable: A LITTLE MORE CAROLINE AND LESS

AGNELLI. Her response was to go scuba diving with the Italian tycoon the next day. (Which at least pleased Cassini, whose swimwear sales soared after Jackie was repeatedly photographed in Italy wearing his colorful one-piece suits.)

"Believe it or not," Betty Spalding said, "Jack was jealous of Jackie seeing any other man, even a pal like Bill Walton, because he was convinced she was doing the same things he was doing. In Jack's mind his other women were always separate and apart from his responsibility to his wife."

After years of suffering Jack's infidelity in relative silence, she relished the idea of putting Jack through the same torment. "What can I do?" she asked coyly. "I have dinner with someone, dance with someone for more than one dance, stay with someone, get photographed with someone without Jack—and everyone automatically says, 'Oh, he must be her new lover.' How can you beat that?"

Was Jackie entirely faithful during their years in the White House? CBS's then-Washington Bureau Chief David Schoenbrun, much admired by JFK, said privately that "nobody should worry about Jackie"—that she was carrying on affairs of her own.

Since the late 1950s much speculation centered on her relationship with Walter Sohier. To be sure, Jackie and the unmarried Washington attorney were extremely close; during the times she felt most abandoned by Jack, she would call on Sohier at his Georgetown house and spend hours with him.

Veteran Washington columnist Betty Beale conceded that "Jackie was no puritan. She obviously enjoyed the company of men other than her husband. It's hard to blame her. I think Jackie loved Jack, but coming from the background he did it's difficult to see how he could really be faithful to one woman."

"Jack was jealous of her," Cassini allowed. "But if she had slept with somebody other than him, it would have been disaster for her." Still, Cassini added, "I always had the feeling that she was irritated, but I never had the feeling she would create a retribution for what he did . . ."

Returning around Labor Day, Jackie hit the ground running once again. In mid-September, she and Jack watched the America's Cup races in Newport, then attended the black tie reception and dinner at the Breakers. That month she also attended the opening of Philharmonic Hall in New York, the first of several massive structures that would eventually make up Lincoln Center.

Leonard Bernstein, who conducted the evening's performance, committed what was for some an unforgivable faux pas when following the concert he kissed Jackie backstage. "Well, I never heard the end of it from the press," Bernstein recalled, "and there was also consternation in the White House because I was so wet. I mean, that sweaty, awful conductor kissing this gorgeous creature, coast to coast on television, was just not permissible. And I'm still living it down. Horrible. But it doesn't seem to have affected our relationship."

On the morning of October 16, 1962, U.S. intelligence experts informed JFK that aerial photos showed the clear presence of offensive nuclear missiles in Cuba. For the next week, top-secret meetings went on behind closed doors at the White House. Without members of the White House staff ever knowing, Pentagon and State Department officials slept behind closed doors on couches and cots. Jack explained the gravity of the situation to his wife, and the importance of conducting business as usual in the White House.

There were few options open to the President—an air strike or invasion, a negotiated settlement through the United Nations, or a naval blockade of the island. At first an angry Jack, his judgment perhaps affected by the amphetamine shots he was now getting to cope with the round-the-clock strategy sessions, leaned toward quick and decisive military intervention.

A voice of reason at National Security Council meetings was Deputy Secretary of Defense Roswell Gilpatric. While presidential advisor McGeorge Bundy argued for an air strike, Gilpatric spoke up. "Essentially, Mr. President," Gilpatric said, "this is a choice between limited action and unlimited action, and most of us think that it's better to start with limited action." JFK nodded in agreement.

The following Sunday, J. B. West was jarred awake by an urgent call from Jackie. When he arrived in the family quarters at the White House, through a back door so as not to arouse suspicion, she was waiting for him. "Thank you for coming, Mr. West," she said calmly. "There's something brewing that might turn out to be a big catastrophe—which means we might have to cancel the dinner and dance for the Maharaja and Maharani of Jaipur Tuesday night."

Even though he was now consumed by the mounting crisis, Jack squeezed out a few extra moments to spend with Caroline and John-John, who to make matters worse was in bed with a temperature of 104. In an uncharacteristically melancholy moment, Jack turned to Jackie. "We've already had a chance," he said. "But what about all the children?"

The next evening the President addressed the nation, announcing that he had ordered a blockade. The Cuban Missile Crisis had begun. While the world teetered on the brink of nuclear holocaust, Jackie, though smoking even more than usual, remained surprisingly self-possessed. With the state dinner canceled, she asked a few friends—Bobby and Ethel, Lee and Stas, and Oleg Cassini—to come by the White House for dinner.

"Jackie tried to be upbeat," Cassini said. "But it was a tense evening." Jack, on the other, hand, was "detached, fatalistic."

Finally, McGeorge Bundy came in to tell the President that a Soviet ship had turned back rather than confront the blockade. "Well," JFK said, "we still have a twenty percent chance to be at war with Russia."

When no one else was around, Cassini asked, "Mr. President, are you saying war is still possible?"

"Oh yes," Jack said without missing a beat. "It's possible, all right."

The crisis lasted a total of thirteen days. Then, on October 24, Russian ships carrying missiles toward Cuba turned back. "We're eyeball to eyeball," Secretary of State Dean Rusk said, "and I think the other guy just blinked." With that historic pronouncement, Rusk signaled the end to the crisis. The world breathed a sigh of relief.

Chuck Spalding was driving from his home in Connecticut to his job in Manhattan when "the news came over the car radio that the Russians had backed down. I pulled over at the nearest phone booth and called the White House. Jack answered. 'You did it! You did it!' I said.

"There was a pause, and he replied, very calmly, 'So I trust the boys on Wall Street are pleased as well?' Here the world had been pulled back from the brink of nuclear destruction, and he was calm enough to make that kind of casual, witty remark."

Jack, meanwhile, could not resist telling friends which of them had made his short list to join the First Family in the subterranean emergency government headquarters thirty miles outside Washington and which hadn't. "I'm afraid," he told Ben and Tony Bradlee over dinner, "neither of you made it."

Apparently saving the world from obliteration was not enough to win the hearts of all his countrymen. Immediately after the crisis, JFK called Baldrige to his office. "I have been thinking," he told her, "you know, none of these people [McGeorge Bundy, Dean Rusk, Sorensen, McNamara, Salinger, Gilpatric, and his other close advisors] have gone to bed. They have all stayed by my side during these thirteen days and I want to record this event somehow for them. I want to give them a present that will remind them of how much it meant to have them stick by me."

He told her to approach her former boss, Tiffany Chairman Walter Hoving, and ask him to make up forty sterling silver calendars showing the month of October with "JFK" at the top and the thirteen critical days circled. When he realized the cost for each came to forty dollars, he told Baldrige to get Tiffany to do a cheaper version in Lucite. Hoving refused.

Then JFK asked for a discount. "Never," Hoving replied. "Abraham Lincoln tried to get a discount from Tiffany on a pearl necklace for his wife and we wouldn't do it. We never give discounts to presidents."

The President erupted. "What? You tell that bastard Hoving," he shouted at Baldrige, "that we will never shop there again—not for state gifts, nothing!" Eventually, JFK calmed down and agreed to pay full price out of his own pocket, and the White House continued to purchase many of its state gifts from Tiffany.

Jack told the Bradlees he felt his "victory" over the Russians was hollow at best. He believed that a fatal misstep between the two superpowers was inevitable, and as a result would wipe out "all of us at this table and our children."

All of Jack's friends were familiar with his fatalistic streak. He often talked of assassination and speculated that he would be shot while riding in an open car through a downtown street "with all the people and the noise . . ."

Larry Newman, their Hyannis Port neighbor, was invited to sit next to Jack during mass one weekend. "Do you think if somebody tried to take a shot at me," he asked matter-of-factly, "they'd get one of you first?"

"No, Mr. President," Newman answered, "but now that I think of it, I won't be sitting with you next Sunday!"

Jack smiled. "That's okay," he said, glancing at the reporters a few rows back. "I still have the press right behind me for protection."

On January 8, 1963, the most famous painting in the world, the *Mona Lisa*, was unveiled at Washington's National Gallery of Art. Largely because of his friendship with Jackie, French Minister of Culture André Malraux agreed to have the Leonardo da Vinci masterpiece removed from the Louvre and lent, not to an American museum, but personally to the President. Reporters covering the unveiling of the portrait noted that Jackie, wearing a bejeweled, strapless mauve gown, upstaged *La Gioconda*.

Three days later, Jackie was dictating a letter to Mary Gallagher when she suddenly stopped. "Mary, would you say I've done enough until now as first lady?"

"Yes, Jackie," Gallagher answered. "I think you have—even more than your share."

It had been a rhetorical question, of course. Jackie had been the most activist first lady the White House had seen since Eleanor Roosevelt, packing more than any of her predecessors had into two years.

She summoned Tish Baldrige to the sitting room. "I am taking the veil!" she announced brightly. For the foreseeable future, Jackie told Baldrige, she was devoting herself to her family. All nonessential outside activity would cease—no more "semiofficial" foreign trips, luncheons, photo opportunities, ship launchings, or hospital visits. She would restrict herself to performing only those duties that her husband deemed essential. She did not tell them the real reason for her decision for drastically curtailing her schedule, but they suspected it just the same. Jackie was pregnant.

The principal "essential duty" Jackie felt obligated to perform was the overseeing of state dinners. After one state dinner honoring Chief Justice Earl Warren and LBJ, and another for the president of Venezuela, the New York cast of *Brigadoon* was brought in that March to entertain a youthful King Hassan II of Morocco. Sol Hurok, Myrna Loy, and Agnes de Mille were among the guests, as was the musical's lyricist, Alan Jay Lerner. (Lerner was also the wordsmith for *My Fair Lady* and for *Camelot,* which would later be used as a metaphor of the Kennedys' thousand days in the White House.)

Tish Baldrige had contingency plans to cover every conceivable problem. Because of the limited space, they had to use taped music instead of the Marine Band. When JFK fretted about the tape breaking, Baldrige proudly pointed out that a backup tape would be running at the same time to prevent just such an eventuality.

But in the middle of the performance, an extra spotlight was turned on and blew a fuse, plunging the East Room into total darkness. Guns drawn, a dozen horror-stricken Secret Service agents sprinted to every window and exit. In the pitch black, the

President calmly turned to his guest of honor and whispered, "Your Majesty, it's part of the show, you know."

The lights went back on two minutes later. Jackie leaned forward in her chair, cast a knowing look at her husband, and winked.

After the performance, Jack thanked Lerner, who had been his classmate at Choate. "And to think," JFK said, "neither of us thought the other would amount to anything."

The blown-fuse episode was not the only major mishap at an official White House function. At a later state dinner for the King of Afghanistan, JFK asked that the eight-minute fireworks display over the White House be squeezed into four minutes. The resulting barrage was so intense that bodyguards and Secret Service agents leapt toward the President and the King to protect them. Washington police were flooded with calls asking if a plane had crashed or the city was under attack.

On another occasion, Metropolitan Opera singers gave a performance of *Così Fan Tutte* for children of the diplomatic corps in the State Dining Room. "The President went over to talk to them," Baldrige recalled. "One of the stars wore a mink turban with large ostrich feathers that went right into the lit candles on the wall sconce and burst forth into a towering mass of flame."

The fire was quickly extinguished, but some of the children began to cry. "The President put his arms around them," Baldrige recalled, "but they kept crying. Then he burst out laughing because there was no more danger, and those frightened children—with the sight of the President laughing and laughing, well, they started laughing too, and soon the whole room was laughing. It showed how really great he was. They all adored him."

On April 18, Jackie made the official announcement from Palm Beach that she was pregnant. One of the first congratulatory notes was from Roswell Gilpatric, the patrician New York lawyer who now served as number two man in the Defense Department under McNamara and had been the voice of reason during the Cuban Missile Crisis. Jackie had taken an obvious liking to Gilpatric, and their cozy behavior at various White House functions had attracted the attention of both Jack and Gilpatric's third wife (out of five), Madelin.

"It was so thoughtful of you to write me about the baby," Jackie responded. "It is such a happy thing and thank you so much for taking the time—And now that I don't have to go to all those ladies' lunches I hope I can come and see you and Madelin some lunch in May or June."

While Jackie and the President relaxed in the Florida sun, Baldrige was left fielding countless requests for the First Lady's presence at various official functions. Outgoing, self-deprecating, and very popular with the Washington press, Baldrige came to represent to Jackie the formidable demands of Jackie's position. And while she had done a great deal to shield her from some of those demands, there were times she simply told Jackie, "You just have to do this."

"I don't 'have' to do anything," Jackie complained to her husband.

"I was in a most unfortunate position," Baldrige said, "being both someone who worked for her and an old friend." After a trip to New York to catch Nureyev and Fonteyn perform at Lincoln Center, Jackie made replacing Baldrige her first order of business. She picked another old friend, in fact her dearest friend, Nancy Tuckerman.

In May, Alan Jay Lerner and Eddie Fisher (both fellow patients of Max Jacobson) staged a forty-sixth birthday celebration for JFK. As in the previous year, this party was a star-studded Democratic party fund-raising event held in New York—this time at the Waldorf-Astoria. Famed trial lawyer Louis Nizer danced in a chorus line with Ed Sullivan; Sugar Ray Robinson, Tony Randall, and Robert Preston were among those who performed.

"Dr. Feelgood" was also among the guests at the party. He discovered from yet another patient at the party, former National Democratic Party Treasurer Nathan Lichtblau, that an unsuspecting Harry Truman had also taken speed while he was in the

White House. "If Max thinks that Kennedy is the first United States president he has treated, he is mistaken," Lichtblau told Nina Jacobson. "I used to share my bottle of vitamins with Harry."

"This came as a complete surprise to me," Jacobson recalled. "But before I could comment about it, Kennedy came over and joined us. We congratulated him on his birthday. He said he was happy to see us and was glad I could tear myself away from the office . . ." After filling them in on the latest antics of Caroline and John-John, he said, "I hope you are all enjoying the party as much as I," and then rushed off to catch the entertainment.

Marilyn Monroe's sexy rendition of "Happy Birthday" on the occasion of JFK's forty-fifth birthday is indelibly etched in the public mind. But few realize that on turning forty-six he was serenaded by yet another of his former lovers. This time it was Audrey Hepburn who brought down the house with her own enticing version of "Happy Birthday, Mr. President."

Toward the end of the evening, Eddie Fisher was "standing in line next to Audrey, waiting to greet the President, and after speaking to her for a moment, he passed right by me without a sign of recognition. But suddenly he did a double take and grasped my hand."

"Well," JFK said with a grin, referring to their last encounter in Max Jacobson's office, "how are you feeling *now?*" It was to be the last time Fisher saw Jack Kennedy.

Jackie had her own birthday party planned for Jack that May 29, a cruise down the Potomac aboard the yacht *Sequoia.* He had wanted the party to take place aboard the *Honey Fitz,* but was told "the boat's got rotting stern timbers—like the rest of us, I guess."

It was raining on the President's birthday, but the small group set out anyway. While lightning and thunder crashed all around, the *Sequoia* sailed downriver and back again a total of five times. The guests—Bobby and Ethel, Teddy, the Bartletts, the Fays, the Bradlees, the Shrivers, Lem Billings, David and Hjordis Niven, an old Boston pol named Clem Norton, Bill Walton, and Mary

Meyer—were drinking and laughing away, oblivious to the storm that raged outside. A three-piece Marine Band kept playing one of the President's favorite tunes, "The Twist," until it was time for the President to open his gifts.

Filter-tipped Salem in hand, Jackie stood by Jack's side as he ripped the wrapping off each package, examining each gift and holding it aloft for the others to see. Her running commentary came to an abrupt halt when an inebriated Clem Norton put his foot right through the rare engraving that had been Jackie's birthday gift to Jack. "There was a moment of stunned silence," Ben Bradlee wrote. "Jackie had scoured galleries to find it, but she greeted its destruction with that veiled expression she assumes . . ."

"That's really too bad, isn't it, Jackie," JFK said as he put it aside. Then he reached for the next present. She merely sighed and said, "Oh, that's all right. I can get it fixed."

"Jackie was almost as unemotional [as Jack] about what would have been, we felt, a disaster to most people," Bradlee observed. "They both so rarely show any emotion, except by laughter."

—

Jackie, who had suffered through a miscarriage, a stillbirth, and two difficult pregnancies, was preoccupied. Jack shared her concern, at least to the extent that he fully supported her decision to spend the summer relaxing in Hyannis Port.

"While our President was busy presumably running the country," said her on-again, off-again friend Truman Capote, "Jackie's moods were swinging this way and that. I mean, she was *always* an extremely moody person. It was almost impossible to know if she was going to just throw her arms around you or walk by like you simply did not exist. Maybe it was just because she was pregnant and all those hormones were doing their thing. Or maybe it had something to do with good ole Dr. Max."

Alarmingly, Jackie, who along with Jack had long ago convinced herself that Max Jacobson's pills and "vitamin" injections were harmless pick-me-ups, continued to unknowingly ingest Dr. Feelgood's amphetamine cocktails throughout her pregnancy.

She also continued to smoke. Although certainly not as much was known at the time about the harmful effects of smoking during pregnancy, the general public was well aware that smoking caused low birth weight. Given Jackie's history of problem pregnancies, her decision to continue to smoke may reflect simple medical ignorance. Or more likely, an addiction to nicotine that—given the stresses arrayed against her—was so powerful she simply could not overcome it.

Jack was touring military bases in California when Jackie first sought comfort, solace, and understanding in the company of one of his most trusted advisors. Black Jack Bouvier's daughter was always more comfortable in the company of men, particularly more mature married men. At fifty-seven, Yale-educated Roswell Gilpatric was a decade older than Jack and twenty-two years older than Jackie.

While Jack was away, she invited Gilpatric, who was going to be leaving his position as number two man in the Defense Department to return to private law practice in New York, to lunch alone with her at Camp David. Jackie and Jack had always assumed FDR's old refuge of Shangri-La in Maryland's Catoctin Mountains—which Ike later renamed Camp David after his grandson—would not be to their liking. But since they had spent a small fortune building their country house, Wexford, they came to the belated decision that Camp David was, in Jackie's words, "just charming."

"I loved my day in Maryland," Jackie later wrote to Gilpatric.

> It made me happy for one whole week—It is only Thursday today—But I know the spell will carry over until tomorrow—and I will go back to Camp David—and see those West Virginia motel shacks with their bomb shelters churning underneath—as great columned houses—

We had some people to dinner last night who had been to another farewell party for you at Anderson House. I always push unpleasant things out of my head on the theory that if you don't think about them they won't happen—but I guess your departure—which I would never let myself realize until tonight—is true—

I feel sorry for whoever succeeds you—(for them)—and I will never really like them—no matter who they turn out to be—and neither will anyone else—They will always live in your shadow—and no one else will be able to have force and kindness at the same time—

But I feel much sorrier for us—In this strange city where everyone comes and goes so quickly you get used to its rather fickle transiency—So when anyone's departure leaves a real void—you should be really proud of that—although you are the last person who would care about such a thing.

I know you will find some peace at last—But I also know that the change of pace will be an awful readjustment. I wish you so well through all of that—Please know Dear Ros that I will wish you well always—Thank you—Jackie.

At one of their intimate White House dinners, Jackie had declared Gilpatric, whose sexual escapades were already known to Washington insiders, as "the second most attractive man in the Defense Department" next to McNamara. "Men can't understand his sex appeal," Jackie said, pointing to Ben Bradlee and her husband. "Look at them. They look just like dogs that have had a plate of food grabbed from under their noses."

Years later, Gilpatric and Jackie would at times be inseparable. Their trip to Mexico to visit the Mayan ruins fueled worldwide speculation that he was to become the next Mr. Jacqueline Kennedy.

Angered by her husband's slavish devotion to Jackie, Madelin filed for divorce in 1970. Were her husband and Jackie having an affair while she was in the White House? "I have my own feelings about that," she said, "but I won't go into them. They were certainly very, very close. Just say it was a particularly close, warm, long-lasting relationship."

Gilpatric would not deny that, though for years he was less than forthcoming on his relationship with Jackie. "Both Jack Kennedy and Jackie told me things in confidence that I will never divulge," he said. But he went on to concede that he and Jackie became "romantically involved" when she was First Lady. "We loved each other. She had certain needs, and I am afraid Jack was capable of giving only so much. I suppose I filled a void in her life, but that does not mean they didn't love each other. If anything, I think they were growing closer toward the end."

At the end of June 1963, Jack embarked on a history-making trip to Europe. In West Berlin, three fifths of the population streamed into the streets to hear JFK make his famous "Ich bin ein Berliner" speech. Unlike Jackie, he had no facility for foreign languages, and had to be coached for over an hour just to pronounce this simple phrase properly. The hysterical response of the multitude thrilled Kennedy, then troubled him. "He always regarded crowds as irrational," Arthur Schlesinger remarked. "Perhaps a German one compounded the irrationality."

Hours later, Jack received a less tumultuous but no less warm greeting on his arrival in Ireland. At Dunganstown in County Wexford, which he had visited sixteen years earlier, JFK was served tea, cookies, and hugs by his distant Irish relatives. After a stopover in England to discuss the Nuclear Test Ban Treaty with Harold Macmillan, he went on to Rome and a private audience with Pope Paul VI. There was speculation as to whether JFK would kneel before the new pontiff and kiss his ring. "Norman Vincent Peale would love that," teased Kennedy, who merely shook the Pope's hand.

Jackie spent most of July reading, painting, and resting in their rented oceanfront home on Squaw Island, not far from the Hyannis Port compound. The Squaw Island house was at the end of a long dirt road, more secluded, more luxurious, and quieter than the houses that were in the Kennedy homestead. Already anticipating life after the birth of her third child, Jackie asked if a vibrating-belt weight loss machine could be installed for her in the White House exercise room.

On August 5, 1963, in what was a crowning achievement of JFK's administration, the Nuclear Test Ban Treaty was signed by Secretary of State Dean Rusk in Moscow. However, Jack and Jackie's sense of euphoria was to be short-lived. On August 7, 1963—five weeks before the baby was due to arrive—Jackie took Caroline and John-John horseback riding at nearby Osterville. On the ride home, she began experiencing labor pains. Thinking they might be false, she went upstairs to lie down and phoned for Dr. John Walsh, who fortunately was vacationing nearby.

At 11 A.M., a Secret Service agent brought the Kennedys' convertible around to the front of the house while Dr. Walsh carefully helped Jackie out the front door. When Dr. Travell, who had also arrived at the scene, asked if she should notify the President, Jackie's response was immediate. "No!" she shouted back at Travell as the car sped away.

With Dr. Walsh and Mary Gallagher at her side, Jackie was heading for the helicopter that would whisk her to the military hospital at Otis Air Force Base. Jackie had been characteristically composed, but suddenly she became emotional. "Dr. Walsh," she said, "you've just got to get me to the hospital on time! I don't want anything to happen to this baby."

"We'll have you there in plenty of time," he said, trying to reassure her.

But Jackie kept pleading, "Please hurry! This baby mustn't be born dead!"

The helicopter arrived minutes later at the hospital, where a special presidential wing had already been set up precisely in the event an emergency like this occurred. At 12:52, Jackie gave birth by cesarean section to a four-pound ten-ounce boy who was promptly placed in an incubator. Although she had twice insisted Jack not be told she was in labor, he had gotten word and arrived at the hospital forty minutes after the boy's birth. Even before the President had arrived, the base chaplain baptized the baby Patrick Bouvier Kennedy, after Jack's grandfather and Black Jack Bouvier.

Before he had a chance to see Jackie, the President was told that the baby suffered from a severe respiratory problem involving the lung's hyaline membrane not uncommon among premature infants.

The decision was made to transport the baby by ambulance to Children's Hospital in Boston, where he could receive better care. But first, Jack wheeled Patrick into Jackie's room, and placed him in Jackie's arms. She held the baby for a few minutes before he was placed back in the incubator. This was the only time Jackie ever held her youngest child, and the last time she saw him. "His hair was dark," said Mary Gallagher, who saw Patrick as he passed in the hallway, "his features well formed."

While Patrick was being driven to Boston, Jack visited Caroline and John-John on Squaw Island, then returned to check on Jackie before flying to Boston. JFK checked into the Ritz Carlton Hotel not far from the hospital, but was soon told the baby was being moved to Harvard's School of Public Health, where he would be placed in an oxygen chamber.

Growing more and more concerned despite doctors' reassurances, Jack visited the baby four times that day. In the afternoon, he flew to Otis Air Force Base to bolster Jackie's spirits, then helicoptered back to Boston. That night, Jack refused to leave the hospital. Instead, he spent the night sleeping in a vacant bed two floors above the room where Patrick lay fighting for his life in the oxygen chamber.

The nation prayed for the recovery of this first baby born to a sitting president, but at 2 A.M. Dave Powers awakened Jack to tell him that the baby's condition had taken a turn for the worse. While he paced the hallway waiting for the elevator to take him downstairs, the President passed the room of a severely burned child. He stopped to ask the night nurse about the child, and paused to write a note to the child's mother. "There he was, with his own baby dying downstairs," Powers said, "but he had to take the time to write a note to that poor woman, asking her to keep her courage up."

Less than three hours later, at 5 A.M. on August 9, 1963, Patrick died. He was forty hours old. "He put up quite a fight," Jack told Powers. "He was a beautiful baby." Then he returned to the vacant hospital room where he had slept the night before, closed the door, sat on the edge of the bed and broke down sobbing.

Jack then rushed to his wife's side at Otis Air Force Base. Jackie, who had already been given the tragic news by Dr. Walsh, at first tried to put on a brave face. But when she saw Jack they broke down together. "Oh, Jack, oh, Jack," she sobbed. "There's only one thing I could not bear now—if I ever lost you."

Jackie was too weak to attend the funeral, but she insisted the tiny coffin be covered in flowers as Black Jack Bouvier's had been. New York's Cardinal Spellman, Bobby and Teddy, Jackie's sister, Lee, and Jamie and Janet Auchincloss were among the few who heard Cardinal Cushing say the Mass of the Angels. When Cushing was finished, Jack stepped forward and placed the St. Christopher medal Jackie had given him on their wedding day into the tiny casket.

"Then they filed out," Cardinal Cushing recalled, "and for the second time I saw tears in the eyes of Jack Kennedy, and they were copious tears. He was the last of the family to leave the little chapel. I was behind him. The casket was there. It was in a white marble case. The President was so overwhelmed with grief that he literally put his arms around that casket as though he was carrying it out. I said, 'Come on, Jack. Let's go. God is good.' "

At Holyhood Cemetery near his Brookline birthplace, an inconsolable Jack reached out to touch the coffin as it was lowered into the ground. Tears were streaming down his cheeks. "Goodbye," he said. "It's awfully lonely down there."

Jackie remained in the hospital for a full week. "The President was very concerned about her," Arthur Schlesinger remembered. "He tried to think of ways to cheer her up." JFK asked Schlesinger to approach his friend Adlai Stevenson. "Jackie is so fond of Adlai," Jack said. "Could you ask him to drop her a note in the hospital? It would mean a lot to her." When the letter arrived, Jackie was "deeply touched," Schlesinger said. "Of course she had no idea that the President was behind it. He was just happy to see her smile." When Jackie did leave the hospital she put up a brave front. "You've been so wonderful to me," she told the nurses as she left the hospital, "that I'm coming back here next year to have another baby."

"They were both shattered by Patrick's death," said Teddy White, who later spoke to Jackie about its impact on their relationship. "And for the first time, Jack reached out to her as he had never done before, had never been *capable* of doing before. There had always been this wall between them, but their shared grief tore that wall down. At long last, they were truly coming closer together. But it would prove to be too late."

Jack also worried about the impact on the children, who had been eagerly awaiting their little brother's arrival. To cheer them up, he returned to Squaw Island from Washington with Shannon, a cocker spaniel puppy. When Jackie arrived home from the hospital, she and Jack were greeted by the sight of Caroline, John-John, and the entire Kennedy canine menagerie—Shannon, Clipper, Charlie, Pushinka's puppies White Tips, Streaker, Butterfly, and Blackie—rolling around on the front lawn.

On September 12, Ben and Tony Bradlee, the Auchinclosses, and a few others helped Jackie and Jack celebrate their tenth anniversary at Hammersmith Farm. The Bradlees rode with JFK in the presidential helicopter, and when they landed they were struck by the new closeness between the Kennedys. "This was the first time we had seen Jackie since the death of little Patrick," Bradlee recalled, "and she greeted JFK with by far the most affectionate embrace we had ever seen them give each other . . . they are the most remote and independent people, so when their emotions do surface it is especially moving."

At the party, Jack presented his wife with a catalog list from the New York antique dealer J. J. Klejman and invited her to pick out one of the items for a thousand dollars and up. After bantering about the prices, she selected a coiled serpent bracelet. She gave him a scrapbook filled with before-and-after photographs of the newly refurbished Rose Garden (of which they were both especially proud)—and a St. Christopher medal to replace the one Jack had placed in Patrick's coffin. Later, he gave her something to remember their tiny son by: a small gold ring with emerald chips—green for Patrick—that she wore on her little finger.

For the benefit of their guests, Jackie and Jack appeared nothing less than ebullient. In truth, neither had come to terms with the loss of Patrick. As late as mid-October, Jack was in Boston watching a Harvard-Columbia football game when at halftime he suddenly turned to Dave Powers and Kenny O'Donnell and told them he wanted to visit Patrick's grave—"alone." They ducked out, eluded the press, and drove to the cemetery. The Secret Service detail kept a respectful distance while the President walked slowly up to the headstone simply marked KENNEDY. "He seems," Jack said to Powers and O'Donnell, "so alone here." (After the assassination, both Patrick and their unnamed stillborn daughter would be reinterred in Arlington National Cemetery alongside their father.)

Lee Radziwill, meantime, was searching for ways to lift her sister's spirits when Aristotle Onassis offered the use of his yacht *Christina* for an Aegean cruise. Famous for his flamboyant lifestyle and shady business dealings, Onassis was hardly the ideal shipmate for the wife of an American president, particularly one facing a tough reelection campaign. Kennedy also wondered if his sister-in-law was merely trying to curry favor with Onassis. Although opera great Maria Callas had long been Onassis's mistress, there were rumors that Lee intended to annul her marriage to the prince and marry Onassis.

"Lee had a sort of romance going with Onassis," Evelyn Lincoln said. "At first Jack didn't like the idea [of Jackie going on the *Christina*] but then he thought maybe it would do her some good." For appearance's sake, Jack sent Under Secretary of Commerce Franklin D. Roosevelt, Jr. and his wife, Suzanne, along as chaperones.

Onassis, aware of the potential for embarrassment, had not intended to go along on the cruise. But Jackie insisted that he come. "I could not accept his generous hospitality," she explained, "and then not let him come along. It would have been too cruel. I just couldn't have done that." In addition to Jackie, Onassis, the Radziwills, and Roosevelts, Ari's sister Artemis and her husband as well as a few other friends joined the cruise.

The ostentatiously appointed 325-foot *Christina,* with its barstools upholstered in whale scrotum and its gold-plated bathroom fixtures, was hardly Jackie's style. But to the surprise of many, the First Lady appeared happier than anyone had seen her in months. Even she had never been pampered to quite such an extent. The *Christina*'s crew of sixty included two chefs, two hairdressers, a Swedish masseuse, and a band.

On board, the champagne flowed and no fewer than eight varieties of caviar were served. When guests weren't dining on foie gras and lobster or bouncing to bouzouki music on the *Christina*'s mosaic-tiled dance floor, they were walking the cobblestone streets of Lesbos, Crete, and Ithaca. Onassis and Jackie spent hours alone on the deck, sharing their thoughts as they gazed up at the star-filled sky.

As they swam, danced, and island-hopped, Jackie kept telling her shipmates, "I just wish Jack could be here with us." And when ship-to-shore phones failed to work, she wrote lengthy letters telling her husband how much she missed him.

But by the time they reached Onassis's private island of Skorpios, Lee was jealous of how surprisingly close he and Jackie had grown in so short a time. To Jack back home, when she was photographed sunbathing on board the *Christina* in a bikini, it began to seem like a replay of her Italian romp with Gianni Agnelli. When they docked at Istanbul so Jackie could visit the Blue Mosque, crowds lined the streets to cheer her. That night, to Lee's chagrin, their host gave Jackie a magnificent diamond and ruby necklace that could be converted into two bracelets.

"Onassis fell for Jackie," said Evelyn Lincoln, "and then it turned out that he became more than just a friend." Did Lincoln think Jackie had an affair with Onassis before the assassination? "I think so, yes. Jackie loved money. Onassis had money. That might have been what she saw in him. And she didn't like President Kennedy's political friends. She didn't like that kind of life . . . Kennedy couldn't change his career because he was a politician. So you shape up or get lost in the shuffle."

Jackie had angered Jack when she told him that, if given a choice, she would rather visit Morocco than Ireland. So after she left Onassis she dropped in on King Hassan of Morocco, who was eager to repay her for her hospitality in Washington. He commanded that she be given any object in the kingdom that seemed to please her. When she got to the airport for her departure, she was stunned to find security guards loading three carloads of gifts onto her plane.

When she arrived home from her overseas idyll, Jackie was greeted by Jack, Caroline, and John-John. "Oh, Jack," she said, rushing up to embrace him, "I'm so glad to be home!"

Jackie turned her attention to Caroline's religious education. Months earlier she had dispatched Miss Grimes, headmistress of the White House School, to the Georgetown Visitation Academy—a cloistered convent—to see if it would be suitable for Caroline and her six Catholic schoolmates. Questions raised by her tiny brother's death made it seem even more imperative that Caroline learn more about God and his mysterious ways.

On the first day of instruction, the parents of all the children came to observe Sister Joanne Frey of the Mission Helpers of the Sacred Heart teach catechism class. But Jackie went to the wrong church, and when she finally did show, recalled Sister Joanne, "she was quite flustered, quite apologetic. 'I'm just so sorry,' she said. 'Would you mind if I stay for class?' Of course I was just looking at her and thinking, 'Oh God . . . '"

While Jackie sat in the back of the classroom, Sister Joanne decided "to begin at the beginning. We discussed the Creation, and then I told them to put their heads down and after they'd thought about it, to draw a picture of what they were thinking.

"I walked around the room, and I saw Caroline with a black crayon, and pretty soon she had covered the whole paper with black. I thought, 'If this is her idea of religion, God' . . . The other kids had all drawn animals, people, Adam and Eve. Caroline's was the only picture in black. But then she took a blue crayon and started coloring over the black."

Finally Sister Joanne asked if any of the children wanted to discuss their drawing, and Caroline's hand shot up. "In the beginning there was nothing but darkness," she said, "but then God put a light up in the sky—and one was a moon." She held it up, and Frey saw that Caroline had left holes in the sky for stars, and a crescent moon. On the back, she had proudly written "Caroline Bouvier Kennedy" in block letters.

When the class was over, Jackie went up to Sister Joanne. "If I had had religion taught to me in that way," she said, "it would have been a much happier experience for me. Would you mind if I take the drawing home to show the President?"

Another time, Sister Joanne asked the children to cut out pictures from a magazine and then tell the class the story the pictures told. "My mommy helped me," Caroline volunteered before showing her teacher a picture of a child about her age, and a mother holding an infant. "This is Mommy," Caroline explained, "this is me, and this would have been Patrick, my baby brother. He's in heaven."

Jackie often accompanied her daughter to the classes, sometimes with John-John in tow. One day in October, her little brother burst into class with a stick over his shoulder. "He thinks he's a soldier," Caroline said, rolling her eyes, "and he doesn't even know how to salute."

"A month later," Sister Joanne said, "like everyone else I cried when I saw him standing there saluting his father's coffin. It was a *perfect* salute. Ironic, isn't it? The most famous salute of all time."

Oddly, the classes remained undetected by the press for the entire eight-month-long period Caroline attended them. "The limos in front of the building were obvious," Sister Joanne Frey said. "It was apparent to anyone who cared to notice that something was going on. But the press never discovered we were there."

Perhaps she was feeling some residual guilt over her trip aboard Onassis's yacht. Or maybe, after thirteen trips abroad, Jackie felt it was time to show the flag as first lady within the borders of the United States. Whatever the reason, Jackie agreed to accompany her husband on a political fence-mending trip to Dallas.

An ongoing feud between the state's liberal Senator Ralph Yarborough and its conservative Governor John Connally was splitting the party down the middle, threatening to hand Texas to the GOP in 1964. The two-day swing through the Lone Star state was to include fund-raising events in San Antonio, Houston, Fort Worth, and Dallas. Then the Kennedys planned to spend the weekend on the Johnson Ranch.

It seemed amazing to those around him that Jack would chose this as his wife's first appearance on the 1964 campaign trail. "I almost fell over when he told me Jackie was coming with us," O'Donnell recalled.

"You know how I hate that sort of thing," Jackie told friends. "But if he wants me there, then that's all that matters. It's a tiny sacrifice on my part for something he feels is very important to him." Asked if, as in the past, ill health might force Jackie to cancel at the last minute, the White House spokesman hedged. "She will help in every way she can," he said, "consistent with other obligations and continuing good health."

Just several weeks earlier, an ugly mob in Dallas had pelted Adlai Stevenson with rotten eggs. Brother Bobby and Arkansas Senator William Fulbright realized JFK felt he had to go, but thought it unnecessary for Jackie to accompany him. "If Jack wants me," she said, "I'll go anywhere."

On November 13, Jack, Jackie, Caroline, and John-John watched from the White House balcony as the kilted Black Watch pipers performed for an audience of seventeen hundred under-privileged youngsters on the South Lawn. The next day, Jack flew to New York to give a speech, sneaking out the side door of the Carlyle later that night to attend a small dinner party at the Fifth Avenue apartment of Stephen and Jean Kennedy Smith.

Over dinner, Adlai Stevenson told of being spat on and threatened by the mob in Dallas, and urged the President not to go—with or without Jackie. As they left the party, Oleg Cassini turned to Jack and asked, "Why do you go? Your own people are saying you should not go." Jack merely shrugged and smiled.

While Jackie went horseback riding in Virginia, the President spent the weekend in Palm Beach, watching the launch of a Po-laris missile at Cape Canaveral, then a football game on televi-sion. That evening after dinner with Dave Powers and Kenny O'Donnell, he sang one of his favorite tunes, "September Song." The lyrics—"And the days dwindle down, to a precious few . . ."—would prove hauntingly prophetic.

George Smathers rode back to Washington with his friend aboard Air Force One. "Damnit to hell, I've got to go out to Texas," Jack told him, half jokingly. "Your friend Lyndon is caus-ing me trouble."

"Lyndon helped you get elected, Jack," Smathers replied. "You owe a lot to him."

"How do I get out of it?" Jack wanted to know.

"You can't get out of it, Mr. President," Smathers insisted. "You've got to go. You're doing the right thing." More than three decades later, Smathers would confess, "I wish to God I hadn't said it."

Pierre Salinger would have similar regrets. Two days before the President's departure, as Salinger was himself preparing to fly with Secretary of State Dean Rusk to Japan, JFK said, "I wish I weren't going to Texas."

"Don't worry about it," Salinger said. "It's going to be a great trip and you're going to draw the biggest crowds ever. Going with Mrs. Kennedy will be terrific." But Salinger neglected to mention that the day before he'd received a letter from a woman in Dallas begging him to tell JFK not to make the trip. "I'm worried about him," she had written. "I think something terrible will happen to him."

The night before they embarked on their fateful journey, Jackie and Jack hosted a reception for the Supreme Court justices and other members of the judicial branch. It was Jackie's first appearance at a formal White House function since Patrick's death—and their last.

"I feel great," Jack told Kenny O'Donnell as he boarded Air Force One the morning of November 21, 1963. "My back feels better than it's felt in years." Their departure had been delayed slightly; in typical fashion, Jackie was running a little late. During the flight, Jack worried about his wife's comfort. The advance weather report they had been given failed to predict the heat wave that was sweeping across the state; Jackie's pastel wool suits would be uncomfortably warm.

But Jack was thrilled with the wild reception they received when they landed in San Antonio. At the airport, someone handed Jackie a bouquet of yellow roses while others waved placards reading BIENVENIDO MR. AND MRS. PRESIDENT and JACKIE COME WATER-SKIING IN TEXAS. As a crowd of 125,000 cheered, JFK turned to his wife and said, "See, you do make a difference."

After speaking at the dedication of the new Air Force School of Aerospace Medicine, Jack made an impromptu stop at an oxygen chamber; he asked one of the scientists if space medicine might someday improve the treatment of premature infants like Patrick.

In Houston, the crowds were even larger and more exuberant. "Mr. President, your crowd here today was about the same as last year's," Dave Powers told him, "but a hundred thousand more people came out to cheer for Jackie." Later there were more cheers, as she gave a speech to the League of United Latin-American Citizens in flawless Spanish.

The next stop was Fort Worth, where they arrived a little after midnight at their two-bedroom suite on the eighth floor of the Texas Hotel. That last night of Jack's life, Jackie went to his room to spend the night with him, but found that his old stomach problem was acting up—probably a nervous reaction to the heavy campaign schedule. Exhausted, they fell into each other's arms, kissed goodnight, and she returned to her separate room.

The next morning in a parking lot across from the hotel, Jack spoke to a crowd that had waited in the rain for hours just to catch a glimpse of Mr. and Mrs. Kennedy. "Where's Jackie? Where's Jackie?" the crowd began chanting.

"Mrs. Kennedy is organizing herself," he told them. "It takes a little longer, but of course, she looks better than us when she does it." Jackie had, in fact, asked Mary Gallagher to remove all her makeup from bags that had already been packed for the trip to Dallas. She felt she needed a last-minute touch-up for the busy day ahead.

Jack returned to the hotel's grand ballroom where he was to speak at a chamber of commerce breakfast. When Jackie finally made her entrance nearly a half hour late wearing a pink wool suit, trademark pillbox hat, and white kid gloves, the crowd of two thousand inside the ballroom gave her a Texas welcome—cheering, hooting, standing on chairs to applaud.

"Two years ago I introduced myself in Paris by saying I was the man who had accompanied Mrs. Kennedy to Paris," Jack said. "I am getting somewhat the same sensation as I travel around Texas. Why is it nobody wonders what Lyndon and I will be wearing?"

Elated by their reception, Jack and Jackie returned to their suite to relax before heading for Dallas. JFK had long ago concluded that together they made a potent combination on the campaign trail, but he had no idea if she intended to sit this one out as she had in 1960.

"They had been through so much together in the last few years, particularly the baby's death," Spalding said. "I think by the time they got to Dallas she saw herself as a full partner."

Kenny O'Donnell came to their hotel room to tell them it was time to leave for Dallas. "I'll go anywhere with you this year," Jackie told her husband.

"How about California in two weeks?" he asked.

"I'll be there." She nodded.

Jack turned to O'Donnell. "Did you hear *that?*" he said, beaming.

Aboard Air Force One minutes later, the President's mood quickly turned dark when he was handed a copy of a black-bordered full-page ad in the *Dallas News*. The ad, paid for by the "American Fact-finding Committee," denounced JFK's "ultra-leftist" policies and called him "fifty times a fool" for signing the Nuclear Test Ban Treaty. "We're heading into nut country today," he told Jackie as he showed her the paper. "But, Jackie, if somebody wants to shoot me from a window with a rifle, nobody can stop it, so why worry about it?"

Thirteen minutes after leaving Fort Worth, Air Force One landed at Dallas's Love Field. The weather had cleared, and as they stepped out into the searing heat and sunshine, the President and his wife were greeted by wild cheers from what appeared to be a very friendly crowd. In a repeat of that day in 1960 when he had returned to Hyannis Port after winning the nomination, someone handed Jackie a bouquet of red roses while Jack headed toward the fence to shake hands.

There was a difference this time; Jackie, now a confident part of his team, joined him. "I tried to stay close to my husband and lots of times you get pushed away, you know, people leaning over and pulling your hand," she would later recall. "They were very friendly."

The presidential motorcade left Love Field at 11:55 A.M. bound for the downtown Trade Mart, where Jack was to speak at a lunch-eon. The Secret Service had wanted a bulletproof bubbletop on their Lincoln, and so did Jackie—if for nothing else, she joked, to protect her bouffant. But Jack was determined not to put anything between himself and the people. Jack sat in the rear right-hand seat, Jackie on the left, the bouquet of roses on the seat between them. Governor Connally sat on the pull-out jump seat in front of Jack while the Governor's wife, Nellie, sat in front of Jackie.

Jack and Jackie were amazed at the response, even friendlier and more enthusiastic than it had been in San Antonio, Houston, and Fort Worth. Cheering crowds lined the streets twelve-deep. Jack stopped the motorcade twice—to shake hands with children and then a group of nuns.

"You certainly can't say that the people of Dallas haven't given you a nice welcome, Mr. President," said Nellie Connally.

"No, you certainly can't," he replied.

Mrs. Connally pointed to the overpass ahead. "We're almost through. The Trade Mart's beyond that." Sweltering in her wool suit, blinded by the light without sunglasses, Jackie thought "good. It will be so cool in that tunnel." She was waving to crowds on the left while her husband waved to crowds on the right, in front of the Texas School Book Depository. In the car behind them, Dave Powers checked his watch. It was 12:30 P.M.

Many millions of words would be written about what happened next—an endless stream of speculation ending in a vast sea of conjecture. But one thing was certain. At that moment Jack and Jackie—the collective entity that had seized the world's imagi-nation—ceased to exist.

The motorcycles that were escorting them had been backfiring, and at first that was what Jackie thought she heard. But then she saw Connally grabbing his arm and beating his fist shouting, "No, no, no, no, no."

"Then Jack turned and I turned," she later told Teddy White. "Then Jack turned back so neatly, his last expression was so neat

... you know that wonderful expression he had ... He looked puzzled, then he slumped forward. He was holding his hand ... I could see a piece of his skull coming off. It was flesh-colored, not white—he was holding out his hand. I can see this perfectly clean piece detaching itself from his head. Then he slumped in my lap, his blood and his brains were in my lap."

It was a full seven seconds before Jackie climbed out onto the back of the car—something she would not remember doing at all. "Dave, what do you think I was trying to do?" she would later ask when Dave Powers showed her photographs of the incredible scene. Whether she was trying to get help or escape the horror hardly mattered. Within seconds, Secret Service agent Clint Hill jumped onto the rear bumper of the Lincoln and she helped him into the car.

Lying in the car with Hill on top shielding them as they sped to Parkland Memorial Hospital six miles away, she pleaded, "Jack, Jack, Jack, can you hear me? I love you, Jack." She held down the top of his head, "trying to keep the brains in ... but I knew he was dead."

When the car got to the hospital, she refused to let go of her husband. "Please, Mrs. Kennedy," said Hill. "We must get the President to a doctor."

"I'm not going to let him go, Mr. Hill," she said, cradling Jack's head in her lap. Her husband's blue eyes were open in a fixed stare. "You know he's dead. Leave me alone."

Then Hill, finally understanding that she did not want anyone to see that the top of Jack's skull was missing, took off his jacket, and wrapped it around JFK's shattered head. Only then did she let Hill, Powers, and another Secret Service agent, Roy Kellerman, carefully lift Jack out of the car and onto a waiting stretcher.

At the hospital, "these big Texas interns" kept trying to lead her away, but Jackie refused to leave her husband's side. "I'm not leaving," she told them firmly. When Jack first arrived, doctors discovered that he was in fact still breathing. As they gave him massive blood transfusions, Jackie sat outside the trauma room chain-smoking cigarettes and wondering if there was even the slimmest chance he might pull through as he had so many times before. But if he miraculously survived, she thought, Jack would be severely brain-damaged, and she remembered what he had said about Joe after his stroke: "Don't let that happen to me." Jackie recalled this one fleeting moment of hope: "I thought, 'I'll take care of him every day of his life, I'll make him happy' . . . but I knew he was dead."

Finally, at one o'clock, Jackie was told that her husband was dead. A priest was called. Jack was now covered by a sheet, and his foot was sticking out, "whiter than the sheet," Jackie would remember. She bent down and kissed his foot. Then she pulled down the sheet. "His mouth was so beautiful," she recalled. "His eyes were open." She kissed his lips, then held Jack's hand while the priest gave him the last rites.

Someone helped Jackie remove her bloody white kid gloves. She took off her wedding ring, also stained with Jack's blood, and slipped it on his finger. Knowing she would have doubts about giving up her wedding ring, however, Kenny O'Donnell later removed it from JFK's finger at Bethesda Naval Hospital and returned the ring to a grateful Jackie.

Caroline learned of her father's death from Maud Shaw. "I can't help crying, Caroline, because I have some very sad news to tell you," the nanny said. "Your father has gone to look after Patrick. Patrick was so lonely in heaven. He didn't know anyone there. Now he has the best friend anybody could have."

When John-John was told, he asked, "Did Daddy take his big plane with him?" Miss Shaw said yes. "I wonder," the boy said, "when he's coming back."

Unable to sleep even under the influence of a powerful sedative, Jackie spent much of that first night in the White House without Jack writing a tear-drenched letter to her dead husband. She had already had the children do the same thing. "You must write a letter to Daddy now," she had instructed Caroline, "and tell him how much you love him." In block letters, Caroline printed, "DEAR DADDY WE ARE ALL GOING TO MISS YOU. DADDY, I LOVE YOU VERY MUCH. CAROLINE." Three-year-old John-John scrawled an *X* on his sister's letter.

With Bobby for support, Jackie went to the East Room where Jack lay in state, surrounded by an honor guard. The coffin was opened, and Jackie placed the letters inside, along with a pair of gold cuff links she had given him and a favorite piece of scrimshaw. Bobby added a rosary, his gold PT-109 tie clip, and a clip of his own hair. An aide brought a pair of scissors, and Jackie gently cut off a lock of her husband's hair.

The images generated over the next few days would be indelibly etched in the national psyche: Jackie, eyes swollen from crying and still wearing the suit stained with her husband's blood ("I want them to see what they've done"), standing next to Lyndon Johnson as he is sworn in as president aboard Air Force One; assassin Lee Harvey Oswald clutching his stomach as he is shot to death by Jack Ruby ("Just one more awful thing," Jackie said); world leaders from Haile Selassie to Charles de Gaulle marching in the funeral procession behind the caisson and the riderless horse named, incredibly, Black Jack; the grieving widow beneath the black veil, kneeling with Caroline in the Capitol rotunda to kiss Daddy's flag-draped coffin; tiny, blue-coated John-John's heartbreaking salute . . .

On the afternoon of November 25 in the family quarters, Caroline ran up to Jackie. "Mommy," she asked, "did they love Daddy?"

"Oh yes, they loved Daddy."

Caroline shook her head. They didn't, she said, "or they wouldn't have done that to him."

Then the little girl, obviously worried, asked, "Do they love you?"

Jackie reassured her daughter that people loved her. Then she said it should come as no surprise that not *everyone* loved Daddy. "After all," Jackie said, "not everybody loved Jesus, did they?" Satisfied, Caroline scampered toward the small party in the family room. It was John-John's third birthday.

At first no one told Joe. Rose made no mention of what the family had taken to calling "the events of November 22." And the servants, to keep Joe from watching the news, unplugged his television set and told him it was out of order.

After two days, the family decided it was time he knew. "I picked up Bobby and Teddy at the Hyannis Airport and drove them to the house," recalled Secret Service agent Ham Brown. "Joe was in bed, and there was a nurse's station outside his door where they could monitor him. Bobby and Ted and Eunice went into Joe's room and we turned off the intercom and left them alone. God knows what went on inside that room when they told him Jack had been assassinated, but I'll tell you there wasn't a dry eye among all of us standing out in the hall. When they came out, they were all crying."

Jackie arrived at Hyannis Port for Thanksgiving with the folded flag that had draped the President's coffin. Once again, they turned off the intercom outside Joe's room. "He was in bed and even given the horrible circumstances," Ham Brown said, "he smiled when Jackie entered the room. Jackie and Joe were buddies.

"We shut the door and they stayed in that room talking for about an hour. Just like before, everybody in the hall was sobbing. Tears everywhere. Secretaries, nurses, secret service agents. We were all a mess. When Jackie opened the door to leave, I looked inside and there was this sad, sad sight of Joe just sitting upright in bed, the triangle of flag still in his lap."

The day after the funeral—four days after she had held her husband's bloody head in her lap—Jackie had invited Lady Bird Johnson to tea at the White House. "Some of the happiest years of my marriage have been spent here. You will be happy here," she told Mrs. Johnson. Before she walked out of the White House for the last time as first lady on December 6, Jackie ordered that a bronze plaque be placed over the mantle in the President's Bedroom. It read: "In this room lived John Fitzgerald Kennedy with his wife Jacqueline—during the two years, ten months and two days he was President of the United States—January 20, 1961–November 22, 1963."

It had been affixed to the wall beneath another plaque that read: "In this room Abraham Lincoln slept during his occupancy at the White House as President of the United States, March 4, 1861–April 13, 1865."

———

By holding herself together, Jackie held a nation together. But at a terrible personal price. Once the dignitaries had departed and she had fulfilled her ceremonial role as living symbol of the world's grief, the reality of what had happened finally hit Jackie. Sister Joanne Frey was telling Caroline's catechism class about Mary Magdalene washing the feet of Christ when all of a sudden Caroline blurted out, "My mommy cries all the time."

"I tried to resume teaching," Sister Joanne recalled, "but Caroline said 'My mommy cries *all* the time' again and again. Obviously the poor little girl didn't know what to do."

Away from the cameras, Jackie was caught in a downward spiral of unrelenting despair. "I'm a living wound. My life is over," she told a friend. "I'm dried up. I have nothing more to give and some days I can't even get out of bed. I cry all day and all night until I'm so exhausted I can't function. Then I drink."

Less than a month after Dallas, Jackie wrote to her friends Ben and Tony Bradlee, "Something that you said in the country stunned me so—that you hoped I would marry again. You were so close to us so many times. There is one thing that you must know. I consider that my life is over and I will spend the rest of it waiting for it really to be over."

On May 23, 1994, Jackie was buried beside Jack, Patrick, and their unnamed stillborn daughter at Arlington National Cemetery. As they had thirty years before, Caroline and John-John bade their beloved parent a poignant yet dignified good-bye.

Did Jack ever love Jackie? Patrick's tragic death only a few months before the assassination was a pivotal event in the lives of the Kennedys, one that redefined the nature of their relationship. For the first time, Jack was able to reach out to his wife in ways he never could before. Did Jackie love Jack? There is no evidence that she ever *stopped* loving him.

Now that both Jack and Jackie are gone, perhaps the hysteria that enveloped them in life will be replaced with reason and understanding. Conceivably, we will be able to strip away the layers of hype and mystique to reveal the often vulnerable, tentative human beings underneath.

He was unquestionably a brilliant man whose vision of a better world continues to inspire millions. By virtue of her beauty, grace, and dignity, she is no less admired here and abroad. But to canonize them does us no less a disservice than to demonize them. For all their Olympian traits, Jack and Jackie argued over money, clothes, furniture, and in-laws. They grappled with infidelity, disease, and drug dependence. They fretted about infertility and childbearing, and both worried about and delighted in the children they had. They shared the death of one parent, the debilitating stroke of another, a miscarriage, a stillbirth, and the most crushing blow of all—the loss of a child.

They were nothing like us and everything like us. Theirs was an American marriage.

Acknowledgments

$\mathcal{L}$auren Bacall and Woody Allen were there. So were Walter Cronkite, Shirley MacLaine, William Styron, Teddy White, Andy Warhol, and Swifty Lazar—to name only a few. It was February 1978, a glittering party inside New York's fortress-like Sixty-seventh Street armory honoring the posthumous publication of James Jones's novel, *Whistle*. And when Jacqueline Kennedy Onassis entered the room, everyone froze, too awe-stricken to approach the icon in their midst. For an awkward minute no one, no matter how revered or celebrated in his or her own field, had the audacity to invade the six feet of personal space that separated Jackie from the other guests. So Jackie simply stood there, totally alone in the center of the room—until my wife, Valerie, and I naïvely walked up and said hello. There was, for one fleeting moment, a look of relief on Jackie's face. There was an equally revealing scene moments later, when we witnessed Lee Radziwill arrive, then make a hasty exit when she realized her sister was there.

Although Jack and Jackie were of my parents' generation, and I grew up not on the East Coast but in the San Francisco Bay Area, our paths had somehow crossed at curious times over the years. On September 12, 1953, my family was taking a drive through Newport, Rhode Island, when suddenly we found our red-and-white Ford station wagon stuck in the middle of Jack and Jackie's wedding procession. Nine years later, I shook hands with President Kennedy when he spoke at Berkeley, and then watched in stunned disbelief as an overzealous fan with a camera leapt from the crowd and was wrestled to the ground not three feet from JFK.

The following year, we were driving through Hyannis when once again we were caught up in a JFK motorcade (the Andersen family car was now a blue Ford Galaxy). Only this time, the President was returning from the hospital where Jackie had just given birth and the premature infant, Patrick, was waging a losing battle for life.

Living and working in Manhattan as a Time Incorporated writer and senior editor, I had other random encounters with Jackie—on a street corner as she hailed a cab, backstage at Shirley MacLaine's Palace Theater opening, at the Park Avenue headquarters of Doubleday, where I happened to be examining the cover of my new book with the art director when Jackie, then a Doubleday editor, suddenly materialized at my side wearing black pants and a black turtleneck.

After talking to those who were closest to Jack and Jackie, I was told again and again that the Kennedys carefully "compartmentalized" their outside relationships. Each friend held only a piece to the intricate jigsaw puzzle that was their life together. As the biographer of their relationship, I was left to sort through those pieces until, finally, they fit.

A tremendous amount of research is necessary for any comprehensive biography, and this was especially true in the case of *Jack and Jackie.* Much time was spent interviewing hundreds of sources: friends, family members, neighbors, classmates, colleagues, political allies and enemies, Jack's former girlfriends, Jackie's ex-fiancé, journalists and photographers who covered them, and those who worked for them before and during their time in the White House. Only a handful of these people asked not to be identified, and I have respected their wishes. When I spoke to Nancy Tuckerman, Jackie's closest confidante and lifelong friend, she regretfully declined—as she has always and vows she will always—to be interviewed at length. However, she was most supportive when we discussed what I hoped to accomplish with *Jack and Jackie,* and I thank her for her kind words of encouragement.

I am particularly grateful to my editor, Will Schwalbe, for his passionate interest in seeing that a balanced biography of Jack and Jackie offset the excesses of the past two decades. This extends to the entire William Morrow family—especially Rebecca Goodhart, Doris Cooper, Jackie Deval, Sharyn Rosenblum, Giulia Melucci, Brad Foltz, Deborah Weaver, Lisa Queen, Willard J. Lubka, and Kathleen Morahan.

Yet again, Ellen Levine has proven herself to be not only a brilliant and dedicated literary agent but also a treasured friend. I am also indebted to Ellen's gifted associate Diana Finch, as well as to Deborah Clifford, Jay Rogers, Louise Quayle, Robert Simpson, and Anne Dubuisson.

Mining the rich vein of archival information contained within the walls of Boston's splendid John Fitzgerald Kennedy Library would have been impossible without the guidance, industry, and insight of historian Michael Foster. I am also indebted to Northeastern University Professor Ray Robinson and to author Laurence Leamer for introducing me to Michael, and to the library's William Johnson, Ron Whealan, Megan Desnoyers, Maura Porter, and June Payne. Special thanks to the JFK Library's audiovisual archivist James B. Hill, who went beyond the call in helping me assemble the photographs for use in the book, many of which have never before been published.

My thanks to noted British television producer and documentary filmmaker Charles Furneaux for his kindness and generous assistance to me as I embarked on *Jack and Jackie.* I am also once again indebted to my talented friend of nearly twenty years, Rosemary McClure.

My beautiful and brilliant daughters, Kate and Kelly, each contributed to the writing of this book in her own way. My parents, Edward and Jeanette Andersen, are always a source of guidance and encouragement, but this time I also thank them for taking a wrong turn and winding up behind Jack and Jackie's wedding car in 1953. And to Valerie, whom I met when we were both under-graduate students at Berkeley in 1967, my love as always, and—equally important—my respect.

Additional thanks to Pierre Salinger, John Kenneth Galbraith, Charles "Chuck" Spalding, Hugh D. "Yusha" Auchincloss, Nancy Dickerson Whitehead, Charles Bartlett, Letitia "Tish" Baldrige, Gore Vidal, Theodore "Ted" Sorensen, Jamie Auchincloss, Sena-tor George Smathers, Oleg Cassini, Jacques Lowe, Paul "Red" Fay, Arthur Schlesinger, Jr., Roswell Gilpatric, John Husted, Pris-cilla McMillan, Sister Joanne Frey, Evelyn Lincoln, Joan Fontaine, Gloria Swanson, Robert Drew, John Davis, Cleveland Amory, Betty Beale, Ham Brown, Patricia S. Lawford, Tony Bradlee, Paula Dranov, Helen Thomas, Vincent Russo, Stephen Corsaro, the late Theodore H. White, Charles Collingwood, Doris Lilly, Dorothy Schoenbrun, Wendy Leigh, the late Truman Capote, Bette Davis, Clare Boothe Luce, John Marion, Michael Gross, To-bias Markowitz, James E. O'Neil, Dorothy Oliger, Tom Freeman, Alfred Eisenstaedt, Bertram S. Brown, Lawrence R. Mulligan, Larry Newman, Charles Whitehouse, Barry Schenck, Susan Crimp, Earl Blackwell, Jeanette Peterson, Clarence Petry, Diana Brooks, Linus Pauling, Cranston Jones, Charles Damore, Steve Michaud, Yvette Reyes, Debbie Goodsite, Betsy Loth, Joy Wan-sley, Steve Karten, Diane Tucker, Dudley Freeman, Valerie Wim-mer, William vanden Heuvel, Hazel Southam, Linda Hanson, Angier Biddle Duke, Lee Wohlfert, Donna Smerlas, Dale Sider, Frank Rigg, Terry L. Birdwhistell, Ronald Grele, Dale Sider, Di-ane Tucker, Drew Middleton, David McGough, Dr. Janet Travell, Sandy Richardson, Albert V. Concordia, David Halberstam, Shir-ley Bombaci, Jim Birchfield, Bill Cooper, Gary Gunderson, Frank Rigg, and Kathy Dolce: and the John Fitzgerald Kennedy Library, Columbia University's Rare Book and Manuscript Library and Butler Library, the Seeley G. Mudd Manuscript Library at Prince-ton University, the Houghton Library at Harvard University, the Robert Drew Archive, the Leukemia Society of America, the Li-brary of Congress, United States Secret Service, the Boston University Library, the Stanford University Archives, the University of Kentucky Library, the Federal Bureau of Investigation, the Choate School Archives, the New York Public Library, the Schlesinger Library, Barraclough Carey Productions, Channel Four Television, Limited, the Columbia University Oral History Project, the Barnstable Public Library, the Redwood Library and Athenaeum of Newport, the Gunn Memorial Library, the New Milford Library, the Southbury Library, Sotheby's, the Bancroft Library at the University of California at Berkeley, Vassar College Library, Winterthur Museum, the Silas Bronson Library, the Brookfield Library, the Amherst College Library, the Lyndon Baines Johnson Library, the Archdiocese of Boston, the Bettmann Archive, the Woodbury Library, the Boston Public Library, Miss Porter's School, Wide World, Movie Star News, the Associated Press, the *New Bedford Standard Times,* and Georgetown University Library.

Sources and Chapter Notes

The following chapter notes are designed to give a general view of the sources drawn upon in preparing *Jack and Jackie*, but they are by no means all-inclusive. The author has respected the wishes of many interviewed subjects to remain anonymous and accordingly has not listed them either here or elsewhere in the text. The archives and oral history collections of, among other institutions, the John Fitzgerald Kennedy Library, the Lyndon Baines Johnson Library, the libraries of Columbia, Harvard, Stanford, and Princeton universities yielded a wealth of information, some of which has been released only since the death of Jacqueline Kennedy Onassis in May 1994. In addition, there have been thousands of news reports and articles concerning the Kennedys published over the past five decades that have served as source material for this book—including press accounts of JFK's political campaigns and his thousand days in the White House that appeared in *The New York Times, The Washington Post, The Boston Globe, Time, Life, Newsweek, Look* magazine, and *The Wall Street Journal* and carried on the AP, UPI, and Reuters wires. Primarily those pieces touching on the personal lives of Jack and Jackie are mentioned here.

Chapter 1

Interview subjects included Hugh D. "Yusha" Auchincloss, Jamie Auchincloss, Charles Bartlett, Paul "Red" Fay, George Smathers, Charles "Chuck" Spalding, John Husted, Betty Beale, Letitia

"Tish" Baldrige, John Davis, and Nancy Dickerson Whitehead. Accounts of the wedding appeared in numerous publications, including *The New York Times, The Boston Globe, The Washington Post, Time, Life,* and *Newsweek.* The author also drew on numerous oral histories, among those given by Janet Auchincloss, Nancy Tuckerman, Eunice Kennedy Shriver, Richard Cardinal Cushing, Torbert MacDonald, John Galvin, Edward C. Berube, and James Farrell.

Chapter 2

For this chapter, the author drew on conversations with John Kenneth Galbraith, Nancy Dickerson Whitehead, Gore Vidal, Gloria Swanson, George Smathers, Dr. Janet Travell, Charles "Chuck" Spalding, Cranston Jones, Cleveland Amory, Clare Boothe Luce, Barrie Schenck, Priscilla McMillan, Susan Crimp, Doris Lilly, Willard K. Rice, Charles Furneaux, and Alfred Eisenstaedt. Among the oral histories: Rose Fitzgerald Kennedy, Ralph Horton, Patrick Munroe, Tom Bilodeau, Mark Dalton, Patrick "Patsy" Mulkern, Robert F. Kennedy, Arthur Krock, Edward M. Gallagher, Joseph Alsop, William O. Douglas, James Farrell, Harold S. Ulen, Harold Tinker, Samuel Bornstein, Dorothy Tubridy, Francis X. Morrissey, Patrick Munroe, Charles B. Garabedian, James Reed, Billy Sutton, and Dinah Bridge.

JFK's medical records and charts, including his navy records as well as documents from the Lahey and Mayo clinics, are from John F. Kennedy's Personal Papers. Also from JFK's Personal Papers are the letters of Inga Arvad and Kirk LeMoyne "Lem" Billings to JFK. See also the papers of Lem Billings at the JFK Library. Much information concerning JFK's affairs with Arvad and others was derived from the files of the Federal Bureau of Investigation, released through the Freedom of Information Act. Other valuable insights into JFK's origins can be found in John Corry, *The Golden Clan* (New York: Houghton Mifflin, 1977) and Joan and Clay Blair, *The Search for JFK* (New York: Berkley, 1976).

See also Mary Billings as quoted by Peter Collier and David Horowitz, *The Kennedys* (New York: Summit Books, 1984).

Other valuable sources for these chapters included the Arthur Krock Papers; the Seeley G. Mudd Manuscript Library, Department of Rare Books and Special Collections; Princeton University libraries; the Laura Bergquist Knebel Papers at Boston University; Stanford University archives; Harvard University's Houghton Library.

Published sources included "Guns v. Butter," *Time,* August 12, 1940; *The New York Times,* April 10, 1946; Nigel Hamilton, *JFK: Reckless Youth* (New York: Random House, 1992); *The New York Times,* June 19, 1946; Robert J. Donovan, *PT 109: John F. Kennedy in World War II* (New York: McGraw-Hill, 1961); "The Secret Files of J. Edgar Hoover," *U.S. News & World Report,* December 19, 1983; Joan Blair and Clay Blair, Jr., *The Search for JFK* (New York: Berkley, 1976).

Chapters 3 to 5

Interview subjects for this period included Hugh D. "Yusha" Auchincloss, Jamie Auchincloss, Charles Bartlett, John Husted, George Smathers, Truman Capote, Charles "Chuck" Spalding, Nancy Dickerson Whitehead, Gore Vidal, Priscilla McMillan, Letitia "Tish" Baldrige, Vincent J. Russo, John Davis, Joan Fontaine, Larry Newman, Patricia Lawford, Oleg Cassini. The author also drew on the John F. Kennedy Memorial Library's oral histories of Rose Fitzgerald Kennedy, Walter Lippmann, Kenneth P. O'Donnell, Thomas "Tip" O'Neill, John W. McCormack, Torbert MacDonald, Dave Powers, Leverett Saltonstall, Robert F. Kennedy, Kaye Halle, Ernest G. Warren, Joseph E. Rosetti, Joanne Barbosa, Anthony Gallucio, Frank E. Dobie, James M. Murphy, Maurice A. Donahue, Mary Colbert, Andrew Dazzi, John Harris, Joseph Deguglliemo, Grace Burke, Benjamin Jacobson, Clement A. Norton, William DeMarco, Dinah Bridge, John F. Dempsey, Joseph Russo, Garrett Byrne, Joseph Casey, John J. Droney, Howard Fitzpatrick,

Daniel O'Brien, Hugh Fraser, John Saltonstall, Foster Furcolo, William F. Kelly, Peter Cloherty, Arthur Krock, James MacGregor Burns, Claiborne Pell.

Mary Lasker's recollections were drawn from her oral history at Columbia University. Articles and other published source materials included *The New York Times,* December 17, 1977; *The Boston Globe,* October 20, 1979; Dave Powers, "I Have Never Met Anyone Like Her," *Life,* August 1995; Mary Van Rensselaer Thayer, *Jacqueline Bouvier Kennedy* (Garden City, N.Y.: Doubleday, 1961); *St. Louis Post-Dispatch,* April 2, 1978; "The Senate's Gay Young Bachelor," *The Saturday Evening Post,* June 13, 1953; John H. Davis, *The Kennedys: Dynasty and Disaster* (New York: McGraw-Hill, 1984); John H. Davis, *The Bouviers: Portrait of an American Family* (New York: Farrar, Straus & Giroux, 1969); "Jackie Kennedy: First Lady at 30?" *U.S. News & World Report,* September 1960; Mary Van Rensselaer Thayer, "First Years of the First Lady," *Ladies' Home Journal,* February 1961; Thomas C. Reeves, *A Question of Character* (New York: Free Press, 1991).

Chapters 6 and 7

The author drew on conversations with Jacques Lowe, Pierre Salinger, Larry Newman, Charles "Chuck" Spalding, George Smathers; Nancy Dickerson Whitehead, Betty Beale, Charles Peters, Clarence Petry, Priscilla McMillan, Sophia Loren, Robert Drew, Jamie Auchincloss, Clare Boothe Luce, Charles Bartlett, Gore Vidal, Hugh D. "Yusha" Auchincloss, Shirley MacLaine, Theodore H. White. Oral histories included Stanley Tretick, Dory Schary, Sargent Shriver, Mark Shaw, Helen Lempart, Jean McGonigle Mannix, John Droney, Barbara Coleman, Dean Acheson, Joanne Barbosa, Fletcher Knebel, Laura Bergquist Knebel, John Kelso, Esther Newberg, Dorothy Tubridy, Lorraine Cooper. Some material regarding Max Jacobson's relationship to the Kennedys is from Jacobson's unpublished memoir. Jacqueline Kennedy Onassis's oral history was done by Terry L. Birdwhistell in New York on May 13, 1981, as part of the John Sherman Cooper Oral History Project of the University of Kentucky Library.

Articles and other published sources for this period included *The New York Times,* September 13, 1953; *The New York Times,* August 7, 13, and 16, 1956; Eleanor Harris, "The Senator Is in a Hurry," *McCalls,* August 1957; Kitty Kelley, *Jackie Oh* (Secaucus, N.J.: Lyle Stuart, 1979); "Pathologist-Sleuth Reopens Kennedy Controversy," *Science News,* July 22, 1967; Herbert Parmet, *Jack: The Struggles of John F. Kennedy* (New York: Dial Press, 1980); "Kennedy Remembered," *Newsweek,* November 28, 1983; *The Washington Post,* May 29, 1987.

Chapters 8 and 9

Author interviews included Pierre Salinger, Gore Vidal, Letitia "Tish" Baldrige, Arthur Schlesinger, Jr., Priscilla McMillan, Ted Sorensen, Roswell Gilpatric, Sister Joanne Frey, Betty Beale, Jacques Lowe, Hugh D. "Yusha" Auchincloss, Paula Dranov, Oleg Cassini, Halston, Bette Davis, Charles "Chuck" Spalding, Robert Drew, Henry Fonda, Teddy White, Alfred Eisenstaedt, Charles Collingwood, Nancy Dickerson Whitehead, Jack Valenti, Charles Damore, Jamie Auchincloss. Those whose oral histories proved especially valuable for these chapters were Angier Biddle Duke, William Walton, Leonard Bernstein, Peter Lawford, Pamela Turnure, Albert Gore, Joseph Alsop, J. B. West, John Sherman Cooper, Stuart Symington, Cyrus Vance, Sister Parish, Stanley Tretick, Maud Shaw, Helen Thomas, Jean McGonigle Mannix, Donald F. Barnes, Roland Evans, Jr., Richard Neuberger, Robert Amory, Jr., Barbara Coleman, Laura Bergquist Knebel, and Godfrey McHugh. Father John C. Cavanaugh's oral history can be found in the Andrew Mellon Library Oral History Collection of the Choate School and the JFK library's oral history collection. Liz Carpenter's and Katharine Graham's oral histories are courtesy of the Lyndon Baines Johnson Library. See also "JFK: The Man, The President," *The Boston Globe* in conjunction with dedication of the John F. Kennedy Library, October 20, 1979.

"This is John Fitzgerald Kennedy," *Newsweek,* June 23, 1958; "Most Talked-About Candidate for 1960," *U.S. News & World Report,* November 8, 1957; "How to Be a Presidential Candidate, *The New York Times Magazine,* July 13, 1958; "Behind the Scenes," *Time,* May 5, 1958; Luella R. Hennessey, "Bringing Up the Kennedys," *Good Housekeeping,* August 1961; Susan Sheehan, "The Happy Jackie, The Sad Jackie, The Bad Jackie, The Good Jackie," *The New York Times Magazine,* May 31, 1970; *New York Post,* January 9, 1961; James Reston, *The New York Times,* January 31, 1961.

Chapters 10 and 11

Information for these chapters was based in part on conversations with Arthur Schlesinger, Jr., John Kenneth Galbraith, Oleg Cassini, George Smathers, Jacques Lowe, Ted Sorensen, Dr. Janet Travell, Pierre Salinger, Letitia "Tish" Baldrige, Nancy Tuckerman, Hugh D. "Yusha" Auchincloss, Roswell Gilpatric, Larry Newman, Charles Bartlett, Gore Vidal, Charles "Chuck" Spalding, Angier Biddle Duke, Ham Brown, Theodore H. White, Sister Joanne Frey, John Davis, Halston, Nancy Dickerson Whitehead, John Husted, Charles Furneaux, Harry Winston, Dorothy Schoenbrun, James Young, Betty Beale, Alan Jay Lerner, Dorothy Oliger, Pat Lawford, Wendy Leigh, Linus Pauling, Evelyn Lincoln, Earl Blackwell. Oral Histories included William Walton, Peter Lawford, Leonard Bernstein, Pamela Turnure, Nancy Tuckerman, Maud Shaw, Tom Wicker, Admiral George G. Burkley, Peter Lisagor, Herve Alphand, Gerald Behn, Traphes Bryant, Gloria Sitrin, Hugh Sidey, Ted Sorensen, Myer Feldman, Walt Rostow, Jacqueline Hirsh, Cordelia Thaxton, Father John C. Cavanaugh, Kenneth Burke, Isaac Avery, Clement Norton, Larry Arata, Joseph Karatis, J. B. West, and Richard Cardinal Cushing.

The voluminous JFK White House Social Files, Secret Service

and White House Staff files were of considerable value, as were the John Fitzgerald Kennedy personal papers and pre-presidential papers, the Jacqueline Kennedy Onassis papers, and the papers of Arthur Schlesinger, Jr., Ted Sorensen, Dean Rusk, Godfrey McHugh, Rose Fitzgerald Kennedy, Joseph P. Kennedy, Paul "Red" Fay, Kenneth O'Donnell, Dave Powers, John Kenneth Galbraith, Lawrence O'Brien, Janet Travell, William Walton, and Theodore H. White. White's papers regarding the assassination and his handwritten notes of his historic "Camelot" interview with Jackie were released in full only in 1995, one year after the death of Jacqueline Kennedy Onassis.

Also from Columbia University's oral history collection: Sarah McClendon, Richard Bolling, Toots Shor, Aaron Shikler, Dave Powers, Larry O'Brien.

Among the published sources consulted: "Joe Kennedy's Feelings About His Son," *Life*, December 19, 1960; Fletcher Knebel, "What You Don't Know About Kennedy," *Look*, January 7, 1961; Philip Nobile and Ron Rosenblum, "The Curious Aftermath of JFK's Best and Brightest Affair," *The New Times Magazine*, July 9, 1976; Arthur Schlesinger, Jr., "What the Thousand Days Wrought," *The New Republic*, November 21, 1983; Mary Barelli Gallagher, *My Life with Jacqueline Kennedy* (New York: David McKay, 1969); "Simply Everywhere," *Time*, February 23, 1962; Hugh Sidey, "The First Lady Brings History and Beauty to the White House," *Life*, September 1, 1961; J. B. West, *Upstairs at the White House* (New York: Coward, McCann & Geoghegan, 1973); "Queen of America," *Time*, March 23, 1962; Anne Taylor Fleming, "The Kennedy Mystique," *The New York Times Magazine*, June 17, 1979; Theodore C. Sorensen, "If Kennedy Had Lived," *Look*, October 19, 1965; Gerri Hirshey, "The Last Act of Judith Exner," *Vanity Fair*, April 1990; "One of Their Own," *Time*, August 31, 1962; Lawrence K. Altman, "Disturbing Issue of Kennedy's Secret Illness," *The New York Times*, October 6, 1992; Ben Bradlee, *Conversations with Kennedy* (New York: W. W. Norton & Co., 1975); Jacqueline Kennedy, "How He Really Was," *Life*, May 29, 1964.

Selected Bibliography

Acheson, Dean. *Power and Diplomacy*. Cambridge, Mass.: Harvard University Press, 1958.

Adams, Cindy, and Susan Crimp. *Iron Rose: The Story of Rose Fitzgerald Kennedy and Her Dynasty*. Beverly Hills, Calif.: Dove Books, 1995.

Amory, Cleveland. *The Proper Bostonians*. New York: E. P. Dutton & Company, Inc., 1947.

Anson, Robert Sam. *"They've Killed the President!": The Search for the Murderers of John F. Kennedy*. New York: Bantam, 1975.

Baldrige, Letitia. *Of Diamonds and Diplomats*. Boston: Houghton Mifflin, 1968.

Beschloss, Michael. *Kennedy and Roosevelt: The Uneasy Alliance*. New York: Norton, 1980.

Birmingham, Stephen. *Real Lace: America's Irish Rich*. New York: Harper & Row, 1973.

———. *Jacqueline Bouvier Kennedy Onassis*. New York: Grosset & Dunlap, 1978.

Bishop, Jim. *The Day Kennedy Was Shot*. New York: Funk & Wagnalls, 1968.

Blair, Joan, and Clay Blair, Jr. *The Search for JFK*. New York: Berkley, 1976.

Bouvier, Jacqueline, and Lee Bouvier. *One Special Summer*. New York: Delacorte Press, 1974.

Bouvier, Kathleen. *To Jack with Love, Black Jack Bouvier: A Remembrance*. New York: Kensington, 1979.

Braden, Joan. *Just Enough Rope*. New York: Villard, 1989.

Bradlee, Ben. *Conversations with Kennedy*. New York: Norton, 1975.

————. *A Good Life*. New York: Simon & Schuster, 1995.

Bryant, Traphes, and Frances Spatz Leighton. *Dog Days at the White House*. New York: Macmillan, 1975.

Buck, Pearl S. *The Kennedy Women: A Personal Appraisal*. New York: Harcourt, 1969.

Burke, Richard E. *My Ten Years with Ted Kennedy*. New York: St. Martin's Press, 1992.

Burns, James MacGregor. *John Kennedy: A Political Profile*. New York: Harcourt, 1960.

————. *Edward Kennedy and the Camelot Legacy*. New York: Norton, 1976.

Cameron, Gail. *Rose: A Biography of Rose Fitzgerald Kennedy*. New York: Putnam, 1971.

Cassini, Oleg. *In My Own Fashion: An Autobiography*. New York: Simon & Schuster, 1987.

————. *A Thousand Days of Magic*. New York: Rizzoli, 1995.

Cheshire, Maxine. *Maxine Cheshire, Reporter*. Boston: Houghton Mifflin, 1978.

Clarke, Gerald. *Capote*. New York: Simon & Schuster, 1988.

Cohn, Roy. *McCarthy*. New York: New American Library, 1968.

Collier, Peter, and David Horowitz. *The Kennedys: An American Drama*. New York: Summit Books, 1984.

Damore, Leo. *The Cape Cod Years of John Fitzgerald Kennedy*. Englewood Cliffs, N.J.: Prentice-Hall, 1967.

Davis, John. *The Bouviers: Portrait of an American Family*. New York. Farrar, Straus, 1969.

————. *The Kennedys: Dynasty and Disaster*. New York: McGraw-Hill, 1984.

DuBois, Diana. *In Her Sister's Shadow: An Intimate Biography of Lee Radziwill*. Boston: Little, Brown, 1995.

Exner, Judith, as told to Ovid Demaris. *My Story*. New York: Grove Press, 1977.

Fay, Paul B. Jr. *The Pleasure of His Company*. New York: Harper & Row, 1966.

Fisher, Eddie. *Eddie: My Life, My Loves.* New York: Harper & Row, 1981.

Fontaine, Joan. *No Bed of Roses: An Autobiography.* New York: William Morrow, 1978.

Frank, Gerold. *Zsa Zsa Gabor, My Story.* New York: World, 1960.

Frischauer, Willi. *Jackie.* London: Michael Joseph, 1967.

Galbraith, John Kenneth. *Ambassador's Journal: A Personal Account of the Kennedy Years.* Boston: Houghton Mifflin, 1969.

Gallagher, Mary Barelli. *My Life with Jacqueline Kennedy.* New York: David McKay, 1969.

Giancana, Antoinette, and Thomas C. Renner. *Mafia Princess: Growing Up in Sam Giancana's Family.* New York: William Morrow, 1984.

Goodwin, Doris Kearns. *The Fitzgeralds and the Kennedys: An American Saga.* New York: Simon & Schuster, 1987.

Granger, Stewart. *Sparks Fly Upward.* New York: Putnam, 1981.

Halberstam, David. *The Best and the Brightest.* New York: Random House, 1969.

Hall, Gordon Langley, and Ann Pinchot. *Jacqueline Kennedy.* New York: Frederick Fell, Inc., 1964.

Hamilton, Nigel. *JFK: Reckless Youth.* New York: Random House, 1992.

Heymann, C. David. *A Woman Named Jackie: An Intimate Biography of Jacqueline Bouvier Kennedy Onassis.* New York: A Lyle Stuart Book/Carol Communications, 1989.

Kelley, Kitty. *Jackie Oh!.* Secaucus, N.J.: Lyle Stuart, 1979.

———. *His Way: The Unauthorized Biography of Frank Sinatra.* New York: Bantam, 1986.

Kennedy, John F. *Why England Slept.* New York: Wilfred Funk, 1940.

———. *Profiles in Courage.* New York: Harper & Row, 1956.

Kennedy, Rose Fitzgerald. *Times to Remember.* Garden City, N.Y.: Doubleday, 1974.

Kessler, Ronald. *Inside the White House.* New York: Pocket Books, 1995.

Koskoff, David E. *Joseph P. Kennedy. A Life and Times,* Englewood Cliffs, N.J.: Prentice-Hall, 1974.

Krock, Arthur. *Memoirs: Sixty Years on the Firing Line.* New York: Funk & Wagnalls, 1968.

Kunhardt Philip B. Jr., ed. *Life in Camelot.* Boston: Little, Brown, 1988.

Lash, Joseph P. *Eleanor and Franklin.* New York: W. W. Norton, 1971.

Latham, Caroline, with Jeannie Sakol. *The Kennedy Encyclopedia.* New York: New American Library, 1989.

Lawford, Patricia Seaton, with Ted Schwarz. *The Peter Lawford Story.* New York: Carroll & Graf, 1988.

Lawliss, Charles. *Jacqueline Kennedy Onassis.* New York: JG Press, 1994.

Leamer, Laurence. *The Kennedy Women: The Saga of an American Family.* New York: Villard, 1994.

Leigh, Wendy. *Prince Charming: The John F. Kennedy Jr. Story.* New York: Signet, 1994.

Lowe, Jacques. *JFK Remembered.* New York: Random House, 1993.

———. *Jacqueline Kennedy Onassis: A Tribute.* New York: A Jacques Lowe Visual Arts Project, 1995.

McCarthy, Joe. *The Remarkable Kennedys.* New York: The Dial Press, 1960.

Mailer, Norman. *Marilyn.* New York: Grosset & Dunlap, 1973.

———. *Of Women and Their Elegance.* New York: Simon & Schuster, 1980.

Manchester, William. *Portrait of a President: John F. Kennedy in Profile.* Boston: Little, Brown, 1962.

———. *The Death of a President.* New York: Harper & Row, 1967.

Martin, Ralph. *A Hero for Our Time.* New York: Ballantine, 1984.

Montgomery, Ruth. *Hail to the Chiefs: My Life and Times with Six Presidents.* New York: Coward-McCann, 1970.

O'Connor, Edwin. *The Last Hurrah.* New York: Bantam Books, 1956.

O'Donnell, Kenneth P., and David F. Powers, with Joe McCarthy. *Johnny We Hardly Knew Ye.* Boston: Little, Brown, 1970.

O'Neill, Tip, with William Novak. *Man of the House: The Life and Political Memoirs of Speaker Tip O'Neill.* New York: Random House, 1987.

Parmet, Herbert S. *Jack: The Struggles of John F. Kennedy.* New York: Dial Press, 1980.

———. *J.F.K.: The Presidency of John F. Kennedy.* New York: Dial, 1983.

Parker, Robert. *Capitol Hill in Black and White.* New York: Dodd, Mead, 1987.

Pepitone, Lena, and William Stadiem. *Marilyn Monroe Confidential.* New York: Pocket Books, 1979.

Reeves, Richard. *President Kennedy: Profile of Power.* New York: Simon & Schuster, 1993.

Reeves, Thomas C. *A Question of Character: A Life of John F. Kennedy.* Rocklin, Calif.: Prima Publishing, 1992.

Salinger, Pierre. *With Kennedy.* Garden City, N.Y.: Doubleday, 1966.

———. *P.S.: A Memoir.* New York: St. Martin's Press, 1995.

Schlesinger, Arthur M., Jr. *A Thousand Days.* Boston: Houghton Mifflin, 1965.

Shulman, Irving. *"Jackie!": The Exploitation of a First Lady.* New York: Trident Press, 1970.

Sidey, Hugh. *John F. Kennedy, President.* New York: Atheneum, 1964.

Sorensen, Theodore C. *Kennedy.* New York: Harper & Row, 1965.

Spada, James. *Peter Lawford: The Man Who Kept the Secrets.* New York: Bantam, 1991.

Stack, Robert, with Mark Evans. *Straight Shooting.* New York: Macmillan, 1980.

Storm, Tempest, with Bill Boyd. *Tempest Storm: The Lady Is a Vamp.* Atlanta: Peachtree, 1987.

Summers, Anthony. *Goddess: The Secret Lives of Marilyn Monroe.* New York: Macmillan, 1985.

Swanson, Gloria. *Swanson on Swanson*. New York: Random House, 1980.

ter Horst, J. F., and Ralph Albertazzie. *The Flying White House*. New York: Coward, McCann & Geoghegan, 1979.

Thayer, Mary Van Rensselaer. *Jacqueline Bouvier Kennedy*. Garden City, N.Y.: Doubleday, 1961.

Thomas, Bob. *Golden Boy: The Untold Story of William Holden*. New York: St. Martin's Press, 1983.

Thomas, Helen. *Dateline: White House*. New York: Macmillan, 1975.

Tierney, Gene, with Mickey Herskowitz. *Self Portrait*. New York: Simon & Schuster, 1979.

Travell, Janet. *Office Hours: Day and Night*. New York: World, 1968.

Vidal, Gore. *Palimpsest: A Memoir*. New York: Random House, 1995.

Warren Report, The. New York: Associated Press, 1964.

Watney, Hedda Lyons. *Jackie*. New York: Leisure Books, 1971.

West, J. B., with Mary Lynn Kotz. *Upstairs at the White House*. New York: Coward, McCann & Geoghegan, 1973.

White, Theodore H. *The Making of the President 1960*. New York: Atheneum, 1961.

———. *In Search of History*. New York: Warner Books, 1978.

Wills, Garry. *The Kennedy Imprisonment*. Boston: Atlantic-Little, Brown, 1981.

INDEX

Fore River shipyard, 19
France, 53, 74, 77
    Jackie in, 84–85, 117–118, 294–295
Frazer, Gertrude, 25
Frey, Sister Joanne, 265, 357–359, 369
Frost, Robert, 248–249, 287, 318
Fulbright, William, 359–360

Gable, Clark, 306
Gabor, Zsa Zsa, 118
Galbraith, John Kenneth, 43, 325, 332
Gallagher, Mary, 103, 114, 186, 188, 232,
    245, 262–263, 330–331, 342–343,
    351, 352, 362
Gargan, Ann, 325
Garland, Judy, 156, 209
Garner, John Nance, 214
George Washington University, 85, 86
Germany, 44, 48–49, 74, 85, 350
Giancana, Sam, 309, 310, 311
Gilpatric, Madelin, 345, 349–350
Gilpatric, Roswell, 339–340, 341, 344–345,
    348–350
Glenn, John, 284
Glen Ora, 275, 284, 329, 330
Gloria Productions, 28, 30–31
Good Life, A (Bradlee), 312
Gore, Albert, Sr., 161, 164
Gore, Thomas, 64
Göring, Hermann, 48–49
Graham, Katharine, 245
Graham, Philip, 245
Grant, Cary, 194
Greece, 303–304
Green, Edith, 201
Gromyko, Andrey, 296

Haley, Jack, 210
Halle, Kay, 15, 152–153
Hammarskjöld, Dag, 300
Hammersmith Farm, 2, 3, 6, 10, 65, 66,
    67, 109, 122, 167, 170, 176, 354
Harper and Brothers, 151, 173
Harriman, Averill, 78
Harriman, Pamela Churchill, 78
Hartington, Billy, 74–75
Harvard University, 17, 18, 22, 25, 38,
    40–45
Hassan II, king of Morocco, 343, 357
Hays, Will, 28
Hayward, Leland, 245
Hayward, Susan, 81

Hearst, William Randolph, 46, 77, 128
Hellman, Lillian, 106
Henie, Sonja, 81
Hennessey, Luella, 235, 237–238, 239
Henry Hentz & Company, 54
Hepburn, Audrey, 100, 103–104, 156, 346
Herbst, William P., 47
Hersey, John, 42, 76
Hewitt, Don, 218
Heymann, C. David, 95
Hickory Hill, 156, 162–163, 169, 170, 175
Hill, Clint, 365
Hitler, Adolf, 44, 49
Hoffa, Jimmy, 175, 309
Holden, William, 103, 104
Hollywood, Calif., 27, 39, 80–82, 141–142,
    172
homosexuality, 37–38, 55, 108, 138, 208–
    209
Honor (TV drama), 172
Hoobler, Jerry, 99
Hoover, Herbert, 64
Hoover, J. Edgar, 51, 192
Hopper, Hedda, 194
Horowitz, David, 116
horseback riding, 55, 58, 60, 62, 63, 87,
    104–105, 111, 136, 182
Horton, Rip, 36, 38, 45
Houghton, Charlie, 40
House of Representatives, U.S., 75–77
Hoving, Walter, 341–342
Humphrey, Hubert, 164, 203, 206, 214,
    237
Huntley, Chet, 166
Hurok, Sol, 343
Husted, Helen, 89, 90
Husted, John, Jackie's engagement to,
    89–91, 96, 97–98
Hyannis Port, Mass., Kennedy home in,
    22, 25, 29, 30, 31, 33, 34, 45, 46,
    112, 121, 129, 131, 153, 173, 176,
    191, 199, 214–216, 224–227, 318,
    326, 347

Inaugural Gala, 245–247
inauguration, 248–254
India, 323, 331–334
Ireland, 85, 350
Italy, 331, 336–338

Jackson, Andrew, 269
Jackson, Henry "Scoop," 213, 214

forty-fifth birthday of, 306–308, 346
forty-sixth birthday of, 345–347
golf playing of, 222–223, 240, 291
gonorrhea of, 47
headaches of, 39, 41
humor and wit of, 35, 37, 105, 108
hunting of, 233–234
injuries and illnesses of, 6, 19–20, 25,
    32–34, 38–41, 46, 47–48, 76–79,
    104, 109, 139–155, 162, 169, 173,
    182–183, 362
isolation and loneliness of, xv, 87, 179,
    322
lateness of, 43, 97
listening skills of, 85, 100
malaria story and, 76–79
male friendship and bonding
    experiences of, 33–37
marriage opposed by, 79–80, 108, 119–
    121
nervous tics of, 139
out-of-wedlock pregnancies due to, 75,
    92, 152
photographs disliked by, 221–222, 276,
    291
political ambitions of, 5, 10, 13, 37, 64,
    75, 77, 82, 96, 104, 117, 151, 164,
    169, 172, 173–174, 189–190, 200–
    201
political campaigns of, 75–77, 88, 93–
    95, 189–191, 200–227, 237
political loss of, 165
as President, 249–256, 262–268, 270–
    280, 289–314, 317
as President-elect, 226–227, 231–240,
    243–248
press relations of, 93, 127, 155, 175,
    189–190, 211, 311–314
profanity used by, 34–35, 47
publicity seeking of, 5, 7, 191, 277–278,
    289
public speaking of, 76, 105, 136–137,
    139, 146, 173, 175, 191, 201, 214,
    229, 247, 249, 350, 362
recklessness of, 44–45, 47, 79, 311, 313–
    314
as senator, 7, 10, 12, 95, 99, 103, 105,
    131–158, 190–199
senior thesis of, 43–44
sexual development of, 30, 31, 34, 36–
    37, 39, 41–42
sloppiness of, 82, 122–123
smoking of, 136, 238
subterfuge of, 291–292
swimming of, 240, 263, 264–265, 279
temper of, 135, 205, 248, 276–277

transition team of, 233, 244
trust fund of, 26–27
TV appearances of, 127, 130–131, 161,
    162, 163
wealth of, 26–27, 105, 117, 171, 237
womanizing of, vii, 17, 23, 30, 37, 48,
    75, 76, 77, 80–83, 92–93, 96, 97,
    98, 100, 103–104, 117–120, 123,
    137–138, 142, 143, 154, 155–156,
    158, 167, 170
in World War II, 41, 48–53, 73–76
see also Kennedy relationship
Kennedy, John Fitzgerald, Jr., 235–236,
    238–239, 243, 250, 252, 351, 352,
    357–360, 370
in White House, 259, 260, 262, 263,
    264, 271–282, 333, 340, 354, 357,
    360, 366–368
Kennedy, Joseph Patrick, Jr., 19, 27–28,
    30
death of, 74–75, 144
education of, 38, 39, 46
JFK compared with, 32, 33, 38, 39, 46
JFK's competition with, 22, 24–25, 74
in World War II, 48, 74, 75
Kennedy, Joseph Patrick, Sr., 17–32, 43,
    82, 88, 146, 150, 171–174, 176, 191,
    250, 309, 323, 368
as ambassador, 44, 45, 51, 154
Arvad and, 50–52
election of 1956 and, 161, 164
as father, 17, 20, 22–28, 30, 32, 38–40,
    43–46, 50, 79, 107, 169
financial and business dealings of, 13,
    17–18, 20, 26–29, 32, 77, 107, 137,
    171, 172, 187, 240, 242, 249–250
Jack and Jackie's wedding and, 5–7, 10,
    11, 12
and Jack as President-elect, 233, 247,
    248
Jackie's relationship with, 13, 114–116,
    171, 172, 187, 275, 325, 326, 368
Jack's campaigns and, 75–77, 94, 167,
    171, 173, 189–190, 208, 210, 211,
    226
and Jack's decision to marry, 13, 107–
    108, 115–116, 118
Jack's illness and, 19–20, 144–145, 148,
    149
prejudice experienced by, 17, 18, 26, 94
Rose's relationship with, 7, 10, 18, 27,
    29, 80, 118
string-pulling of, 43–46, 48, 52, 74, 75,
    77, 156, 157, 208
stroke of, 325–327
traveling of, 21, 23, 27, 29, 32

Leigh, Janet, 209, 246
Lerner, Alan Jay, 343, 344, 345
Lester, Samuel, 58
Levine, Joseph E., 193
Lichtblau, Nathan, 346–347
Life, 95, 121, 191, 196, 219, 220–221, 242, 275, 297
Lincoln, Abraham, 247, 254, 260, 269, 272, 341–342, 357, 369
Lincoln, Evelyn, 96–97, 108, 118, 127, 133, 134, 144, 185, 304, 310–311, 355–356
Lisagor, Peter, 204, 205
Little Foxes, The (Hellman), 106
Lodge, Henry Cabot, 88, 94
London School of Economics, 39
Longworth, Alice Roosevelt, 244
Look, 162, 175, 191, 204, 275–276
Loren, Sophia, 194
Lowe, Ann, 9
Lowe, Jacques, 189, 191–192, 197, 203, 213–216, 219, 226, 237, 246, 254–255, 257, 263, 266, 271, 276, 285, 291, 327
Loy, Myrna, 343
Luce, Clare Booth, 154, 171, 189, 208, 211, 214
Luce, Henry, 45, 171, 208

McCarthy, Joseph, 146, 150, 163
McClellan, John L., 175
McCoy, Tim, 50
MacDonald, Torby, 123
McDonnell, Charlotte, 43, 79
McGuire, Phyllis, 309
McKinley, William, 272
MacLaine, Shirley, 189, 246
Macmillan, Harold, 297, 318, 350
McMillan, Priscilla, 59, 71, 80, 105, 135–138, 140–143, 167, 212, 223
McNamara, Robert, 233, 284, 323–324, 341, 344, 349
Madison, Dolley, 271, 272, 287
Mafia, 309–311
Mahoney, Florence, 83
Maidstone Club, 55, 56, 63
Mailer, Norman, 273
Malcolm, Durie, 80
Malraux, André, 294, 319, 323, 336, 342
Mann, Harvey, 301–302
Mansfield, Jayne, 305
Marquand, John, Sr., 84
Marquand, John Phillips, Jr., 84–85, 117–118

Martin, Dean, 209
Marvin, Langdon "Don," 120, 137, 240
Mayflower Hotel, 156, 190, 249–250
Mead, George, 46
"Meanwhile in Massachusetts Jack Kennedy Dreamed" (Jackie Kennedy), 129–130
Meet the Press (TV show), 199
Mellon, Bunny, 187, 271
Mellon, Paul, 283
Merrywood, 3, 4, 65–66, 88, 89, 90, 95, 97–98, 99, 109, 131, 134, 136, 151, 174, 175
Mesta, Perle, 117, 164
Mexico, 12–13, 127–128, 196, 336, 349
Meyer, Cord, 313
Meyer, Mary Pinchot, 196, 311–312, 313, 335, 346–347
Miller, Arthur, 195, 319
Miss Porter's School, 69–70, 89
Modern Screen, 216
Mohammed Reza Pahlavi, shah of Iran, 323, 335
Mona Lisa (Leonardo da Vinci), 342
Monroe, James, 269, 270
Monroe, Marilyn, 91, 121, 141–142, 194–195, 210, 211, 214, 305–310, 312, 313, 334–335, 336, 346
Montand, Yves, 195, 210
Moore, Eddie, 24
Morrissey, Frank, 214
Morrissey, Michael, 169
Mortimer, Stanley, 111
Mountbatten, Lord Louis, 297
Mount Vernon, 317–318, 333
movies, 27, 28, 30–31, 92, 103, 265
Mowinckel, Letizia, 187
Muckers Club, 35, 38
Mulkern, Patrick "Patsy," 76, 78–79, 94
Muñoz Marín, Luis, 319
Murphia, 135, 136, 174
Murrow, Edward R., 130–131
Mussolini, Benito, 44

Naval Intelligence Office, U.S., 48, 49
Navy, U.S., 48, 49, 73–76
Nehru, Jawaharlal, 323, 331–332
Neville, Mike, 77
New Frontier, 236
Newman, Larry, 119, 153, 212, 214–215, 224–225, 342
Newsweek, 277, 322
New York *Daily News*, 60, 120–121
New York Herald Tribune, 284

New York Stock Exchange, 54, 175–176
New York Times, 5–6, 10, 74, 90, 176, 181, 269
New York *Times-Herald,* 78
New York Times Sunday Magazine, 276
Niven, David, 346–347
Niven, Hjordis, 346–347
Nixon, Pat, 77, 213, 220, 248
Nixon, Richard Milhous, 77, 91, 99, 146–147, 248, 296
    in election of 1960, 202, 213, 215, 217–220, 222, 224, 225, 226, 231, 237
Nixon, Tricia, 91
Nizer, Louis, 345
Norris, George W., 150
Norton, Clem, 346–347
Novak, Kim, 254
Nuclear Test Ban Treaty (1963), 350, 351, 363
Nureyev, Rudolf, 319, 345

O'Donnell, Kenneth P., 10, 136, 159, 163, 198–199, 201, 202, 210, 219, 233, 234, 253, 264–265, 355, 359, 360, 361, 363, 366
O'Leary, Mugsy, 198
Olivier, Laurence, 245–246
Onassis, Aristotle, 154, 355–357, 359
O'Neill, Thomas P. "Tip," 224
Oswald, Lee Harvey, 367
Otash, Fred, 309
Our Forebears (Bouvier), 53
Outlook (TV show), 166

Pakistan, 333–334
Paley, Babe Cushing, 111
Paley, William S., 111
Palm Beach, Fla., Kennedy villa in, 29, 39, 112–116, 148–150, 222–223, 233, 234, 238–243, 279, 303, 328, 360
Parades, Providencia "Provi," 185
Parish, Sister, 174, 243–244, 259–260, 267
Parra, Fernando, 254
Pauling, Linus, 320
Paul VI, pope, 350
Pavlick, Richard B., 239
Peale, Rembrandt, 271
Pearl (Jackie's cook), 262
Pearson, Drew, 170–171, 189
Person to Person (TV show), 130–131
Peskin, Hy, 121

Peters, Charles, 206
Petry, Clarence, 206
Philip, Duke of Edinburgh, 297
Pitcairn, Mary, 31
Pius XII, pope, 8, 153
Plimpton, George, 84, 325
Ponti, Carlo, 194
Pooh ("P"), 167, 168
Porter, Cole, 55
Powers, Dave, 79, 96, 99–100, 110, 136, 148–149, 154, 173, 202, 219, 225, 310, 352–353, 355, 360, 362, 364, 365
    as Jack's swim partner, 263, 264–265
Powers, Jo, 110
Preston, Robert, 346
Price, Harriet, 47
Princeton University, 38, 39, 40
Pritchett, Florence, 240
Profiles in Courage (J. F. Kennedy), 150–151, 156–158, 161
Prohibition, 26
prostitutes, 36, 156
PT-109 incident, 73–74, 76, 161, 250
Purdom, Alicja Darr, 92–93, 121
Purdom, Edmund, 92
Pursuit of Happiness (film), 161, 163
Putnam, Harrington, 5
Putnam, Michelle Bouvier, 5

Queen Elizabeth, 86, 88
Queen Kelly (movie), 30–31
Queen Mary, 72–73, 78

Radziwill, Anna Christina, 252, 297
Radziwill, Lee, 2, 8, 69, 71, 88, 112, 170, 174, 176, 182, 188, 211, 219, 259, 297, 298, 302, 303, 331, 334, 336, 340, 353, 355–357
    childhood of, 58–62, 64
    Jackie compared with, 59, 60
    Jackie's relationship with, ix, 59, 170, 173, 252, 334, 356
    marriages of, 4, 99, 211
Radziwill, Prince Stanislas "Stas," 211, 298, 302–303, 336, 340, 355, 356
Randall, Tony, 346
Rayburn, Sam, 162, 248
Remick, Lee, 156, 193–194
Renty, Countess de, 84
Republicans, Republican Party, 7, 13, 190, 334, 359

in election of 1960, 202, 213, 215, 217–
    220, 222, 224, 225, 226, 231, 237
Ribbentrop, Joachim von, 49
Ribicoff, Abraham, 162
Robinson, Sugar Ray, 345
Roosevelt, Eleanor, 68, 162, 163, 214, 334,
    343
Roosevelt, Franklin D., 19, 38, 51, 68,
    144, 270, 291, 334, 348
Roosevelt, Franklin D., Jr., 206, 279–280,
    356
Roosevelt, Selwa "Lucky," 71
Roosevelt, Suzanne, 356
Roosevelt, Theodore, 302, 319
Roosevelt (Burns), 157
Rose Elizabeth (yacht), 30
Rousmaniere, James, 42
Ruby, Jack, 367
Rusk, Dean, 233, 296, 323, 341, 351, 361
Russo, Joseph, 77
Ryan, "Toodles," 18

Sadie Thompson (movie), 28
Salinger, Pierre, 204, 216, 224, 226, 231,
    235, 239, 251, 262, 268, 277–278,
    281–282, 285, 291, 299, 302, 304,
    312–313, 341, 360–361
Sargent, John Singer, 261
Saturday Evening Post, 84, 119, 175, 191
Schary, Dore, 161
Schlesinger, Arthur, Jr., 162, 272, 275,
    279, 296, 321, 325, 350, 353–354
Schoellkopf, Judith, 337
Schoenbrun, David, 338
Scouten, Rex, 146
Secret Service, 231–232, 235, 240, 244,
    245, 246, 273–274, 275, 281, 289,
    291, 293, 301, 305, 326, 336, 343,
    344, 351, 364, 365
Securities and Exchange Commission
    (SEC), 13, 38, 108
Senate, U.S., 77, 146
  JFK in, 7, 10, 12, 95, 99, 103, 105, 131–
    158, 190–199
  JFK's campaign for, 88, 93–95
Shaw, Mark, 217
Shaw, Maud, 184, 185, 220, 225, 234, 243,
    260, 262, 263, 271, 280, 320, 366
Sheppard, Eugenia, 284
Shevlin, Thomas, Jr., 80
Shriver, Eunice Kennedy, 19, 21, 22, 26,
    31, 35, 111, 117, 123, 146, 163,
    199, 226, 302, 346–347, 368
Shriver, Sargent, 117, 163, 226, 346–347

Sidey, Hugh, 243, 267
Signoret, Simone, 210
Simmons, Jean, 92, 193
Sinatra, Frank, 156, 194, 199, 209, 210,
    245, 247, 253
Smathers, Frank, 149
Smathers, George, 11, 14, 23, 60, 81, 106,
    113, 119, 139, 140, 149, 165–169,
    291, 293, 311, 323, 328, 360
  on Jackie's spending, 187–188
  Jack's womanizing and, 77, 97, 120,
    137, 155–156, 167, 194, 211, 311,
    312, 314, 329, 336–337
Smith, Earl, 240
Smith, Jean Ann Kennedy, 19, 22, 26, 29,
    202, 360
Smith, Stephen, 202, 360
Social Register, 53, 56
Sohier, Walter, 211–213, 338
Solgrave Club, 72, 89
Song, Mickey, 307
Sorensen, Ted, 147, 162, 203, 225, 276,
    321, 341
Soviet Union, 289, 295–297, 300, 339–342,
    351
Spalding, Betty, 101, 113, 185, 197, 251,
    338
Spalding, Chuck, xv, 5, 9, 46, 61, 79, 81,
    87, 92, 106, 111, 115, 123, 128,
    146, 153, 154, 165, 191, 223, 231–
    232, 267, 279, 293, 323, 327, 341
  on election of 1960, 204, 206–207, 217–
    218
  on Jack's womanizing, 23, 104, 190,
    200, 297, 305, 306, 312, 314, 329
  Jacobsen and, 217–218, 302, 303
  on Kennedy marriage, 120, 124
Spalding, Elizabeth, 279
Spalding, Josie, 279
Sparkman, John, 248
Special Summer, A (Bouvier and Bouvier),
    88
Spellman, Francis Cardinal, 353
Spindel, Bernard, 309
Stack, Robert, 46, 141
Standard Oil Company, 64
Stanford School of Business
    Administration, 46
State Department, U.S., 44
Steers, Newton, 175
Steers, Nina Auchincloss "Nini," 3, 64,
    97–98, 175
Stevenson, Adlai, 148, 161–165, 209, 210,
    214, 307, 308, 354, 359, 360
Stravinsky, Igor, 320
Styron, William, 84

Sullivan, Ed, 346
Summers, Anthony, 310
Swanson, Gloria, 10, 28–32, 57
Symington, Stuart, 144, 209, 213, 214, 219

Taft, Robert, 150
Texas, 303, 311, 359–366
Thayer, Mary Van Rensselaer, 233
Thomas, Evan, 151
Thomas, George, 76, 134, 137, 264
Thomas, Helen, 313
Thompson, Bill, 156
Tierney, Gene, 82–83, 92, 123, 150, 237
Tiffany, 341–342
Time, 171, 175, 256, 284, 294, 337
Travell, Janet, 41, 151–152, 183, 209, 261,
    292, 298, 299, 351
Tretick, Stanley, 221–222, 271, 275–276,
    278, 280, 281
Truman, Harry S, 208, 233, 261, 272,
    345–346
Tuckerman, Nancy, x–xi, 12, 70
Tunney, Gene, 83–84
Turner, Lana, 81
Turnure, Pamela, 195–196, 251

United Nations, 75, 300, 339

Van Buren, Martin, 270
Vassar College, 70, 71, 85
Vena, Luigi, 8
venereal disease, 36, 39, 47, 152, 169
Verdon, René, 262, 317
Vidal, Gore, 3, 37, 65, 66, 84, 85, 110,
    132, 139–140, 145, 171–175, 200,
    201, 231–232, 299–300, 305, 311,
    324–325, 329
  on money, 69, 106, 110, 171
Vienna summit (1961), 295–297
Vogue, 85, 86, 216

Wade, Preston, 183
Waldrop, Frank, 48, 78, 88–89, 90
Walsh, John, 234, 351, 353
Walton, William, 91–92, 234, 244, 267,
    308, 322, 323, 346–347
Ward, Peter, 170
War Department, U.S., 48
Warren, Earl, 249, 343
Washington Post, 164, 168
Washington Star, 195
Washington *Times-Herald,* 48, 88–91, 99,
    116–117
Watson, Philip, 305–306
Watson, Tom, 41
Webster, Daniel, 150
Weir, Priscilla "Fiddle," 304
Wenner-Gren, Axel, 49
West, J. B., 238, 251, 255, 259–264, 268,
    274, 275, 325, 340
Wexford, 330, 348
While England Slept (Churchill), 43
White, John, 91–92
White, Theodore, 208, 334, 336, 354, 364
White House, 234, 248, 250–252, 254–256,
    259–285, 292–293, 304–305, 310,
    334–335
  as American Versailles, 317–325
  Jackie's tours of, 237–238, 243, 252,
    273
  restoration of, 244–245, 256, 259–262,
    267–273, 289
Why England Slept (J. F. Kennedy), 43–46
Williams, Tennessee, 37, 319
Wilson, Philip D., 144
Wilson, Woodrow, 270
Winchell, Walter, 72
World War I, 19, 53
World War II, 41, 43, 47–53, 67, 73–76
Wrightsman, Charles, 289
Wrightsman, Jane, 268, 289
Wyeth, Andrew, 319

Yarborough, Ralph, 359
York, Dick, 172